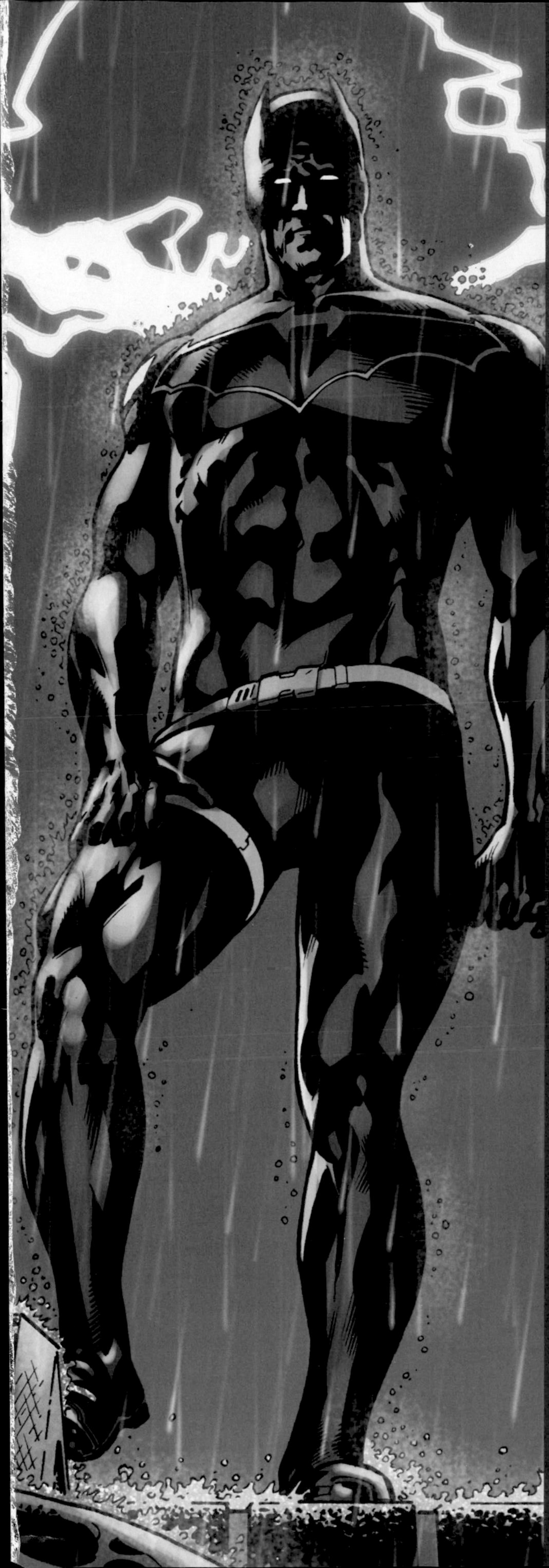

VOLUME 9
GORDON AT WAR

BATMAN – DETECTIVE COMICS

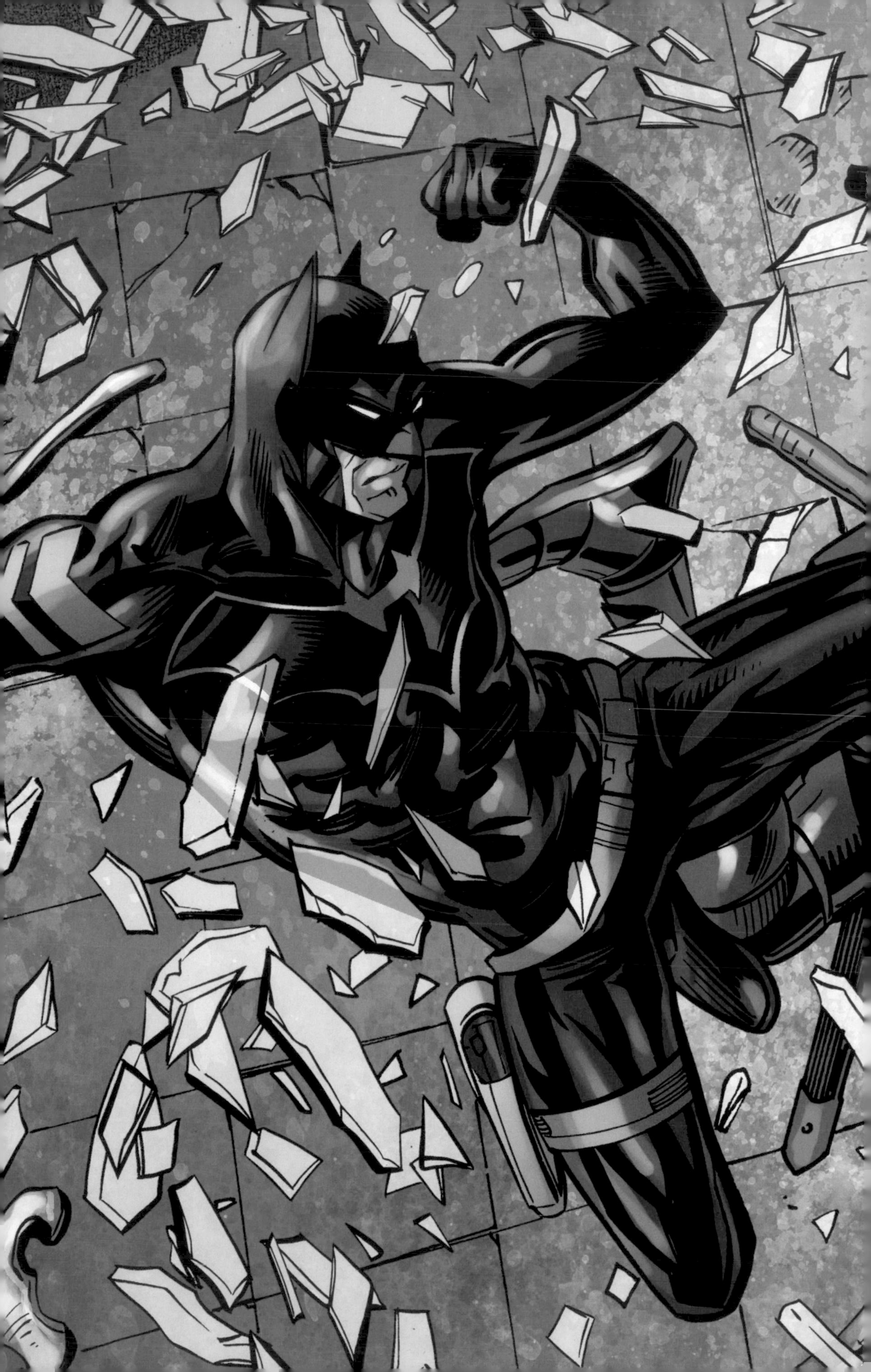

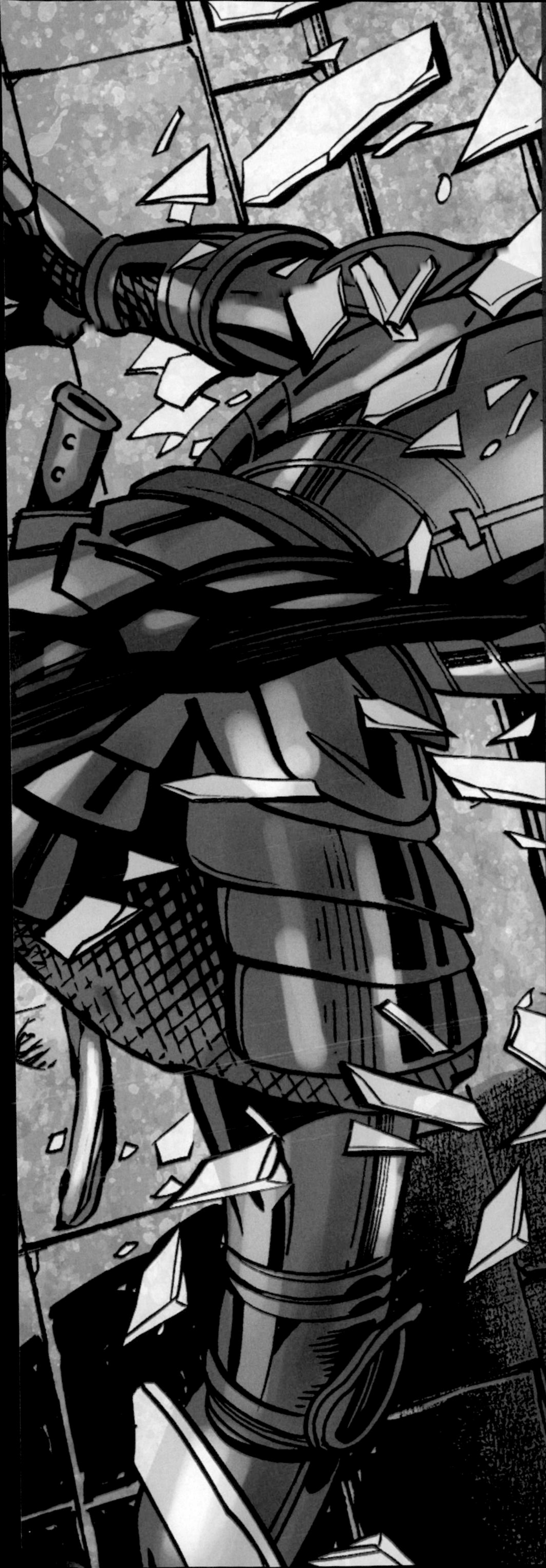

BATMAN – DETECTIVE COMICS

VOLUME 9
GORDON AT WAR

WRITTEN BY
PETER J. TOMASI

PENCILS BY
FERNANDO PASARIN
SCOT EATON

INKS BY
MATT RYAN
WAYNE FAUCHER

COLOR BY
CHRIS SOTOMAYOR

LETTERS BY
WES ABBOTT

COLLECTION COVER ART BY
ANDREW ROBINSON

BATMAN CREATED BY
BOB KANE WITH **BILL FINGER**

MARK DOYLE Editor – Original Series
REBECCA TAYLOR Associate Editor – Original Series
JEB WOODARD Group Editor – Collected Editions
SUZANNAH ROWNTREE Editor – Collected Edition
STEVE COOK Design Director – Books
DAMIAN RYLAND Publication Design

BOB HARRAS Senior VP – Editor-in-Chief, DC Comics

DIANE NELSON President
DAN DiDIO Publisher
JIM LEE Publisher
GEOFF JOHNS President & Chief Creative Officer
AMIT DESAI Executive VP – Business & Marketing Strategy, Direct to Consumer & Global Franchise Management
SAM ADES Senior VP – Direct to Consumer
BOBBIE CHASE VP – Talent Development
MARK CHIARELLO Senior VP – Art, Design & Collected Editions
JOHN CUNNINGHAM Senior VP – Sales & Trade Marketing
ANNE DePIES Senior VP – Business Strategy, Finance & Administration
DON FALLETTI VP – Manufacturing Operations
LAWRENCE GANEM VP – Editorial Administration & Talent Relations
ALISON GILL Senior VP – Manufacturing & Operations
HANK KANALZ Senior VP – Editorial Strategy & Administration
JAY KOGAN VP – Legal Affairs
THOMAS LOFTUS VP – Business Affairs
JACK MAHAN VP – Business Affairs
NICK J. NAPOLITANO VP – Manufacturing Administration
EDDIE SCANNELL VP – Consumer Marketing
COURTNEY SIMMONS Senior VP – Publicity & Communications
JIM (SKI) SOKOLOWSKI VP – Comic Book Specialty Sales & Trade Marketing
NANCY SPEARS VP – Mass, Book, Digital Sales & Trade Marketing

BATMAN – DETECTIVE COMICS VOLUME 9 GORDON AT WAR

DC Comics, 2900 West Alameda Ave., Burbank, CA 91505
Printed by LSC Communications, Salem, VA, USA. 10/28/16. First Printing.
ISBN: 978-1-4012-6923-4

Library of Congress Cataloging-in-Publication Data

Names: Tomasi, Peter, author. | Eaton, Scot, penciller. | Pasarin, Fernando, penciller. | Faucher, Wayne, inker. | Ryan, Matt, inker. | Sotomayor, Chris, colorist. | Abbott, Wes, letterer. | Robinson, Andrew (Andrew C.) artist.
Title: Batman/Detective Comics. Volume 9: Gordon at war / Peter J. Tomasi, writer ; Scot Eaton, Fernando Pasarin, pencillers ; Wayne Faucher, Matt Ryan, inkers ; Chris Sotomayor, colorist ; Wes Abbott, letterer ; Andrew Robinson, collection cover artist.
Other titles: Gordon at war
Description: Burbank, CA : DC Comics, [2016] | "Batman created by Bob Kane with Bill Finger"
Identifiers: LCCN 2016039971 | ISBN 9781401269234 (hardback)
Subjects: LCSH: Comic books, strips, etc. | BISAC: COMICS & GRAPHIC NOVELS / Superheroes.
Classification: LCC PN6728.B36 T666 2016 | DDC 741.5/973—dc23
LC record available at https://lccn.loc.gov/2016039971

PEFC Certified
Printed on paper from sustainably managed forests, controlled sources
PEFC
PEFC/29-31-337
www.pefc.org

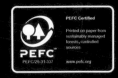

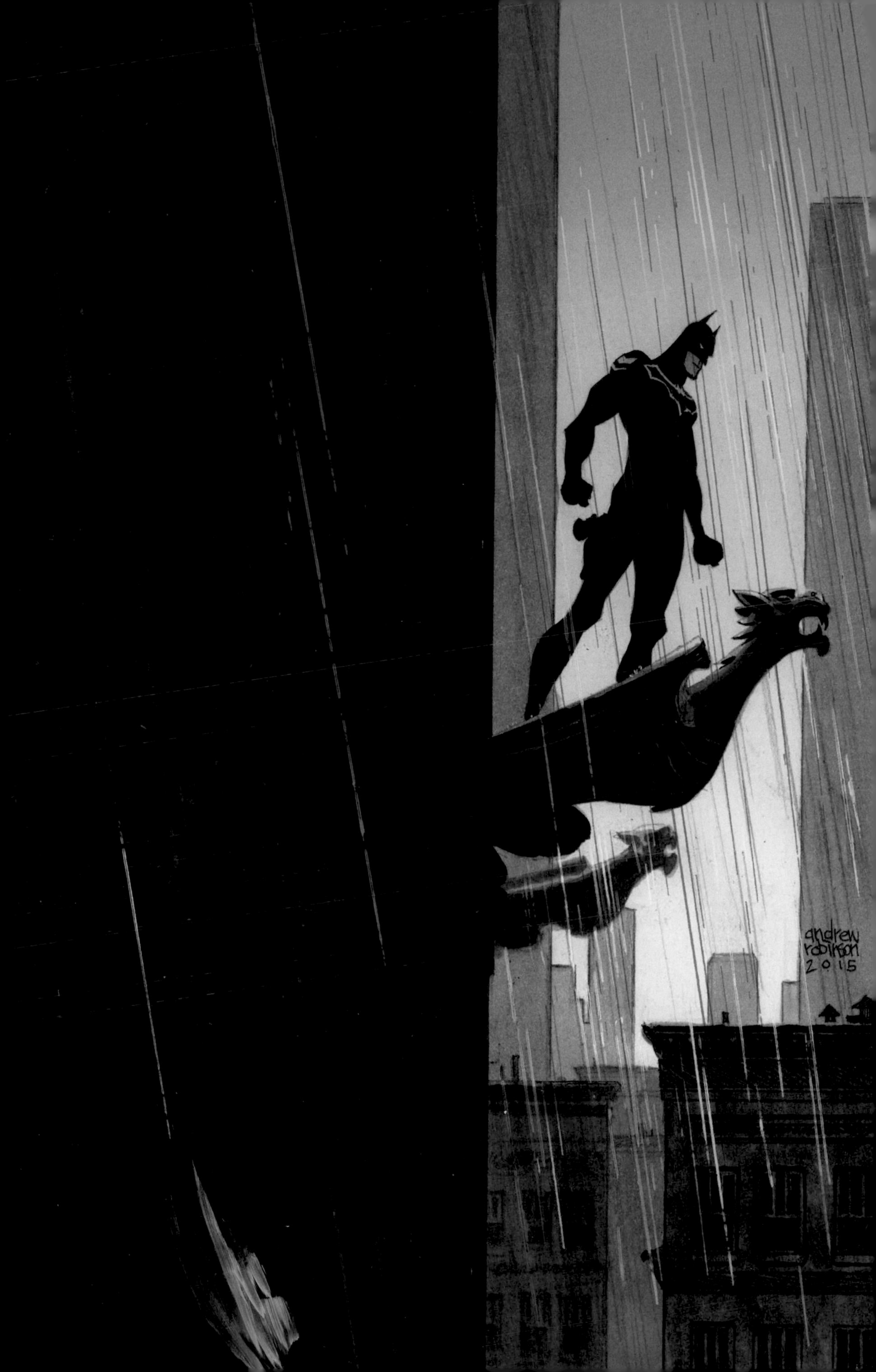
andrew robinson 2015

THE BRONZE AGE: BLOOD OF HEROES

PETER J. TOMASI writer **FERNANDO PASARIN** penciller **MATT RYAN** inker **CHRIS SOTOMAYOR** colorist **WES ABBOTT** letterer **ANDREW ROBINSON** cover

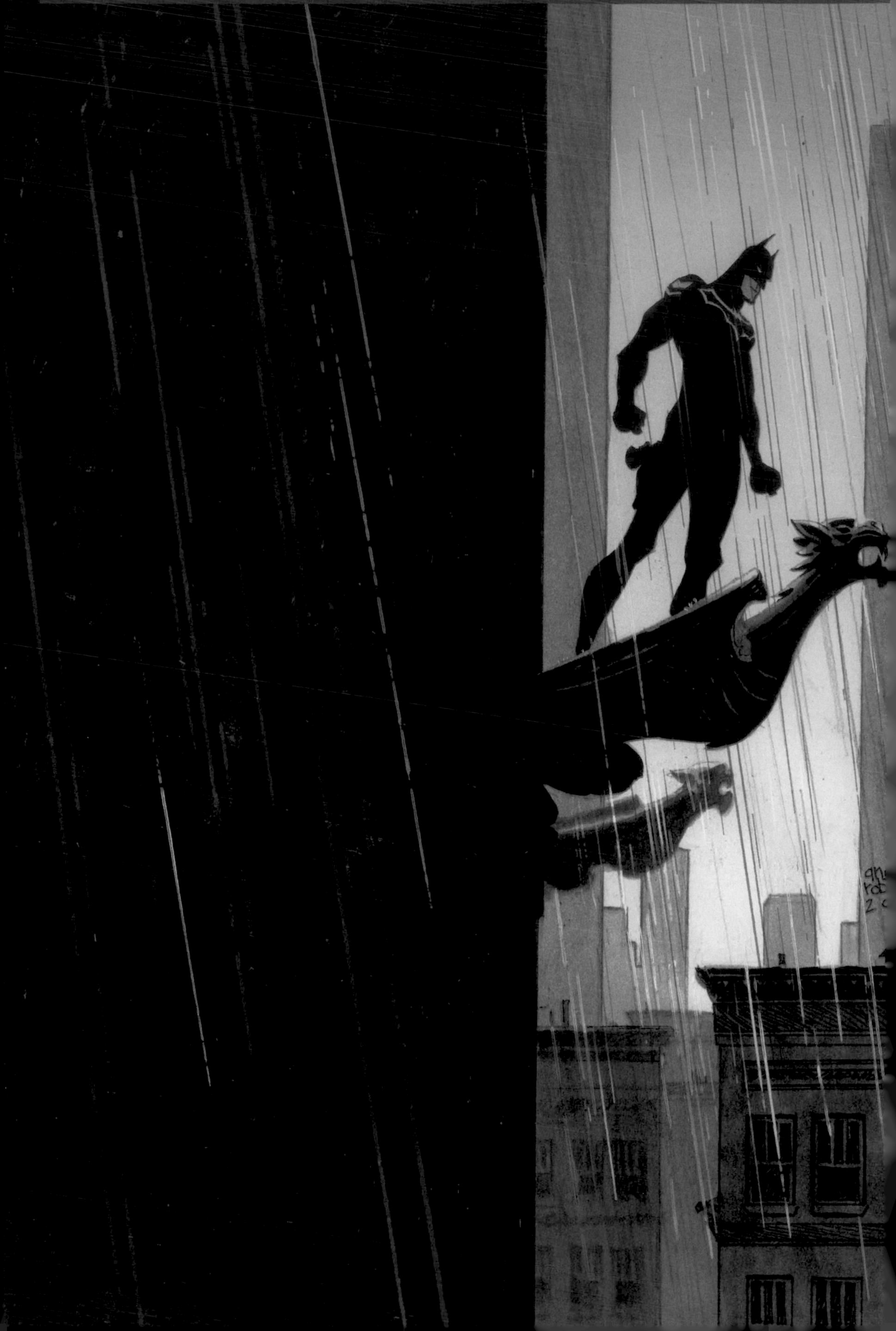

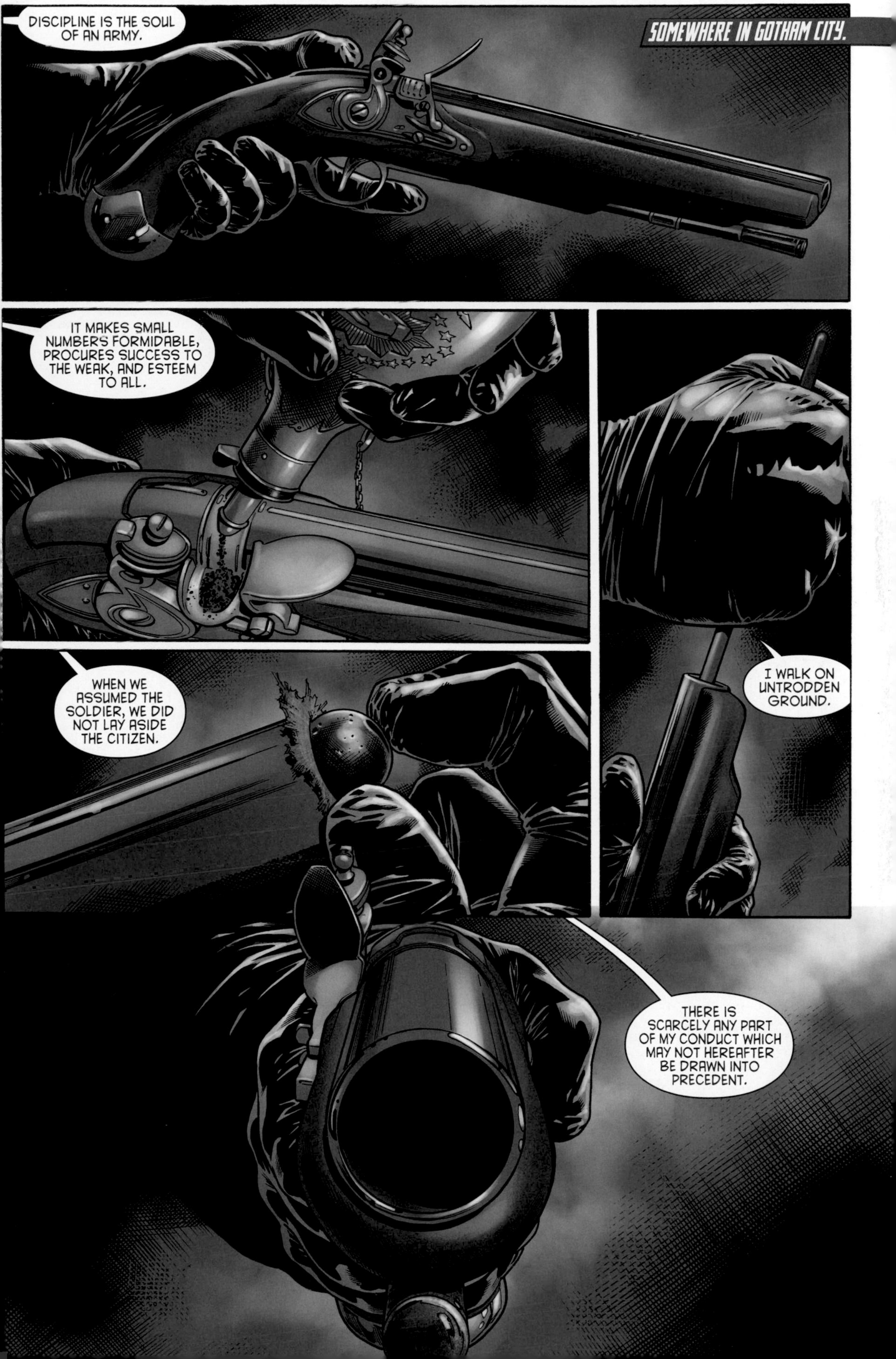
SOMEWHERE IN GOTHAM CITY.
DISCIPLINE IS THE SOUL OF AN ARMY.
IT MAKES SMALL NUMBERS FORMIDABLE, PROCURES SUCCESS TO THE WEAK, AND ESTEEM TO ALL.
I WALK ON UNTRODDEN GROUND.
WHEN WE ASSUMED THE SOLDIER, WE DID NOT LAY ASIDE THE CITIZEN.
THERE IS SCARCELY ANY PART OF MY CONDUCT WHICH MAY NOT HEREAFTER BE DRAWN INTO PRECEDENT.

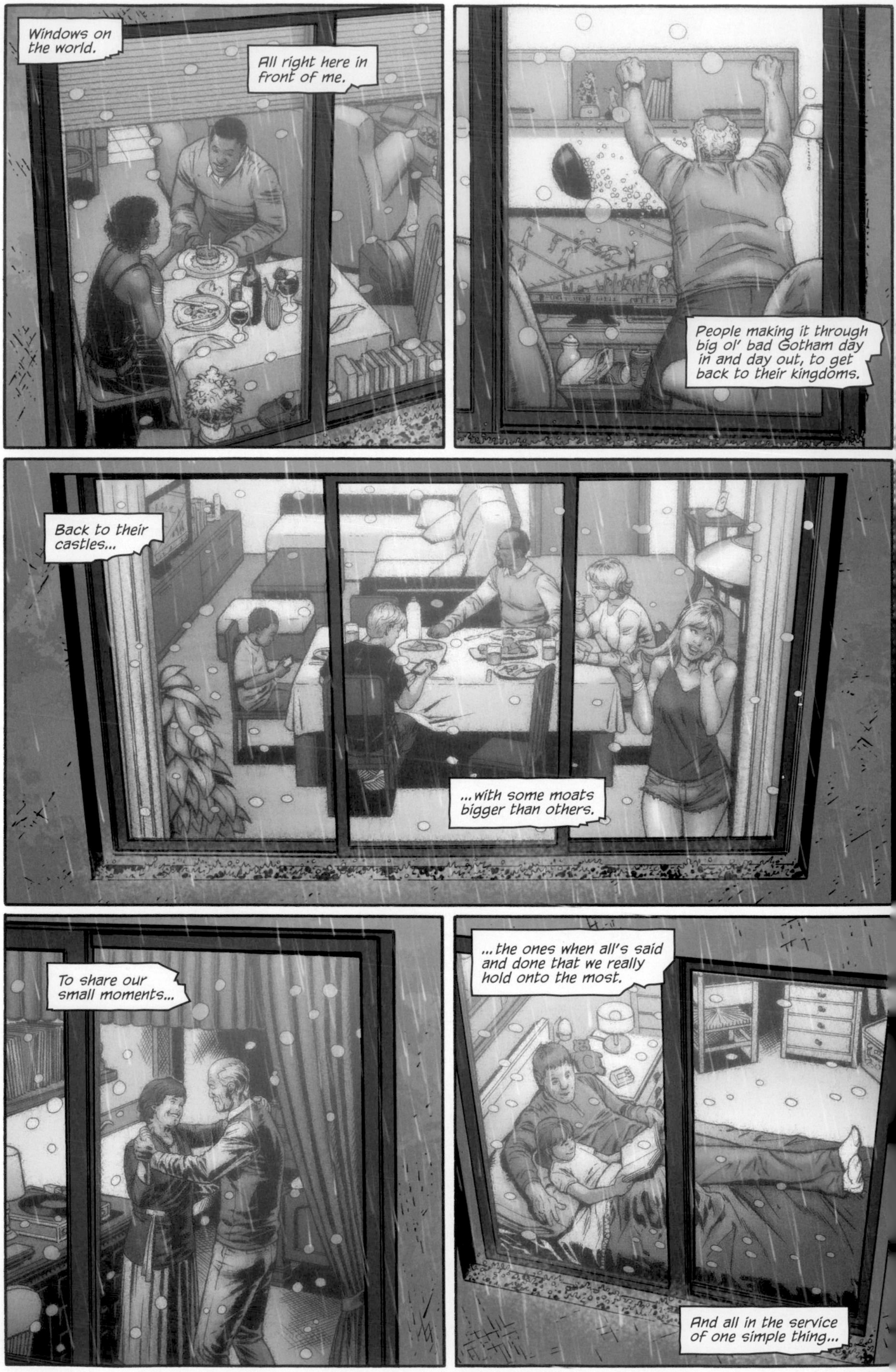
Windows on the world.
All right here in front of me.
People making it through big ol' bad Gotham day in and day out, to get back to their kingdoms.
Back to their castles...
...with some moats bigger than others.
To share our small moments...
...the ones when all's said and done that we really hold onto the most.
And all in the service of one simple thing...

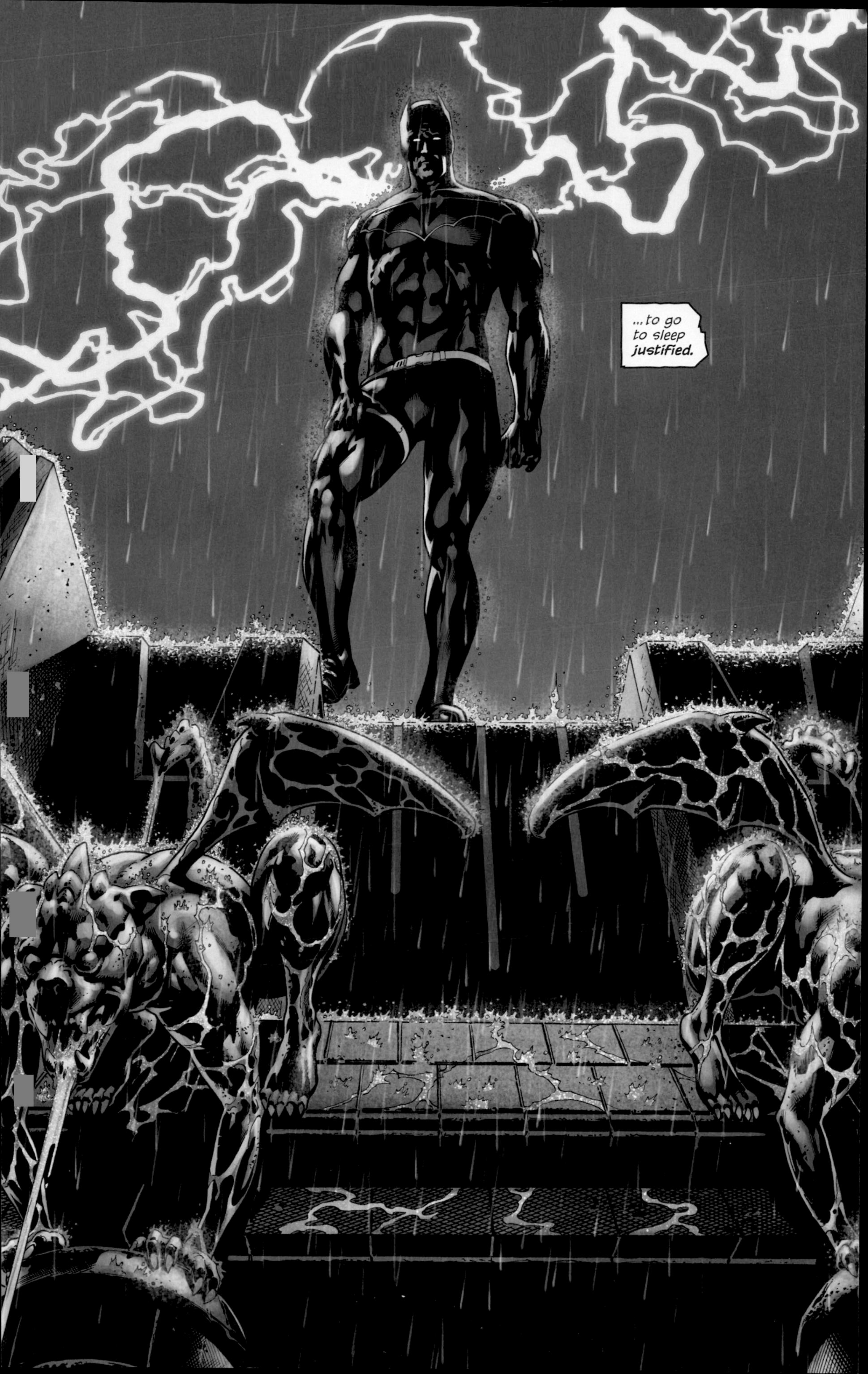
...to go to sleep justified.

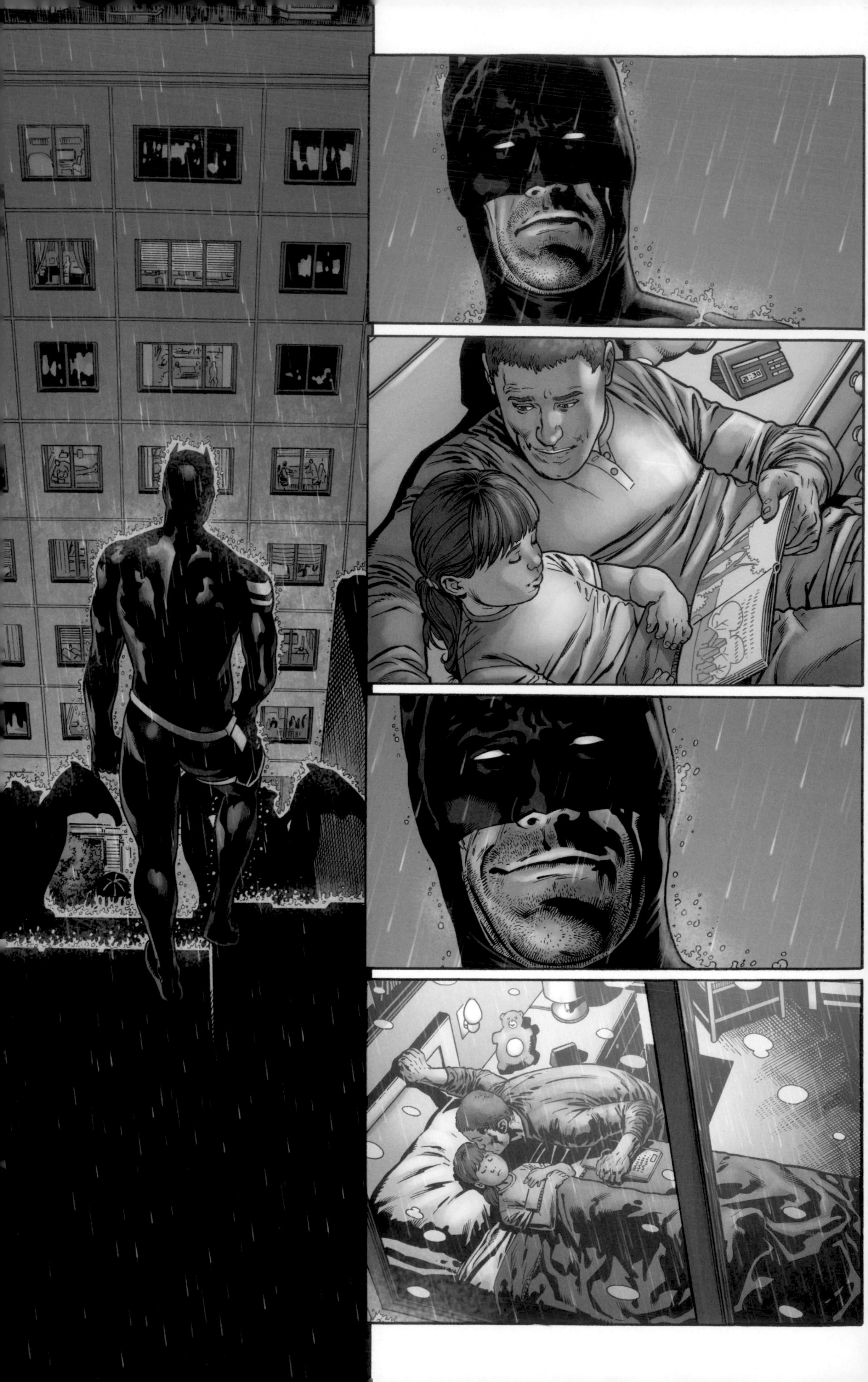

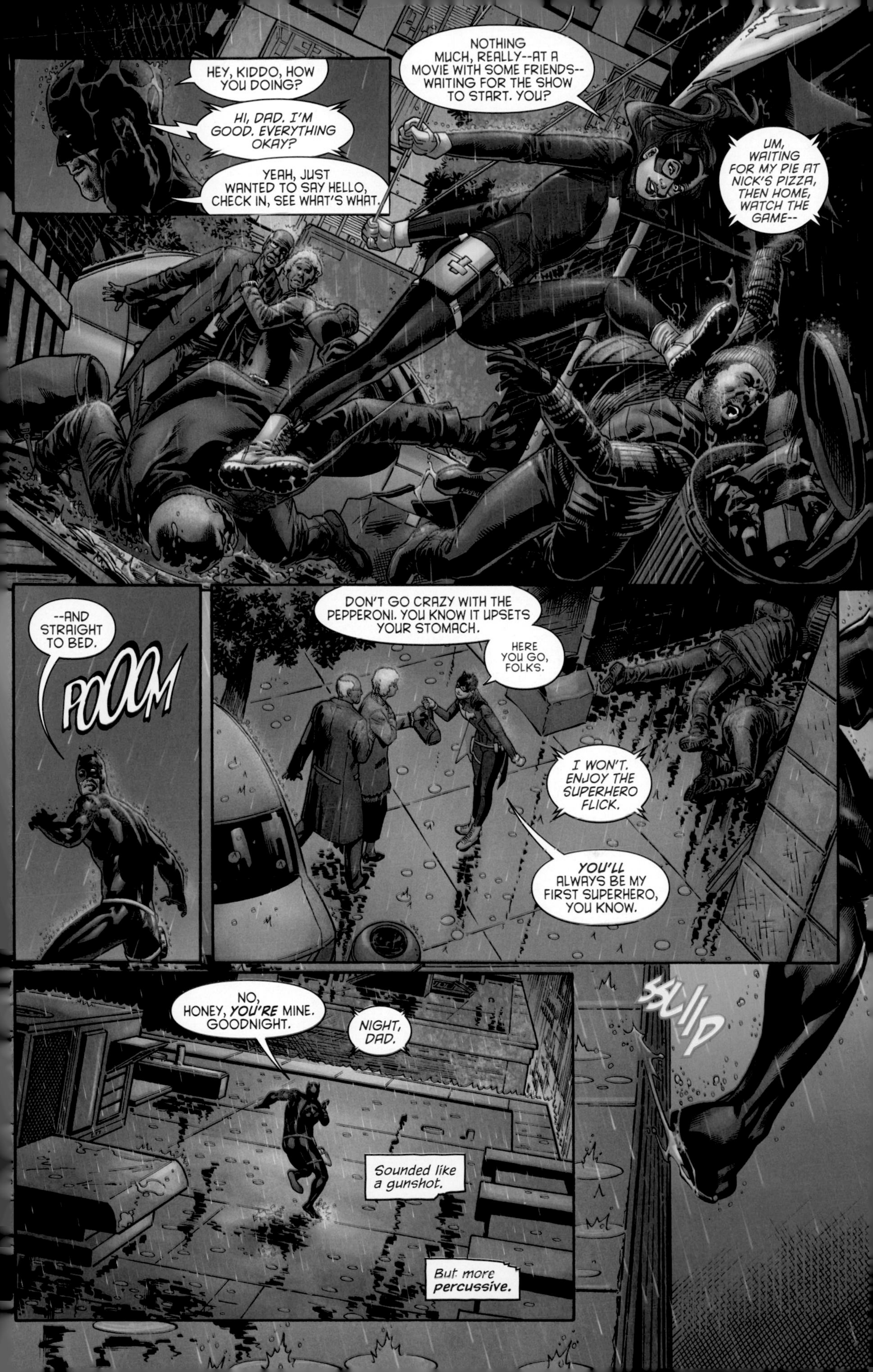
HEY, KIDDO, HOW YOU DOING?
HI, DAD. I'M GOOD. EVERYTHING OKAY?
YEAH, JUST WANTED TO SAY HELLO, CHECK IN, SEE WHAT'S WHAT.
NOTHING MUCH, REALLY--AT A MOVIE WITH SOME FRIENDS--WAITING FOR THE SHOW TO START. YOU?
UM, WAITING FOR MY PIE AT NICK'S PIZZA, THEN HOME, WATCH THE GAME--
--AND STRAIGHT TO BED.
POOOM
DON'T GO CRAZY WITH THE PEPPERONI. YOU KNOW IT UPSETS YOUR STOMACH.
HERE YOU GO, FOLKS.
I WON'T. ENJOY THE SUPERHERO FLICK.
YOU'LL ALWAYS BE MY FIRST SUPERHERO, YOU KNOW.
NO, HONEY, YOU'RE MINE. GOODNIGHT.
NIGHT, DAD.
SSLIIP
Sounded like a gunshot.
But more percussive.

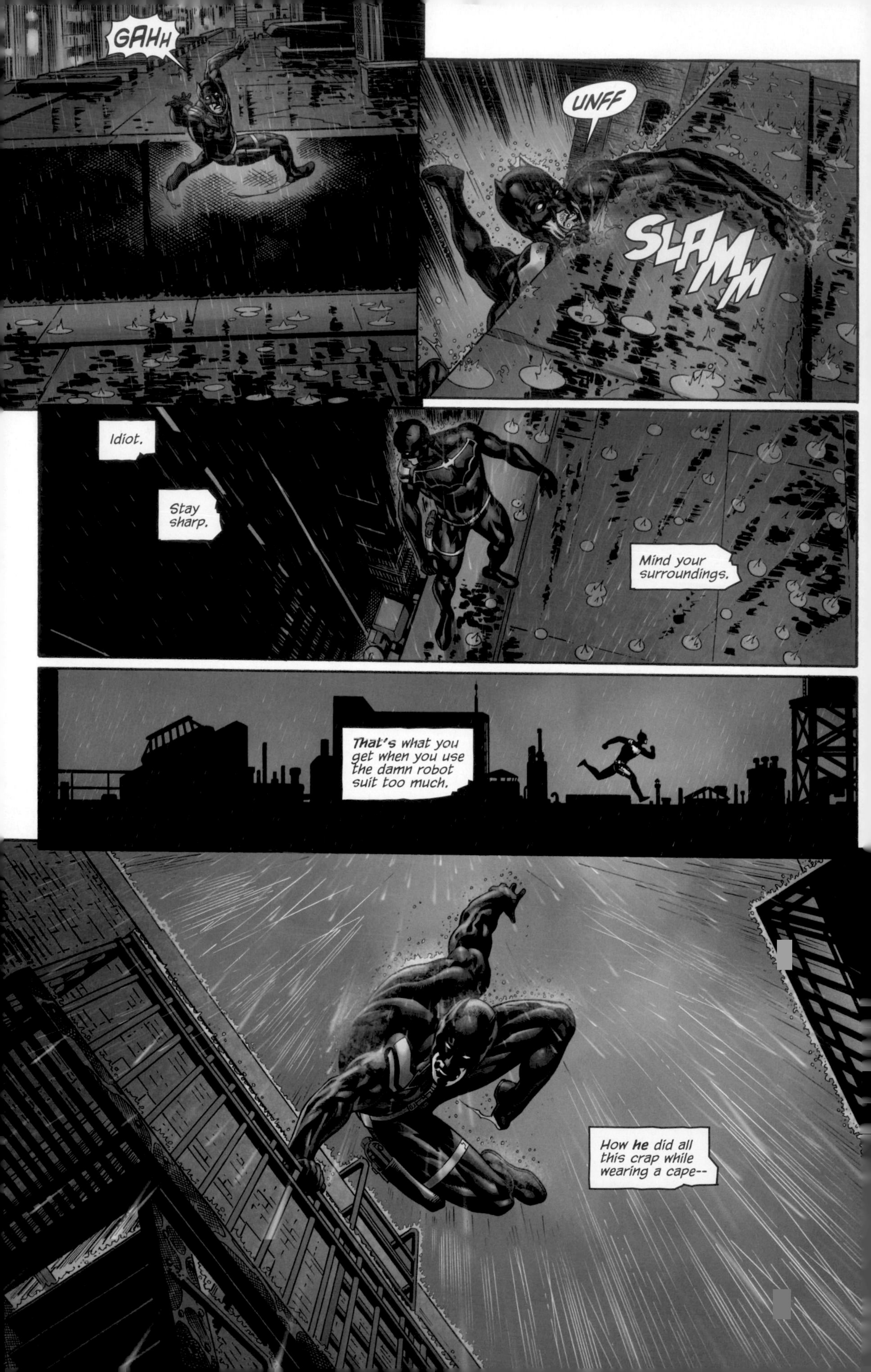
GAHH
UNFF
SLAMMM
Idiot.
Stay sharp.
Mind your surroundings.
That's what you get when you use the damn robot suit too much.
How he did all this crap while wearing a cape--

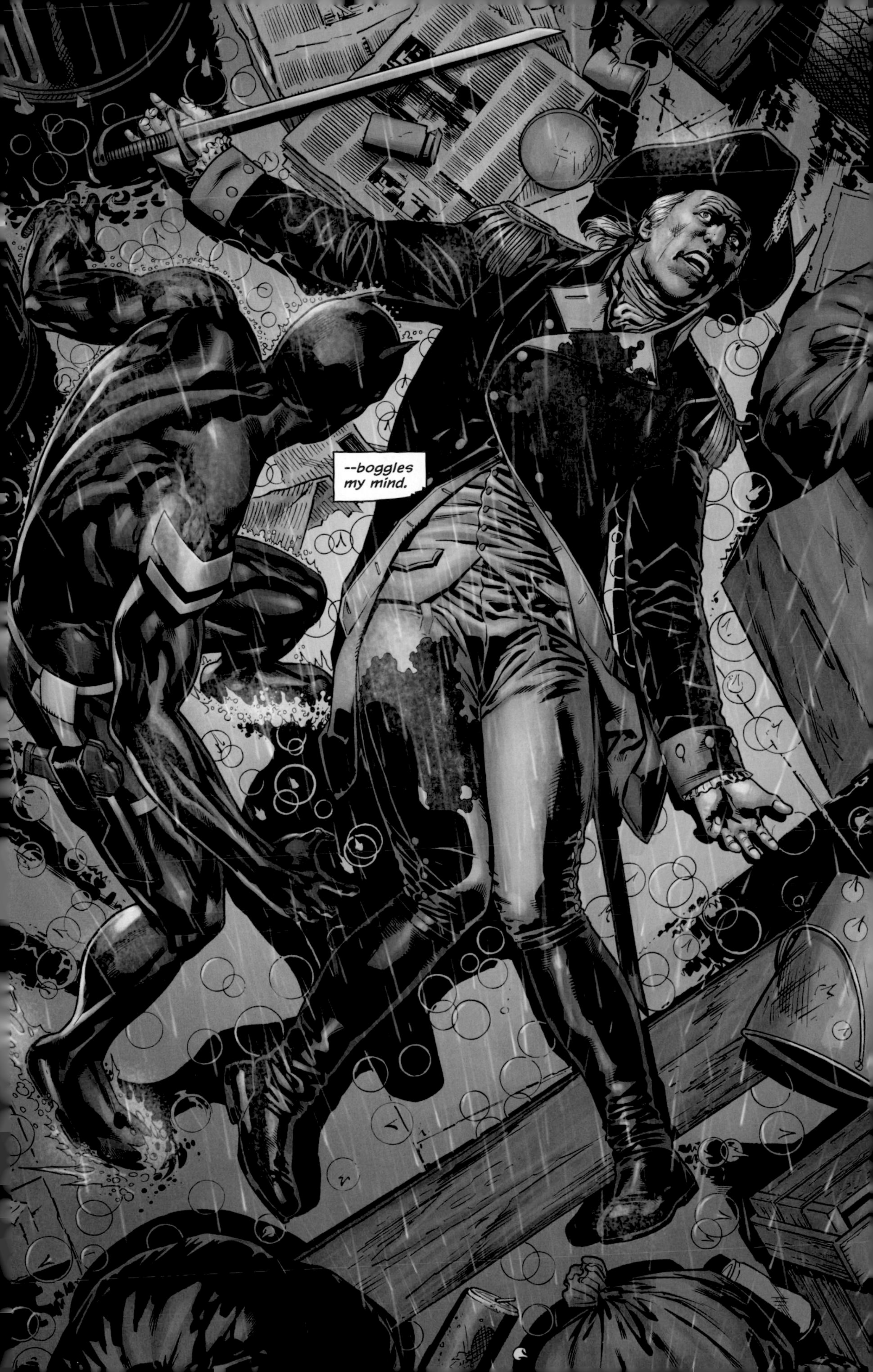
--boggles my mind.

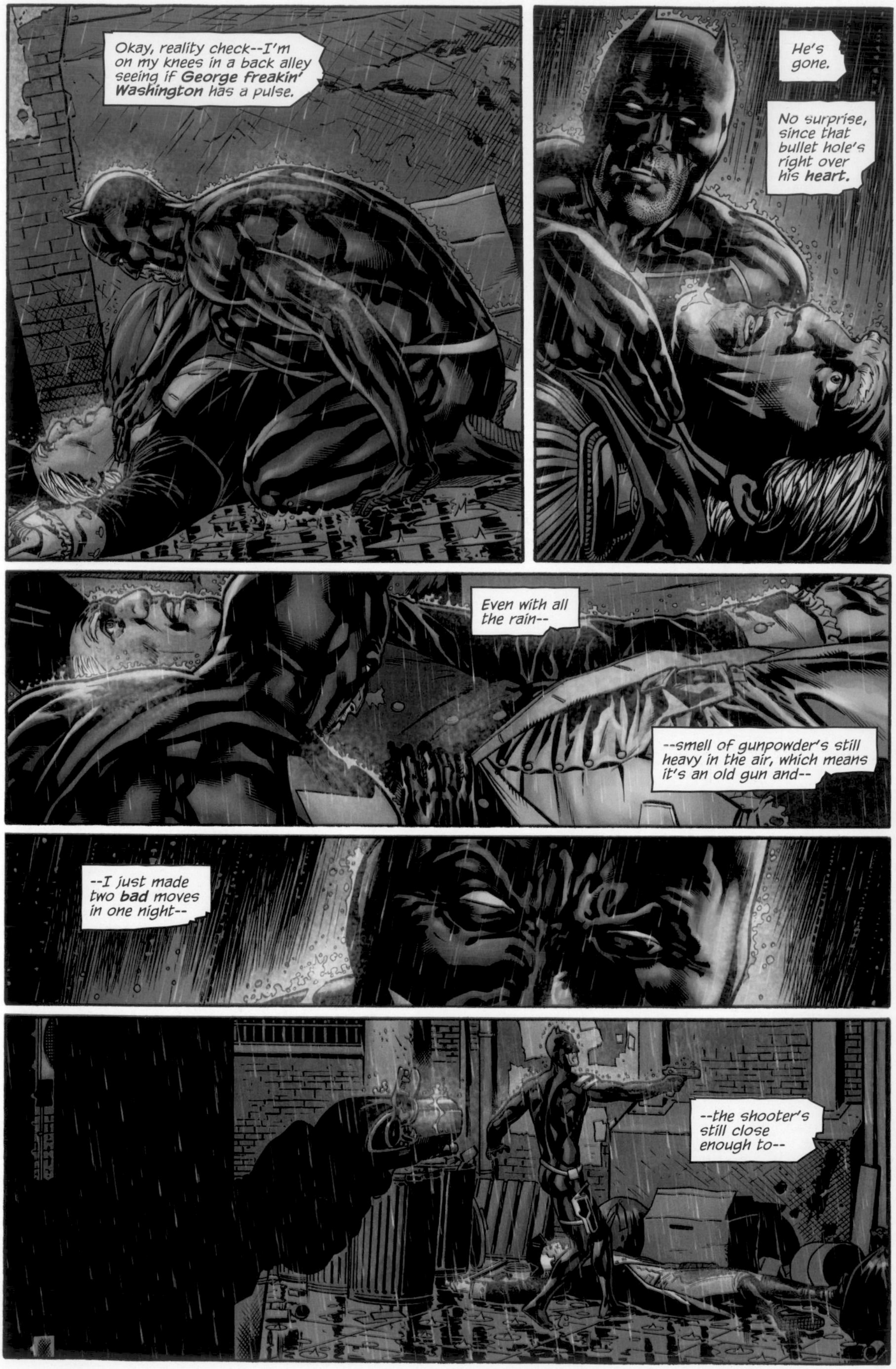
Okay, reality check--I'm on my knees in a back alley seeing if George freakin' Washington has a pulse.
He's gone.
No surprise, since that bullet hole's right over his heart.
Even with all the rain--
--smell of gunpowder's still heavy in the air, which means it's an old gun and--
--I just made two bad moves in one night--
--the shooter's still close enough to--

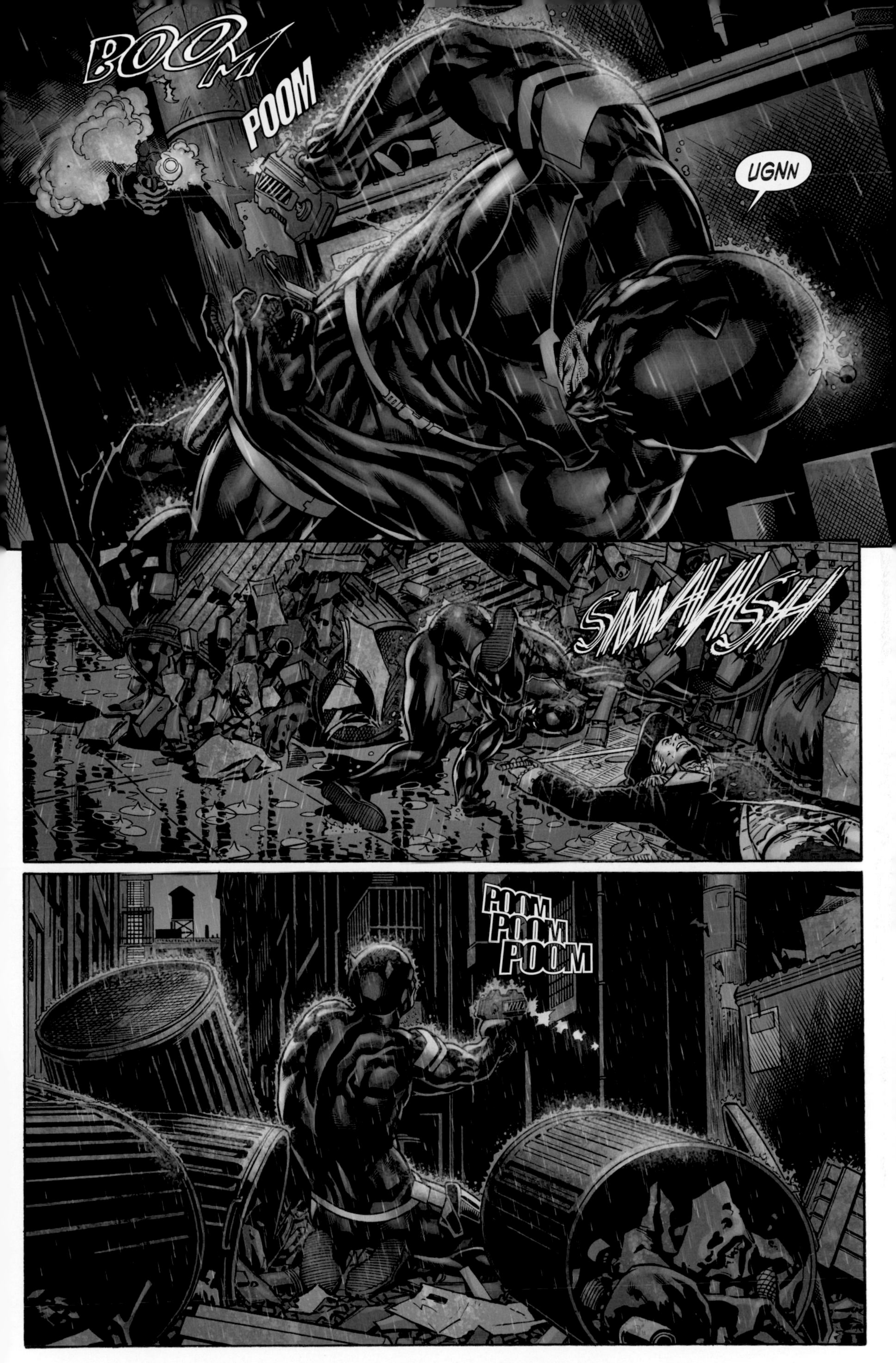
BOOM
POOM
UGNN
SMASH
POOM
POOM
POOM

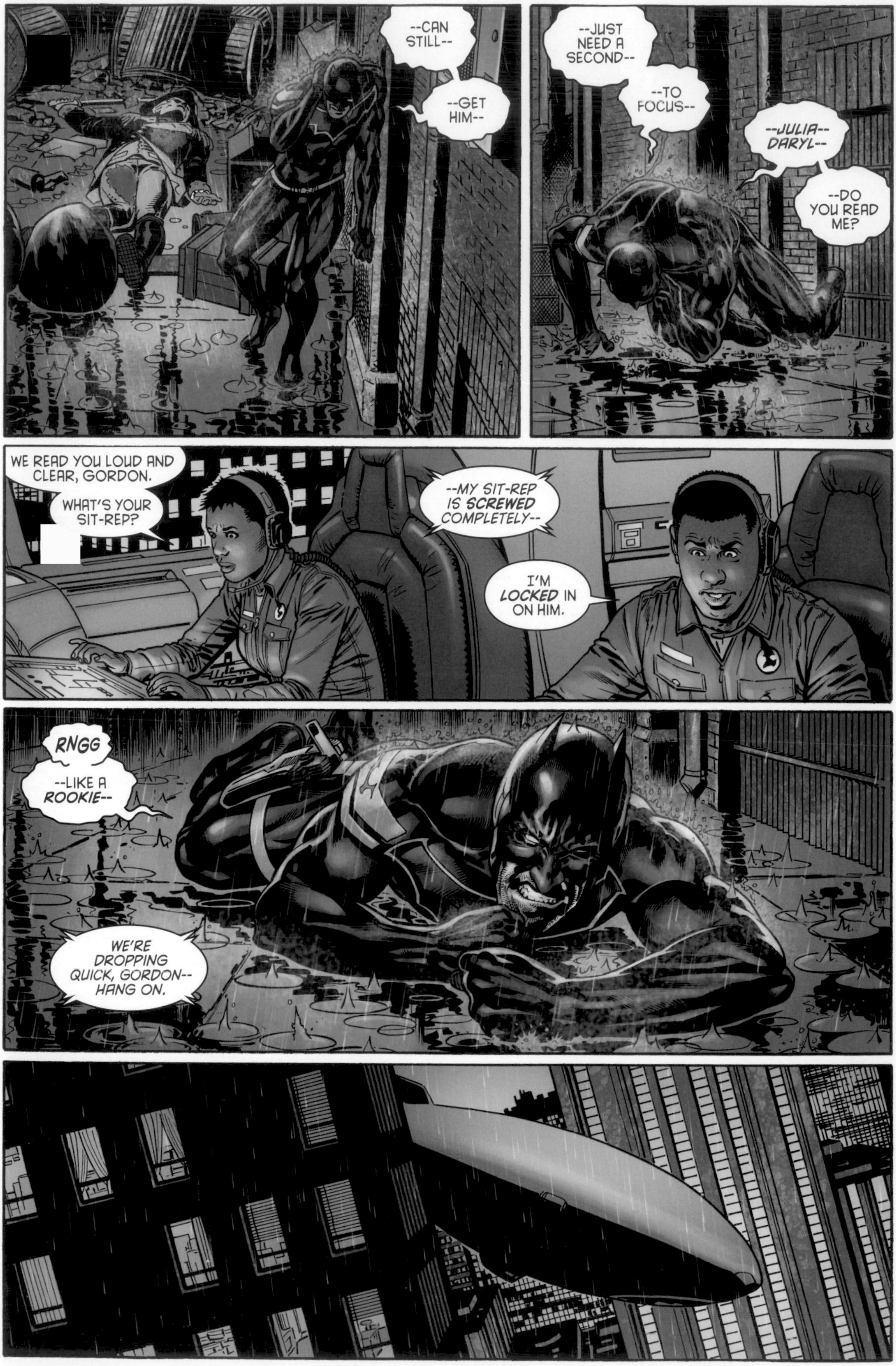
[redacted]
--CAN STILL--
--GET HIM--
--JUST NEED A SECOND--
--TO FOCUS--
--JULIA-- DARYL--
--DO YOU READ ME?
WE READ YOU LOUD AND CLEAR, GORDON.
WHAT'S YOUR SIT-REP?
--MY SIT-REP IS SCREWED COMPLETELY--
I'M LOCKED IN ON HIM.
RNGG
--LIKE A ROOKIE--
WE'RE DROPPING QUICK, GORDON-- HANG ON.

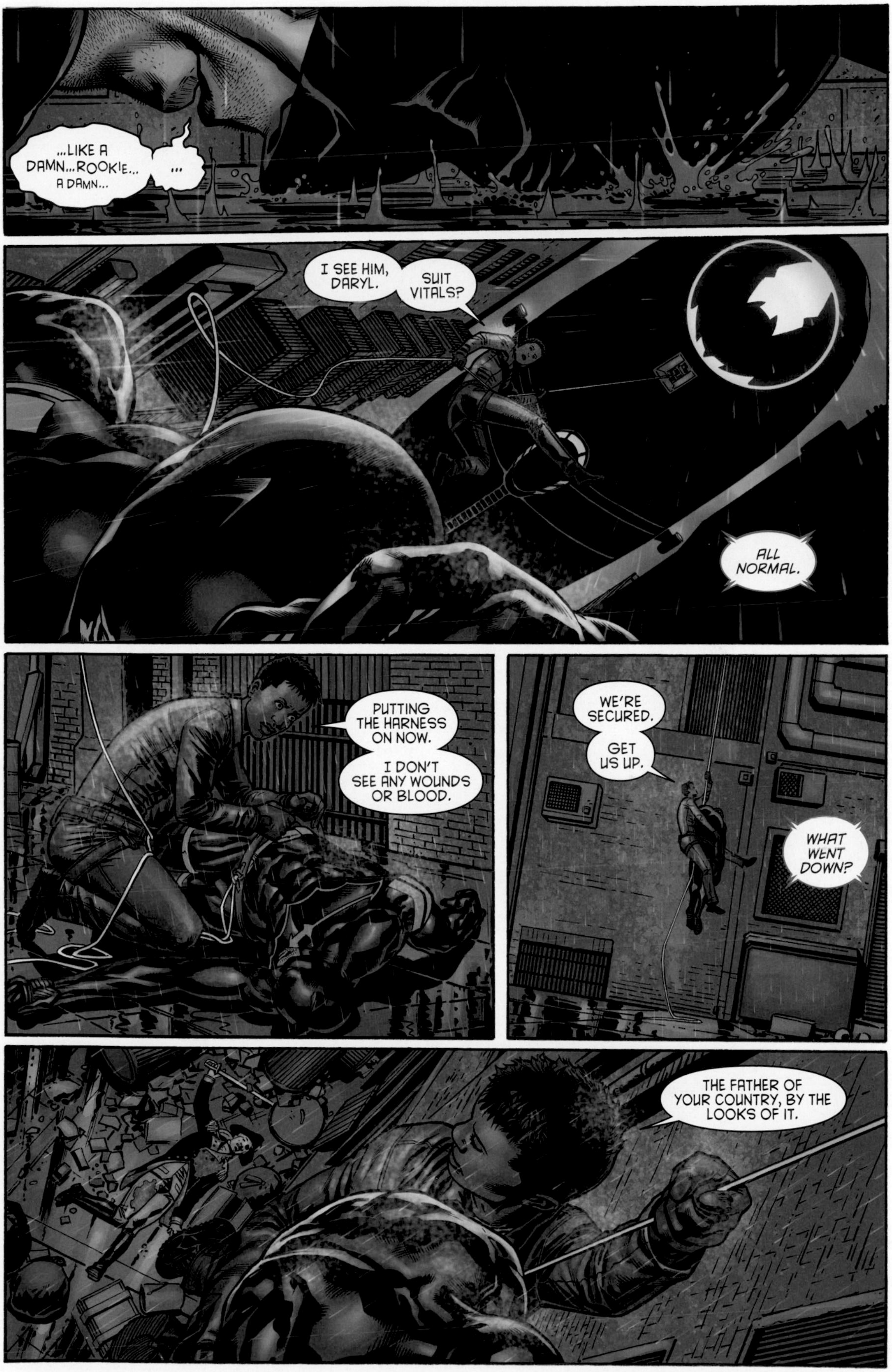
...LIKE A DAMN...ROOKIE... A DAMN...
...
I SEE HIM, DARYL.
SUIT VITALS?
ALL NORMAL.
PUTTING THE HARNESS ON NOW.
I DON'T SEE ANY WOUNDS OR BLOOD.
WE'RE SECURED.
GET US UP.
WHAT WENT DOWN?
THE FATHER OF YOUR COUNTRY, BY THE LOOKS OF IT.

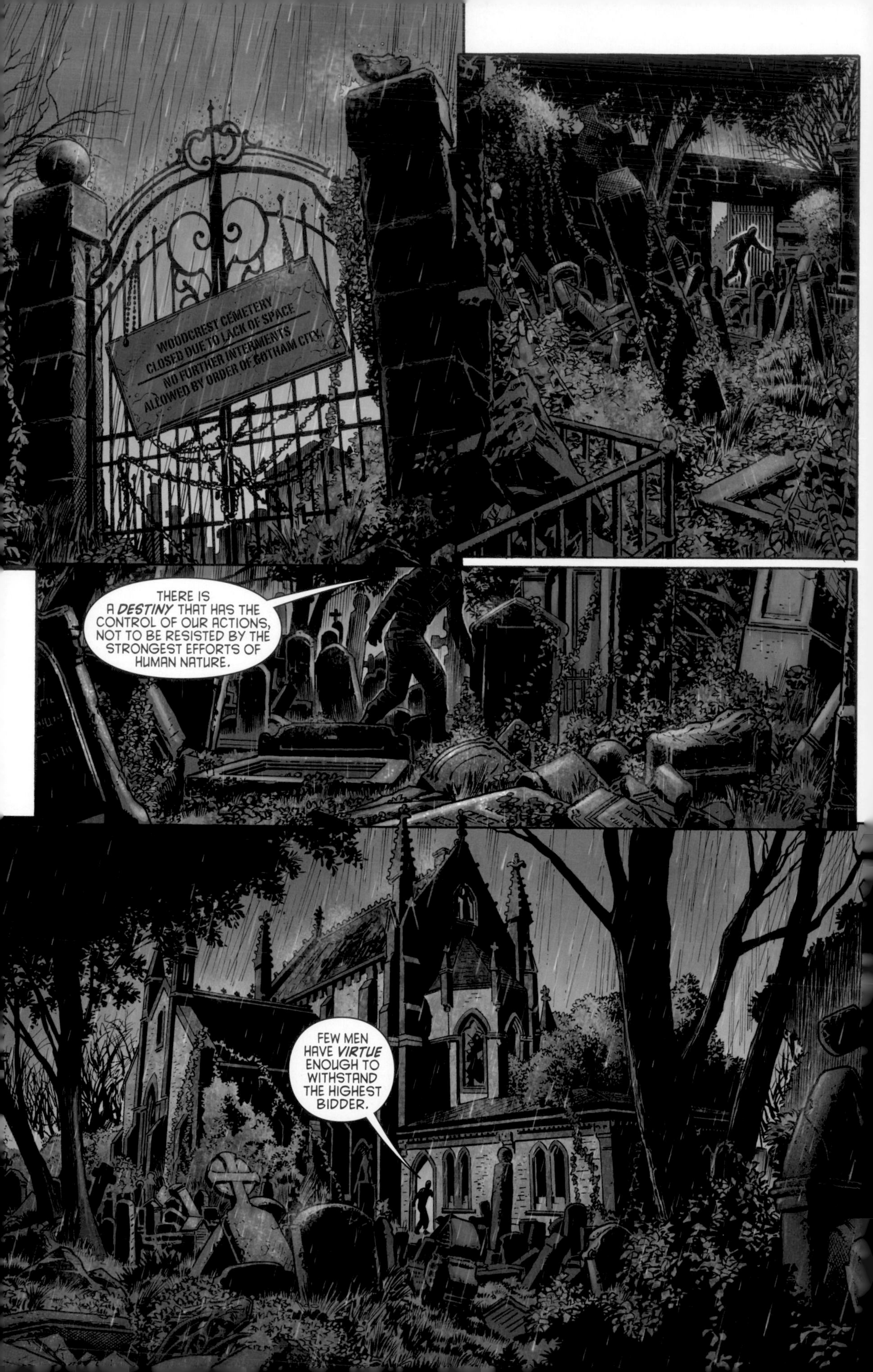
WOODCREST CEMETERY
CLOSED DUE TO LACK OF SPACE
NO FURTHER INTERMENTS
ALLOWED BY ORDER OF GOTHAM CITY
THERE IS A DESTINY THAT HAS THE CONTROL OF OUR ACTIONS, NOT TO BE RESISTED BY THE STRONGEST EFFORTS OF HUMAN NATURE.
FEW MEN HAVE VIRTUE ENOUGH TO WITHSTAND THE HIGHEST BIDDER.

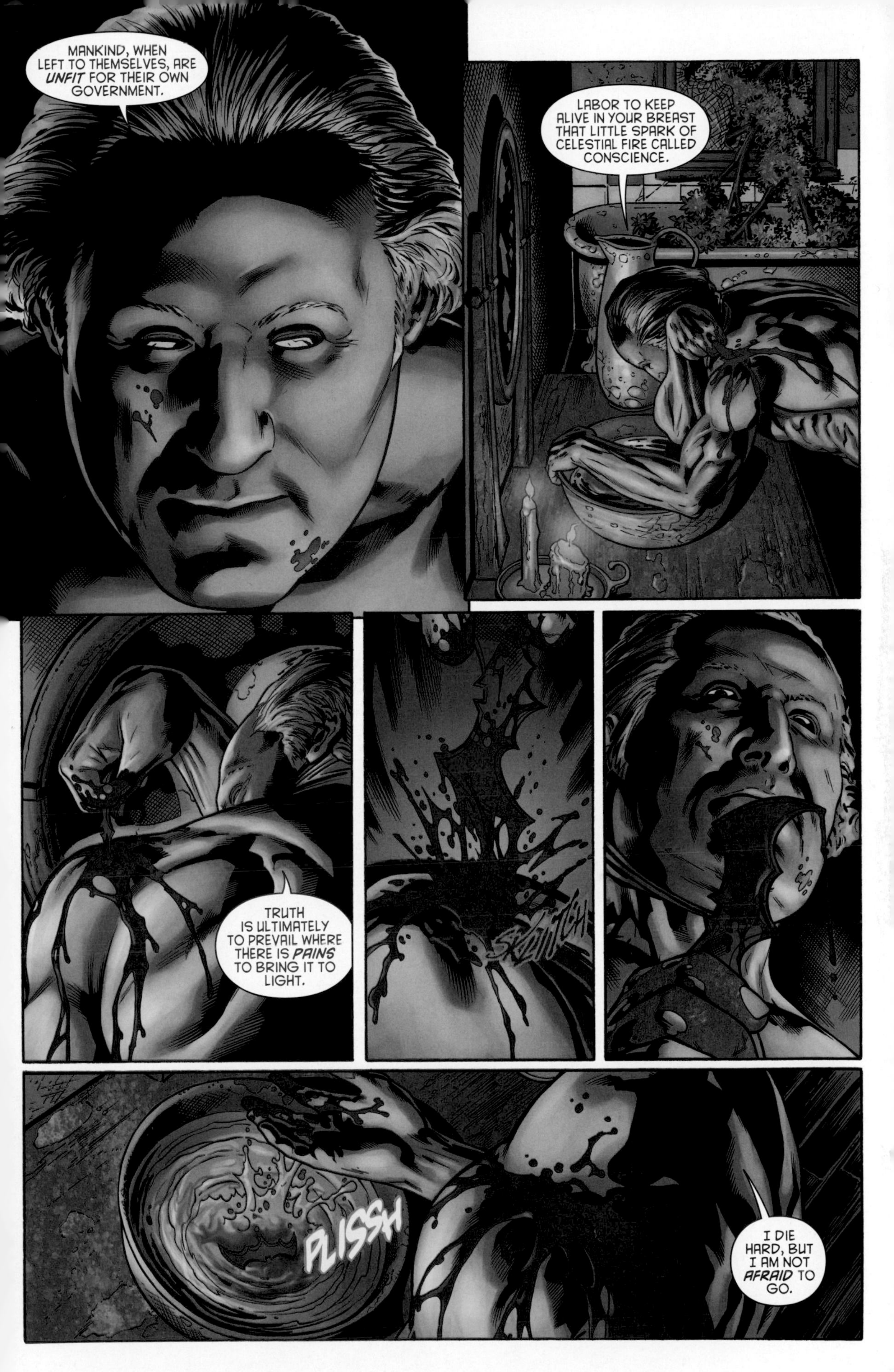
MANKIND, WHEN LEFT TO THEMSELVES, ARE *UNFIT* FOR THEIR OWN GOVERNMENT.
LABOR TO KEEP ALIVE IN YOUR BREAST THAT LITTLE SPARK OF CELESTIAL FIRE CALLED CONSCIENCE.
TRUTH IS ULTIMATELY TO PREVAIL WHERE THERE IS *PAINS* TO BRING IT TO LIGHT.
PLISSH
I DIE HARD, BUT I AM NOT *AFRAID* TO GO.

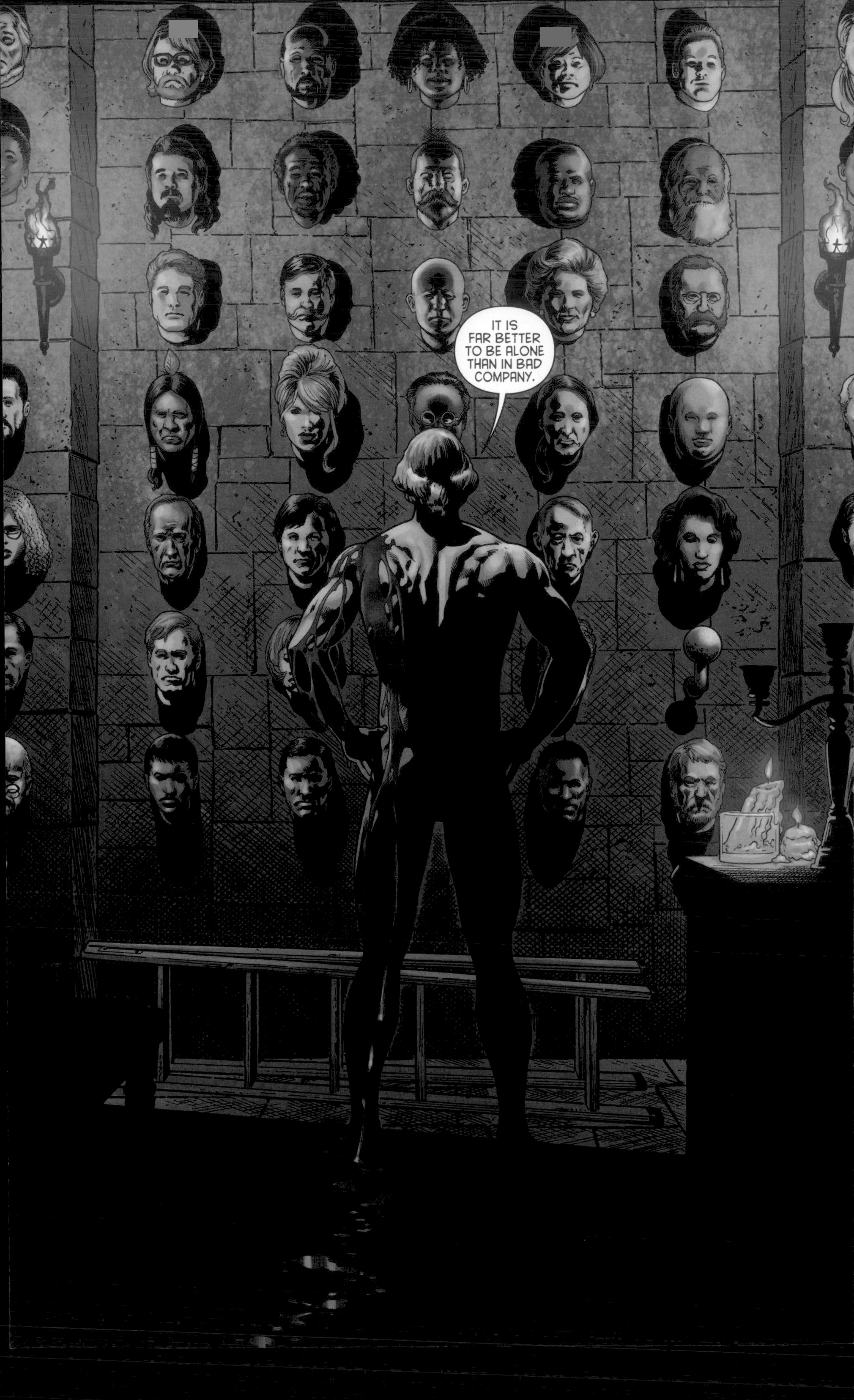
IT IS FAR BETTER TO BE ALONE THAN IN BAD COMPANY.

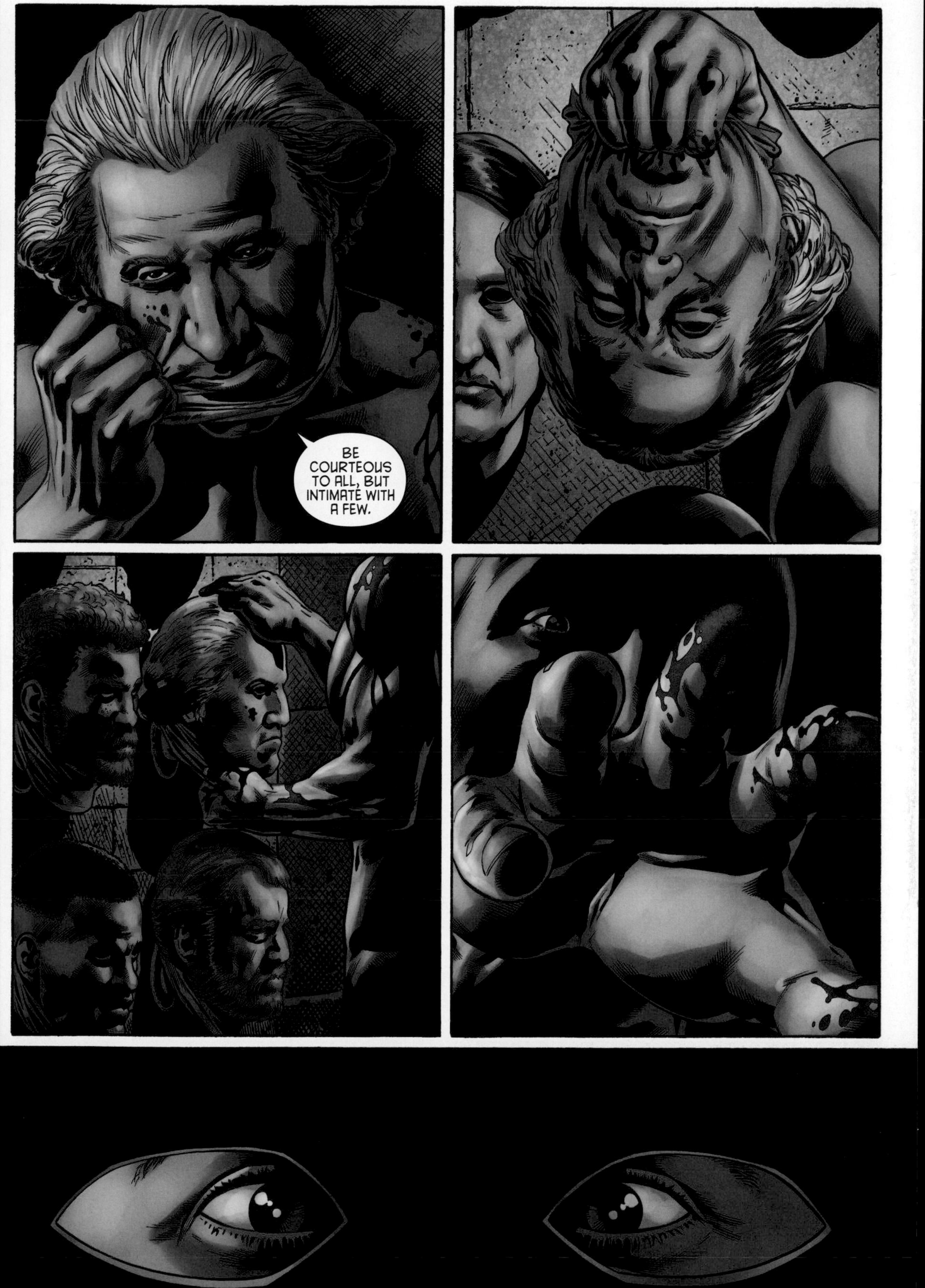
BE COURTEOUS TO ALL, BUT INTIMATE WITH A FEW.

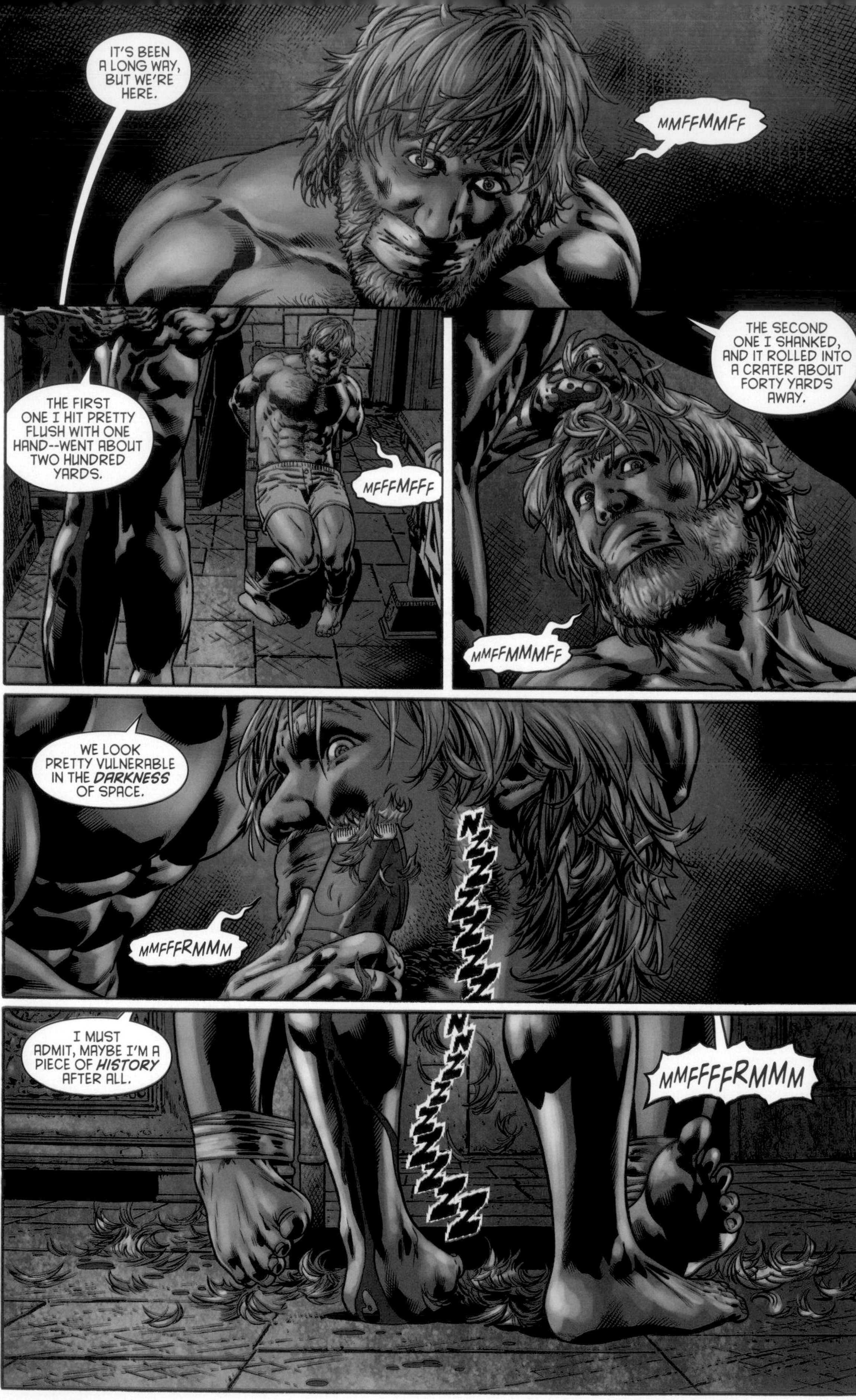
IT'S BEEN A LONG WAY, BUT WE'RE HERE.
MMFFMMFF
THE FIRST ONE I HIT PRETTY FLUSH WITH ONE HAND--WENT ABOUT TWO HUNDRED YARDS.
MFFFMFFF
THE SECOND ONE I SHANKED, AND IT ROLLED INTO A CRATER ABOUT FORTY YARDS AWAY.
MMFFMMMFF
WE LOOK PRETTY VULNERABLE IN THE DARKNESS OF SPACE.
MMFFFRMMM
NZZZZZZZZ
I MUST ADMIT, MAYBE I'M A PIECE OF HISTORY AFTER ALL.
MMFFFFRMMM
NNZZZZZZZZZ

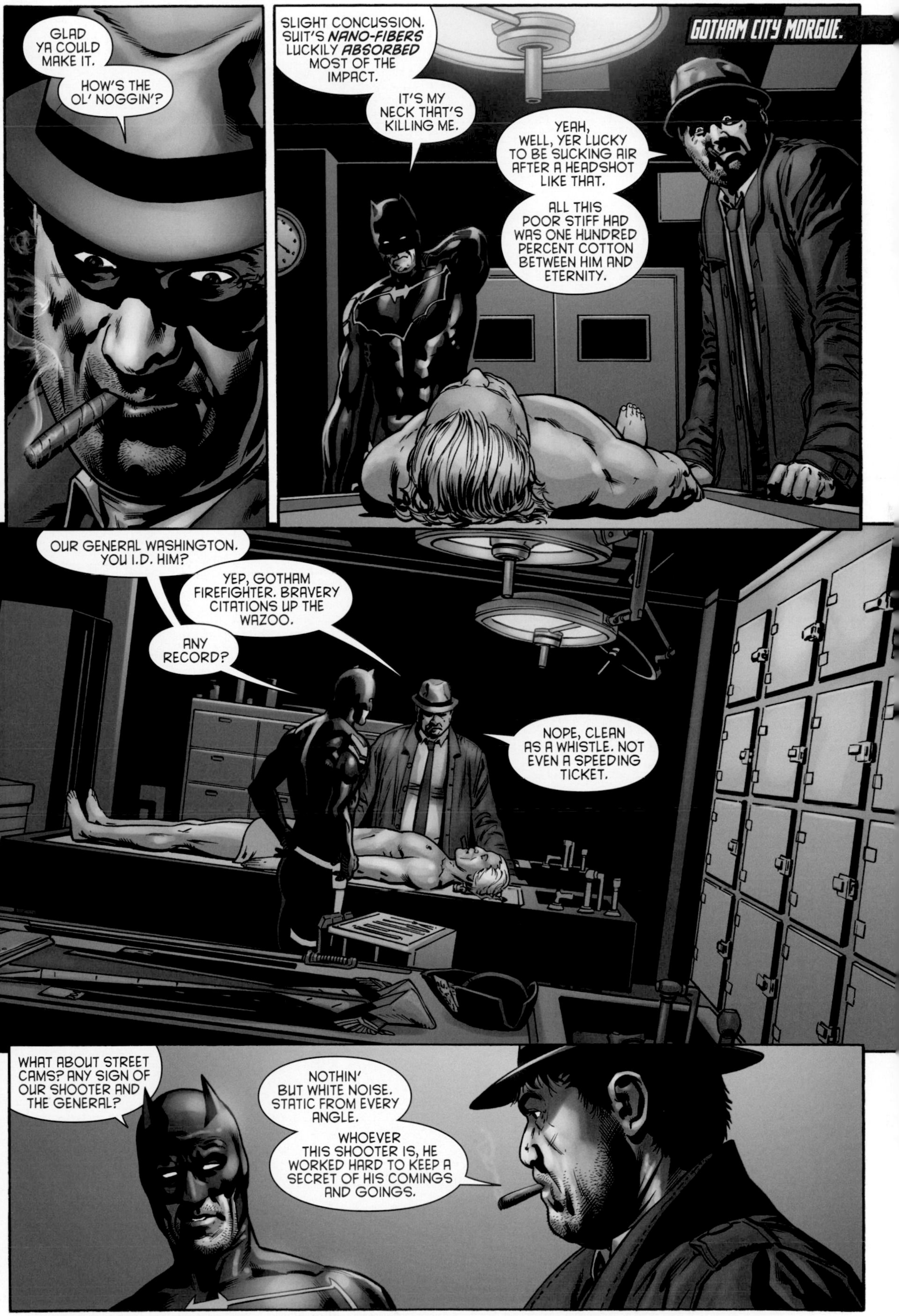
GLAD YA COULD MAKE IT.
HOW'S THE OL' NOGGIN'?
GOTHAM CITY MORGUE.
SLIGHT CONCUSSION. SUIT'S NANO-FIBERS LUCKILY ABSORBED MOST OF THE IMPACT.
IT'S MY NECK THAT'S KILLING ME.
YEAH, WELL, YER LUCKY TO BE SUCKING AIR AFTER A HEADSHOT LIKE THAT.
ALL THIS POOR STIFF HAD WAS ONE HUNDRED PERCENT COTTON BETWEEN HIM AND ETERNITY.
OUR GENERAL WASHINGTON. YOU I.D. HIM?
YEP, GOTHAM FIREFIGHTER. BRAVERY CITATIONS UP THE WAZOO.
ANY RECORD?
NOPE, CLEAN AS A WHISTLE. NOT EVEN A SPEEDING TICKET.
WHAT ABOUT STREET CAMS? ANY SIGN OF OUR SHOOTER AND THE GENERAL?
NOTHIN' BUT WHITE NOISE. STATIC FROM EVERY ANGLE.
WHOEVER THIS SHOOTER IS, HE WORKED HARD TO KEEP A SECRET OF HIS COMINGS AND GOINGS.

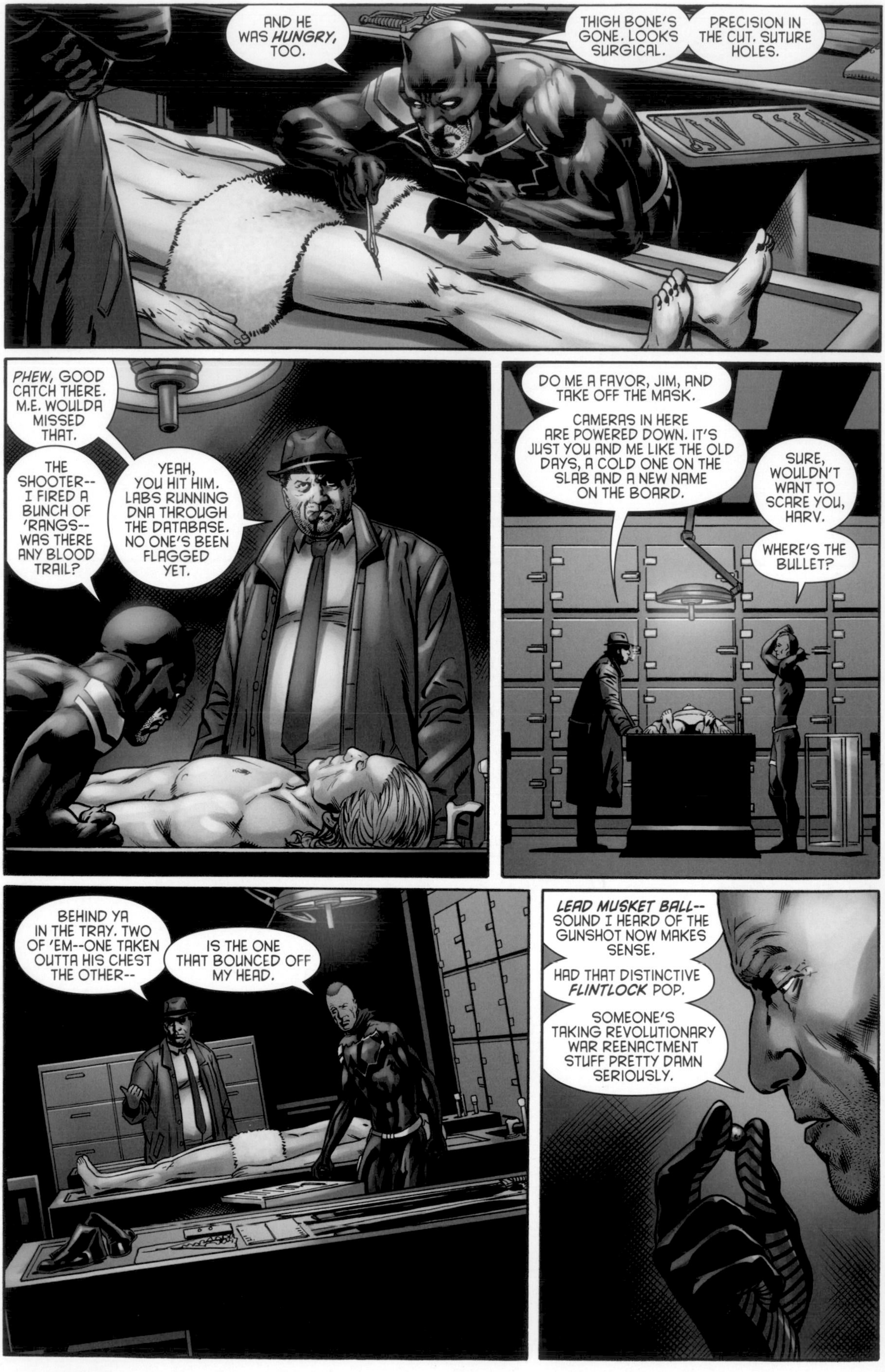

AND HE WAS HUNGRY, TOO.
THIGH BONE'S GONE. LOOKS SURGICAL.
PRECISION IN THE CUT. SUTURE HOLES.
PHEW, GOOD CATCH THERE. M.E. WOULDA MISSED THAT.
THE SHOOTER-- I FIRED A BUNCH OF 'RANGS-- WAS THERE ANY BLOOD TRAIL?
YEAH, YOU HIT HIM. LABS RUNNING DNA THROUGH THE DATABASE. NO ONE'S BEEN FLAGGED YET.
DO ME A FAVOR, JIM, AND TAKE OFF THE MASK.
CAMERAS IN HERE ARE POWERED DOWN. IT'S JUST YOU AND ME LIKE THE OLD DAYS, A COLD ONE ON THE SLAB AND A NEW NAME ON THE BOARD.
SURE, WOULDN'T WANT TO SCARE YOU, HARV.
WHERE'S THE BULLET?
BEHIND YA IN THE TRAY. TWO OF 'EM--ONE TAKEN OUTTA HIS CHEST THE OTHER--
IS THE ONE THAT BOUNCED OFF MY HEAD.
LEAD MUSKET BALL-- SOUND I HEARD OF THE GUNSHOT NOW MAKES SENSE.
HAD THAT DISTINCTIVE FLINTLOCK POP.
SOMEONE'S TAKING REVOLUTIONARY WAR REENACTMENT STUFF PRETTY DAMN SERIOUSLY.

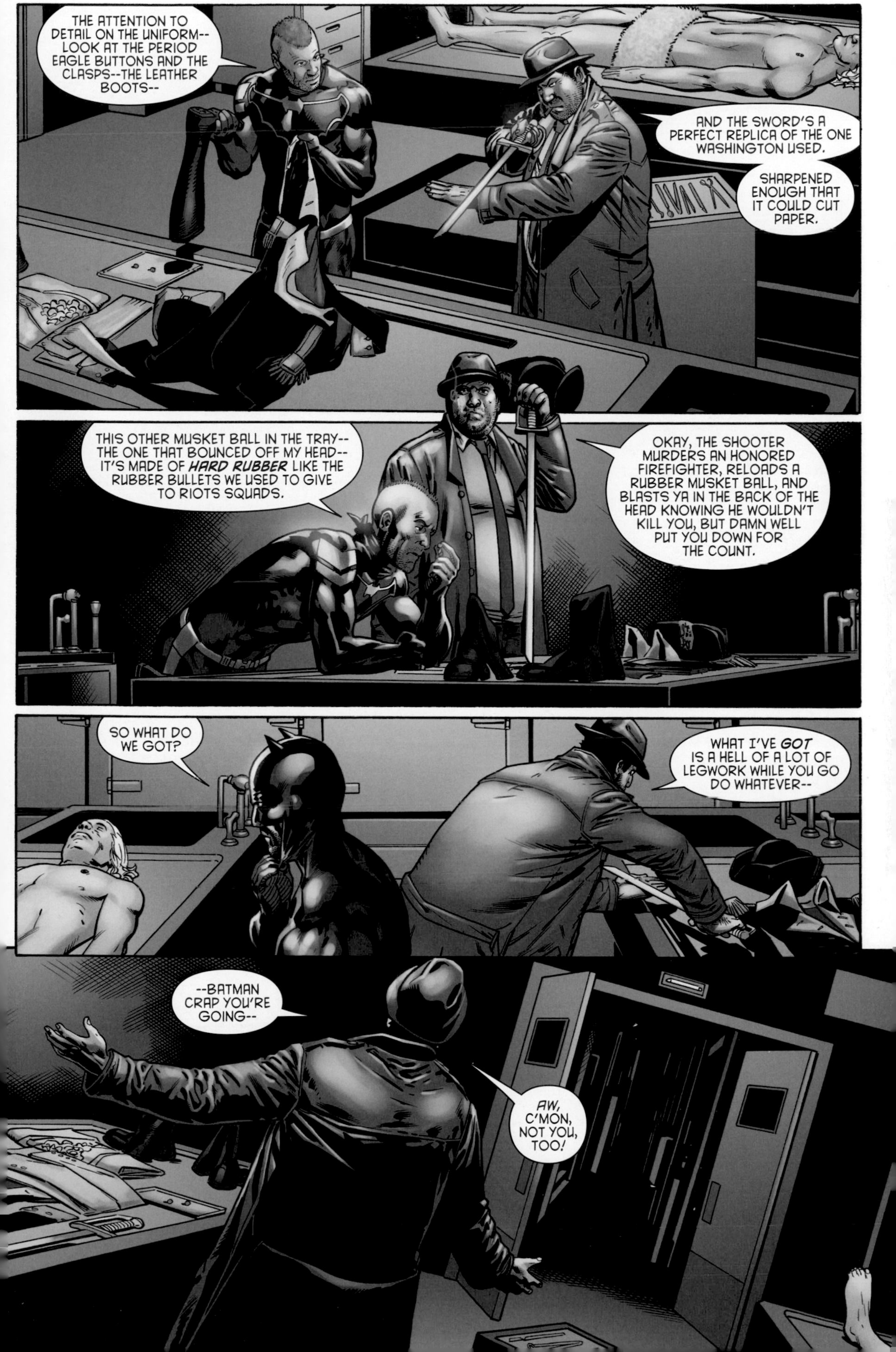

THE ATTENTION TO DETAIL ON THE UNIFORM-- LOOK AT THE PERIOD EAGLE BUTTONS AND THE CLASPS--THE LEATHER BOOTS--
AND THE SWORD'S A PERFECT REPLICA OF THE ONE WASHINGTON USED.
SHARPENED ENOUGH THAT IT COULD CUT PAPER.
THIS OTHER MUSKET BALL IN THE TRAY-- THE ONE THAT BOUNCED OFF MY HEAD-- IT'S MADE OF *HARD RUBBER* LIKE THE RUBBER BULLETS WE USED TO GIVE TO RIOTS SQUADS.
OKAY, THE SHOOTER MURDERS AN HONORED FIREFIGHTER, RELOADS A RUBBER MUSKET BALL, AND BLASTS YA IN THE BACK OF THE HEAD KNOWING HE WOULDN'T KILL YOU, BUT DAMN WELL PUT YOU DOWN FOR THE COUNT.
SO WHAT DO WE GOT?
WHAT I'VE *GOT* IS A HELL OF A LOT OF LEGWORK WHILE YOU GO DO WHATEVER--
--BATMAN CRAP YOU'RE GOING--
AW, C'MON, NOT YOU, TOO!

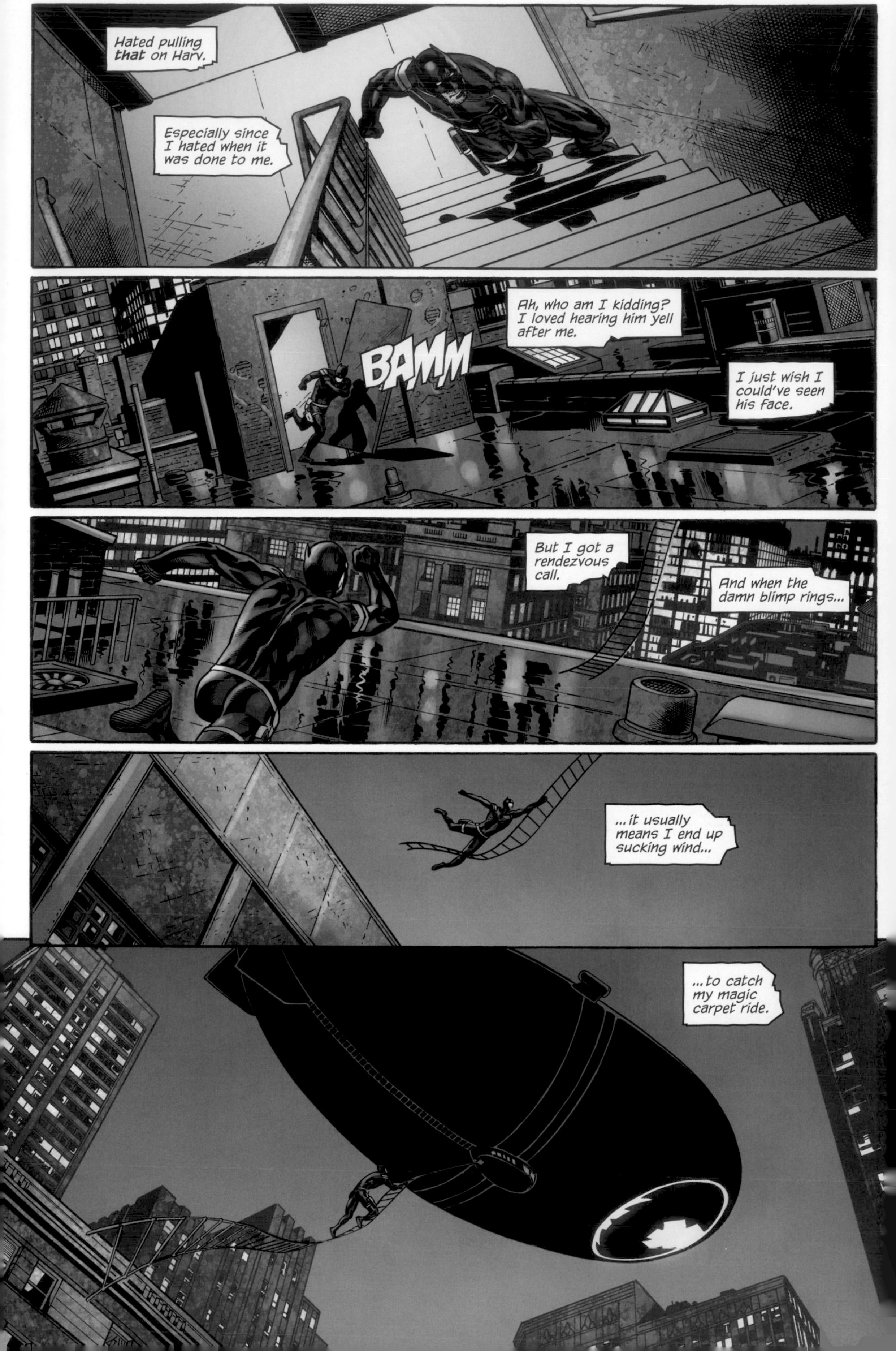
Hated pulling that on Harv.
Especially since I hated when it was done to me.
BAMM
Ah, who am I kidding? I loved hearing him yell after me.
I just wish I could've seen his face.
But I got a rendezvous call.
And when the damn blimp rings...
...it usually means I end up sucking wind...
...to catch my magic carpet ride.

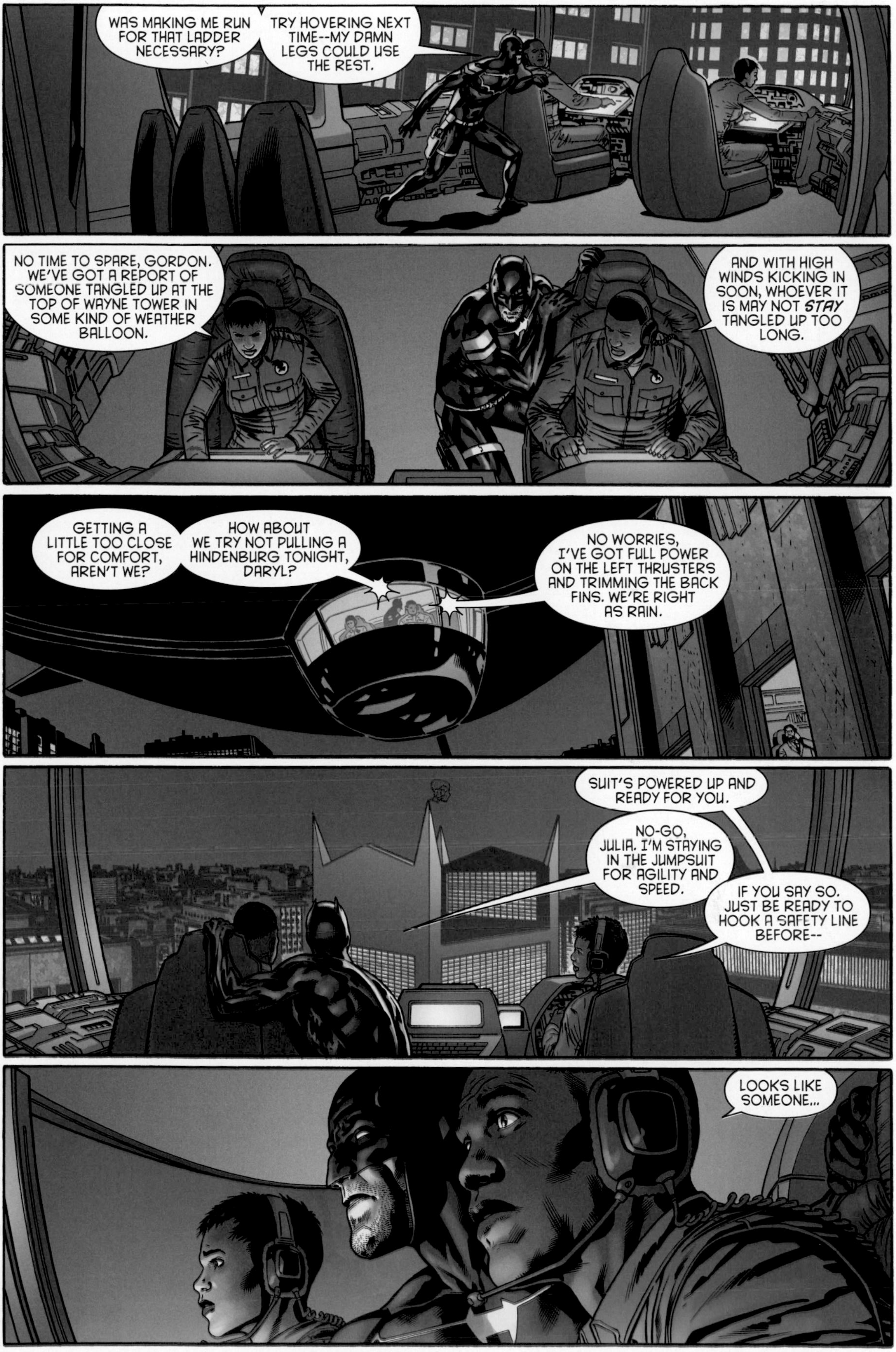
WAS MAKING ME RUN FOR THAT LADDER NECESSARY?
TRY HOVERING NEXT TIME--MY DAMN LEGS COULD USE THE REST.
NO TIME TO SPARE, GORDON. WE'VE GOT A REPORT OF SOMEONE TANGLED UP AT THE TOP OF WAYNE TOWER IN SOME KIND OF WEATHER BALLOON.
AND WITH HIGH WINDS KICKING IN SOON, WHOEVER IT IS MAY NOT *STAY* TANGLED UP TOO LONG.
GETTING A LITTLE TOO CLOSE FOR COMFORT, AREN'T WE?
HOW ABOUT WE TRY NOT PULLING A HINDENBURG TONIGHT, DARYL?
NO WORRIES, I'VE GOT FULL POWER ON THE LEFT THRUSTERS AND TRIMMING THE BACK FINS. WE'RE RIGHT AS RAIN.
SUIT'S POWERED UP AND READY FOR YOU.
NO-GO, JULIA. I'M STAYING IN THE JUMPSUIT FOR AGILITY AND SPEED.
IF YOU SAY SO. JUST BE READY TO HOOK A SAFETY LINE BEFORE--
LOOKS LIKE SOMEONE...

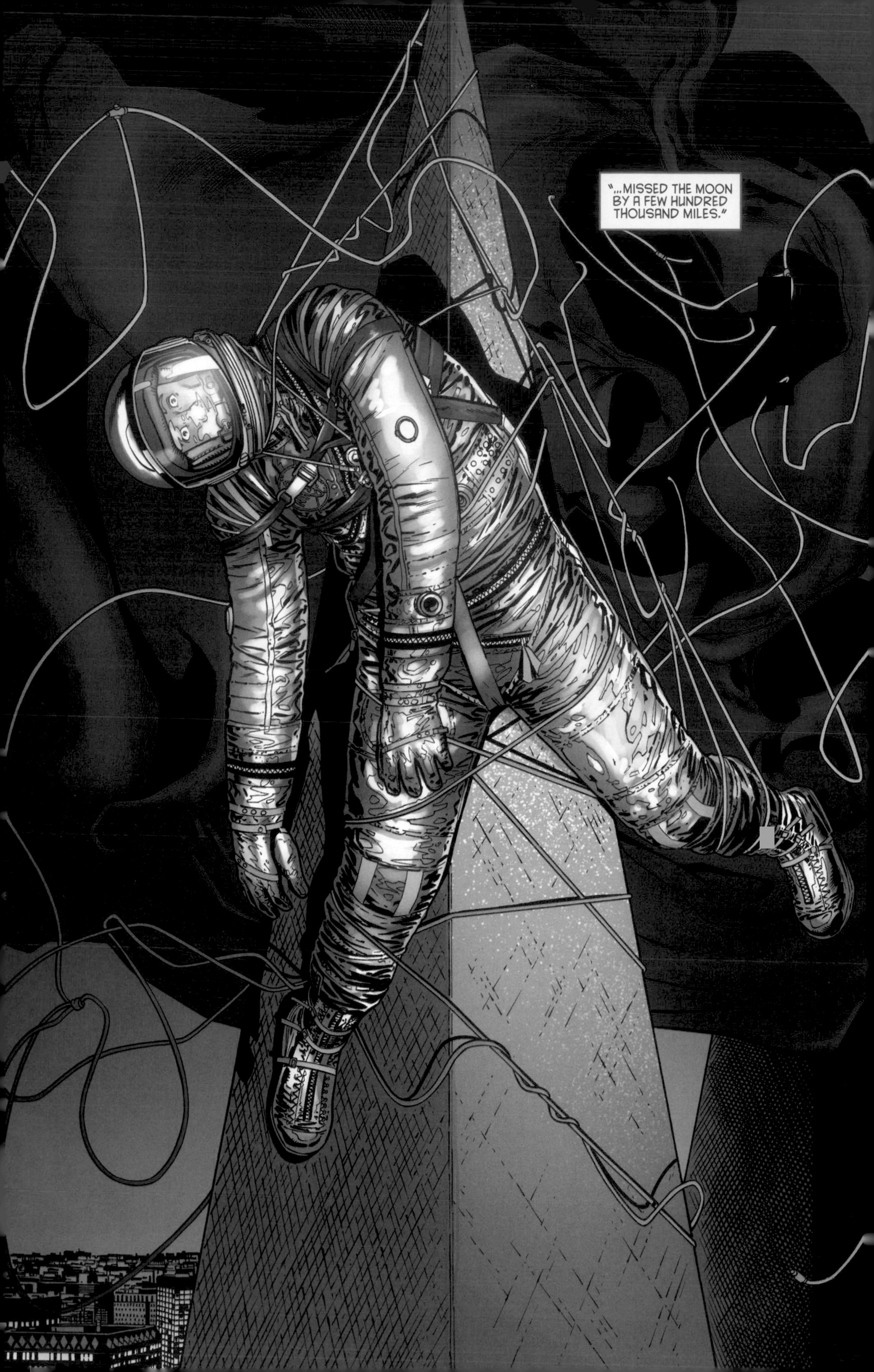
"...MISSED THE MOON BY A FEW HUNDRED THOUSAND MILES."

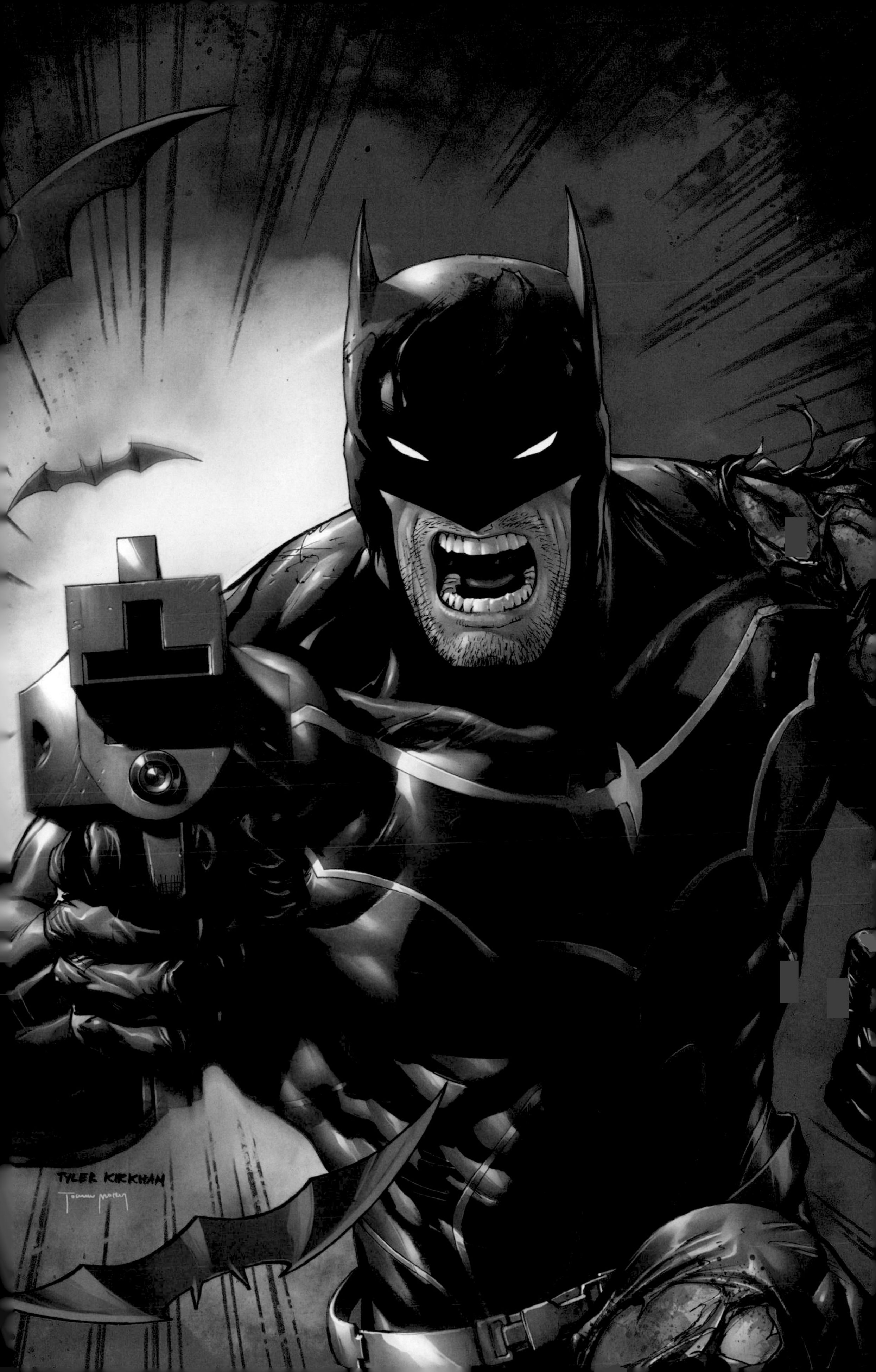
TYLER KIRKHAM

THE BRONZE AGE: SALT OF THE EARTH

PETER J. TOMASI writer FERNANDO PASARIN penciller MATT RYAN inker CHRIS SOTOMAYOR colorist WES ABBOTT letterer TYLER KIRKHAM TOMEU MOREY cover

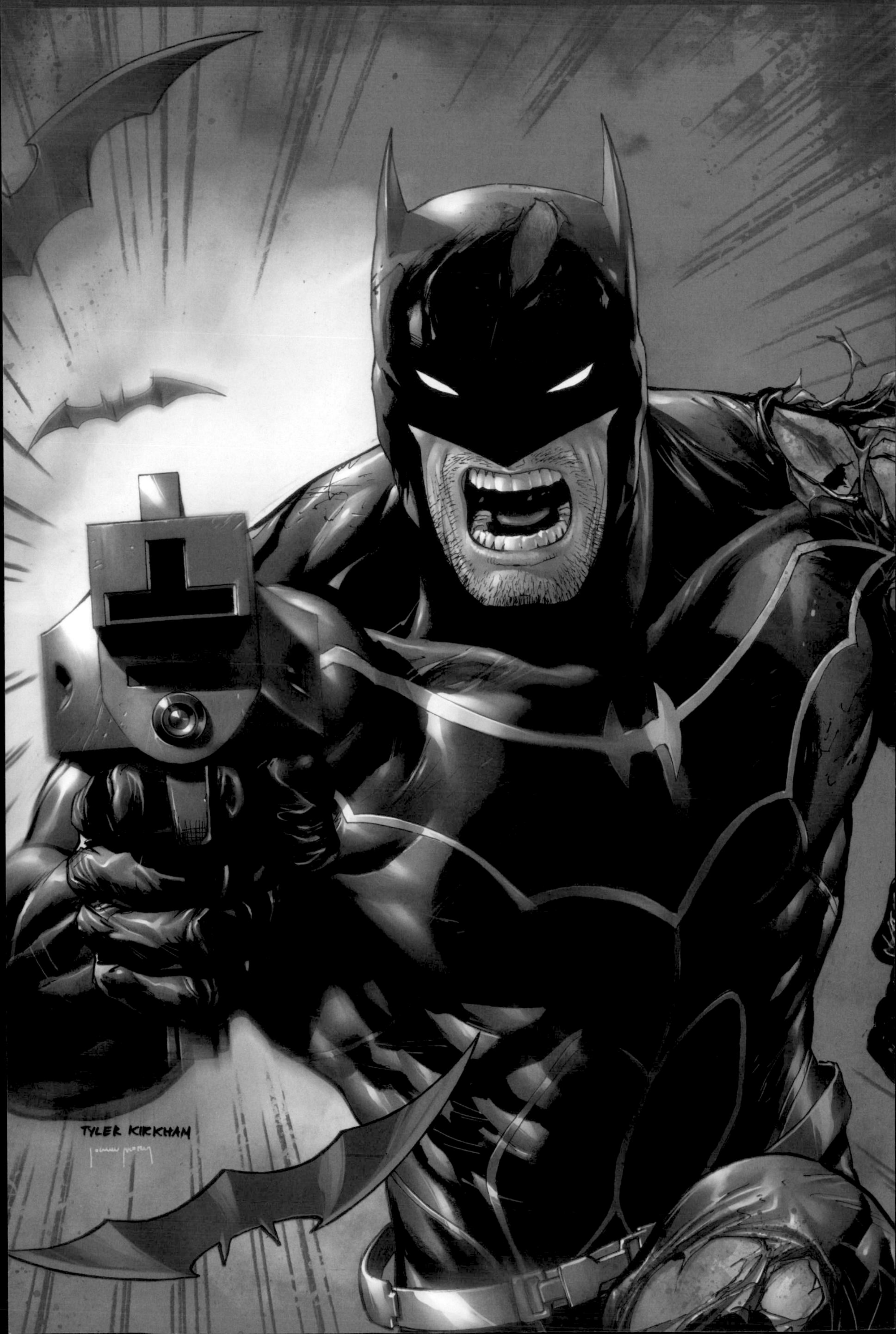
TYLER KIRKHAM

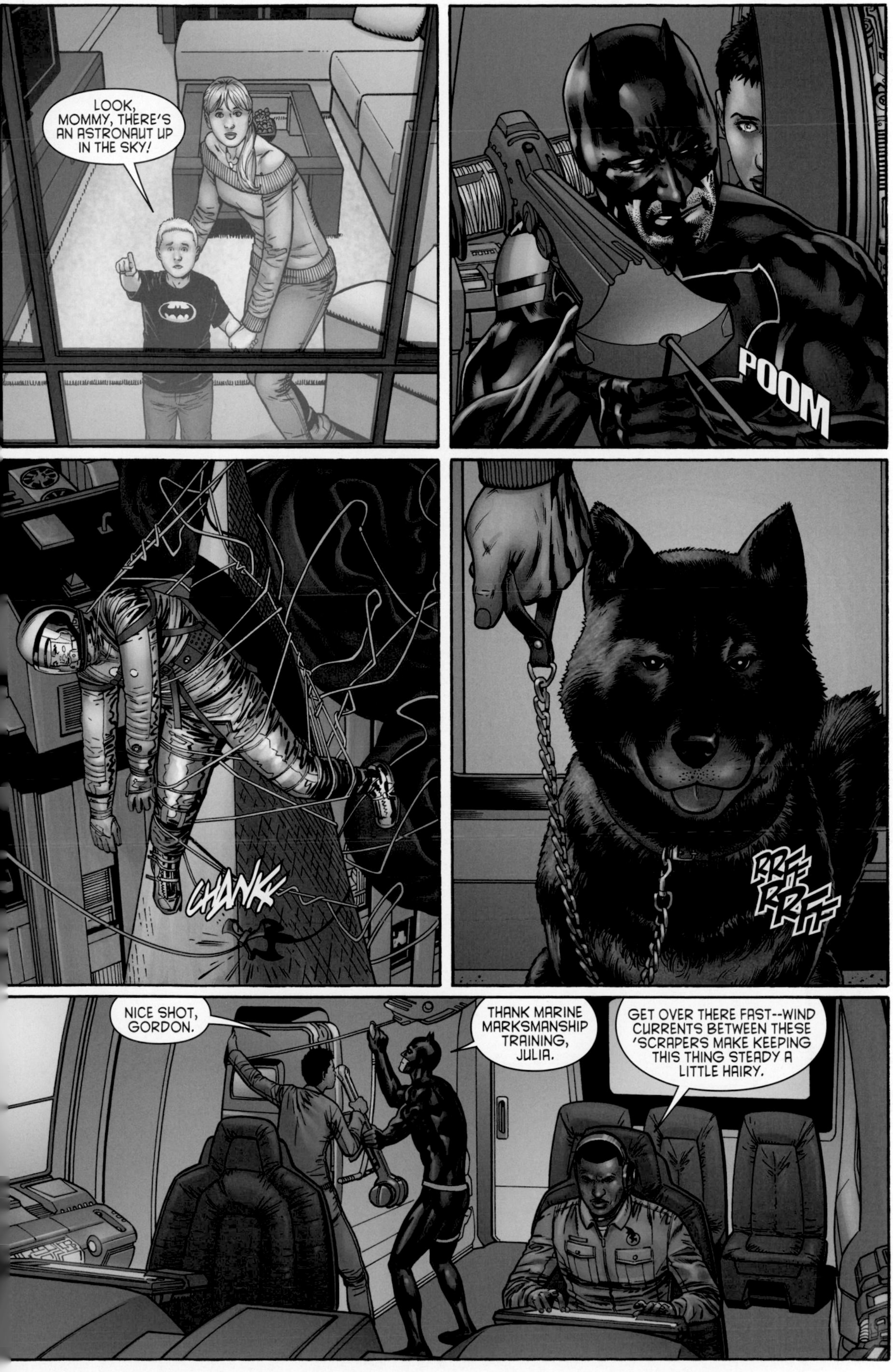

LOOK, MOMMY, THERE'S AN ASTRONAUT UP IN THE SKY!
POOM
CHANK
RRFF RRFF
NICE SHOT, GORDON.
THANK MARINE MARKSMANSHIP TRAINING, JULIA.
GET OVER THERE FAST--WIND CURRENTS BETWEEN THESE 'SCRAPERS MAKE KEEPING THIS THING STEADY A LITTLE HAIRY.

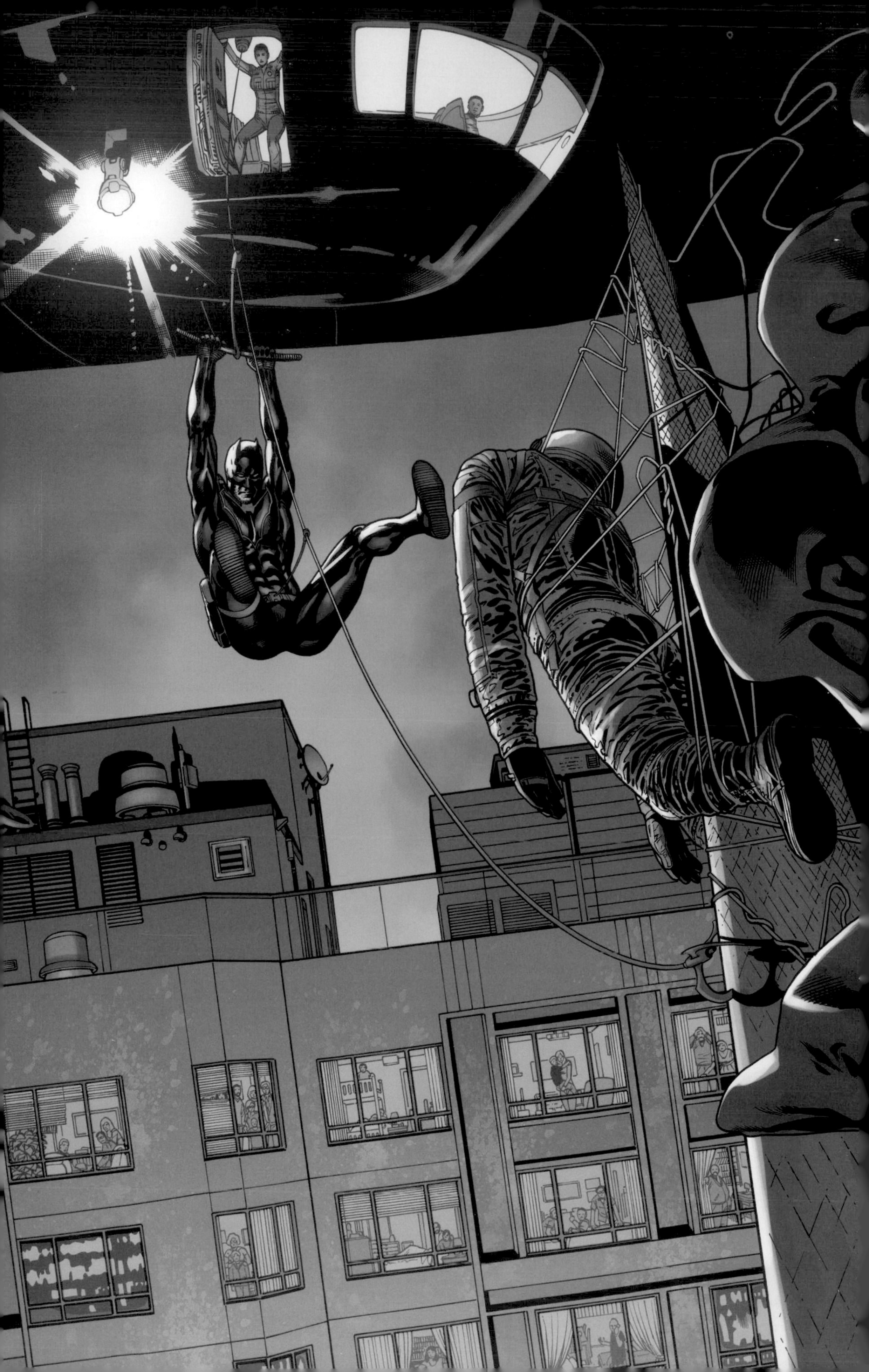

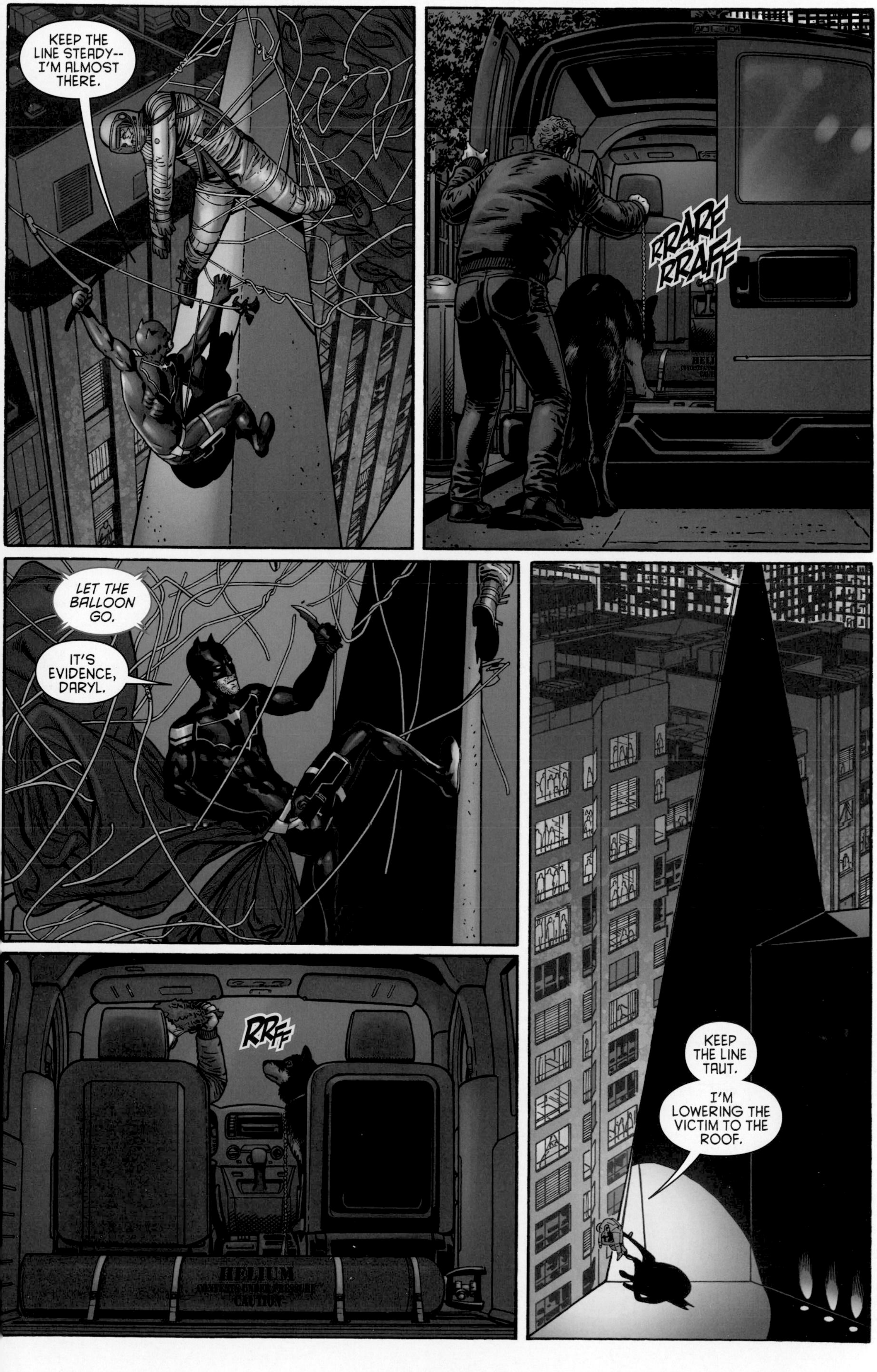
KEEP THE LINE STEADY-- I'M ALMOST THERE.
RRARF RRAFF
LET THE BALLOON GO.
IT'S EVIDENCE, DARYL.
RRFF
HELIUM
CAUTION
KEEP THE LINE TAUT.
I'M LOWERING THE VICTIM TO THE ROOF.

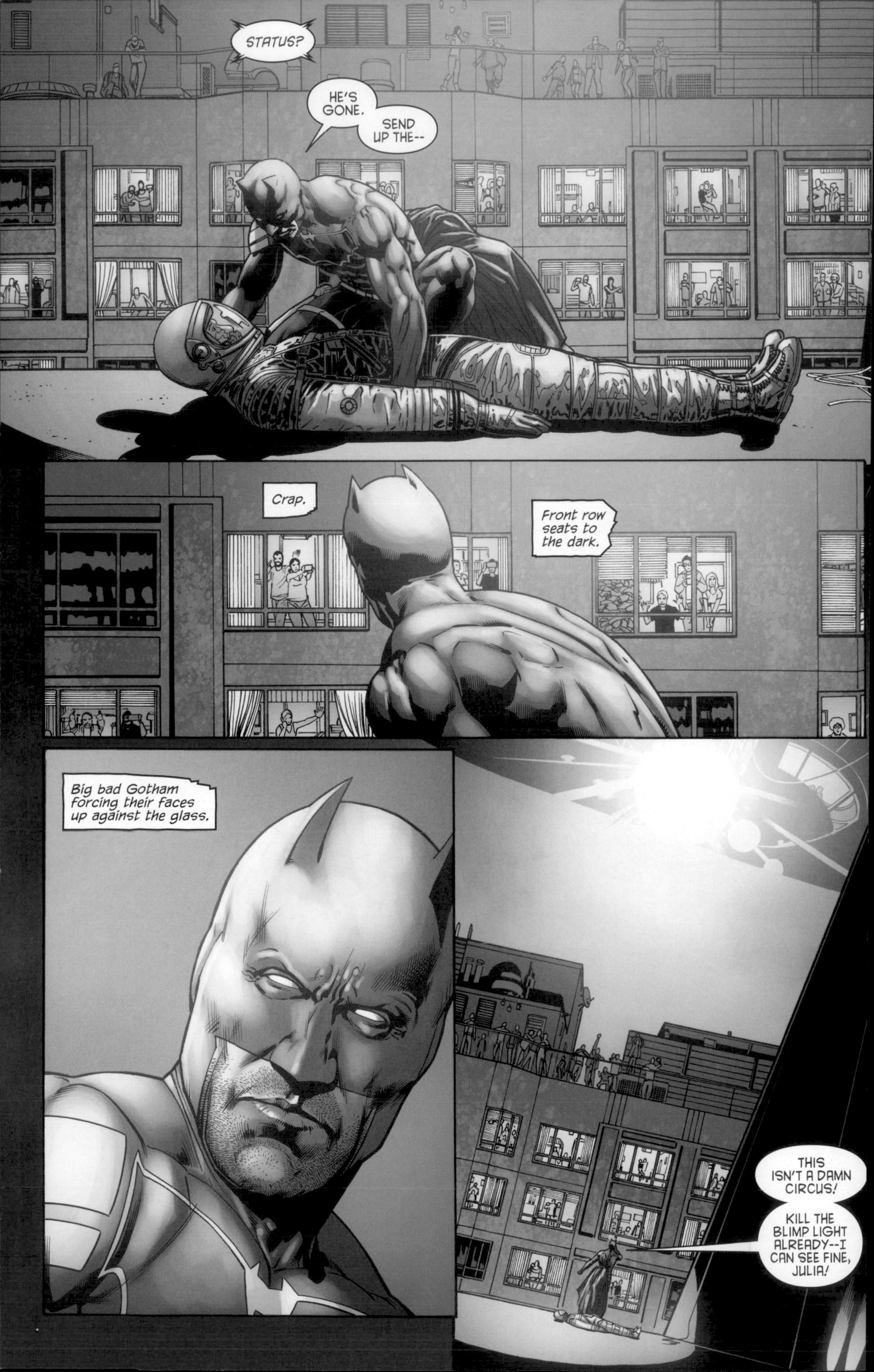
STATUS?
HE'S GONE.
SEND UP THE--
Crap.
Front row seats to the dark.
Big bad Gotham forcing their faces up against the glass.
THIS ISN'T A DAMN CIRCUS!
KILL THE BLIMP LIGHT ALREADY--I CAN SEE FINE, JULIA!

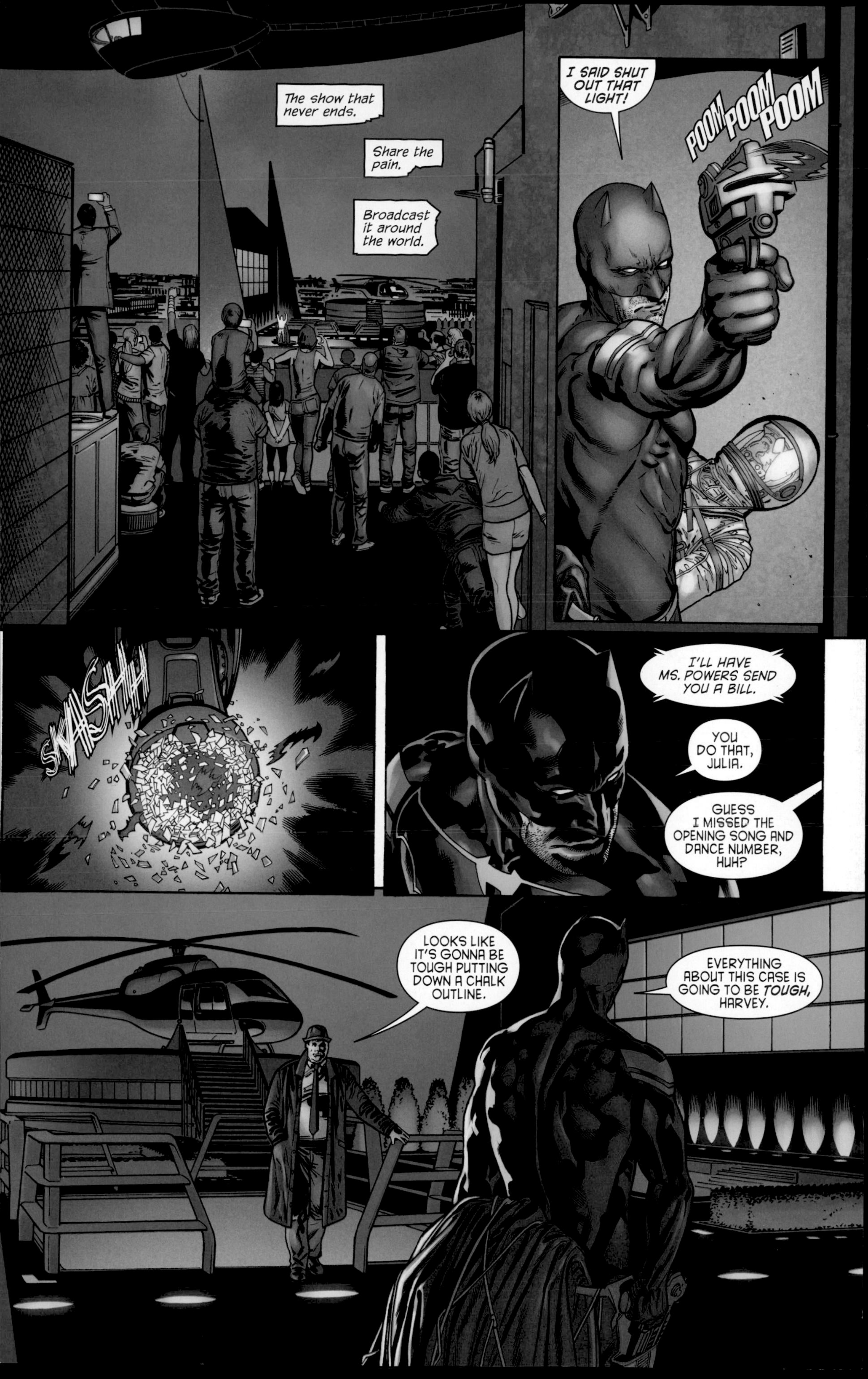

The show that never ends.
Share the pain.
Broadcast it around the world.
I SAID SHUT OUT THAT LIGHT!
POOM POOM POOM
SKASHHH
I'LL HAVE MS. POWERS SEND YOU A BILL.
YOU DO THAT, JULIA.
GUESS I MISSED THE OPENING SONG AND DANCE NUMBER, HUH?
LOOKS LIKE IT'S GONNA BE TOUGH PUTTING DOWN A CHALK OUTLINE.
EVERYTHING ABOUT THIS CASE IS GOING TO BE *TOUGH,* HARVEY.

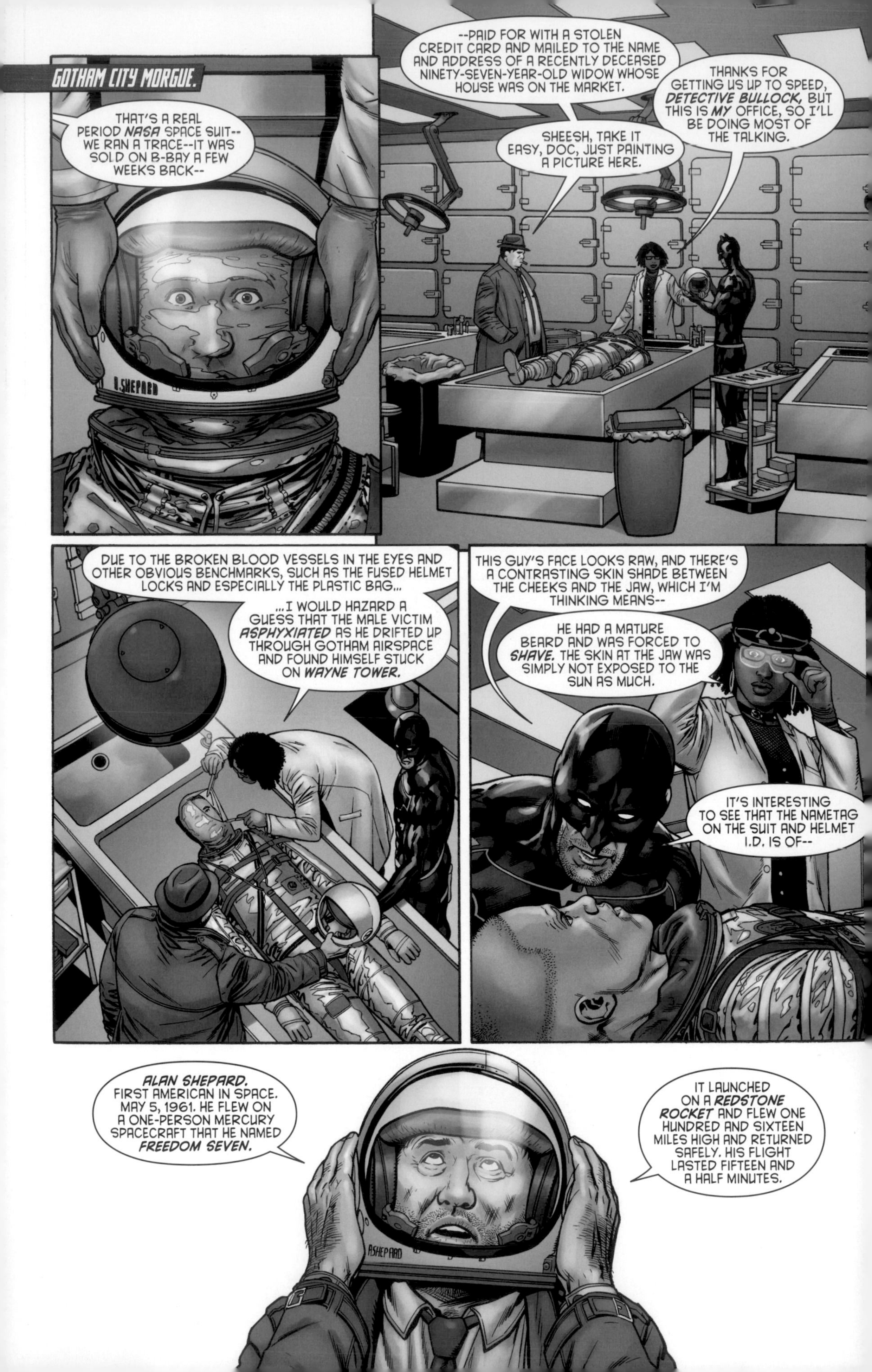
GOTHAM CITY MORGUE.
THAT'S A REAL PERIOD NASA SPACE SUIT--WE RAN A TRACE--IT WAS SOLD ON B-BAY A FEW WEEKS BACK--
--PAID FOR WITH A STOLEN CREDIT CARD AND MAILED TO THE NAME AND ADDRESS OF A RECENTLY DECEASED NINETY-SEVEN-YEAR-OLD WIDOW WHOSE HOUSE WAS ON THE MARKET.
THANKS FOR GETTING US UP TO SPEED, DETECTIVE BULLOCK, BUT THIS IS MY OFFICE, SO I'LL BE DOING MOST OF THE TALKING.
SHEESH, TAKE IT EASY, DOC, JUST PAINTING A PICTURE HERE.
DUE TO THE BROKEN BLOOD VESSELS IN THE EYES AND OTHER OBVIOUS BENCHMARKS, SUCH AS THE FUSED HELMET LOCKS AND ESPECIALLY THE PLASTIC BAG...
...I WOULD HAZARD A GUESS THAT THE MALE VICTIM ASPHYXIATED AS HE DRIFTED UP THROUGH GOTHAM AIRSPACE AND FOUND HIMSELF STUCK ON WAYNE TOWER.
THIS GUY'S FACE LOOKS RAW, AND THERE'S A CONTRASTING SKIN SHADE BETWEEN THE CHEEKS AND THE JAW, WHICH I'M THINKING MEANS--
HE HAD A MATURE BEARD AND WAS FORCED TO SHAVE. THE SKIN AT THE JAW WAS SIMPLY NOT EXPOSED TO THE SUN AS MUCH.
IT'S INTERESTING TO SEE THAT THE NAMETAG ON THE SUIT AND HELMET I.D. IS OF--
ALAN SHEPARD. FIRST AMERICAN IN SPACE. MAY 5, 1961. HE FLEW ON A ONE-PERSON MERCURY SPACECRAFT THAT HE NAMED FREEDOM SEVEN.
IT LAUNCHED ON A REDSTONE ROCKET AND FLEW ONE HUNDRED AND SIXTEEN MILES HIGH AND RETURNED SAFELY. HIS FLIGHT LASTED FIFTEEN AND A HALF MINUTES.

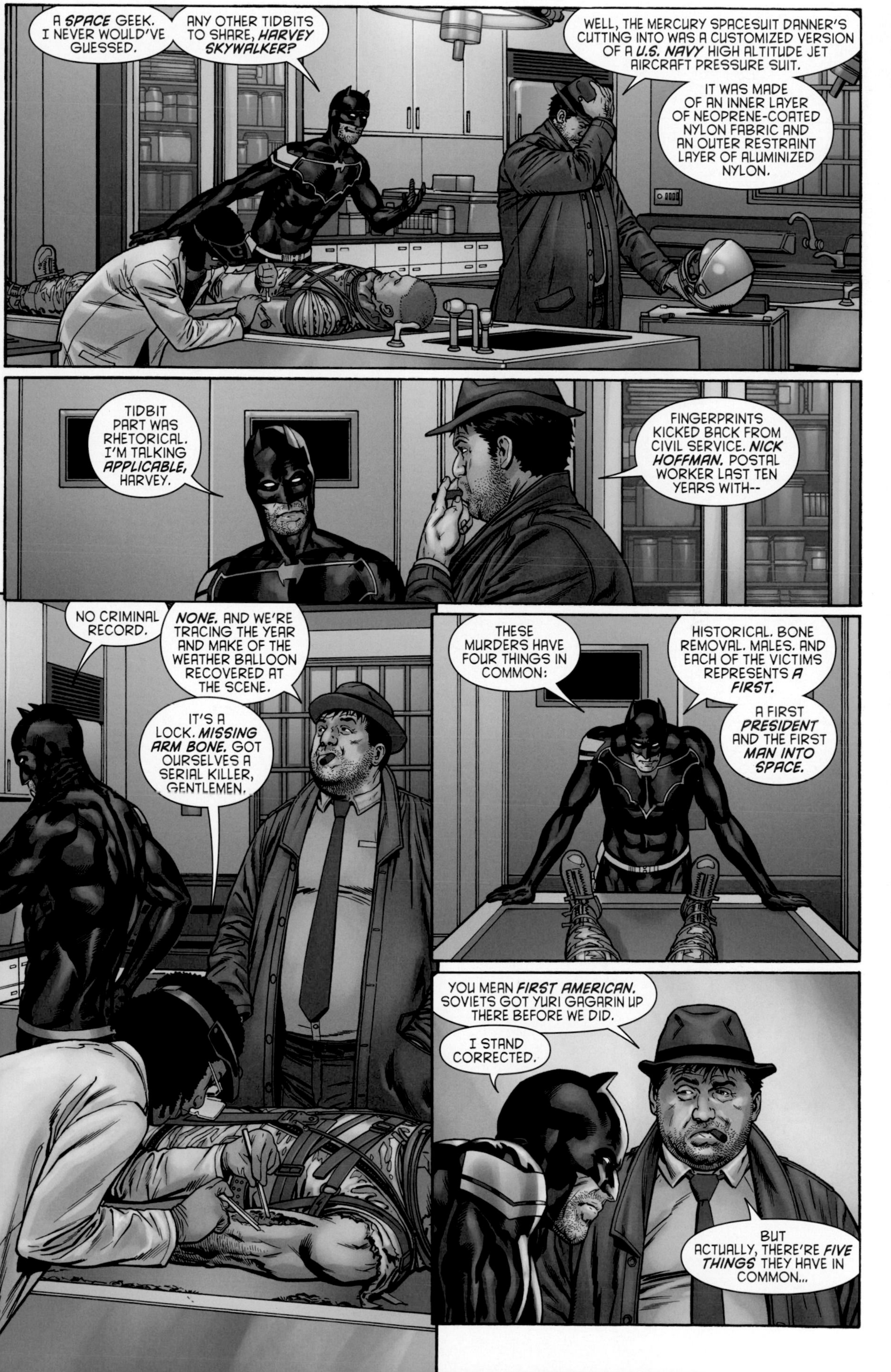
A *SPACE* GEEK. I NEVER WOULD'VE GUESSED.
ANY OTHER TIDBITS TO SHARE, *HARVEY SKYWALKER?*
WELL, THE MERCURY SPACESUIT DANNER'S CUTTING INTO WAS A CUSTOMIZED VERSION OF A *U.S. NAVY* HIGH ALTITUDE JET AIRCRAFT PRESSURE SUIT.
IT WAS MADE OF AN INNER LAYER OF NEOPRENE-COATED NYLON FABRIC AND AN OUTER RESTRAINT LAYER OF ALUMINIZED NYLON.
TIDBIT PART WAS RHETORICAL. I'M TALKING *APPLICABLE,* HARVEY.
FINGERPRINTS KICKED BACK FROM CIVIL SERVICE. *NICK HOFFMAN.* POSTAL WORKER LAST TEN YEARS WITH--
NO CRIMINAL RECORD.
NONE. AND WE'RE TRACING THE YEAR AND MAKE OF THE WEATHER BALLOON RECOVERED AT THE SCENE.
IT'S A LOCK. *MISSING ARM BONE.* GOT OURSELVES A SERIAL KILLER, GENTLEMEN.
THESE MURDERS HAVE FOUR THINGS IN COMMON:
HISTORICAL. BONE REMOVAL. MALES. AND EACH OF THE VICTIMS REPRESENTS *A FIRST.*
A FIRST *PRESIDENT* AND THE FIRST *MAN INTO SPACE.*
YOU MEAN *FIRST AMERICAN.* SOVIETS GOT YURI GAGARIN UP THERE BEFORE WE DID.
I STAND CORRECTED.
BUT ACTUALLY, THERE'RE *FIVE THINGS* THEY HAVE IN COMMON...

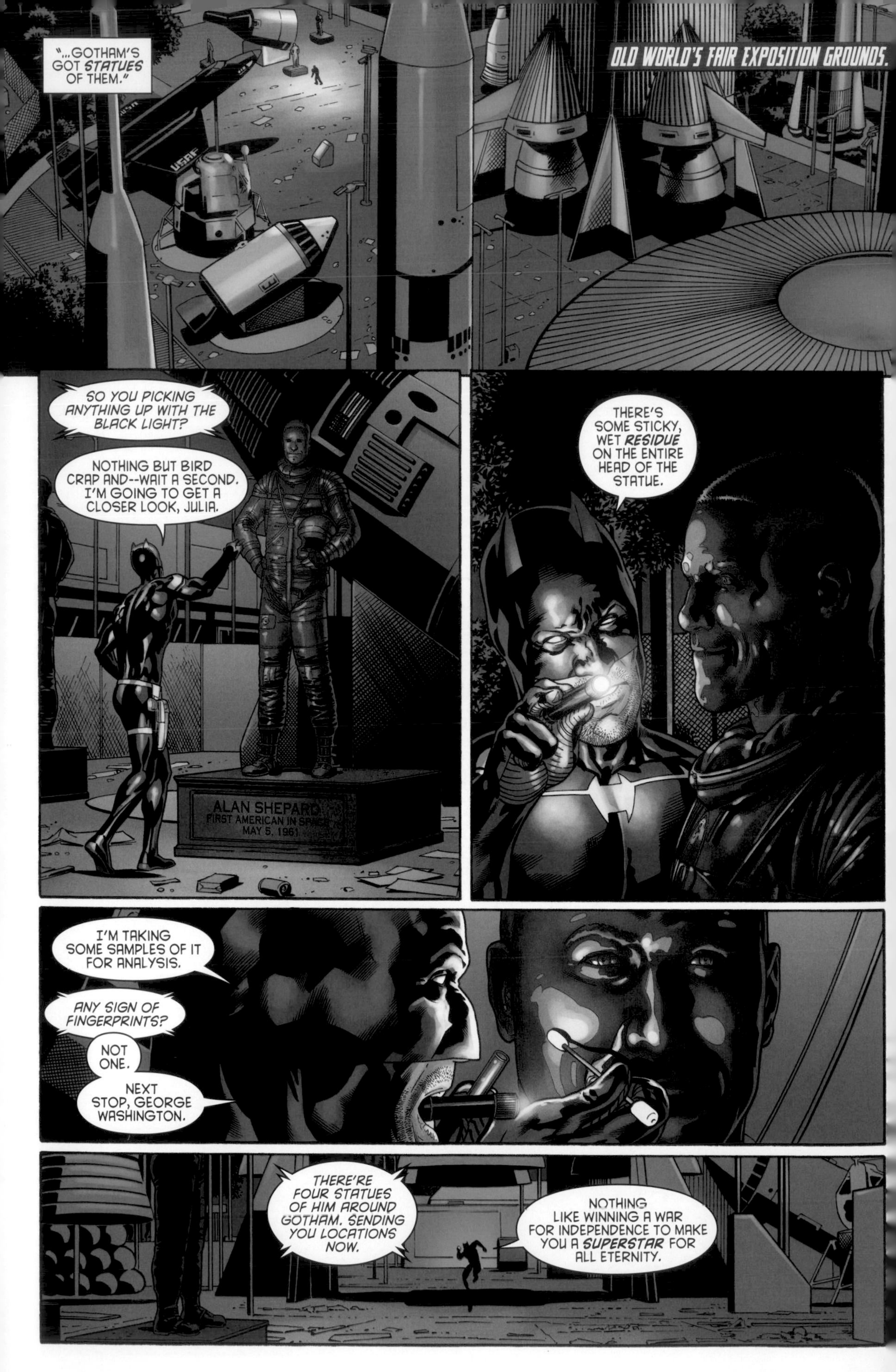
"...GOTHAM'S GOT STATUES OF THEM."
OLD WORLD'S FAIR EXPOSITION GROUNDS.
SO YOU PICKING ANYTHING UP WITH THE BLACK LIGHT?
NOTHING BUT BIRD CRAP AND--WAIT A SECOND. I'M GOING TO GET A CLOSER LOOK, JULIA.
ALAN SHEPARD
FIRST AMERICAN IN SPACE
MAY 5, 1961
THERE'S SOME STICKY, WET RESIDUE ON THE ENTIRE HEAD OF THE STATUE.
I'M TAKING SOME SAMPLES OF IT FOR ANALYSIS.
ANY SIGN OF FINGERPRINTS?
NOT ONE.
NEXT STOP, GEORGE WASHINGTON.
THERE'RE FOUR STATUES OF HIM AROUND GOTHAM. SENDING YOU LOCATIONS NOW.
NOTHING LIKE WINNING A WAR FOR INDEPENDENCE TO MAKE YOU A SUPERSTAR FOR ALL ETERNITY.

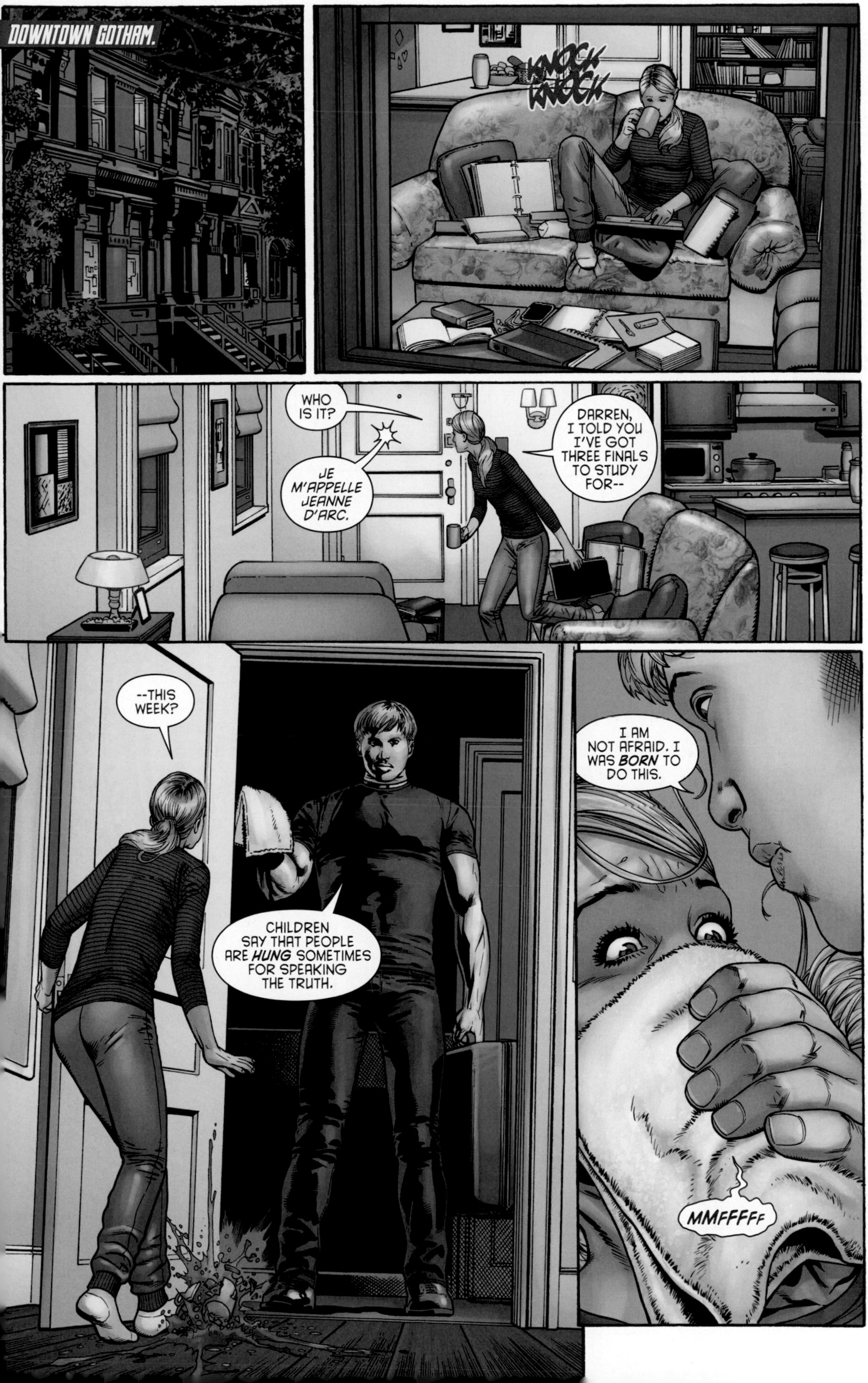
DOWNTOWN GOTHAM.
KNOCK KNOCK
WHO IS IT?
JE M'APPELLE JEANNE D'ARC.
DARREN, I TOLD YOU I'VE GOT THREE FINALS TO STUDY FOR--
--THIS WEEK?
CHILDREN SAY THAT PEOPLE ARE HUNG SOMETIMES FOR SPEAKING THE TRUTH.
I AM NOT AFRAID. I WAS BORN TO DO THIS.
MMFFFFF

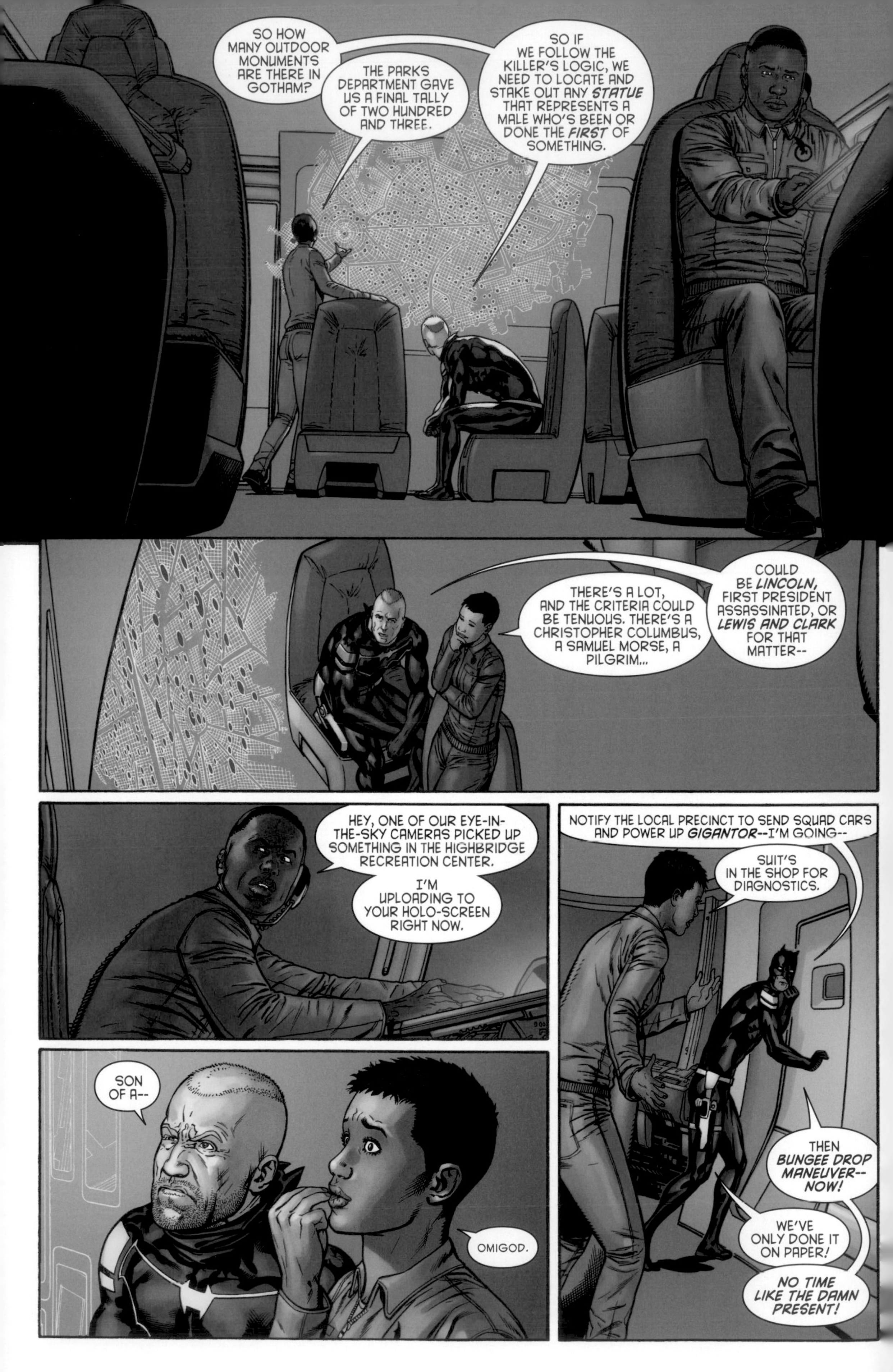
SO HOW MANY OUTDOOR MONUMENTS ARE THERE IN GOTHAM?
THE PARKS DEPARTMENT GAVE US A FINAL TALLY OF TWO HUNDRED AND THREE.
SO IF WE FOLLOW THE KILLER'S LOGIC, WE NEED TO LOCATE AND STAKE OUT ANY STATUE THAT REPRESENTS A MALE WHO'S BEEN OR DONE THE FIRST OF SOMETHING.
THERE'S A LOT, AND THE CRITERIA COULD BE TENUOUS. THERE'S A CHRISTOPHER COLUMBUS, A SAMUEL MORSE, A PILGRIM...
COULD BE LINCOLN, FIRST PRESIDENT ASSASSINATED, OR LEWIS AND CLARK FOR THAT MATTER--
HEY, ONE OF OUR EYE-IN-THE-SKY CAMERAS PICKED UP SOMETHING IN THE HIGHBRIDGE RECREATION CENTER.
I'M UPLOADING TO YOUR HOLO-SCREEN RIGHT NOW.
SON OF A--
OMIGOD.
NOTIFY THE LOCAL PRECINCT TO SEND SQUAD CARS AND POWER UP GIGANTOR--I'M GOING--
SUIT'S IN THE SHOP FOR DIAGNOSTICS.
THEN BUNGEE DROP MANEUVER--NOW!
WE'VE ONLY DONE IT ON PAPER!
NO TIME LIKE THE DAMN PRESENT!

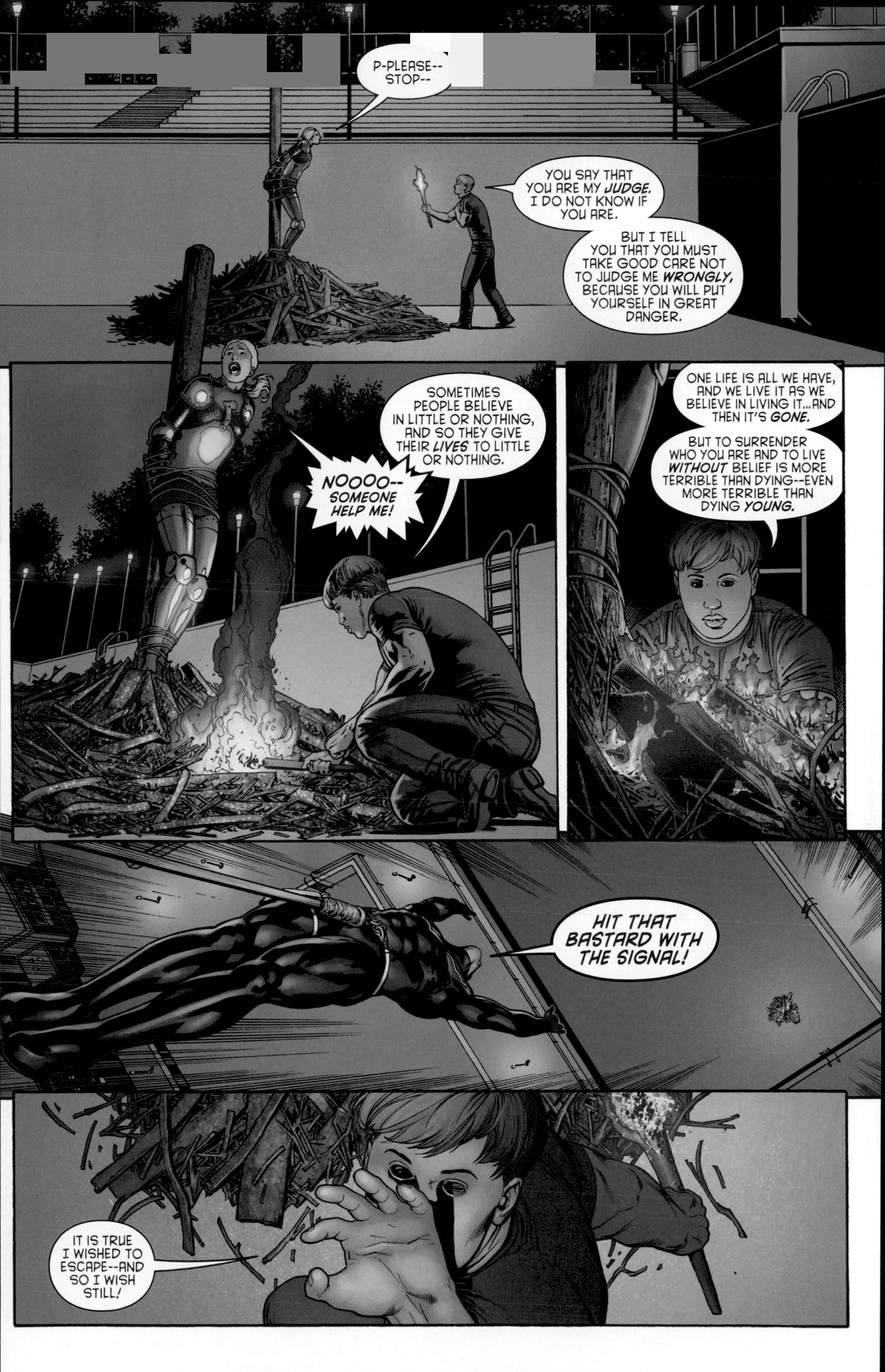
P-PLEASE--
STOP--
YOU SAY THAT YOU ARE MY JUDGE. I DO NOT KNOW IF YOU ARE.
BUT I TELL YOU THAT YOU MUST TAKE GOOD CARE NOT TO JUDGE ME WRONGLY, BECAUSE YOU WILL PUT YOURSELF IN GREAT DANGER.
SOMETIMES PEOPLE BELIEVE IN LITTLE OR NOTHING, AND SO THEY GIVE THEIR LIVES TO LITTLE OR NOTHING.
NOOOO-- SOMEONE HELP ME!
ONE LIFE IS ALL WE HAVE, AND WE LIVE IT AS WE BELIEVE IN LIVING IT...AND THEN IT'S GONE.
BUT TO SURRENDER WHO YOU ARE AND TO LIVE WITHOUT BELIEF IS MORE TERRIBLE THAN DYING--EVEN MORE TERRIBLE THAN DYING YOUNG.
HIT THAT BASTARD WITH THE SIGNAL!
IT IS TRUE I WISHED TO ESCAPE--AND SO I WISH STILL!

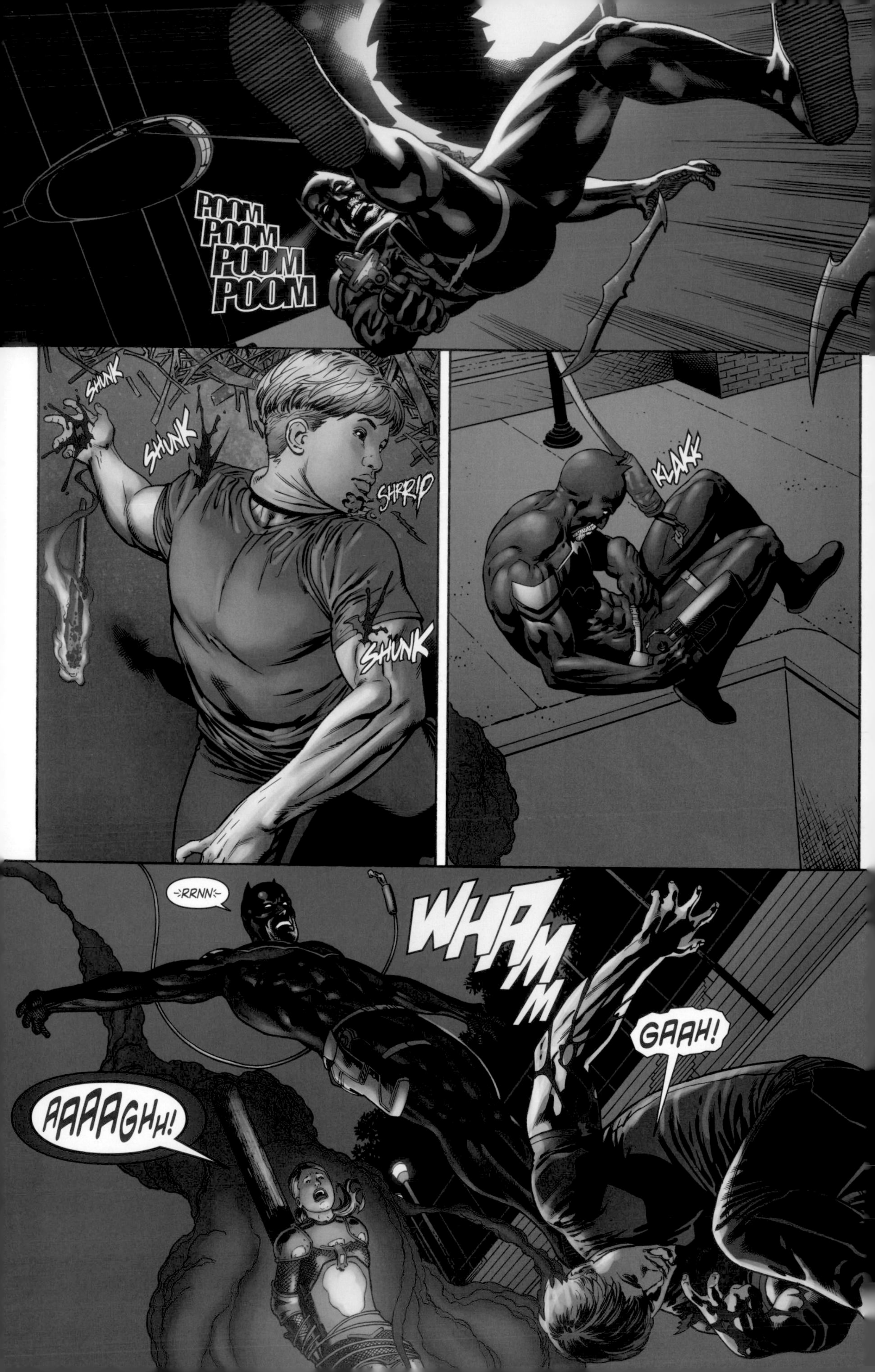
POOM
POOM
POOM
POOM
SHUNK
SHUNK
SHRRIP
SHUNK
KLAKK
-RRNN-
WHAMM
GAAH!
AAAAGHH!

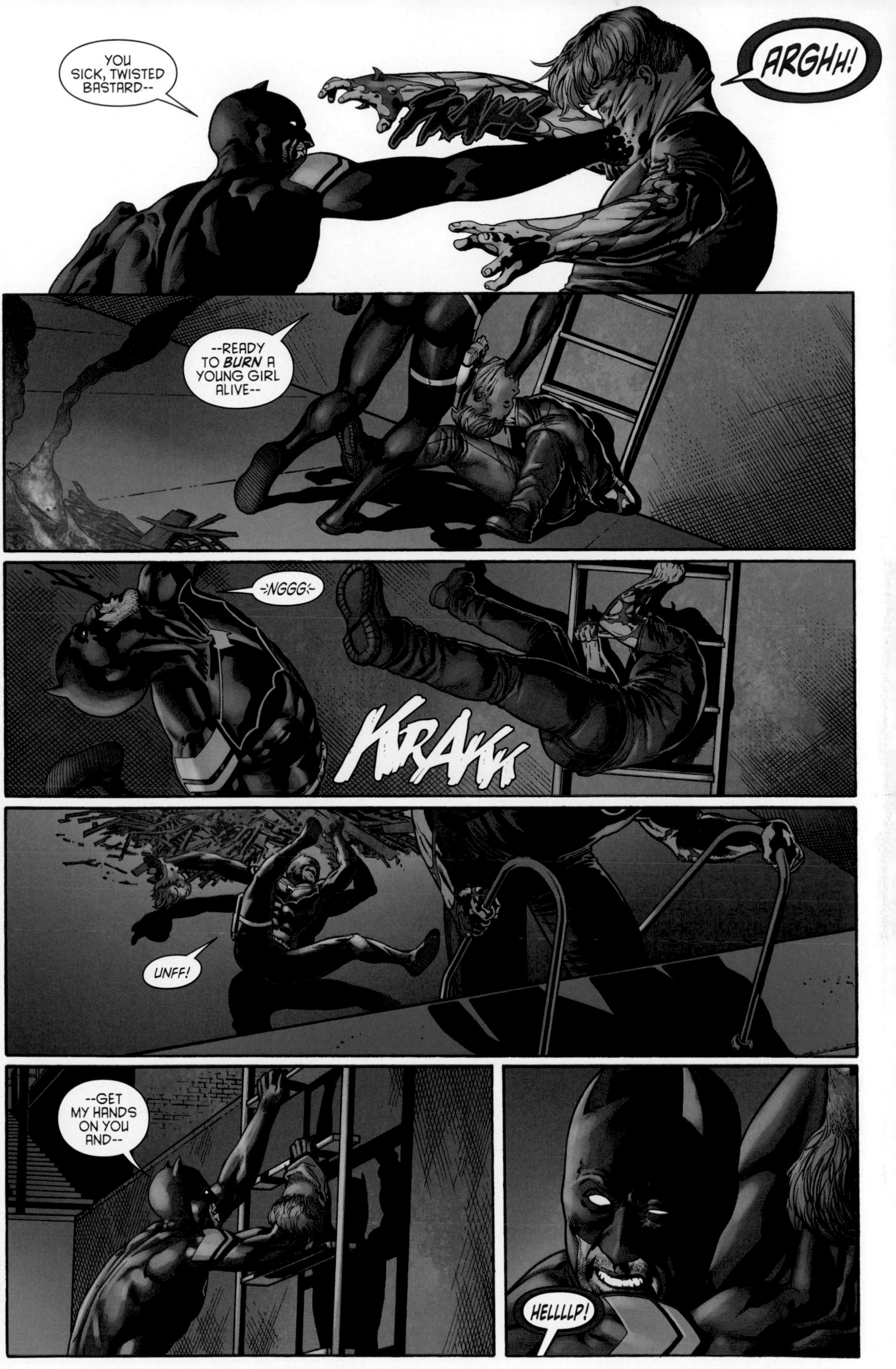
YOU SICK, TWISTED BASTARD--
FRAKK
ARGHH!
--READY TO BURN A YOUNG GIRL ALIVE--
-NGGG-
KRAKK
UNFF!
--GET MY HANDS ON YOU AND--
HELLLLP!

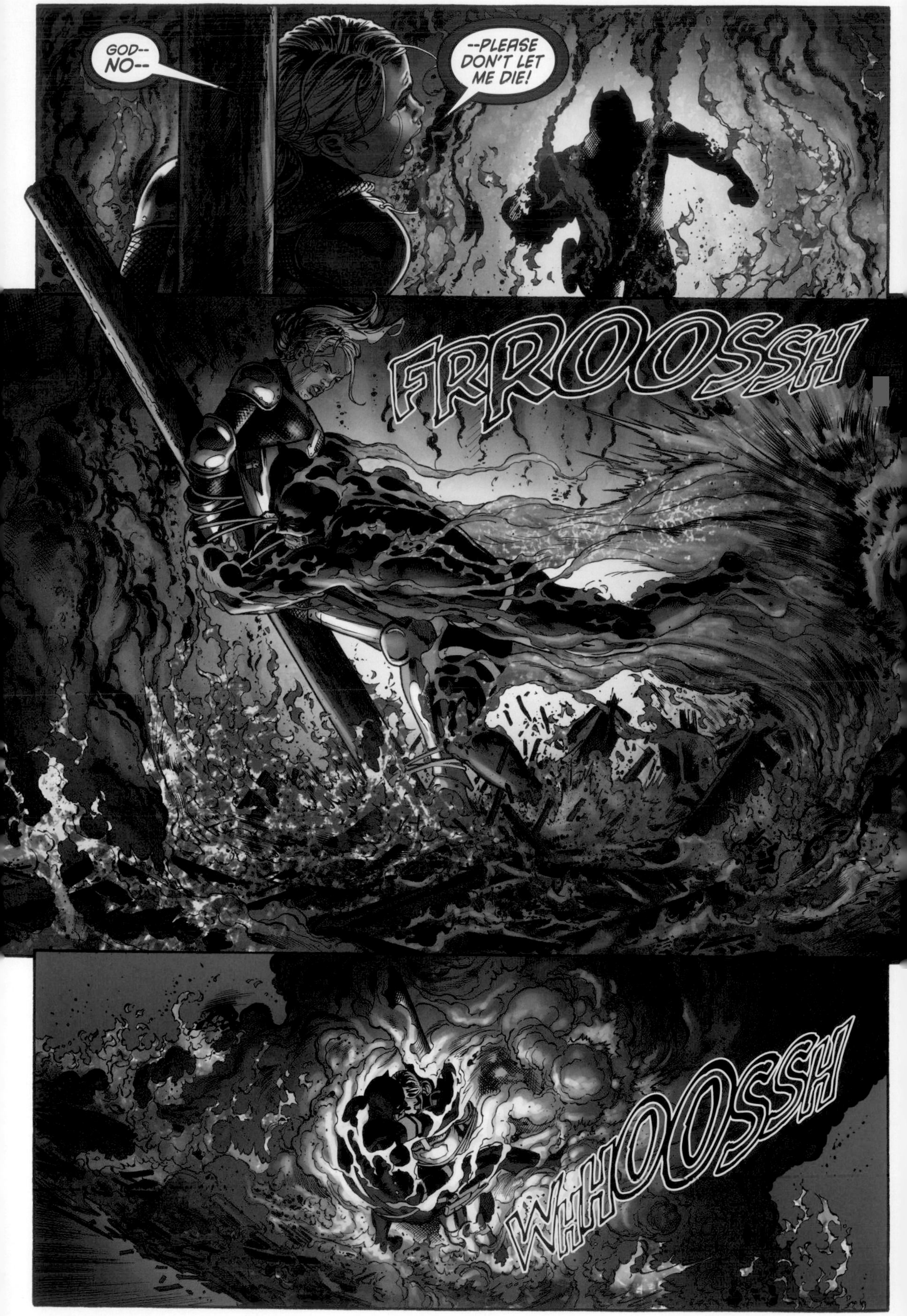
GOD--
NO--
--PLEASE DON'T LET ME DIE!
FRROOSSH
WHHOOSSH

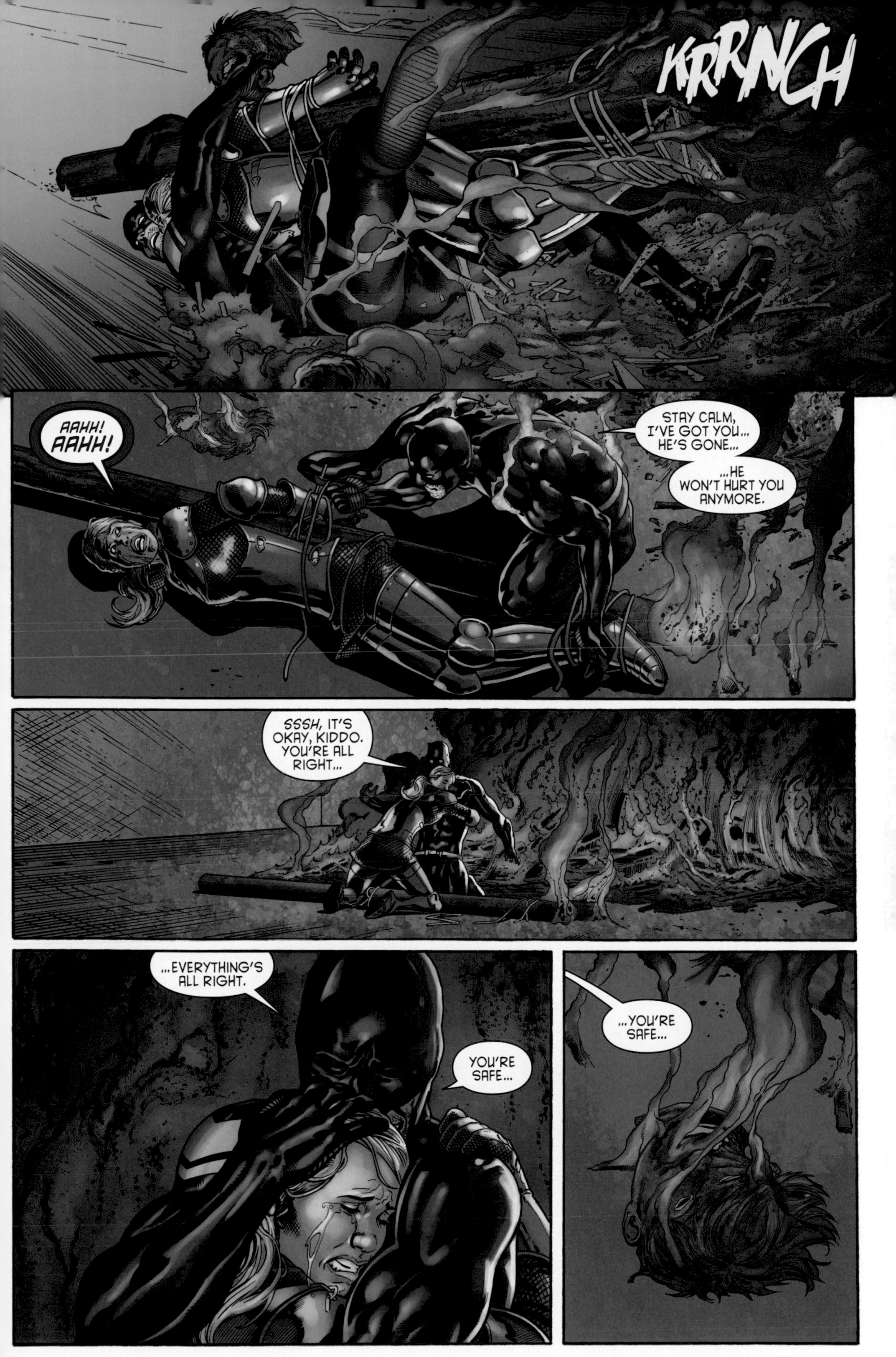
KRRNCH
AAHH! AAHH!
STAY CALM, I'VE GOT YOU... HE'S GONE...
...HE WON'T HURT YOU ANYMORE.
SSSH, IT'S OKAY, KIDDO. YOU'RE ALL RIGHT...
...EVERYTHING'S ALL RIGHT.
YOU'RE SAFE...
...YOU'RE SAFE...

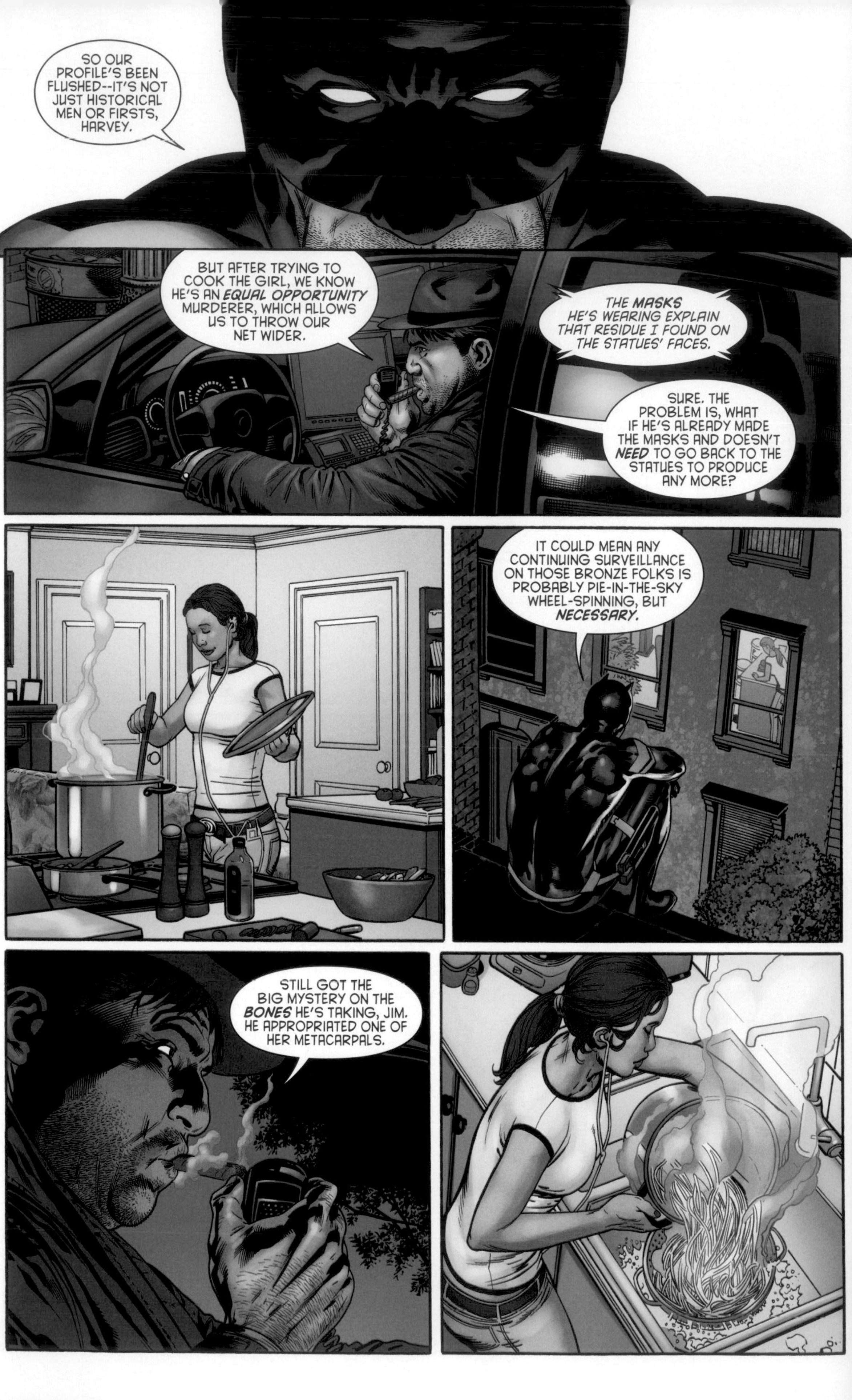
SO OUR PROFILE'S BEEN FLUSHED--IT'S NOT JUST HISTORICAL MEN OR FIRSTS, HARVEY.
BUT AFTER TRYING TO COOK THE GIRL, WE KNOW HE'S AN EQUAL OPPORTUNITY MURDERER, WHICH ALLOWS US TO THROW OUR NET WIDER.
THE MASKS HE'S WEARING EXPLAIN THAT RESIDUE I FOUND ON THE STATUES' FACES.
SURE. THE PROBLEM IS, WHAT IF HE'S ALREADY MADE THE MASKS AND DOESN'T NEED TO GO BACK TO THE STATUES TO PRODUCE ANY MORE?
IT COULD MEAN ANY CONTINUING SURVEILLANCE ON THOSE BRONZE FOLKS IS PROBABLY PIE-IN-THE-SKY WHEEL-SPINNING, BUT NECESSARY.
STILL GOT THE BIG MYSTERY ON THE BONES HE'S TAKING, JIM. HE APPROPRIATED ONE OF HER METACARPALS.

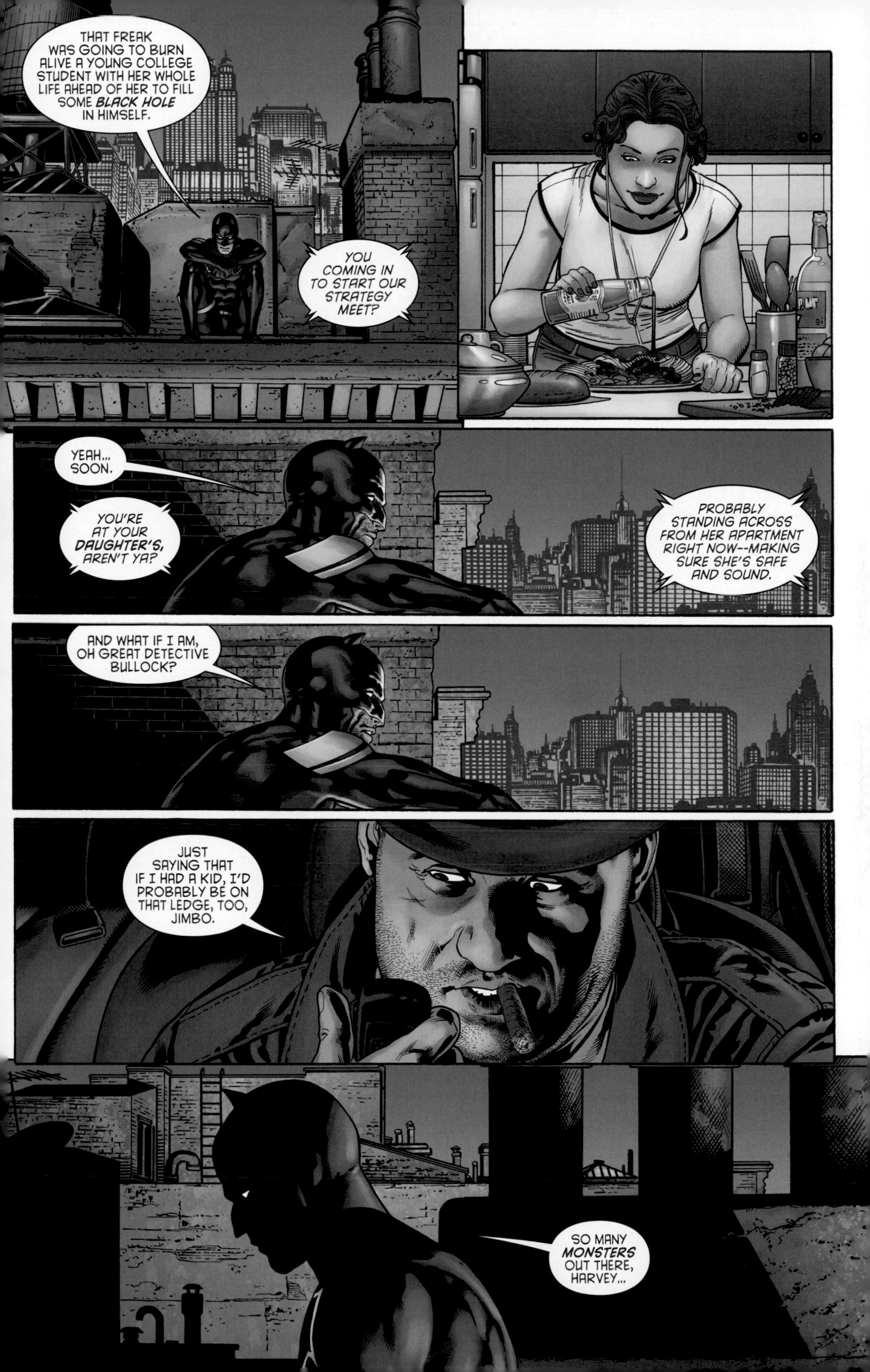
THAT FREAK WAS GOING TO BURN ALIVE A YOUNG COLLEGE STUDENT WITH HER WHOLE LIFE AHEAD OF HER TO FILL SOME BLACK HOLE IN HIMSELF.
YOU COMING IN TO START OUR STRATEGY MEET?
YEAH... SOON.
YOU'RE AT YOUR DAUGHTER'S, AREN'T YA?
PROBABLY STANDING ACROSS FROM HER APARTMENT RIGHT NOW--MAKING SURE SHE'S SAFE AND SOUND.
AND WHAT IF I AM, OH GREAT DETECTIVE BULLOCK?
JUST SAYING THAT IF I HAD A KID, I'D PROBABLY BE ON THAT LEDGE, TOO, JIMBO.
SO MANY MONSTERS OUT THERE, HARVEY...

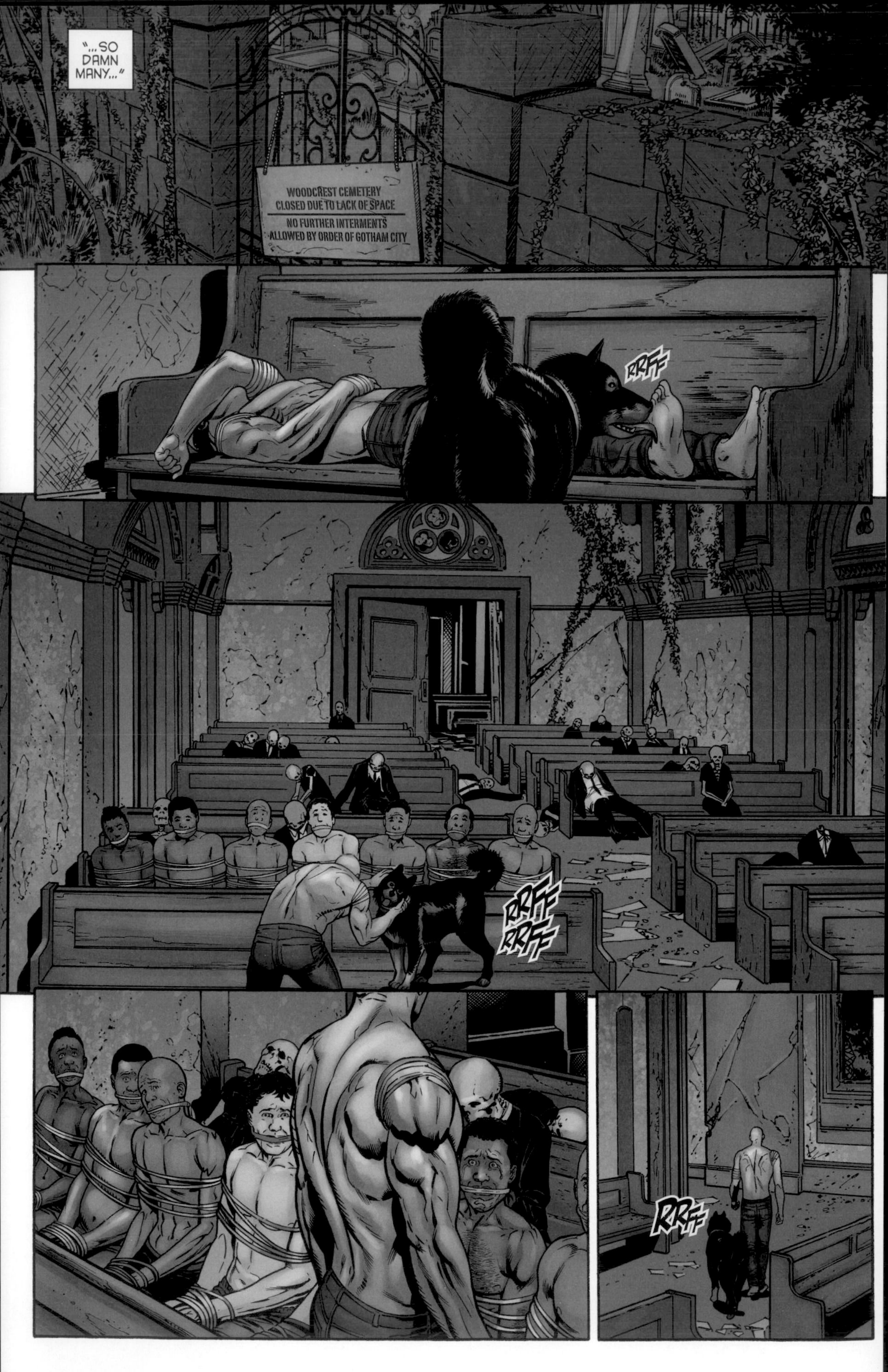
"...SO DAMN MANY..."
WOODCREST CEMETERY
CLOSED DUE TO LACK OF SPACE
NO FURTHER INTERMENTS
ALLOWED BY ORDER OF GOTHAM CITY
RRFF
RRFF
RRFF
RRFF

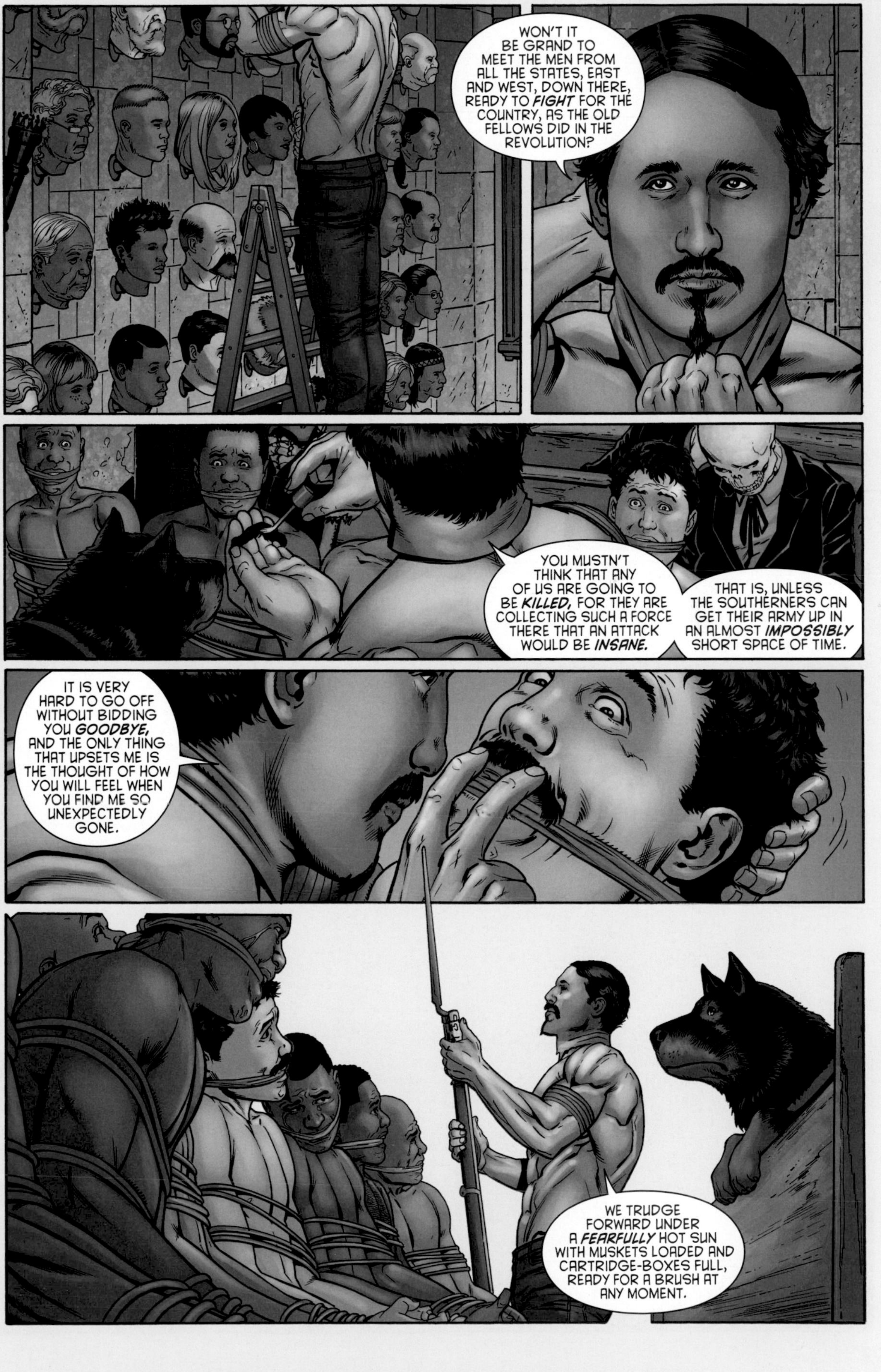
WON'T IT BE GRAND TO MEET THE MEN FROM ALL THE STATES, EAST AND WEST, DOWN THERE, READY TO FIGHT FOR THE COUNTRY, AS THE OLD FELLOWS DID IN THE REVOLUTION?
YOU MUSTN'T THINK THAT ANY OF US ARE GOING TO BE KILLED, FOR THEY ARE COLLECTING SUCH A FORCE THERE THAT AN ATTACK WOULD BE INSANE.
THAT IS, UNLESS THE SOUTHERNERS CAN GET THEIR ARMY UP IN AN ALMOST IMPOSSIBLY SHORT SPACE OF TIME.
IT IS VERY HARD TO GO OFF WITHOUT BIDDING YOU GOODBYE, AND THE ONLY THING THAT UPSETS ME IS THE THOUGHT OF HOW YOU WILL FEEL WHEN YOU FIND ME SO UNEXPECTEDLY GONE.
WE TRUDGE FORWARD UNDER A FEARFULLY HOT SUN WITH MUSKETS LOADED AND CARTRIDGE-BOXES FULL, READY FOR A BRUSH AT ANY MOMENT.

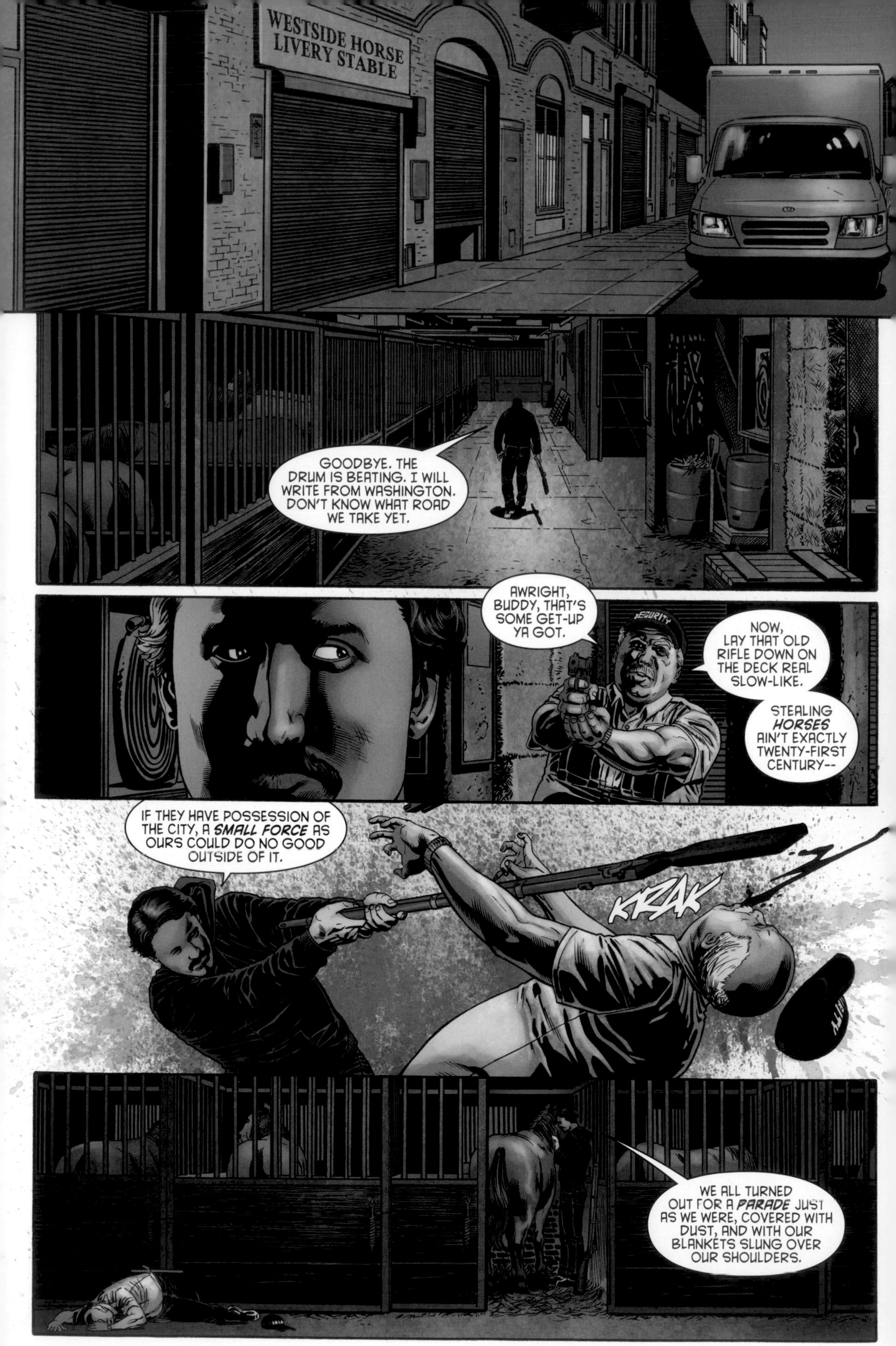
WESTSIDE HORSE LIVERY STABLE
GOODBYE. THE DRUM IS BEATING. I WILL WRITE FROM WASHINGTON. DON'T KNOW WHAT ROAD WE TAKE YET.
AWRIGHT, BUDDY, THAT'S SOME GET-UP YA GOT.
NOW, LAY THAT OLD RIFLE DOWN ON THE DECK REAL SLOW-LIKE.
STEALING *HORSES* AIN'T EXACTLY TWENTY-FIRST CENTURY--
IF THEY HAVE POSSESSION OF THE CITY, A *SMALL FORCE* AS OURS COULD DO NO GOOD OUTSIDE OF IT.
KRAK
WE ALL TURNED OUT FOR A *PARADE* JUST AS WE WERE, COVERED WITH DUST, AND WITH OUR BLANKETS SLUNG OVER OUR SHOULDERS.

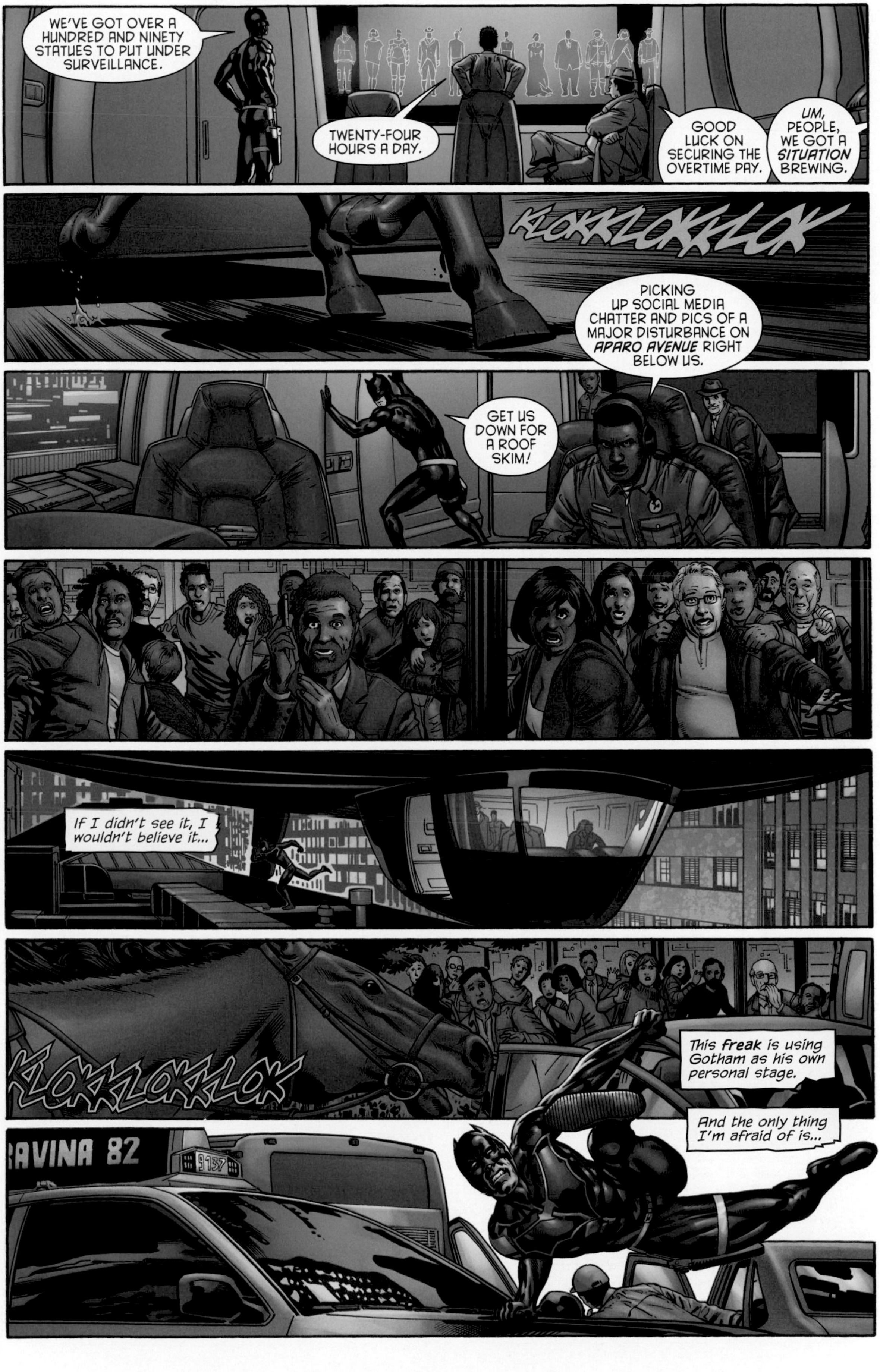
WE'VE GOT OVER A HUNDRED AND NINETY STATUES TO PUT UNDER SURVEILLANCE.
TWENTY-FOUR HOURS A DAY.
GOOD LUCK ON SECURING THE OVERTIME PAY.
UM, PEOPLE, WE GOT A SITUATION BREWING.
KLOKKLOKKLOK
PICKING UP SOCIAL MEDIA CHATTER AND PICS OF A MAJOR DISTURBANCE ON APARO AVENUE RIGHT BELOW US.
GET US DOWN FOR A ROOF SKIM!
If I didn't see it, I wouldn't believe it...
KLOKKLOKKLOK
This freak is using Gotham as his own personal stage.
And the only thing I'm afraid of is...
RAVINA 82
9137

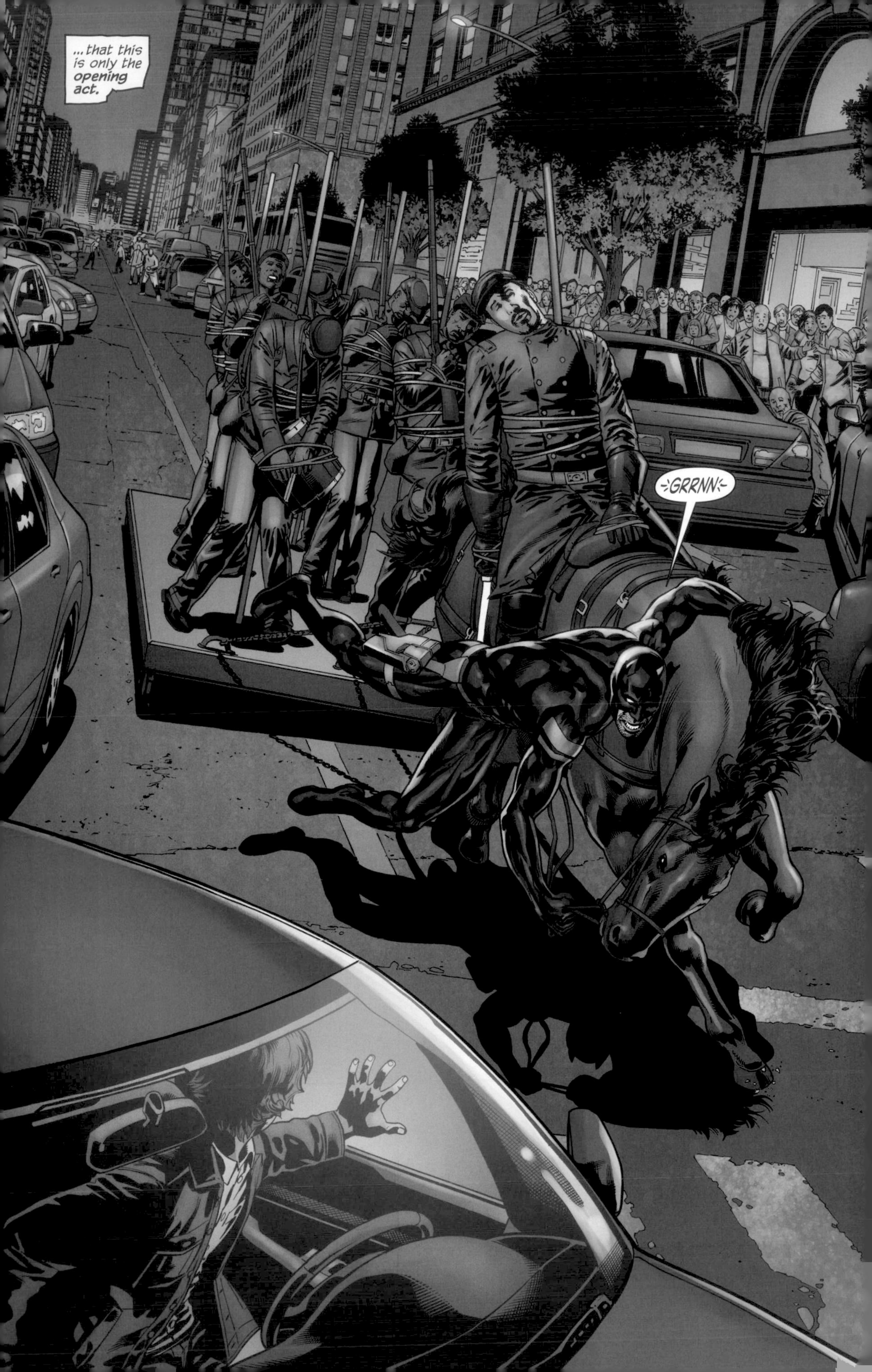
...that this is only the opening act.
-GRRNN-

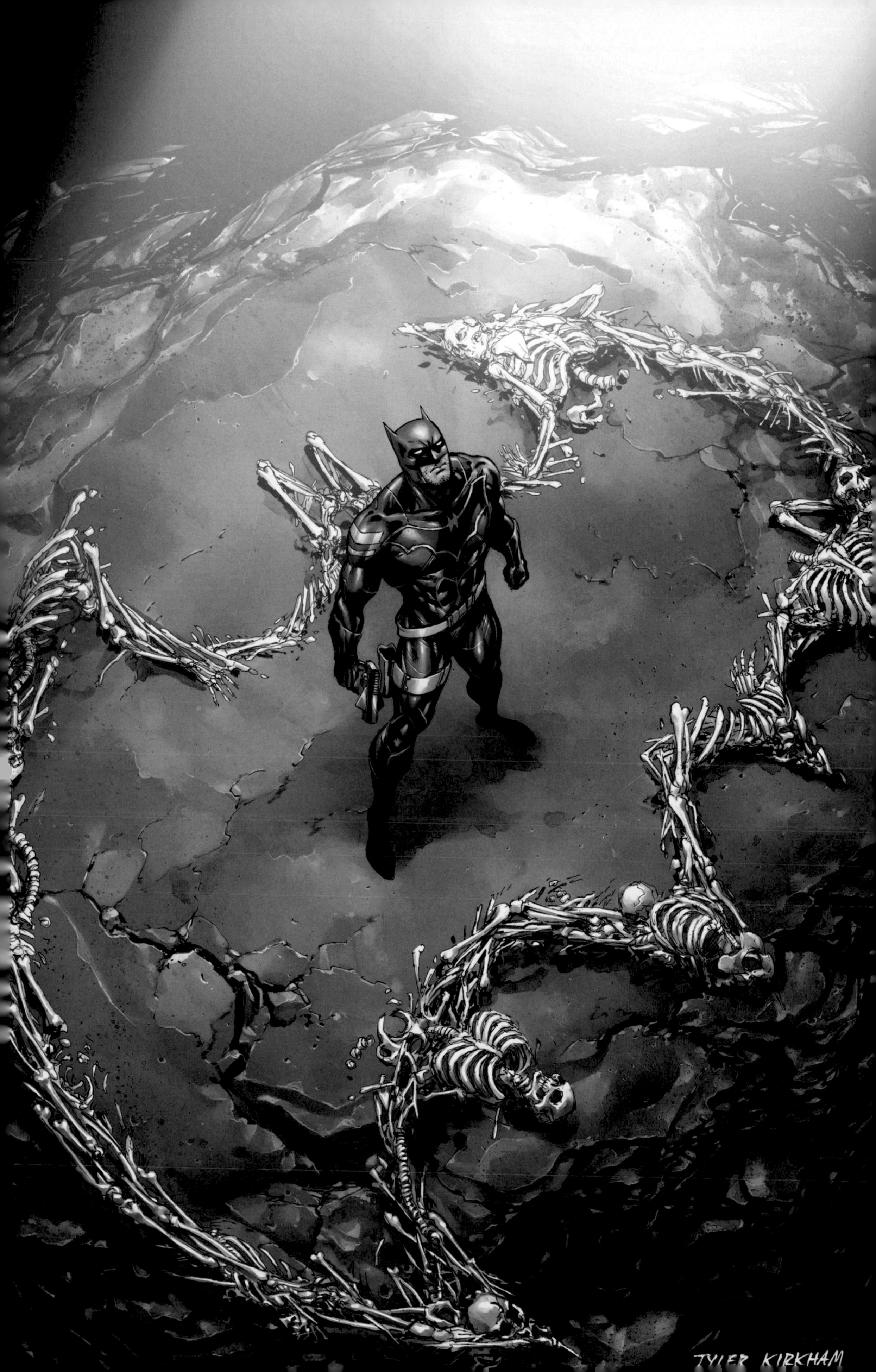
TYLER KIRKHAM

THE BRONZE AGE: MARTYRS AND MADMEN

PETER J. TOMASI writer **FERNANDO PASARIN SCOT EATON** pencillers **MATT RYAN WAYNE FAUCHER** inkers **CHRIS SOTOMAYOR** colorist **WES ABBOTT** letterer **TYLER KIRKHAM TOMEU MOREY** cover

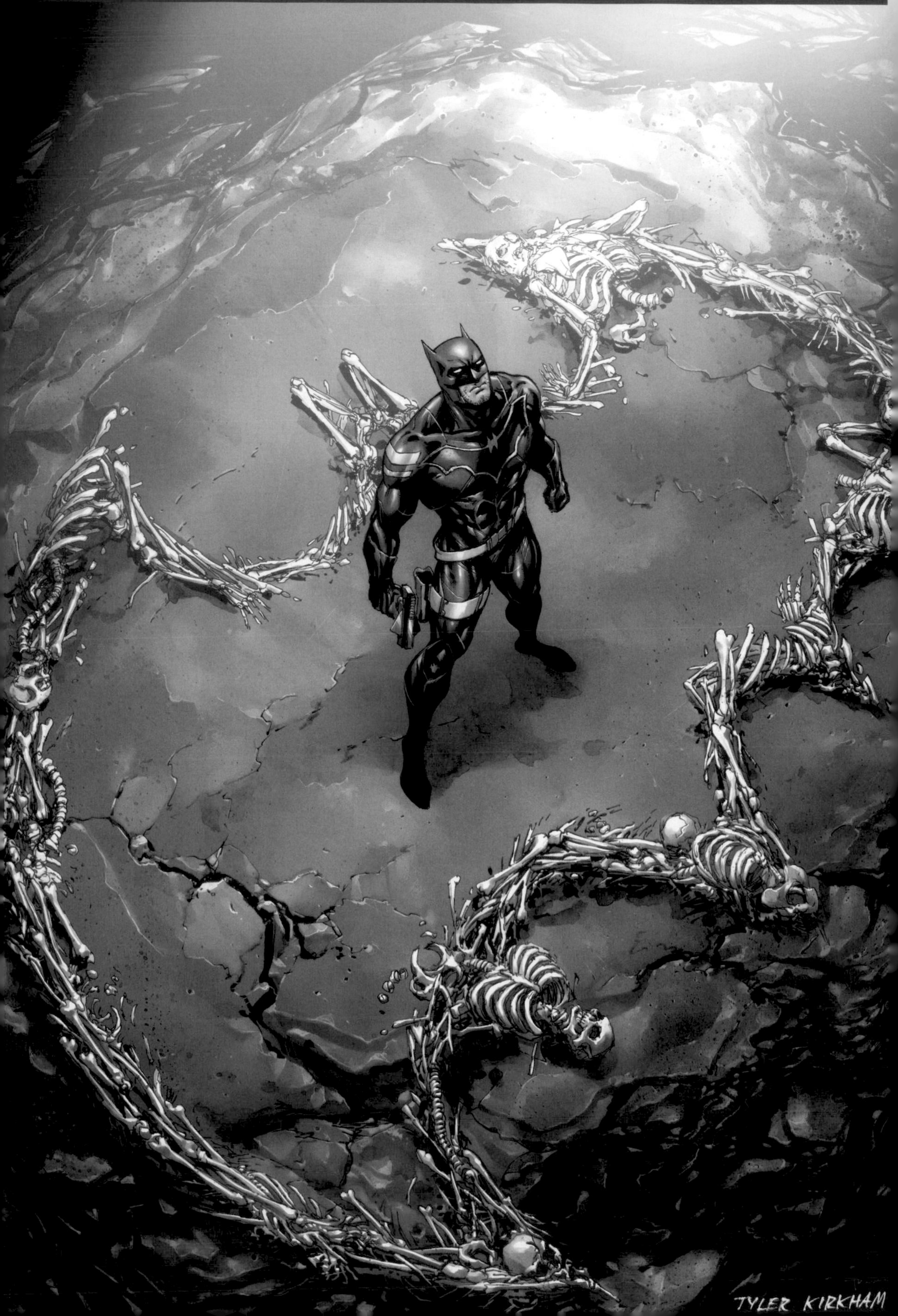
TYLER KIRKHAM

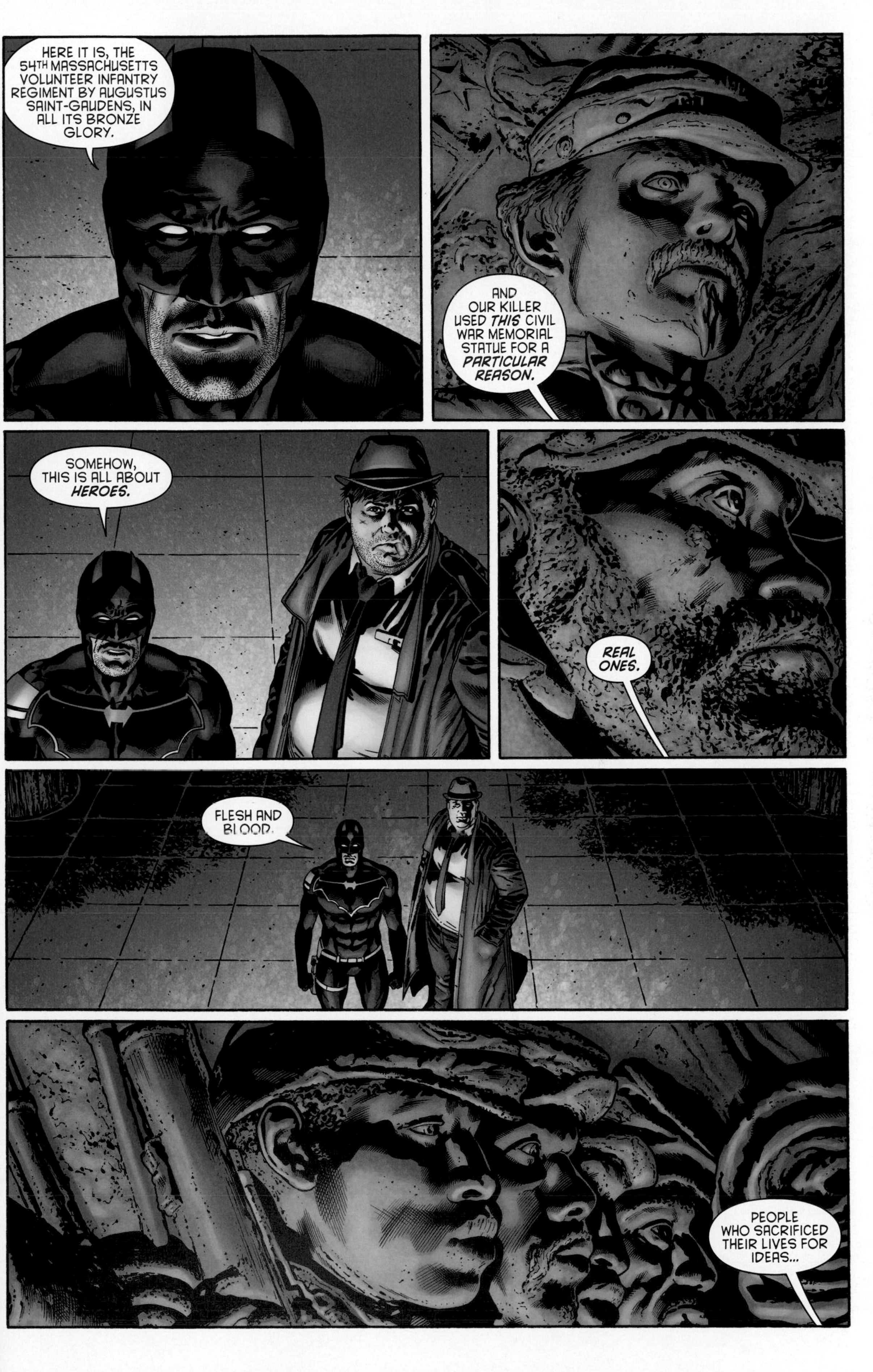
HERE IT IS, THE 54TH MASSACHUSETTS VOLUNTEER INFANTRY REGIMENT BY AUGUSTUS SAINT-GAUDENS, IN ALL ITS BRONZE GLORY.
AND OUR KILLER USED *THIS* CIVIL WAR MEMORIAL STATUE FOR A *PARTICULAR REASON.*
SOMEHOW, THIS IS ALL ABOUT *HEROES.*
REAL ONES.
FLESH AND BLOOD.
PEOPLE WHO SACRIFICED THEIR LIVES FOR IDEAS...

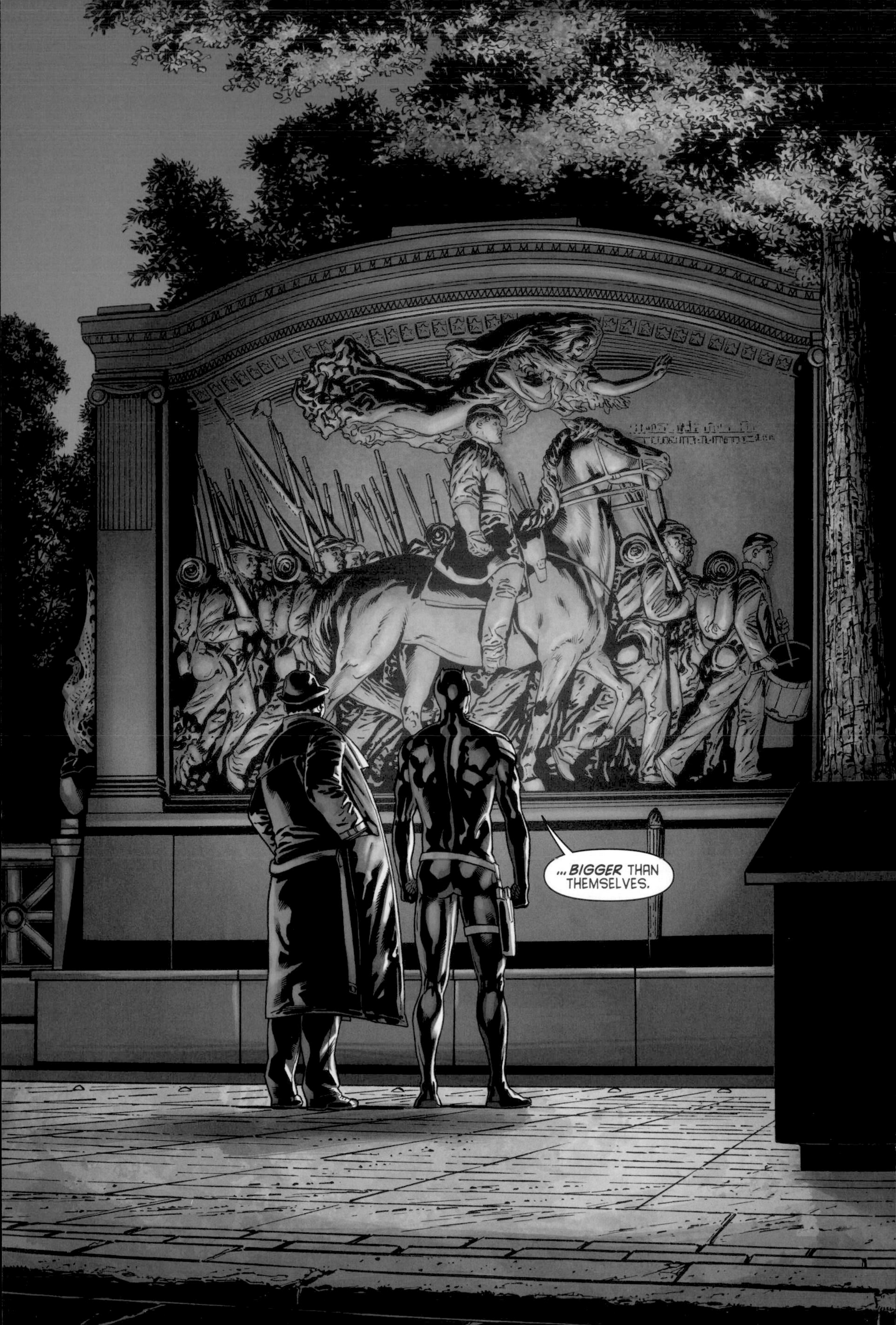
...BIGGER THAN THEMSELVES.

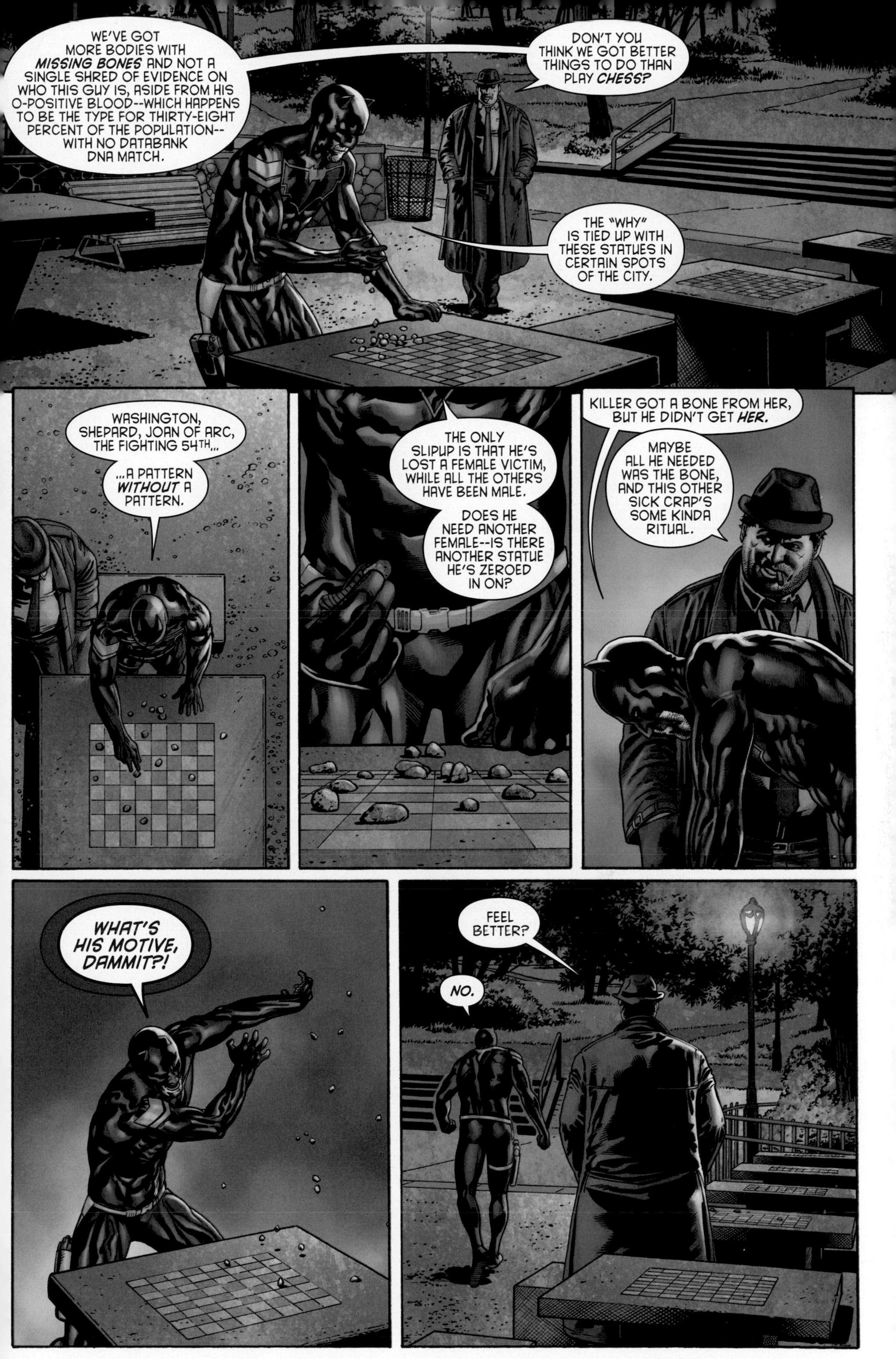
WE'VE GOT MORE BODIES WITH MISSING BONES AND NOT A SINGLE SHRED OF EVIDENCE ON WHO THIS GUY IS, ASIDE FROM HIS O-POSITIVE BLOOD--WHICH HAPPENS TO BE THE TYPE FOR THIRTY-EIGHT PERCENT OF THE POPULATION--WITH NO DATABANK DNA MATCH.
DON'T YOU THINK WE GOT BETTER THINGS TO DO THAN PLAY CHESS?
THE "WHY" IS TIED UP WITH THESE STATUES IN CERTAIN SPOTS OF THE CITY.
WASHINGTON, SHEPARD, JOAN OF ARC, THE FIGHTING 54TH...
...A PATTERN WITHOUT A PATTERN.
THE ONLY SLIPUP IS THAT HE'S LOST A FEMALE VICTIM, WHILE ALL THE OTHERS HAVE BEEN MALE.
DOES HE NEED ANOTHER FEMALE--IS THERE ANOTHER STATUE HE'S ZEROED IN ON?
KILLER GOT A BONE FROM HER, BUT HE DIDN'T GET HER.
MAYBE ALL HE NEEDED WAS THE BONE, AND THIS OTHER SICK CRAP'S SOME KINDA RITUAL.
WHAT'S HIS MOTIVE, DAMMIT?!
FEEL BETTER?
NO.

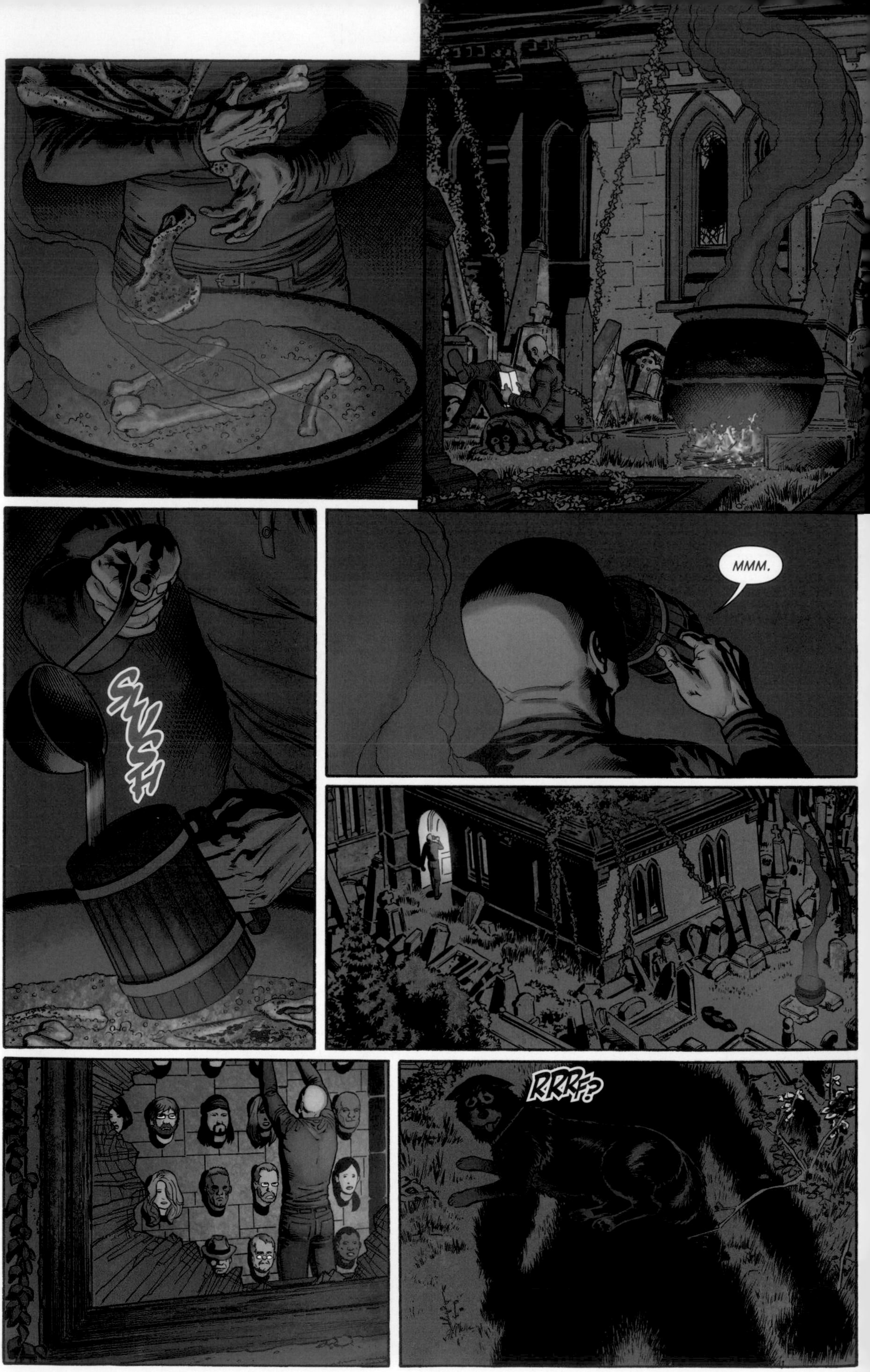
SHLUSH
MMM.
RRRF?

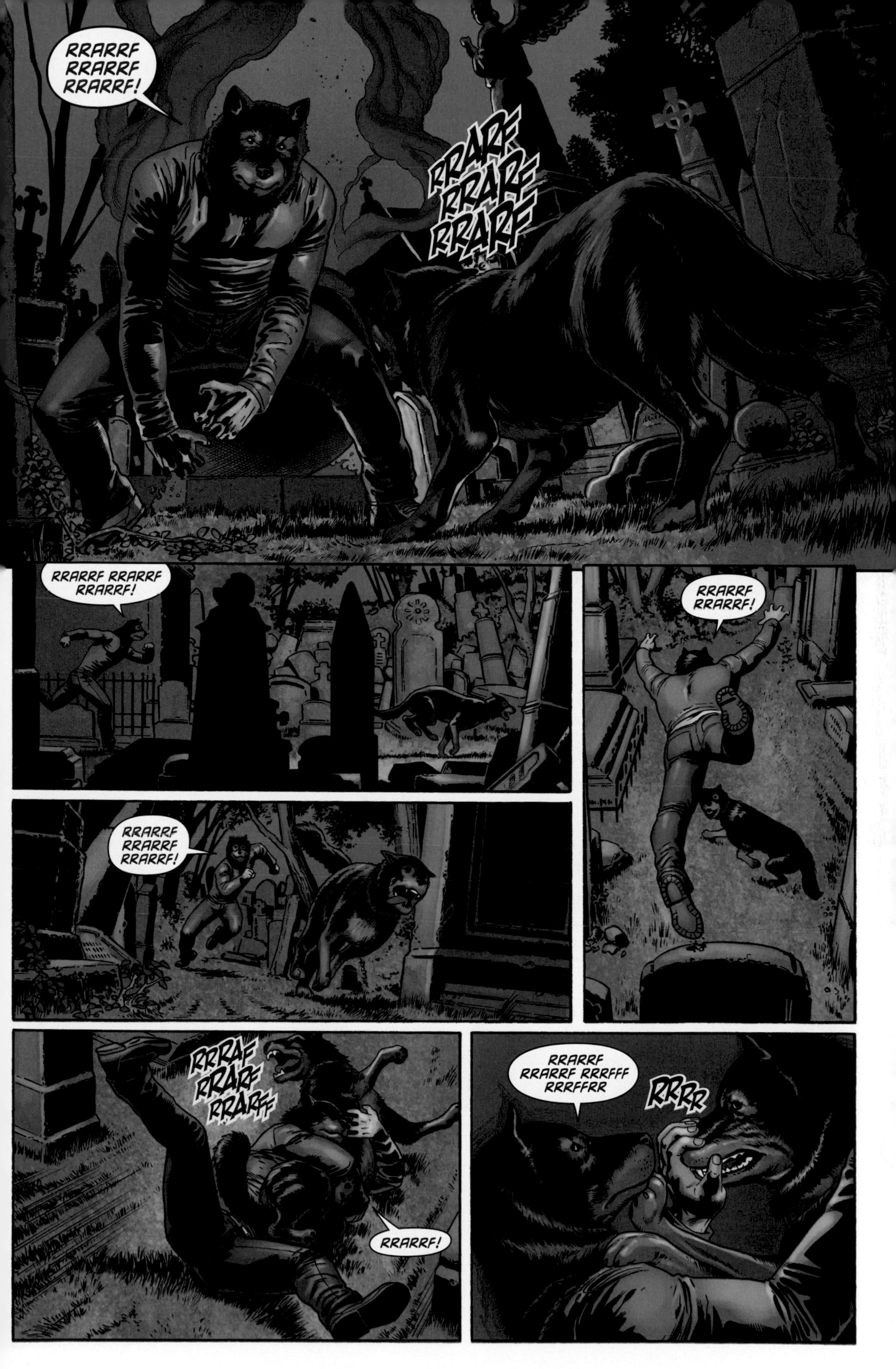
RRARRF RRARRF RRARRF!
RRARF RRARF RRARF
RRARRF RRARRF RRARRF!
RRARRF RRARRF!
RRARRF RRARRF RRARRF!
RRRAF RRARF RRARFF
RRARRF!
RRARRF RRARRF RRRFFF RRRFFRR
RRRR

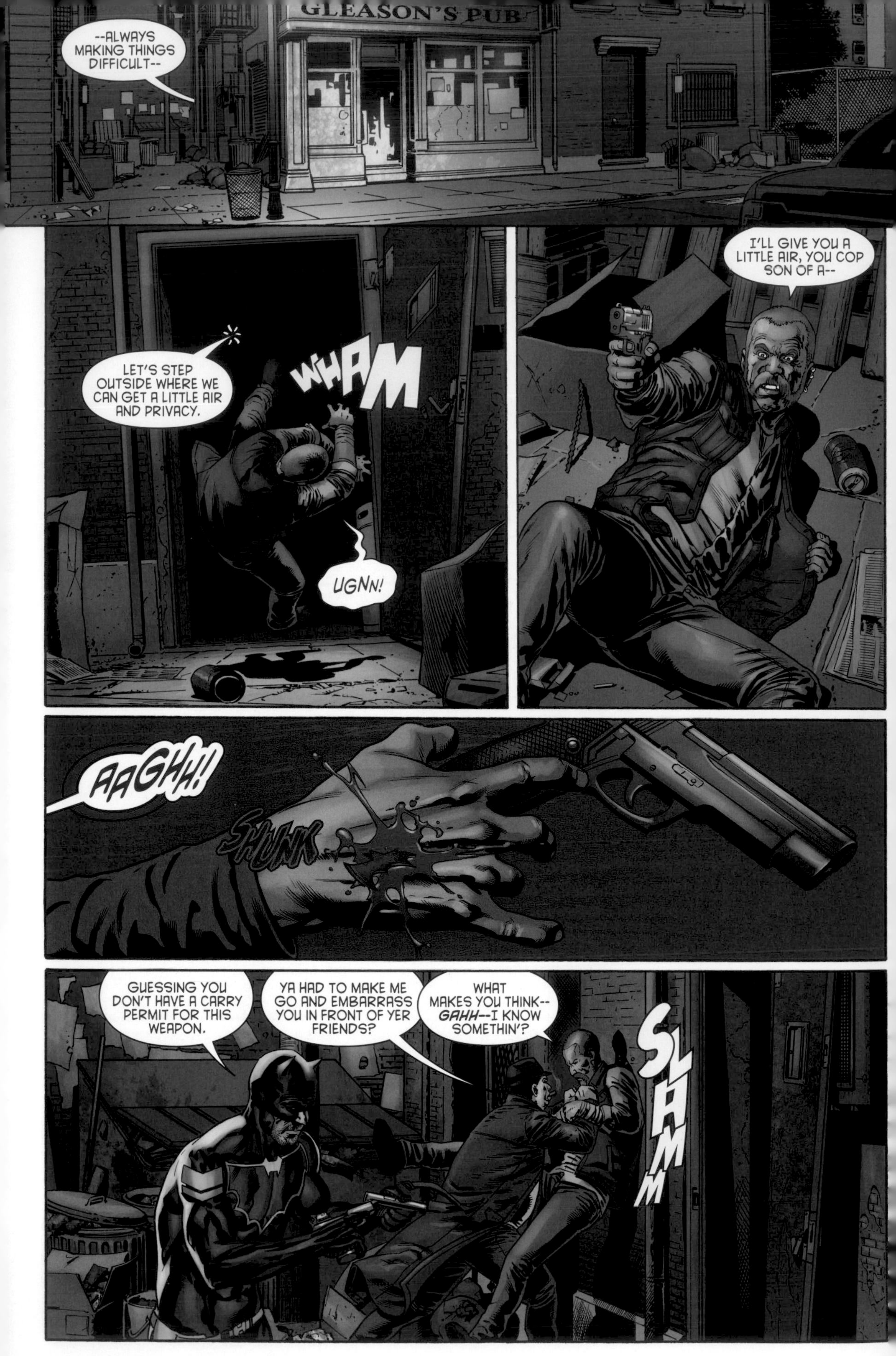
GLEASON'S PUB
--ALWAYS MAKING THINGS DIFFICULT--
LET'S STEP OUTSIDE WHERE WE CAN GET A LITTLE AIR AND PRIVACY.
WHAM
UGNN!
I'LL GIVE YOU A LITTLE AIR, YOU COP SON OF A--
AAGHH!
SHUNK
GUESSING YOU DON'T HAVE A CARRY PERMIT FOR THIS WEAPON.
YA HAD TO MAKE ME GO AND EMBARRASS YOU IN FRONT OF YER FRIENDS?
WHAT MAKES YOU THINK-- GAHH--I KNOW SOMETHIN'?
SLAMM

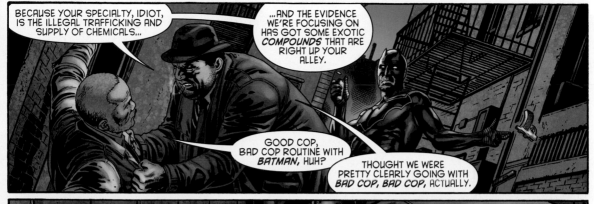

BECAUSE YOUR SPECIALTY, IDIOT, IS THE ILLEGAL TRAFFICKING AND SUPPLY OF CHEMICALS...

...AND THE EVIDENCE WE'RE FOCUSING ON HAS GOT SOME EXOTIC *COMPOUNDS* THAT ARE RIGHT UP YOUR ALLEY.

GOOD COP, BAD COP ROUTINE WITH *BATMAN*, HUH?

THOUGHT WE WERE PRETTY CLEARLY GOING WITH *BAD COP, BAD COP*, ACTUALLY.

SAY *"AH."*

AH.

WE WANT A LIST OF YOUR BUYERS FOR THE LAST SIX MONTHS.

YOUR POINT BEING?

tha' cou' ge' ee dead.

GOTHAM ZOO, GENTLEMEN. GET THERE IMMEDIATELY.

SLEEP ON IT--

KRAK

--AND WE'LL GET BACK TO YOU.

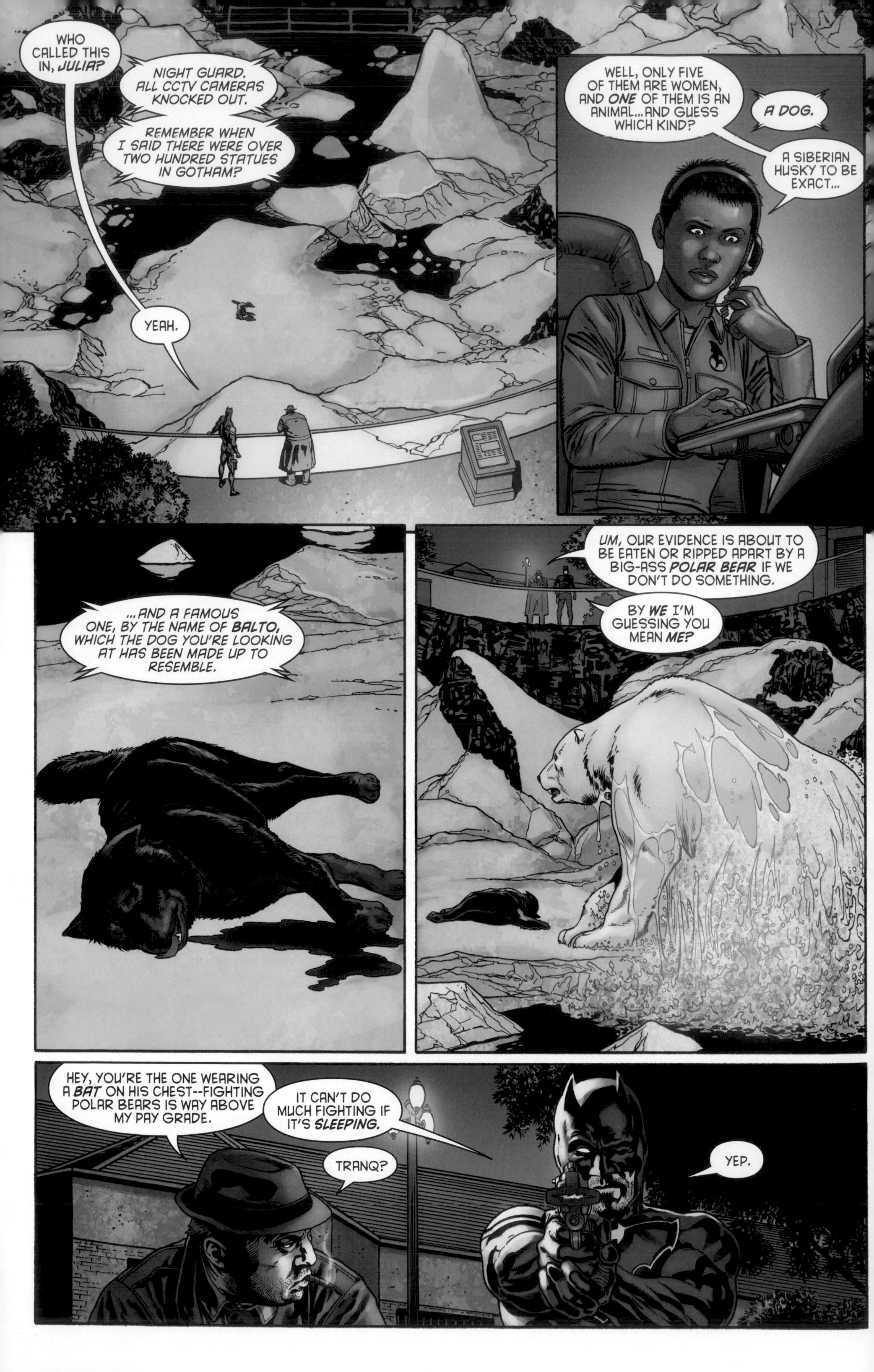
WHO CALLED THIS IN, JULIA?
NIGHT GUARD. ALL CCTV CAMERAS KNOCKED OUT.
REMEMBER WHEN I SAID THERE WERE OVER TWO HUNDRED STATUES IN GOTHAM?
YEAH.
WELL, ONLY FIVE OF THEM ARE WOMEN, AND ONE OF THEM IS AN ANIMAL...AND GUESS WHICH KIND?
A DOG.
A SIBERIAN HUSKY TO BE EXACT...
...AND A FAMOUS ONE, BY THE NAME OF BALTO, WHICH THE DOG YOU'RE LOOKING AT HAS BEEN MADE UP TO RESEMBLE.
UM, OUR EVIDENCE IS ABOUT TO BE EATEN OR RIPPED APART BY A BIG-ASS POLAR BEAR IF WE DON'T DO SOMETHING.
BY WE I'M GUESSING YOU MEAN ME?
HEY, YOU'RE THE ONE WEARING A BAT ON HIS CHEST--FIGHTING POLAR BEARS IS WAY ABOVE MY PAY GRADE.
IT CAN'T DO MUCH FIGHTING IF IT'S SLEEPING.
TRANQ?
YEP.

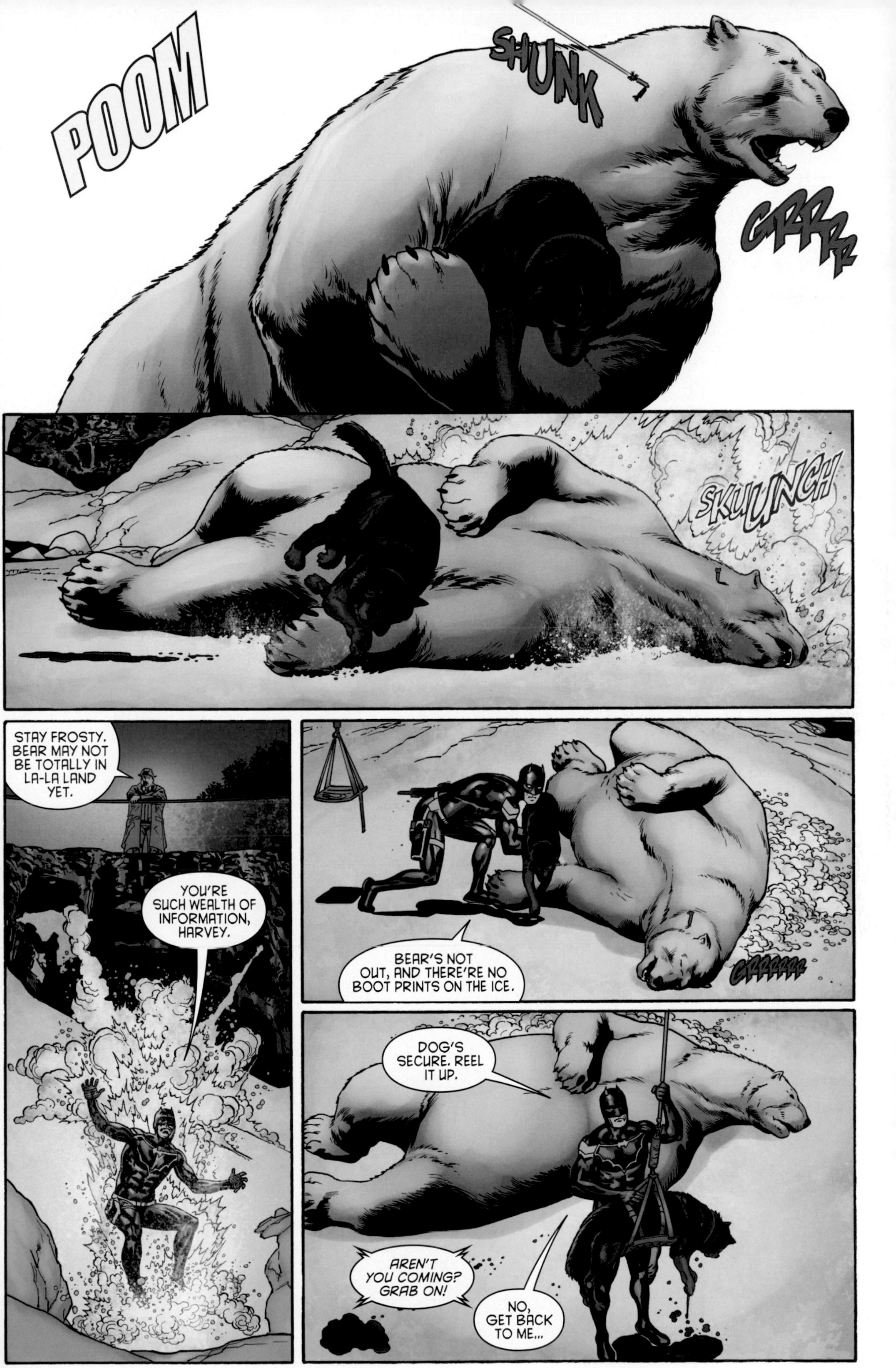
POOM
SHUNK
GRRRR
SKUUNCH
STAY FROSTY. BEAR MAY NOT BE TOTALLY IN LA-LA LAND YET.
YOU'RE SUCH WEALTH OF INFORMATION, HARVEY.
BEAR'S NOT OUT, AND THERE'RE NO BOOT PRINTS ON THE ICE.
GRRRRRR
DOG'S SECURE. REEL IT UP.
AREN'T YOU COMING? GRAB ON!
NO, GET BACK TO ME...

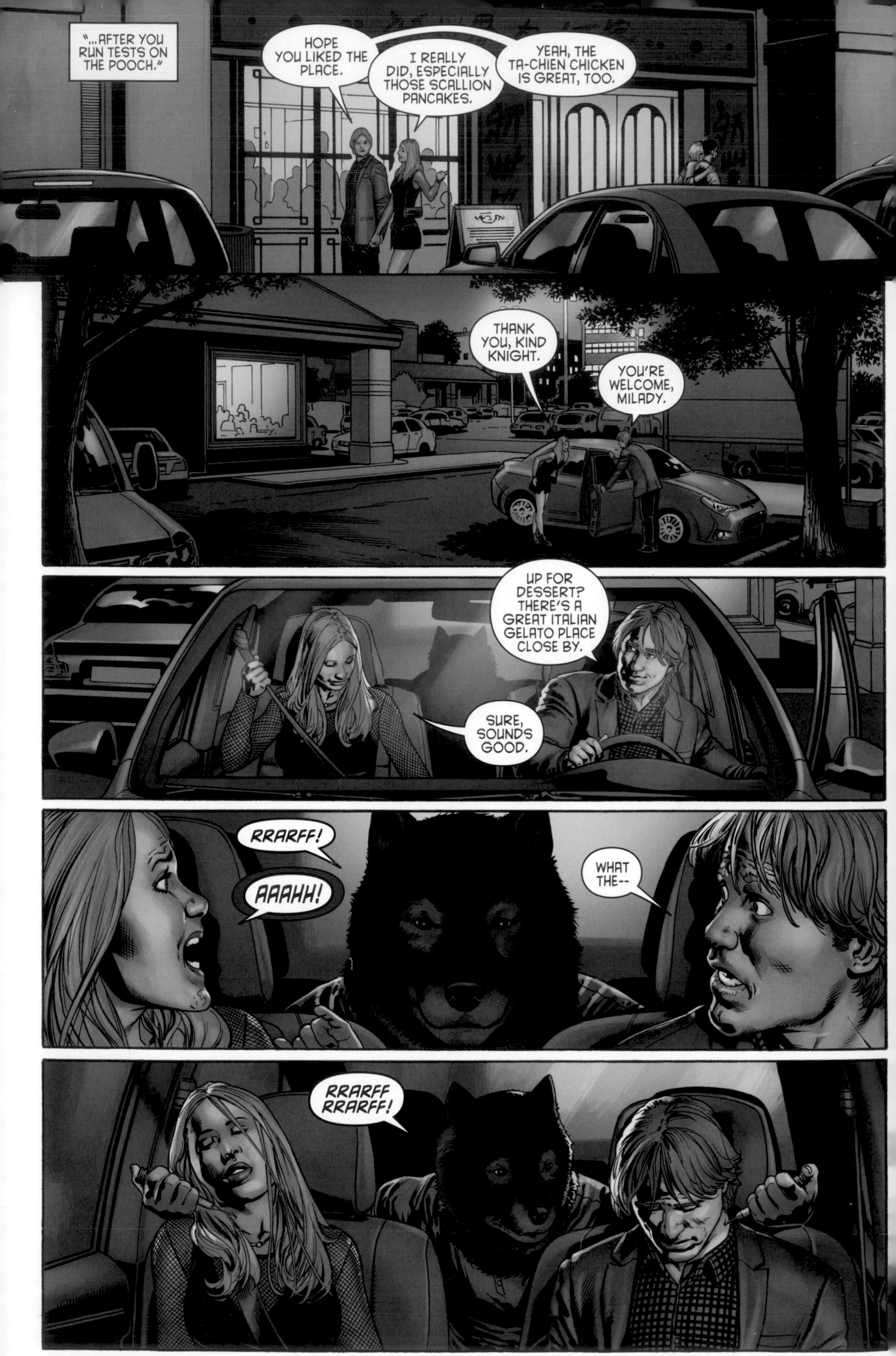
"...AFTER YOU RUN TESTS ON THE POOCH."
HOPE YOU LIKED THE PLACE.
I REALLY DID, ESPECIALLY THOSE SCALLION PANCAKES.
YEAH, THE TA-CHIEN CHICKEN IS GREAT, TOO.
THANK YOU, KIND KNIGHT.
YOU'RE WELCOME, MILADY.
UP FOR DESSERT? THERE'S A GREAT ITALIAN GELATO PLACE CLOSE BY.
SURE, SOUNDS GOOD.
RRARFF!
AAAHH!
WHAT THE--
RRARFF RRARFF!

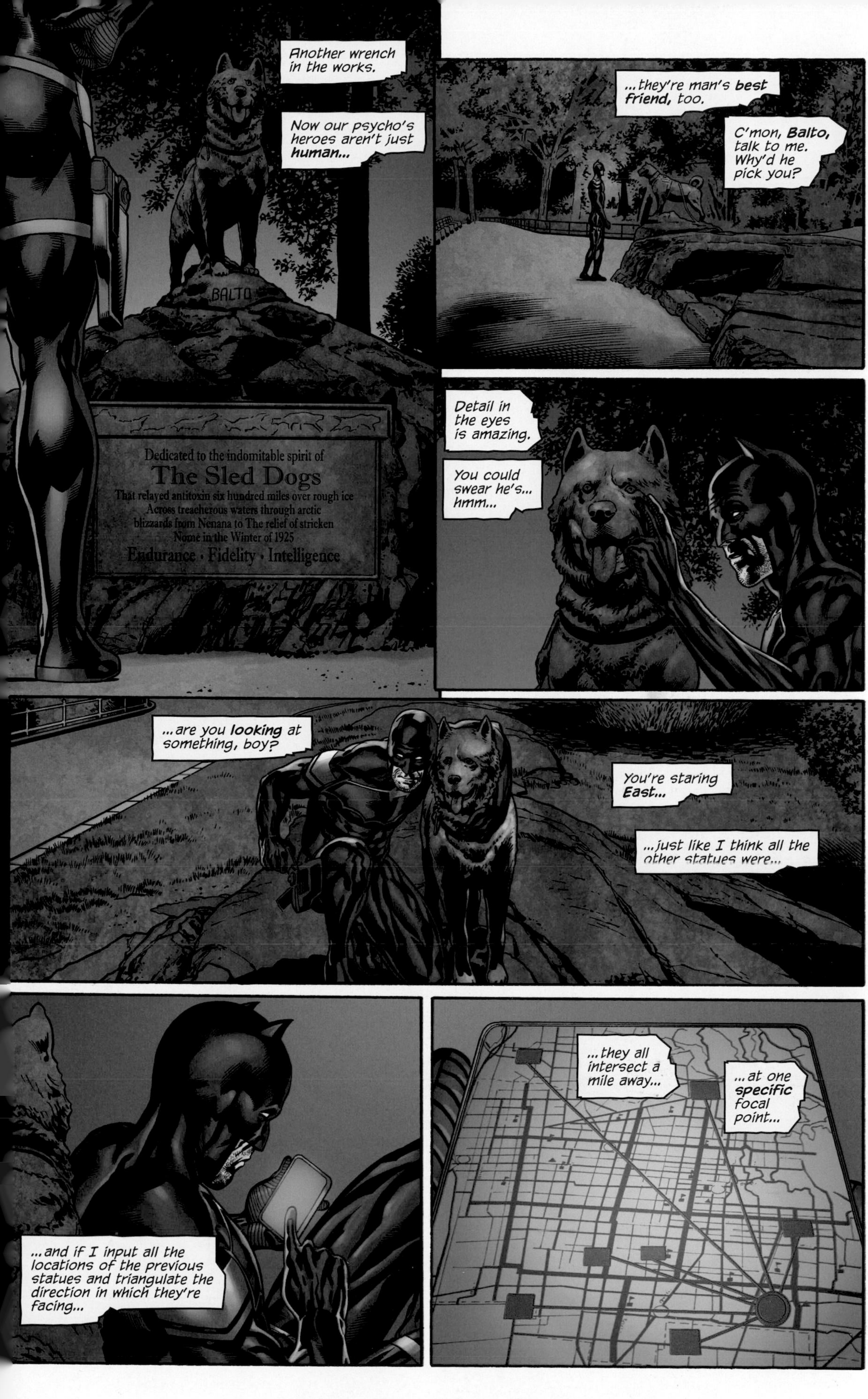

Another wrench in the works.
Now our psycho's heroes aren't just human...
BALTO
Dedicated to the indomitable spirit of
The Sled Dogs
That relayed antitoxin six hundred miles over rough ice
Across treacherous waters through arctic
blizzards from Nenana to The relief of stricken
Nome in the Winter of 1925
Endurance · Fidelity · Intelligence
...they're man's best friend, too.
C'mon, Balto, talk to me. Why'd he pick you?
Detail in the eyes is amazing.
You could swear he's... hmm...
...are you looking at something, boy?
You're staring East...
...just like I think all the other statues were...
...and if I input all the locations of the previous statues and triangulate the direction in which they're facing...
...they all intersect a mile away...
...at one specific focal point...

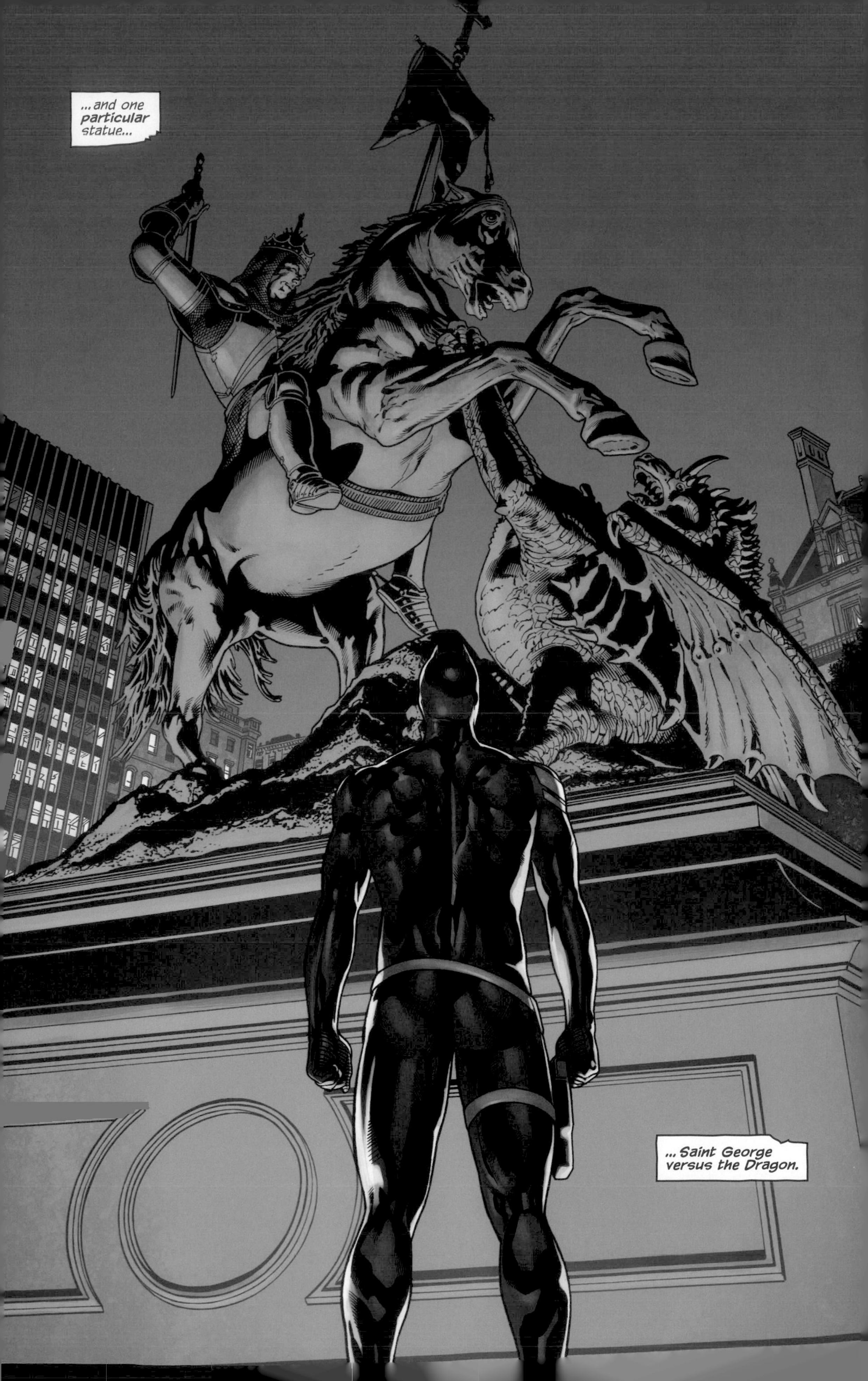
...and one particular statue...
...Saint George versus the Dragon.

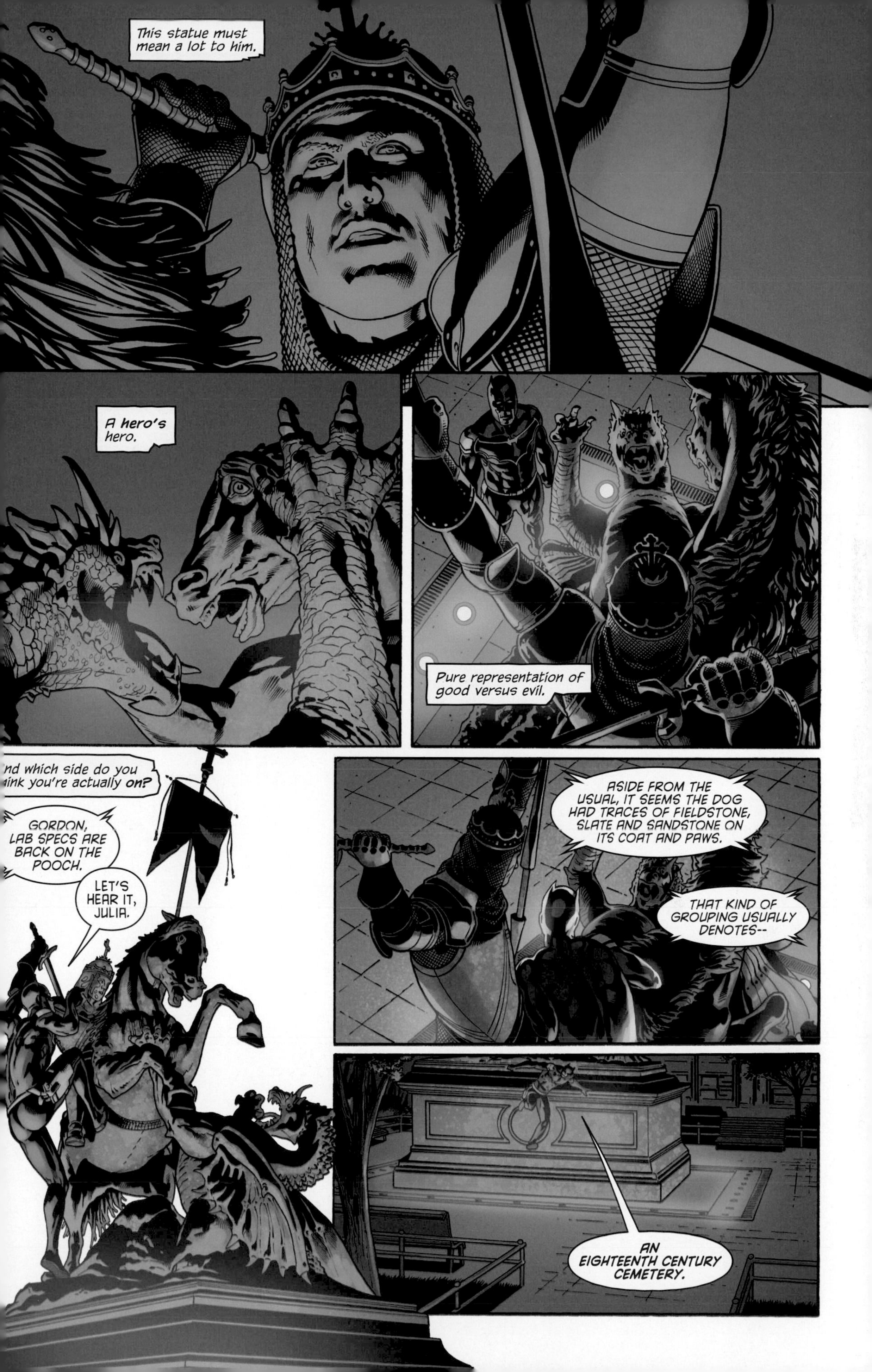
This statue must mean a lot to him.
A hero's hero.
Pure representation of good versus evil.
nd which side do you nink you're actually on?
GORDON, LAB SPECS ARE BACK ON THE POOCH.
LET'S HEAR IT, JULIA.
ASIDE FROM THE USUAL, IT SEEMS THE DOG HAD TRACES OF FIELDSTONE, SLATE AND SANDSTONE ON ITS COAT AND PAWS.
THAT KIND OF GROUPING USUALLY DENOTES--
AN EIGHTEENTH CENTURY CEMETERY.

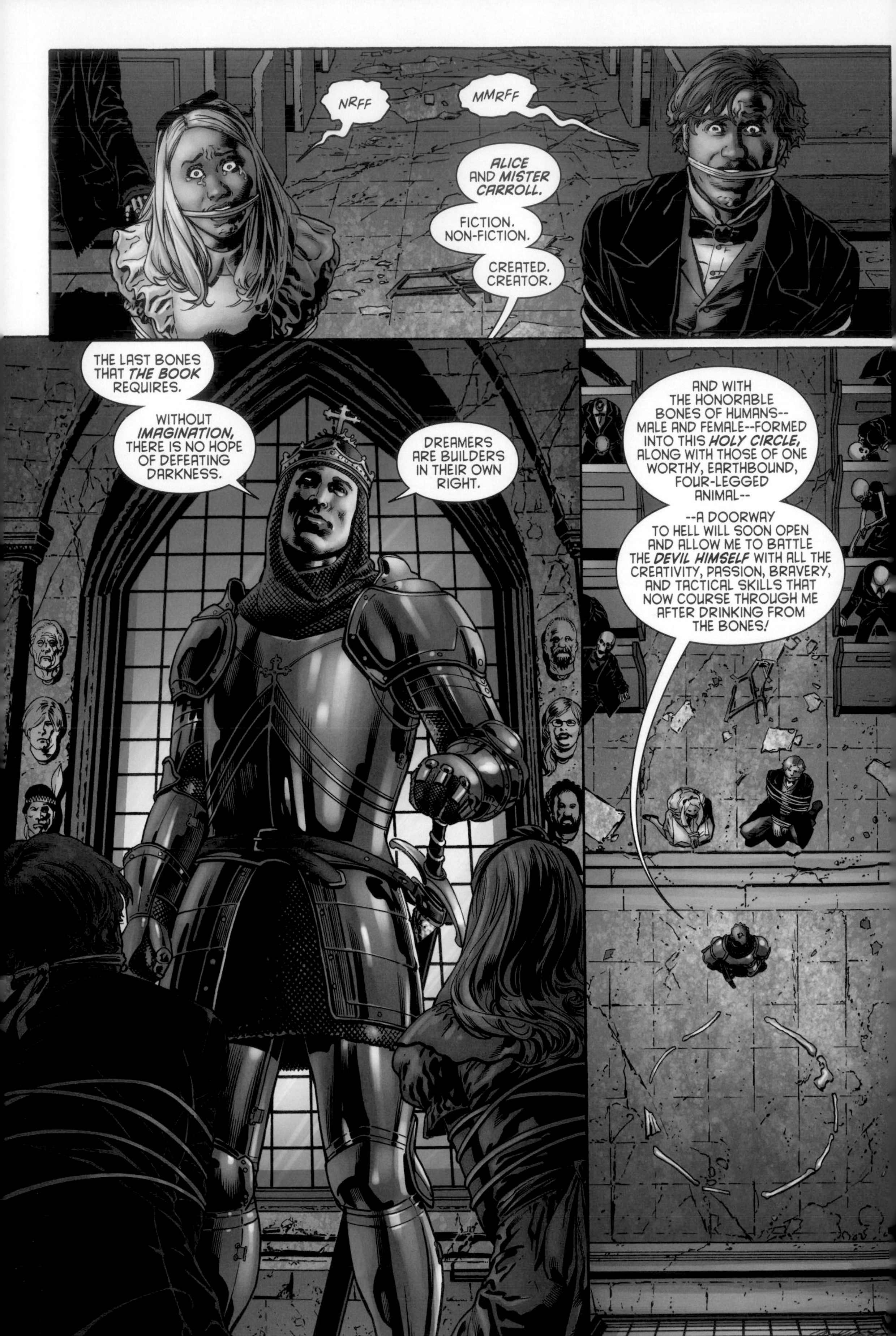
NRFF
MMRFF
ALICE AND MISTER CARROLL.
FICTION. NON-FICTION.
CREATED. CREATOR.
THE LAST BONES THAT THE BOOK REQUIRES.
WITHOUT IMAGINATION, THERE IS NO HOPE OF DEFEATING DARKNESS.
DREAMERS ARE BUILDERS IN THEIR OWN RIGHT.
AND WITH THE HONORABLE BONES OF HUMANS--MALE AND FEMALE--FORMED INTO THIS HOLY CIRCLE, ALONG WITH THOSE OF ONE WORTHY, EARTHBOUND, FOUR-LEGGED ANIMAL--
--A DOORWAY TO HELL WILL SOON OPEN AND ALLOW ME TO BATTLE THE DEVIL HIMSELF WITH ALL THE CREATIVITY, PASSION, BRAVERY, AND TACTICAL SKILLS THAT NOW COURSE THROUGH ME AFTER DRINKING FROM THE BONES!

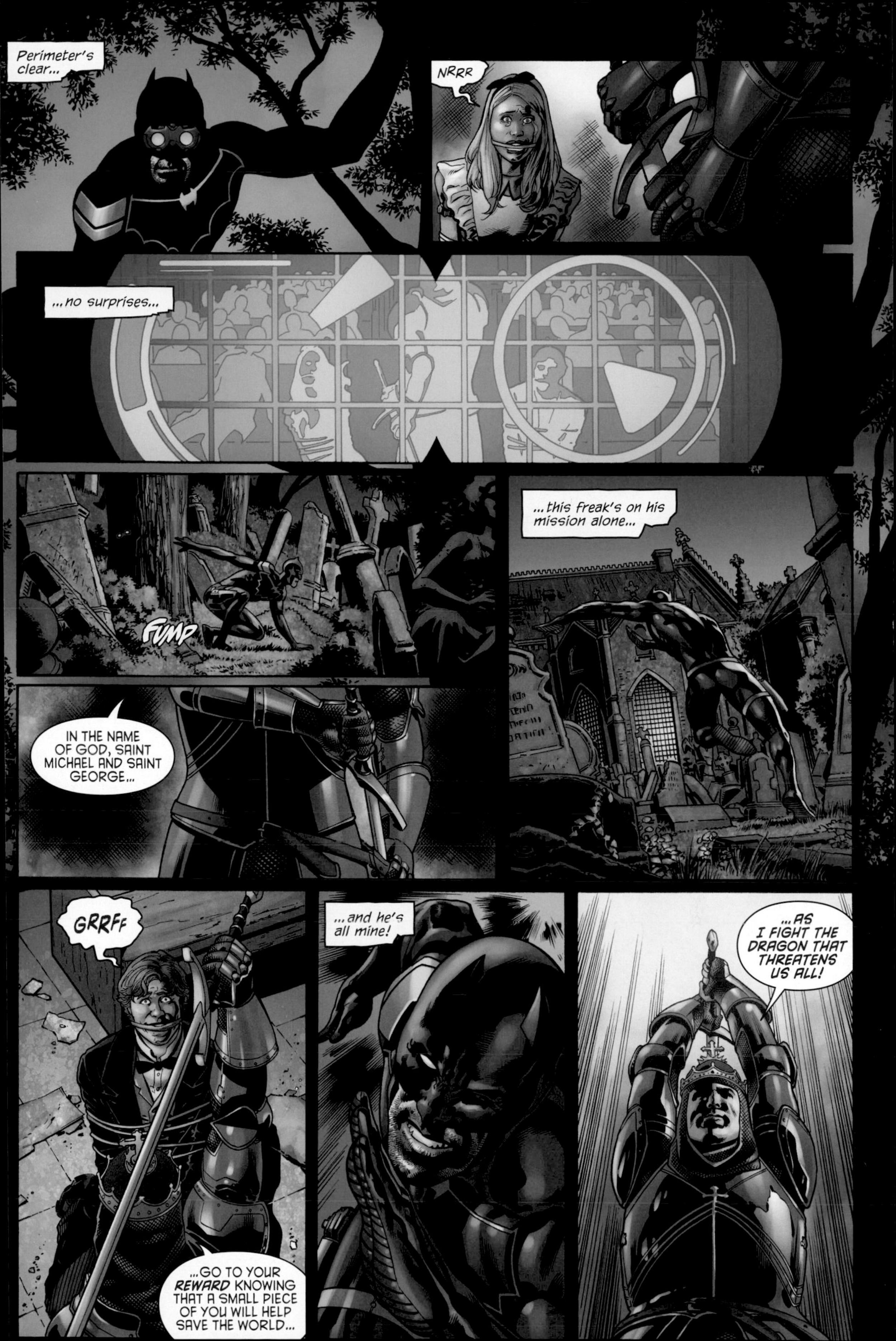
Perimeter's clear...
NRRR
...no surprises...
FUMP
...this freak's on his mission alone...
IN THE NAME OF GOD, SAINT MICHAEL AND SAINT GEORGE...
GRRFF
...GO TO YOUR REWARD KNOWING THAT A SMALL PIECE OF YOU WILL HELP SAVE THE WORLD...
...and he's all mine!
...AS I FIGHT THE DRAGON THAT THREATENS US ALL!

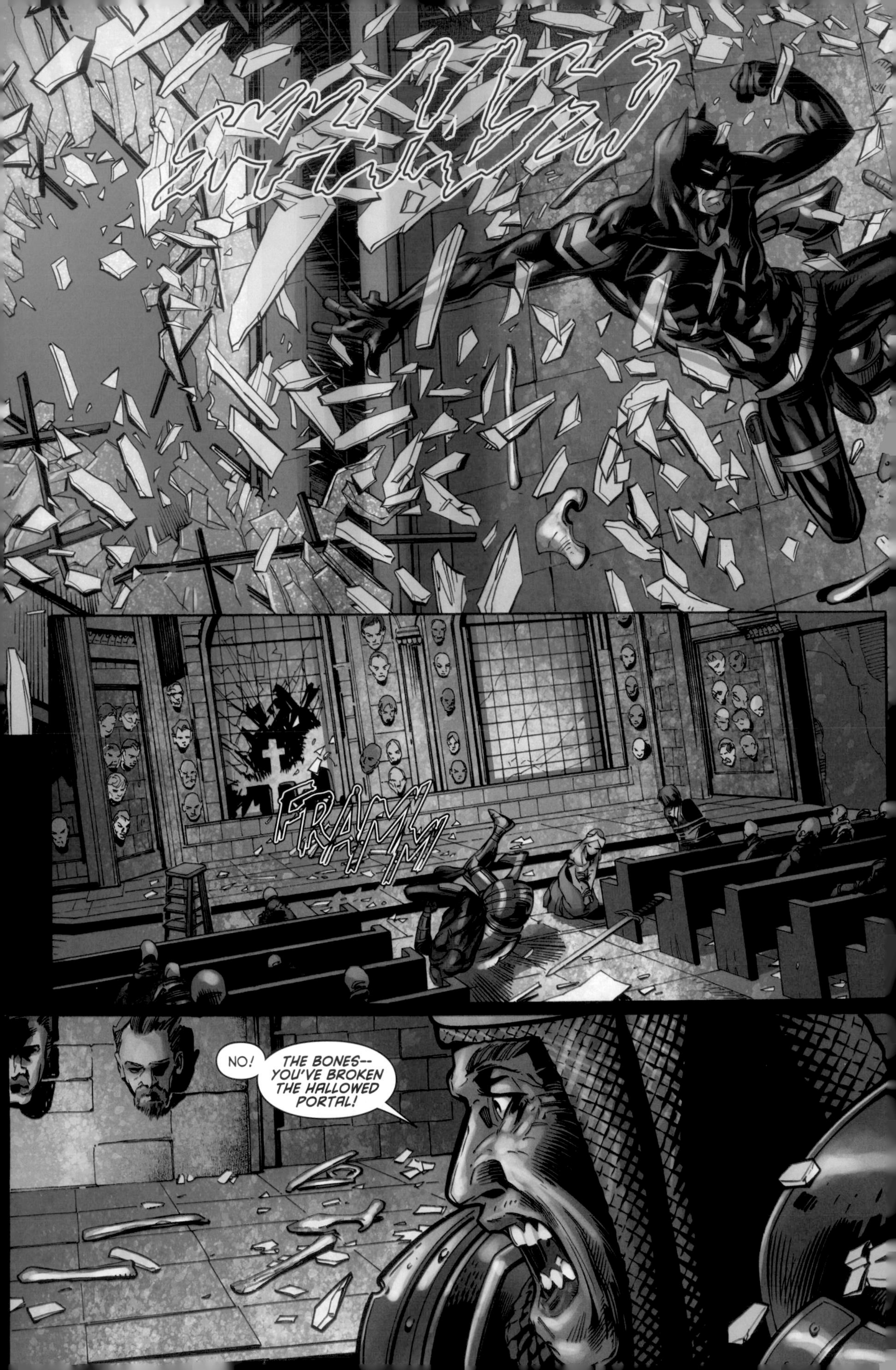
FRAMM
NO!
THE BONES-- YOU'VE BROKEN THE HALLOWED PORTAL!

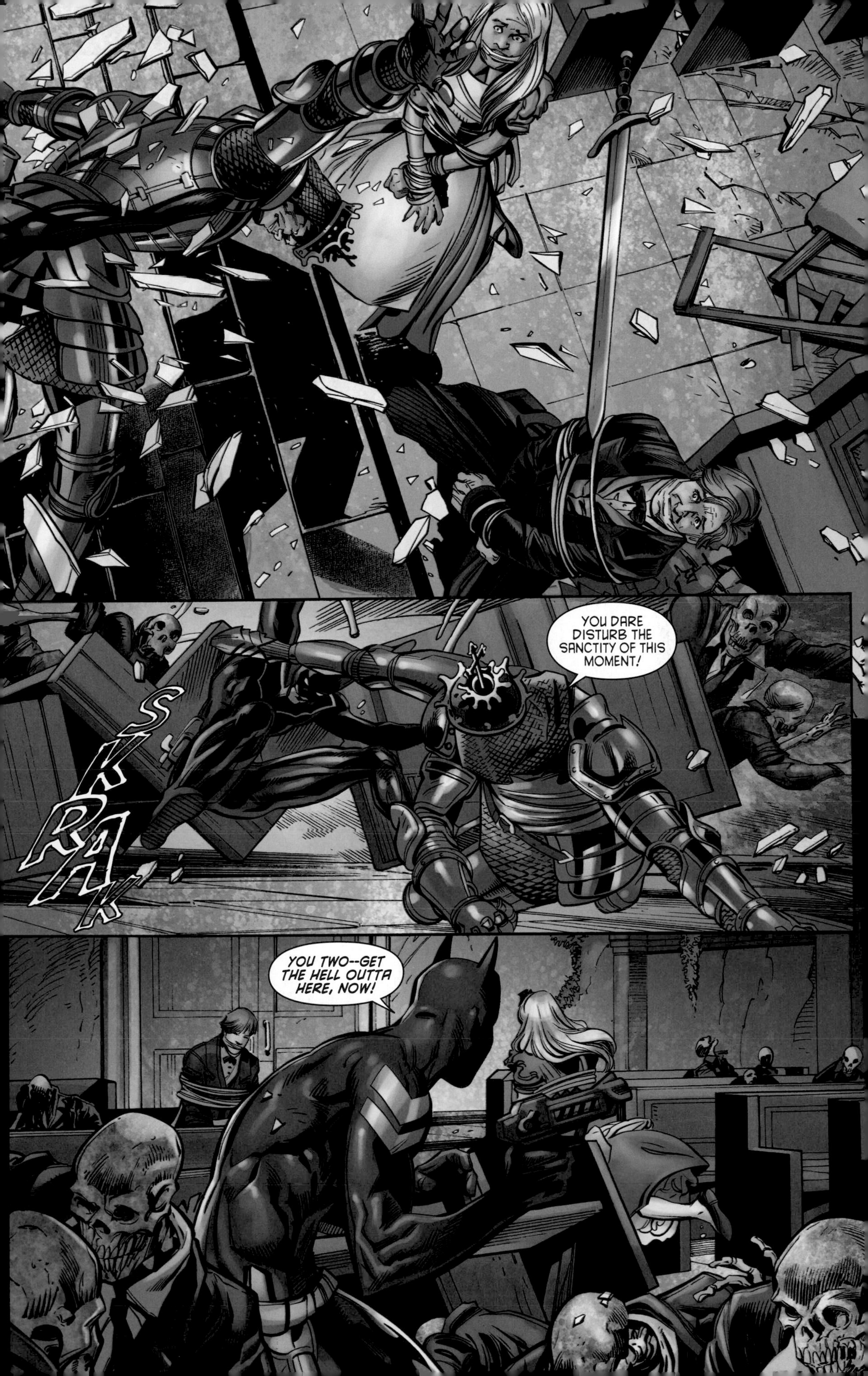
YOU DARE DISTURB THE SANCTITY OF THIS MOMENT!
SKRAK
YOU TWO--GET THE HELL OUTTA HERE, NOW!

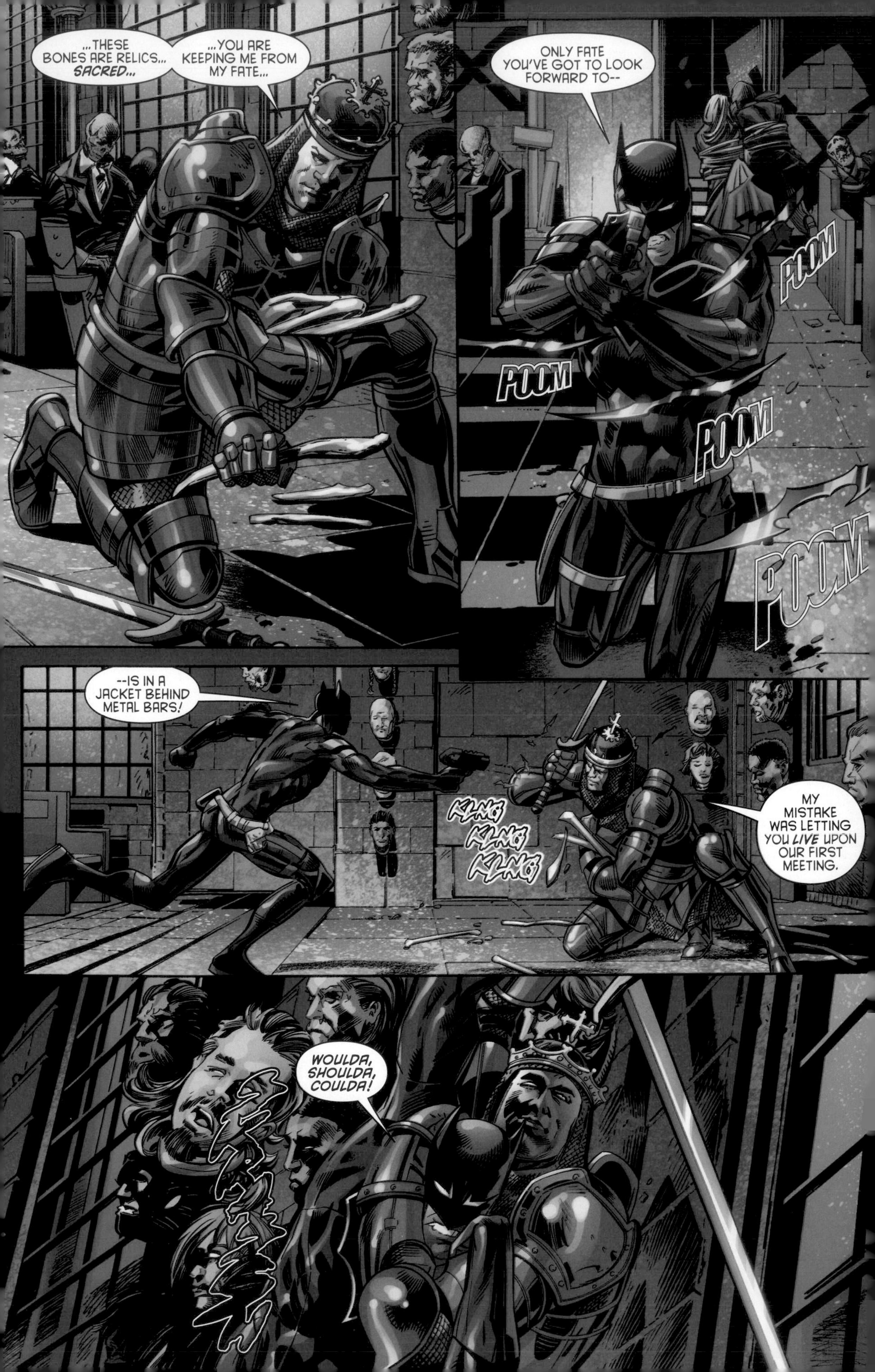

...THESE BONES ARE RELICS... SACRED...
...YOU ARE KEEPING ME FROM MY FATE...
ONLY FATE YOU'VE GOT TO LOOK FORWARD TO--
POOM
POOM
POOM
POOM
--IS IN A JACKET BEHIND METAL BARS!
KLNG KLNG KLNG
MY MISTAKE WAS LETTING YOU LIVE UPON OUR FIRST MEETING.
WOULDA, SHOULDA, COULDA!

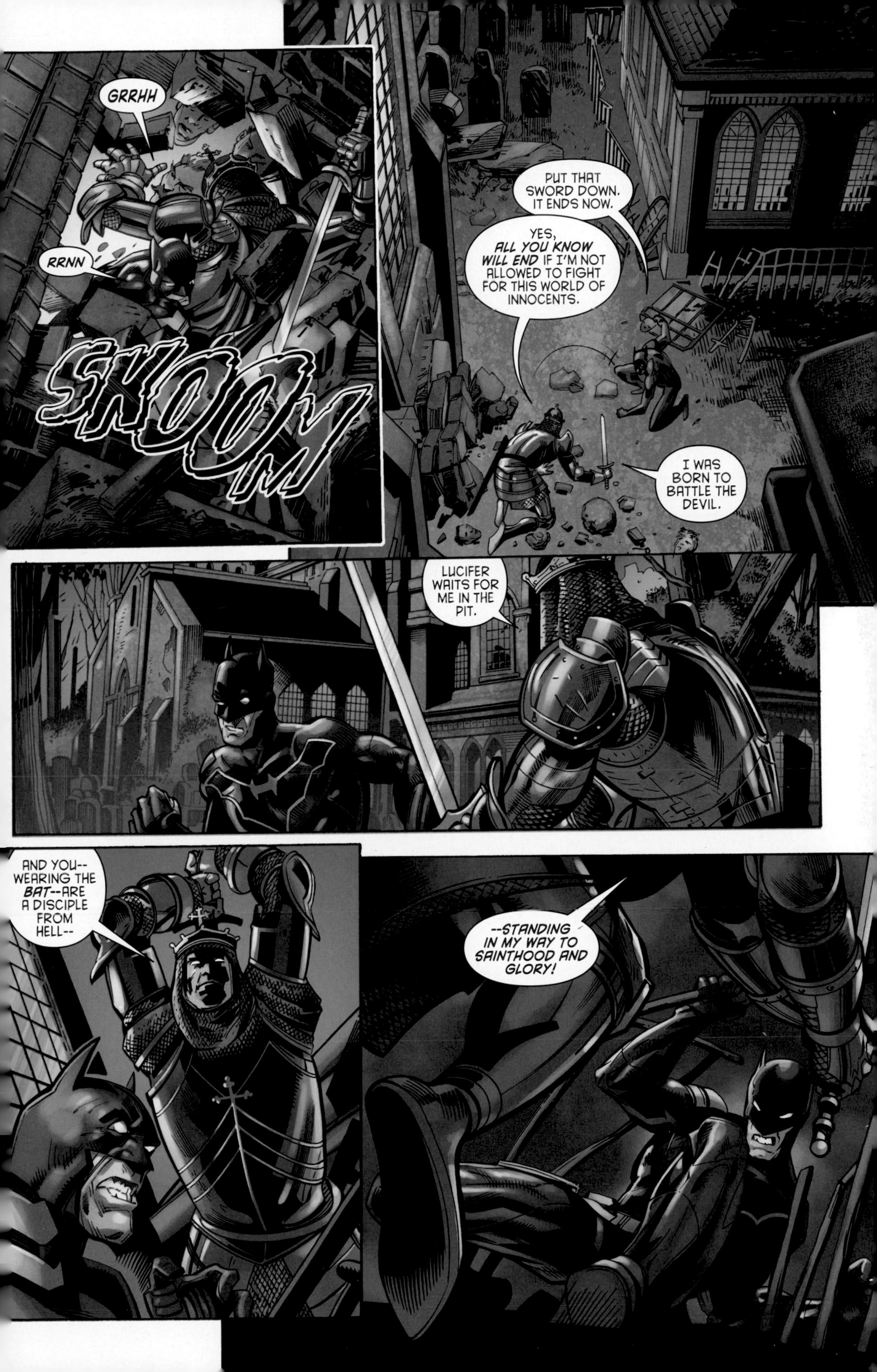
GRRHH
RRNN
SKOOM
PUT THAT SWORD DOWN. IT ENDS NOW.
YES, ALL YOU KNOW WILL END IF I'M NOT ALLOWED TO FIGHT FOR THIS WORLD OF INNOCENTS.
I WAS BORN TO BATTLE THE DEVIL.
LUCIFER WAITS FOR ME IN THE PIT.
AND YOU-- WEARING THE BAT--ARE A DISCIPLE FROM HELL--
--STANDING IN MY WAY TO SAINTHOOD AND GLORY!

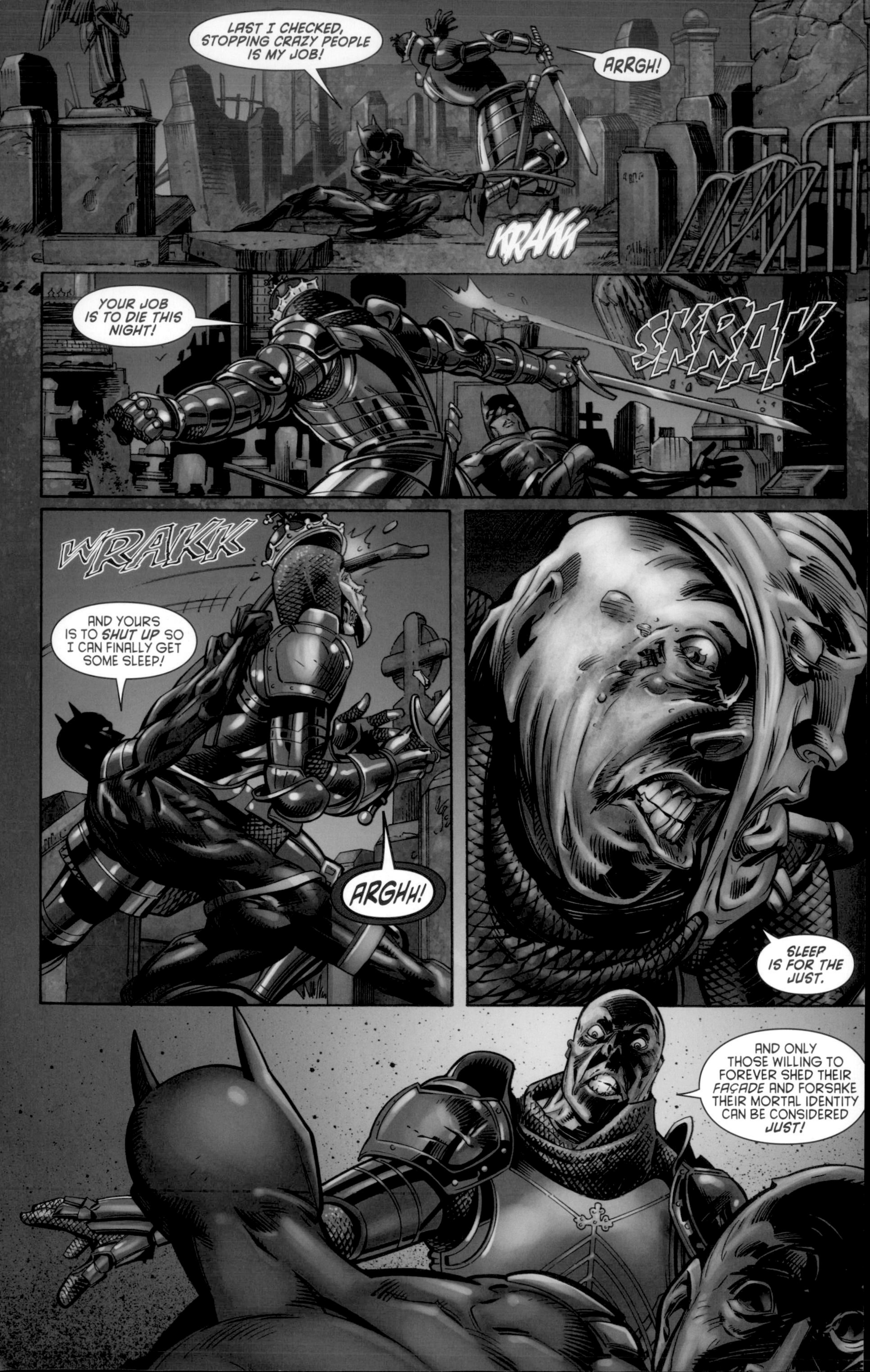

LAST I CHECKED, STOPPING CRAZY PEOPLE IS MY JOB!
ARRGH!
KRAKK
YOUR JOB IS TO DIE THIS NIGHT!
SKRAK
WRAKK
AND YOURS IS TO SHUT UP SO I CAN FINALLY GET SOME SLEEP!
ARGHH!
SLEEP IS FOR THE JUST.
AND ONLY THOSE WILLING TO FOREVER SHED THEIR FAÇADE AND FORSAKE THEIR MORTAL IDENTITY CAN BE CONSIDERED JUST!

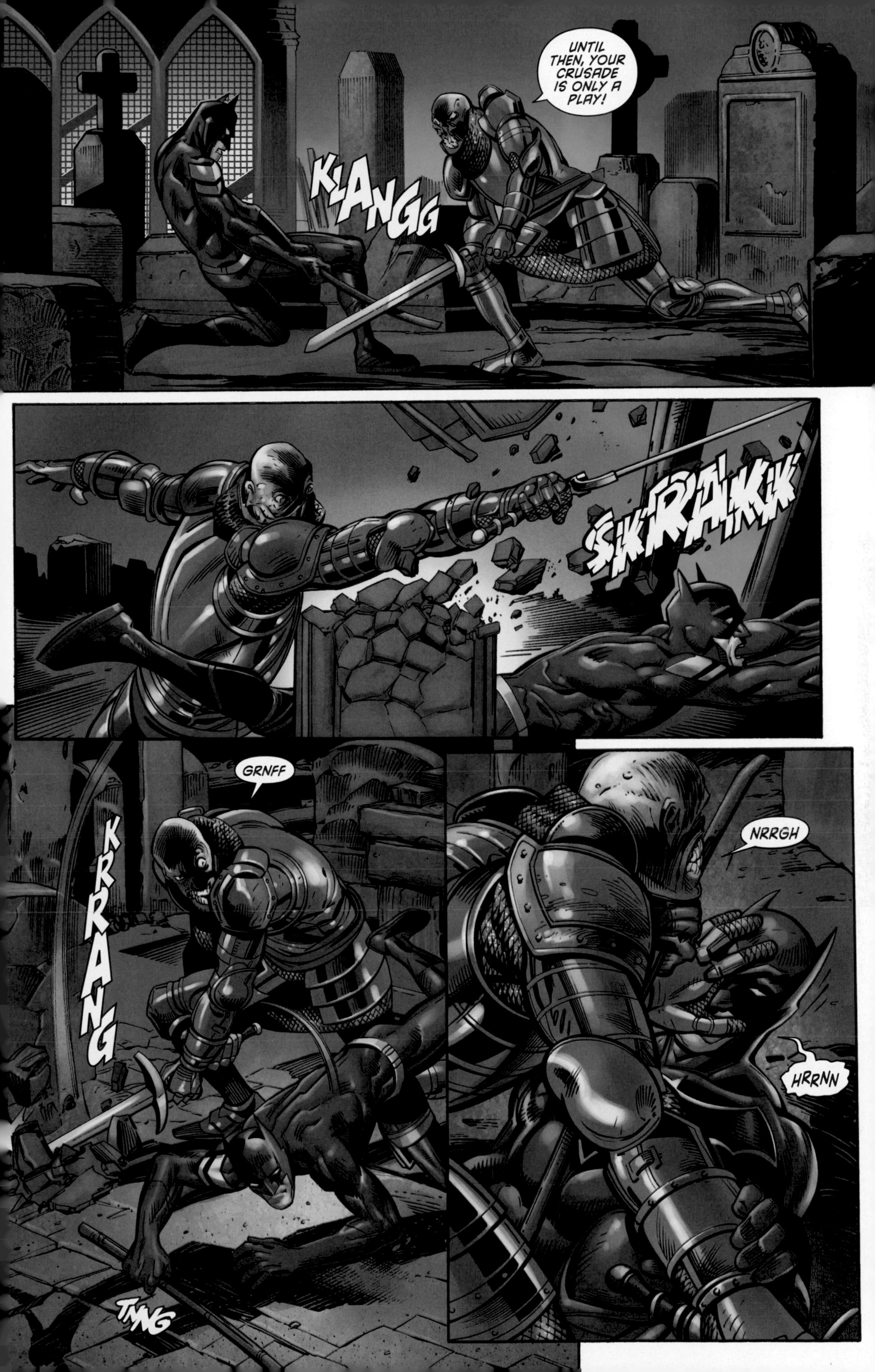
UNTIL THEN, YOUR CRUSADE IS ONLY A PLAY!
KLANGG
SKRAKK
GRNFF
KRRANG
TNNG
NRRGH
HRRNN

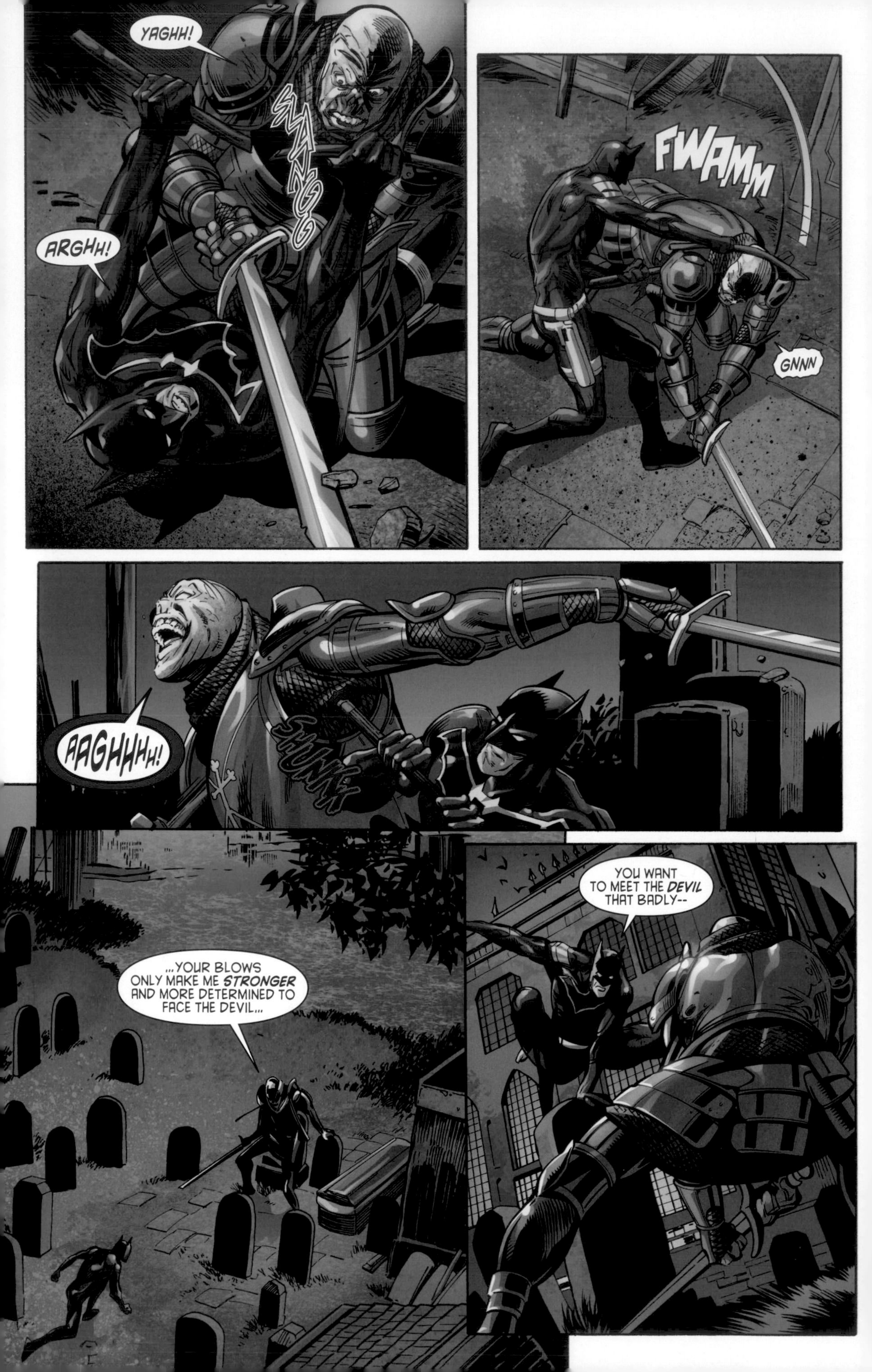
YAGHH!
SWANGG
ARGHH!
FWAMM
GNNN
AAGHHHH!
SHUNKK
...YOUR BLOWS ONLY MAKE ME *STRONGER* AND MORE DETERMINED TO FACE THE DEVIL...
YOU WANT TO MEET THE *DEVIL* THAT BADLY--

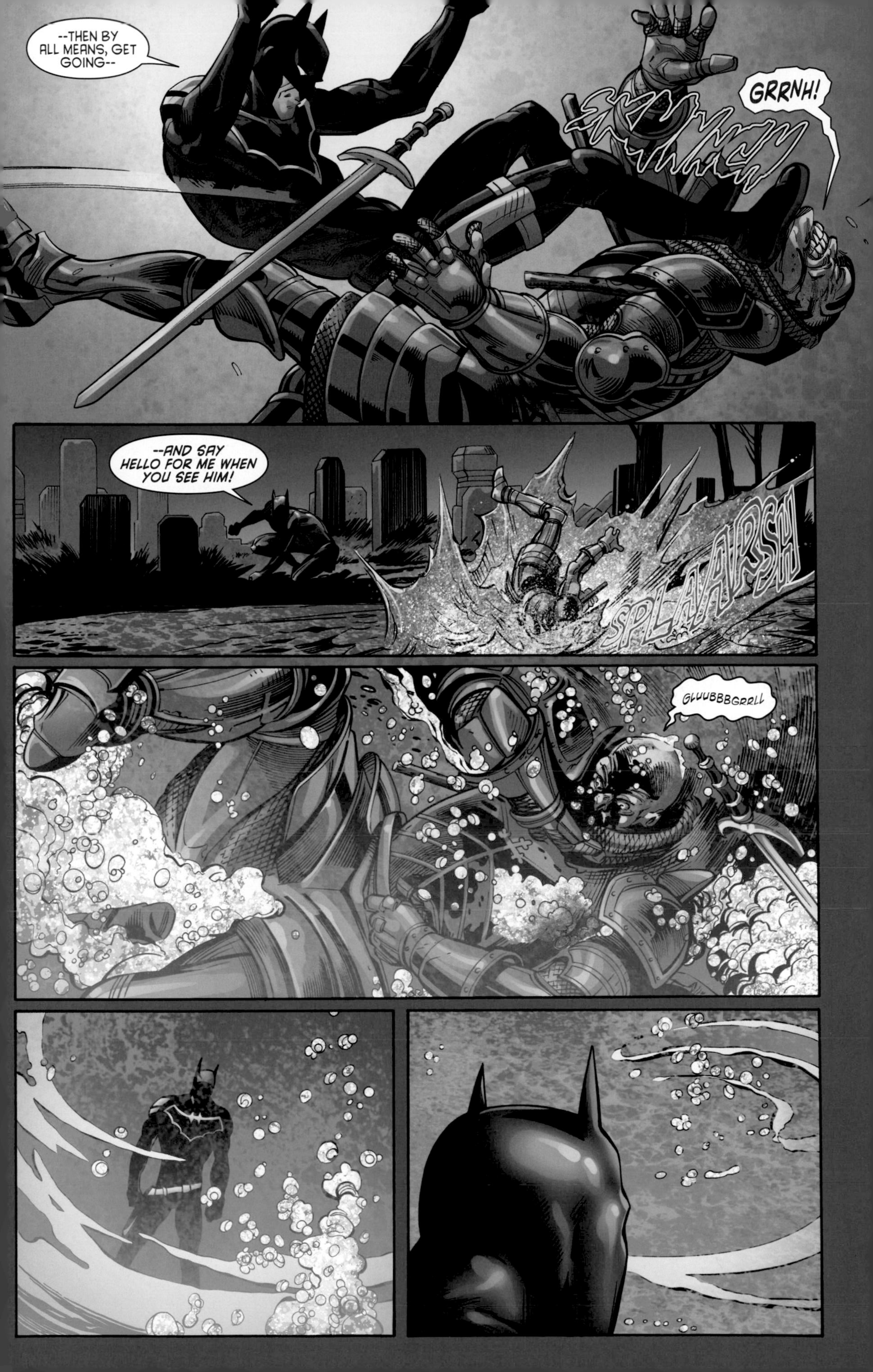
--THEN BY ALL MEANS, GET GOING--
GRRNH!
--AND SAY HELLO FOR ME WHEN YOU SEE HIM!
SPLAVRSH
GLUUBBBGRRLL

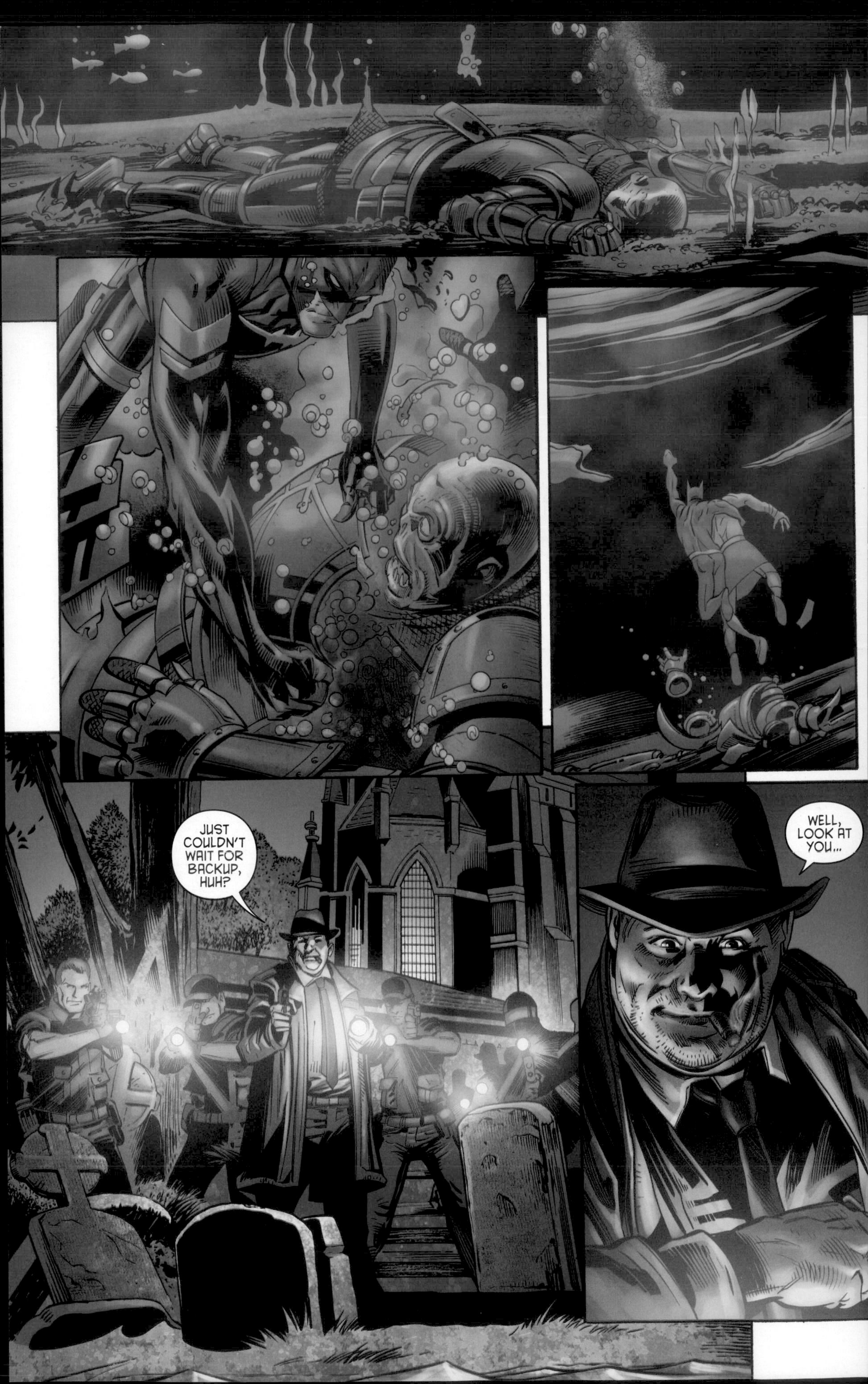
JUST COULDN'T WAIT FOR BACKUP, HUH?
WELL, LOOK AT YOU...

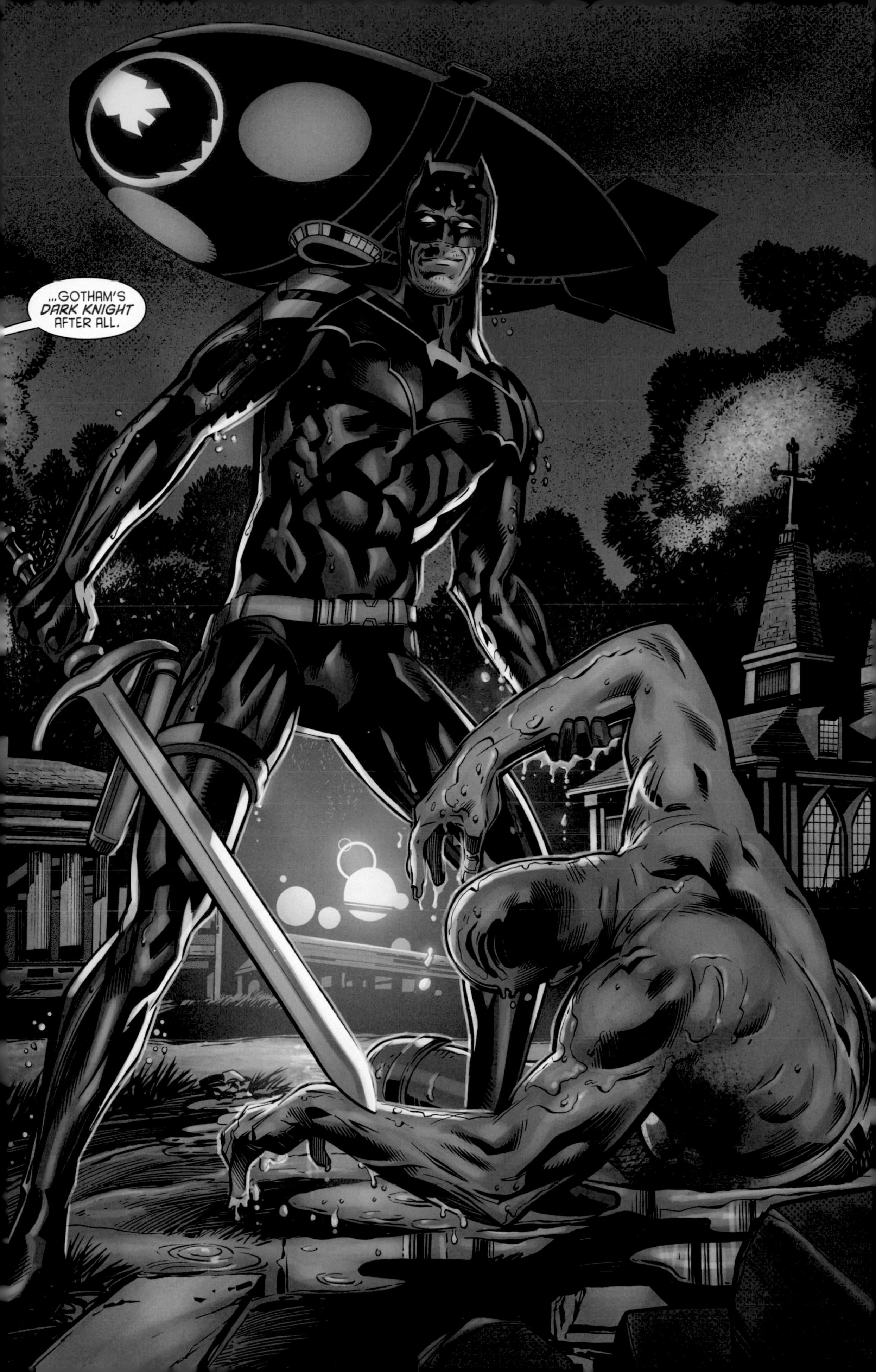
...GOTHAM'S DARK KNIGHT AFTER ALL.

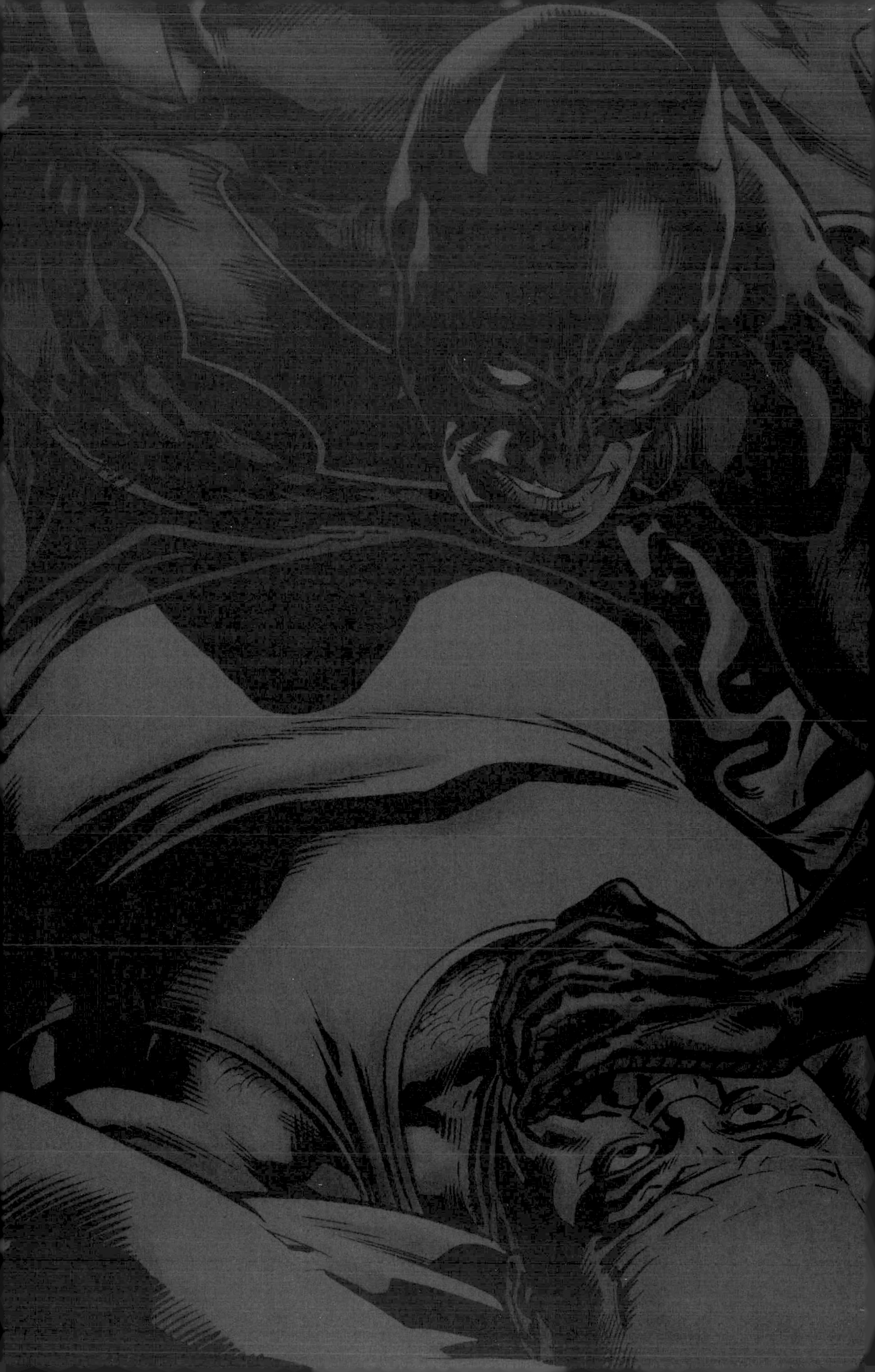

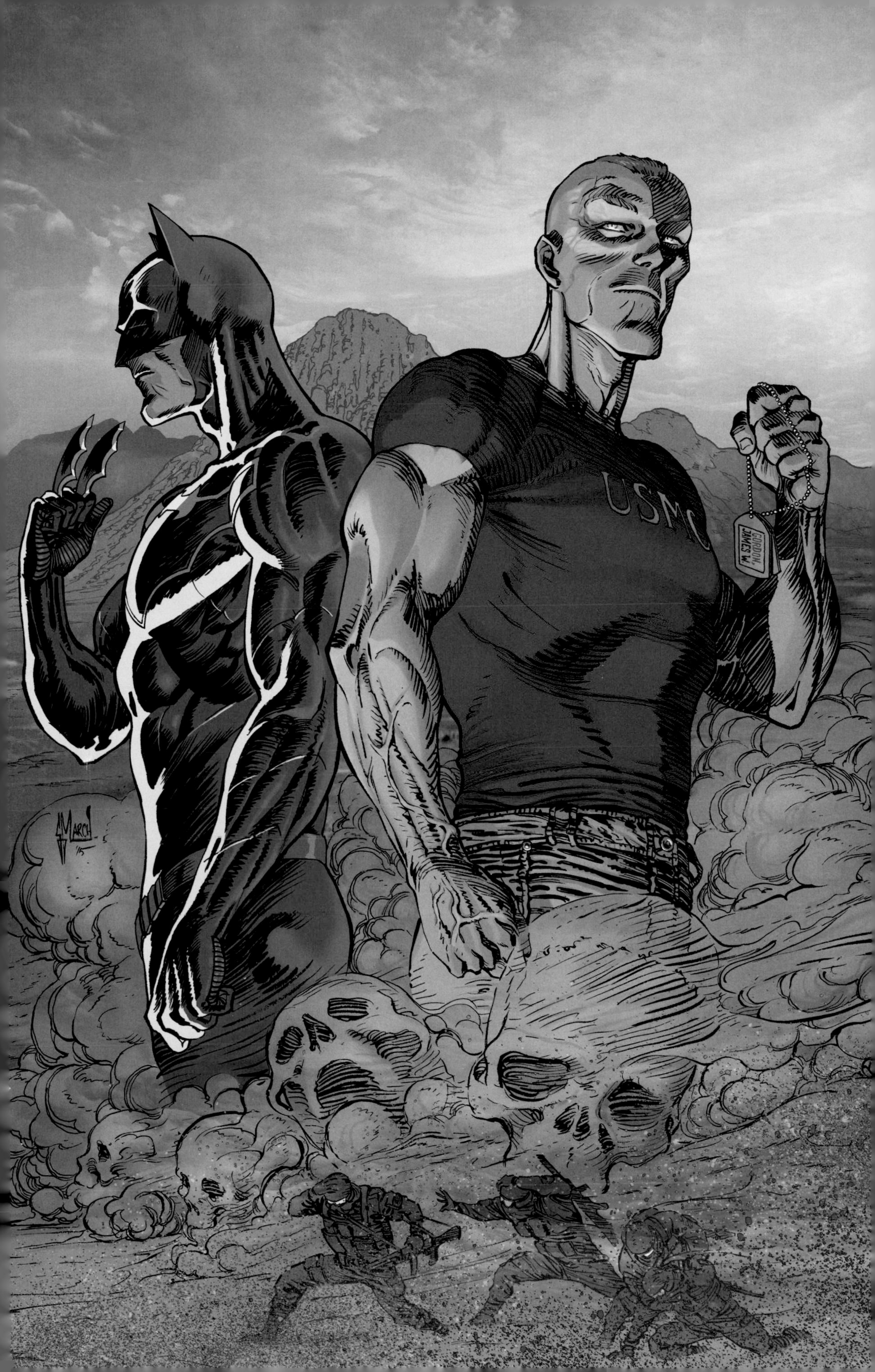
USMC
GORDON, JAMES W.
MARCH

OUR GORDON AT WAR, PART 1

PETER J. TOMASI writer **FERNANDO PASARIN** penciller **MATT RYAN** inker **CHRIS SOTOMAYOR** colorist **WES ABBOTT** letterer **GUILLEM MARCH** cover

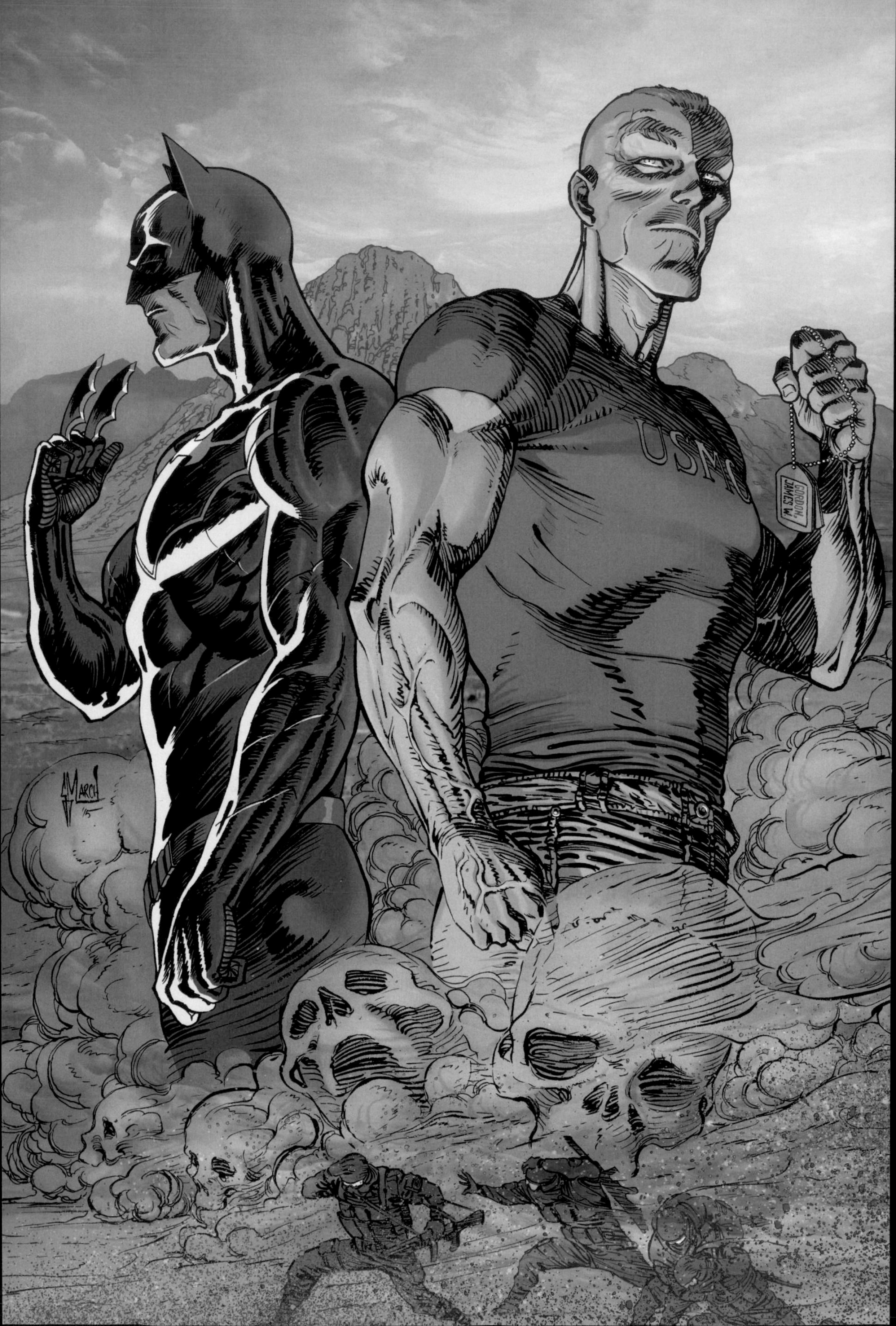

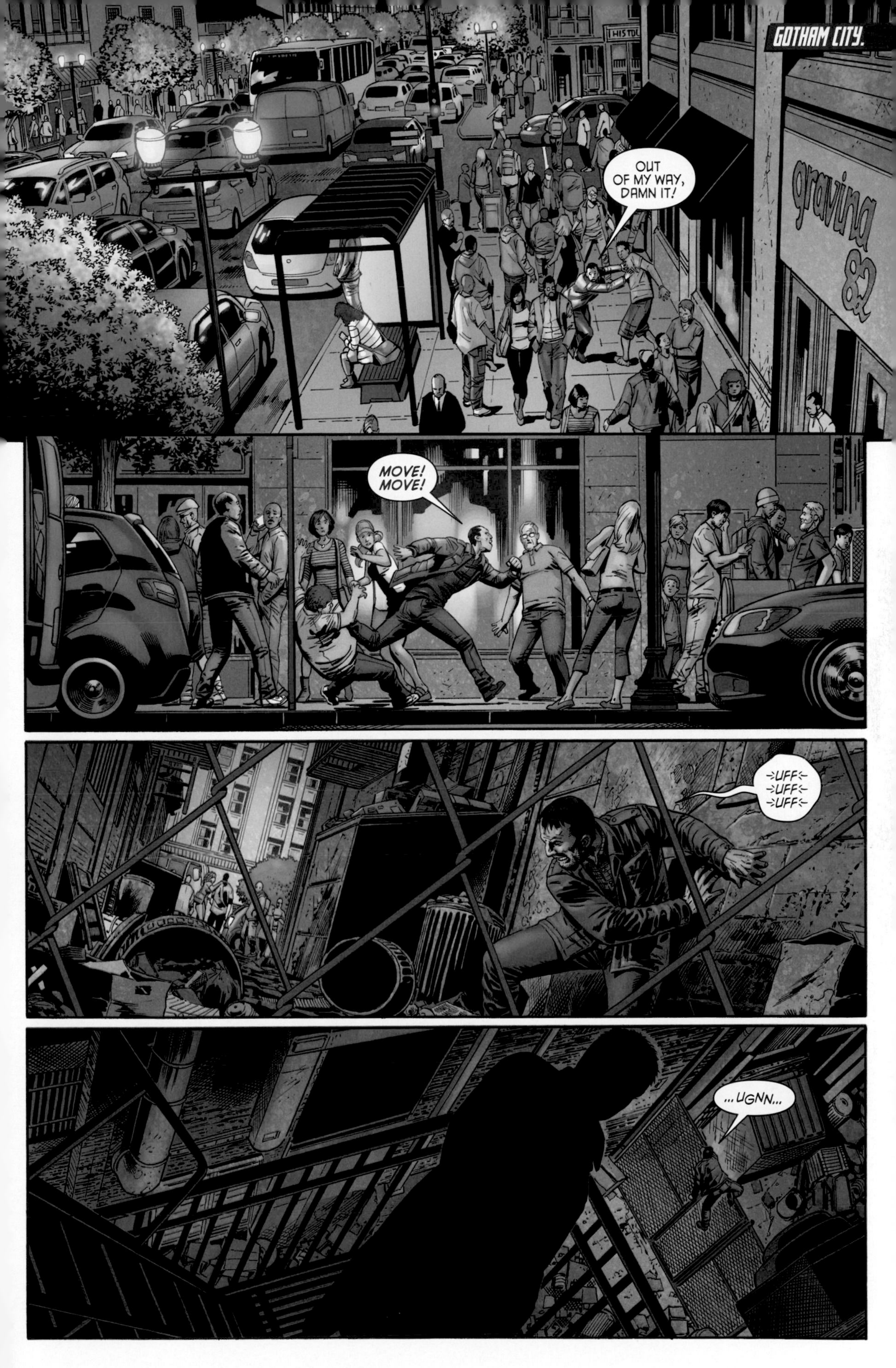
GOTHAM CITY.
OUT OF MY WAY, DAMN IT!
gravina 82
MOVE! MOVE!
UFF UFF UFF
...UGNN...

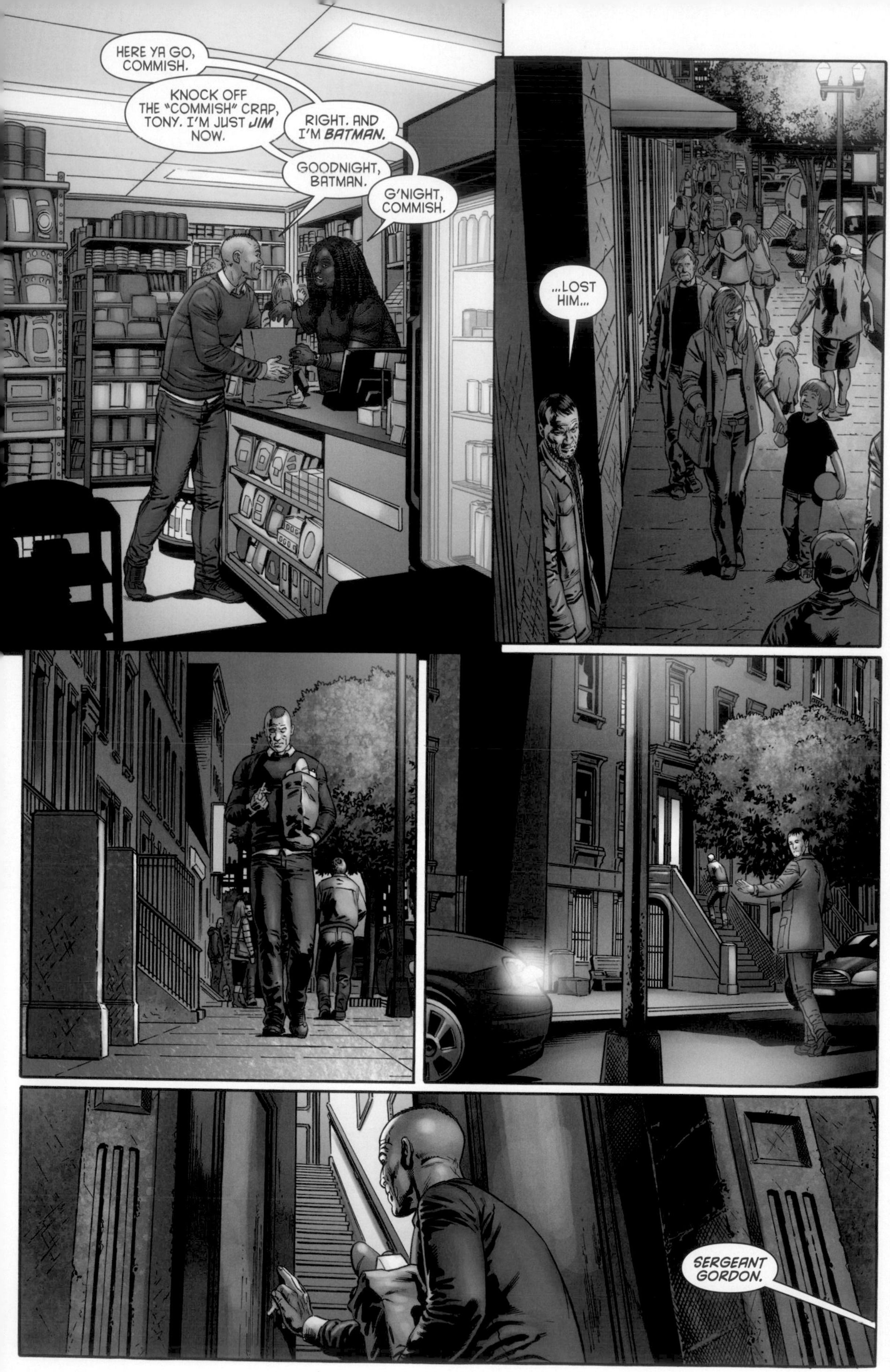
HERE YA GO, COMMISH.
KNOCK OFF THE "COMMISH" CRAP, TONY. I'M JUST *JIM* NOW.
RIGHT. AND I'M *BATMAN.*
GOODNIGHT, BATMAN.
G'NIGHT, COMMISH.
...LOST HIM...
SERGEANT GORDON.

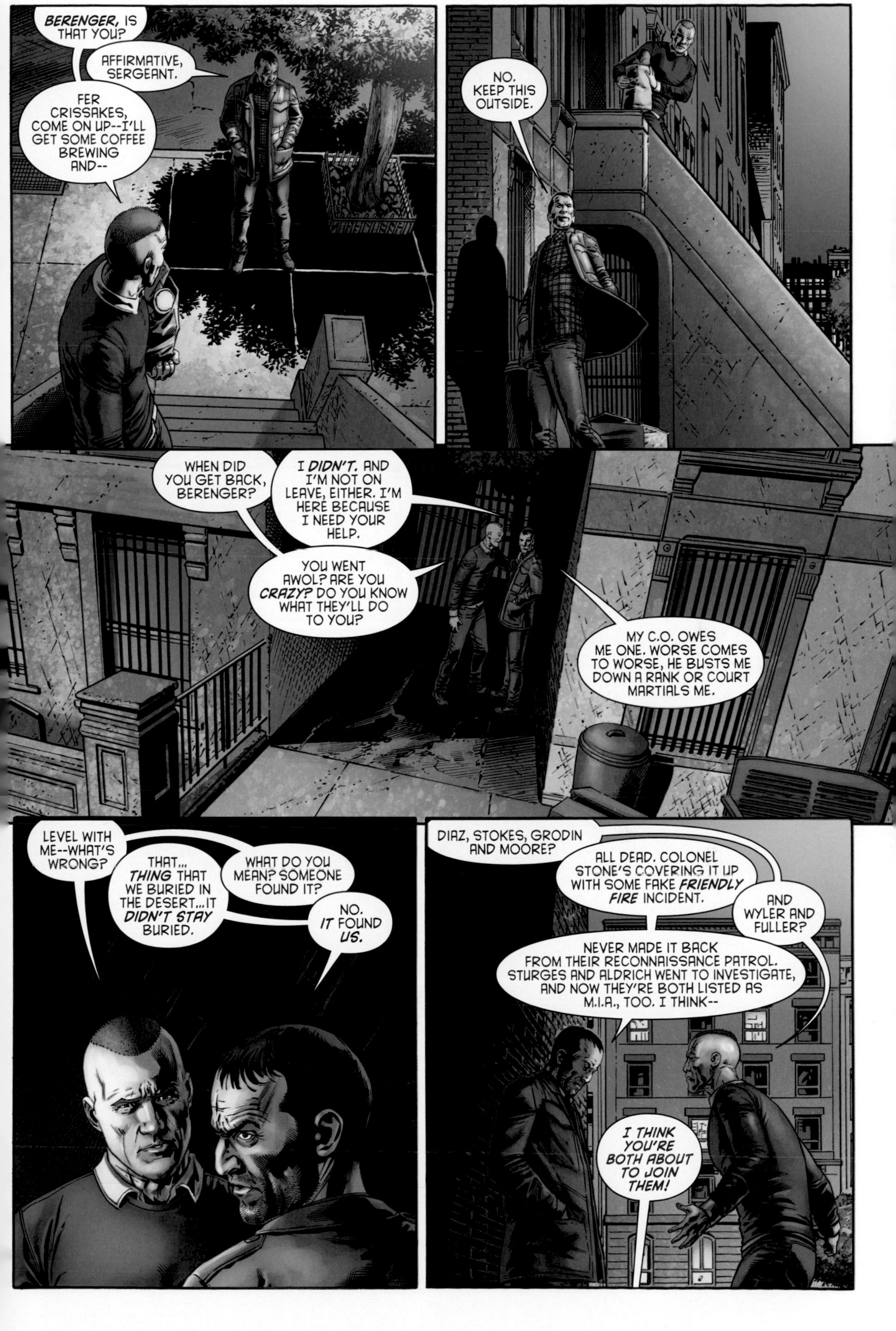
BERENGER, IS THAT YOU?
AFFIRMATIVE, SERGEANT.
FER CRISSAKES, COME ON UP--I'LL GET SOME COFFEE BREWING AND--
NO. KEEP THIS OUTSIDE.
WHEN DID YOU GET BACK, BERENGER?
I DIDN'T. AND I'M NOT ON LEAVE, EITHER. I'M HERE BECAUSE I NEED YOUR HELP.
YOU WENT AWOL? ARE YOU CRAZY? DO YOU KNOW WHAT THEY'LL DO TO YOU?
MY C.O. OWES ME ONE. WORSE COMES TO WORSE, HE BUSTS ME DOWN A RANK OR COURT MARTIALS ME.
LEVEL WITH ME--WHAT'S WRONG?
THAT... THING THAT WE BURIED IN THE DESERT...IT DIDN'T STAY BURIED.
WHAT DO YOU MEAN? SOMEONE FOUND IT?
NO. IT FOUND US.
DIAZ, STOKES, GRODIN AND MOORE?
ALL DEAD. COLONEL STONE'S COVERING IT UP WITH SOME FAKE FRIENDLY FIRE INCIDENT.
AND WYLER AND FULLER?
NEVER MADE IT BACK FROM THEIR RECONNAISSANCE PATROL. STURGES AND ALDRICH WENT TO INVESTIGATE, AND NOW THEY'RE BOTH LISTED AS M.I.A., TOO. I THINK--
I THINK YOU'RE BOTH ABOUT TO JOIN THEM!

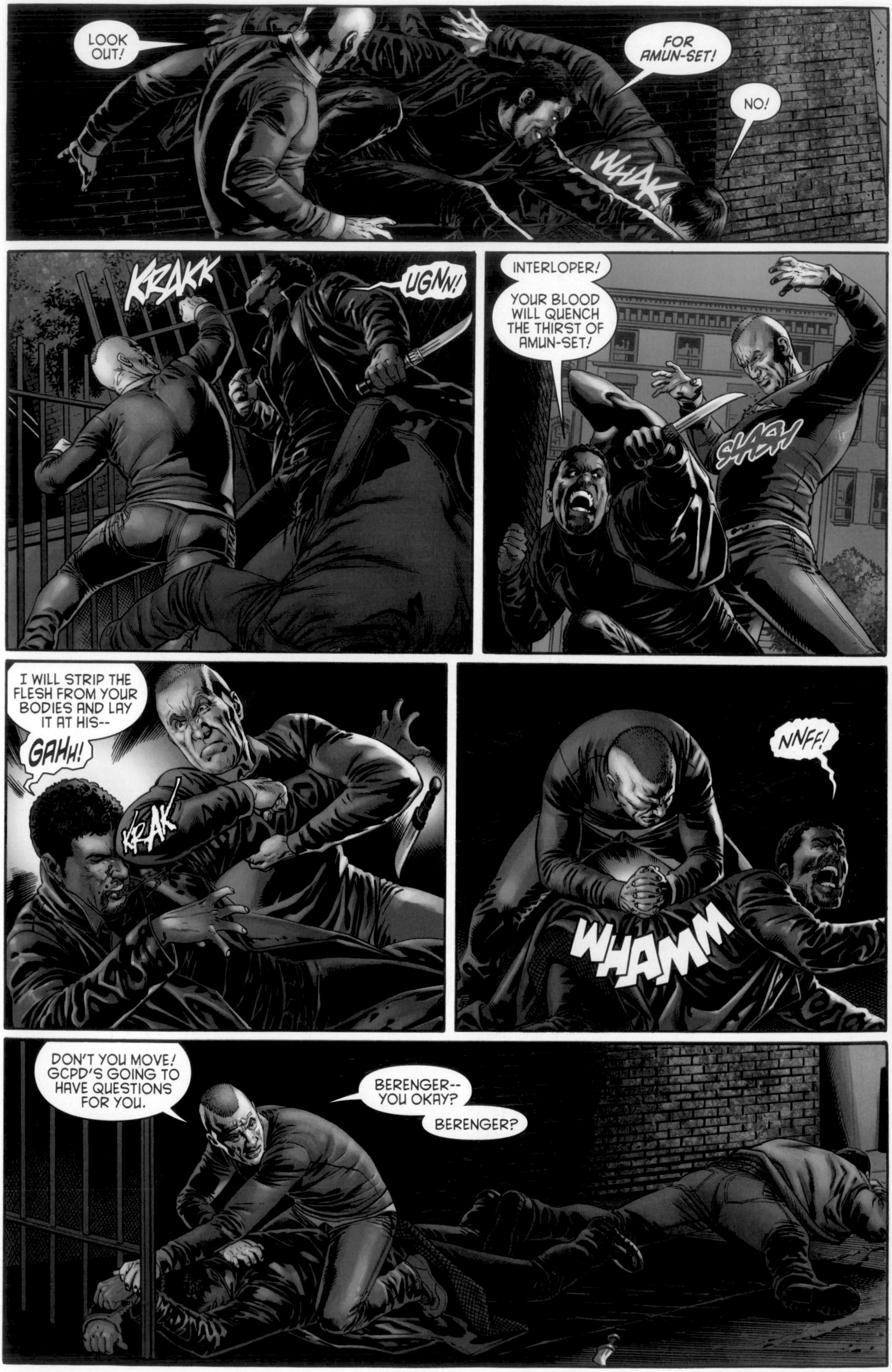
LOOK OUT!
FOR AMUN-SET!
NO!
WHAK
KRAKK
UGNN!
INTERLOPER!
YOUR BLOOD WILL QUENCH THE THIRST OF AMUN-SET!
SLASH
I WILL STRIP THE FLESH FROM YOUR BODIES AND LAY IT AT HIS--
GAHH!
KRAK
NNFF!
WHAMM
DON'T YOU MOVE! GCPD'S GOING TO HAVE QUESTIONS FOR YOU.
BERENGER-- YOU OKAY?
BERENGER?

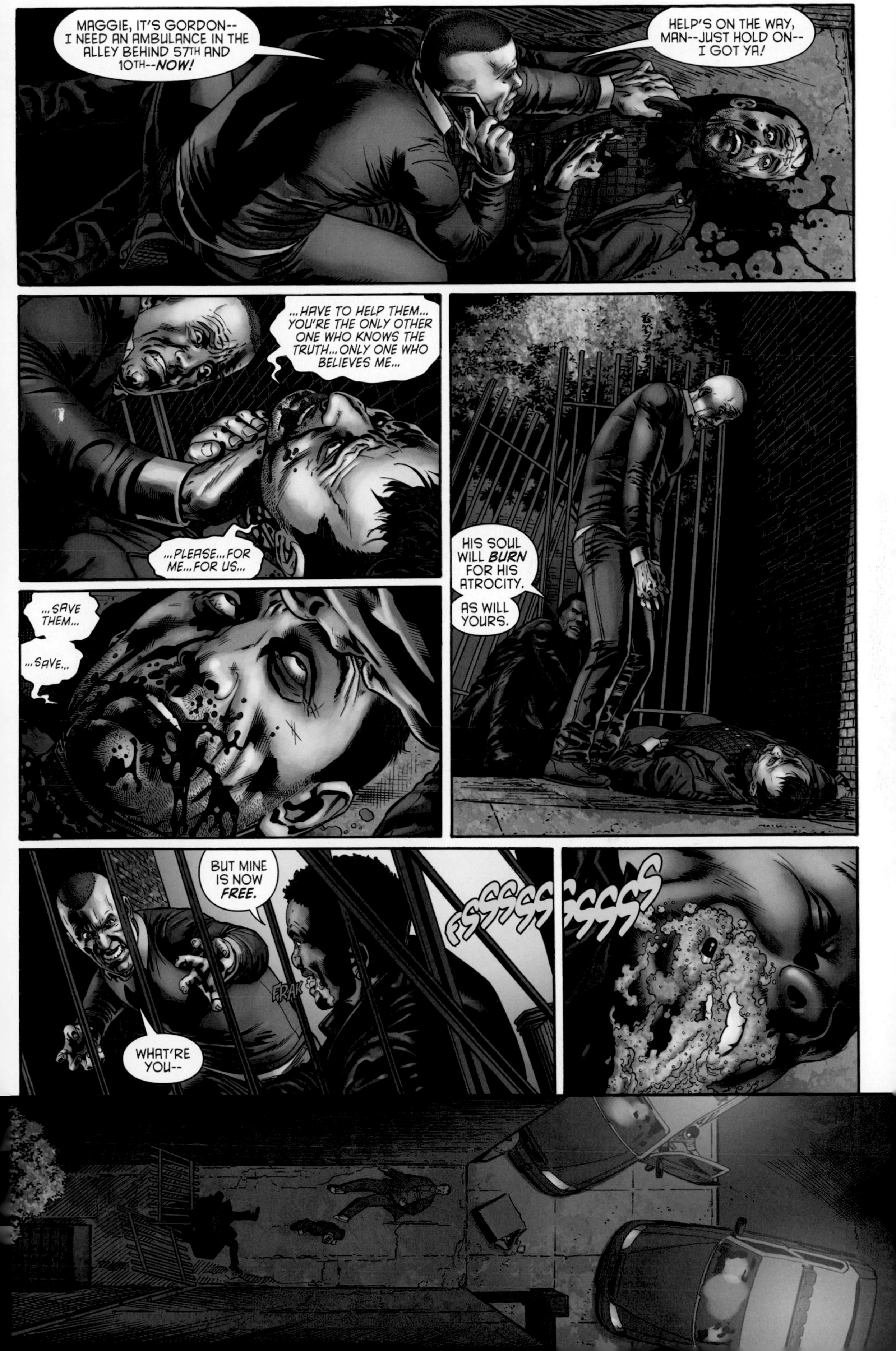
MAGGIE, IT'S GORDON-- I NEED AN AMBULANCE IN THE ALLEY BEHIND 57TH AND 10TH--NOW!
HELP'S ON THE WAY, MAN--JUST HOLD ON-- I GOT YA!
...HAVE TO HELP THEM... YOU'RE THE ONLY OTHER ONE WHO KNOWS THE TRUTH...ONLY ONE WHO BELIEVES ME...
...PLEASE...FOR ME...FOR US...
HIS SOUL WILL BURN FOR HIS ATROCITY.
AS WILL YOURS.
...SAVE THEM...
...SAVE...
BUT MINE IS NOW FREE.
FRAK
WHAT'RE YOU--
FSSSSSSSSS

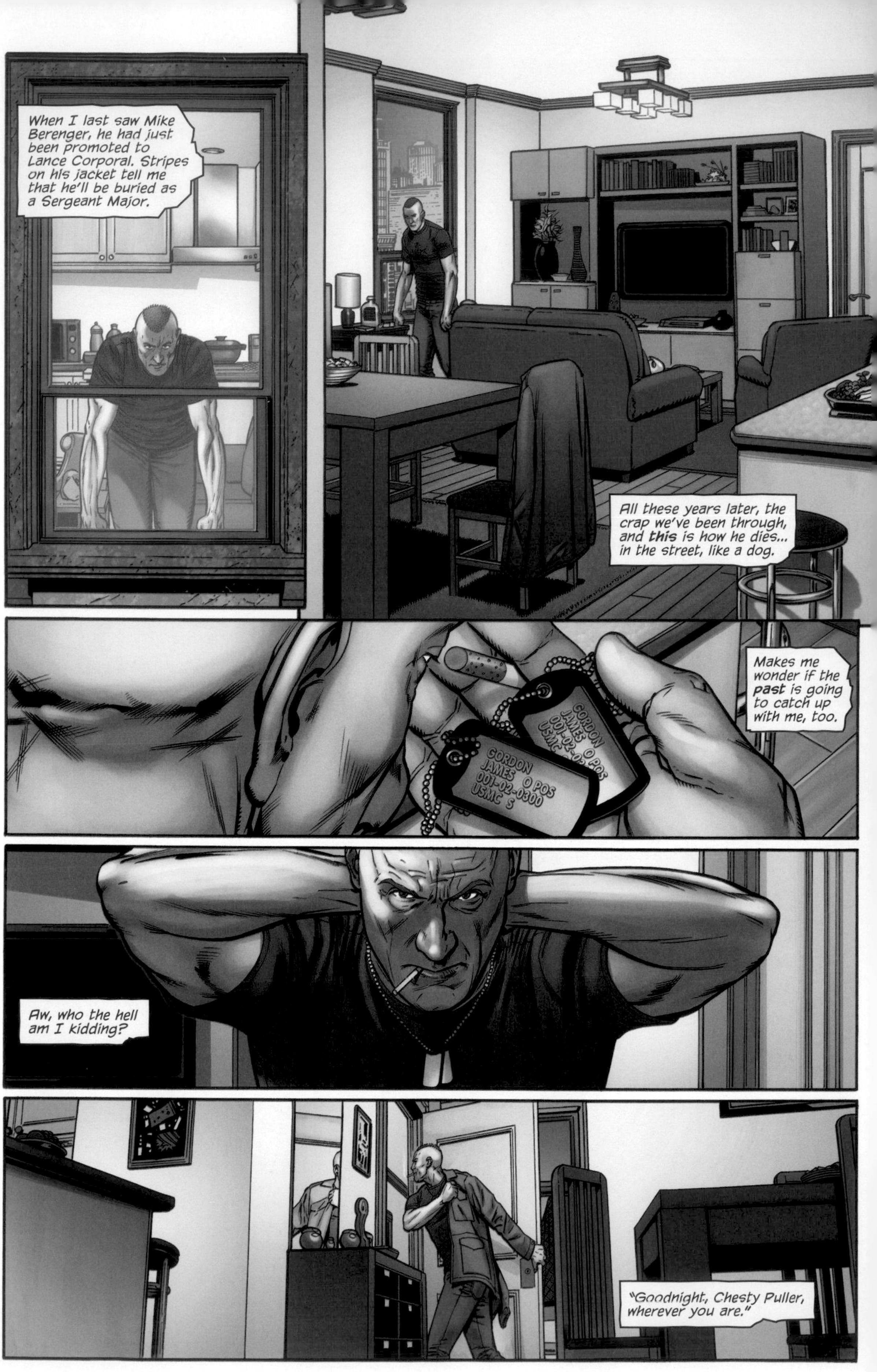
When I last saw Mike Berenger, he had just been promoted to Lance Corporal. Stripes on his jacket tell me that he'll be buried as a Sergeant Major.
All these years later, the crap we've been through, and **this** is how he dies... in the street, like a dog.
Makes me wonder if the **past** is going to catch up with me, too.
GORDON
JAMES O POS
001-02-0300
USMC S
Aw, who the hell am I kidding?
"Goodnight, Chesty Puller, wherever you are."

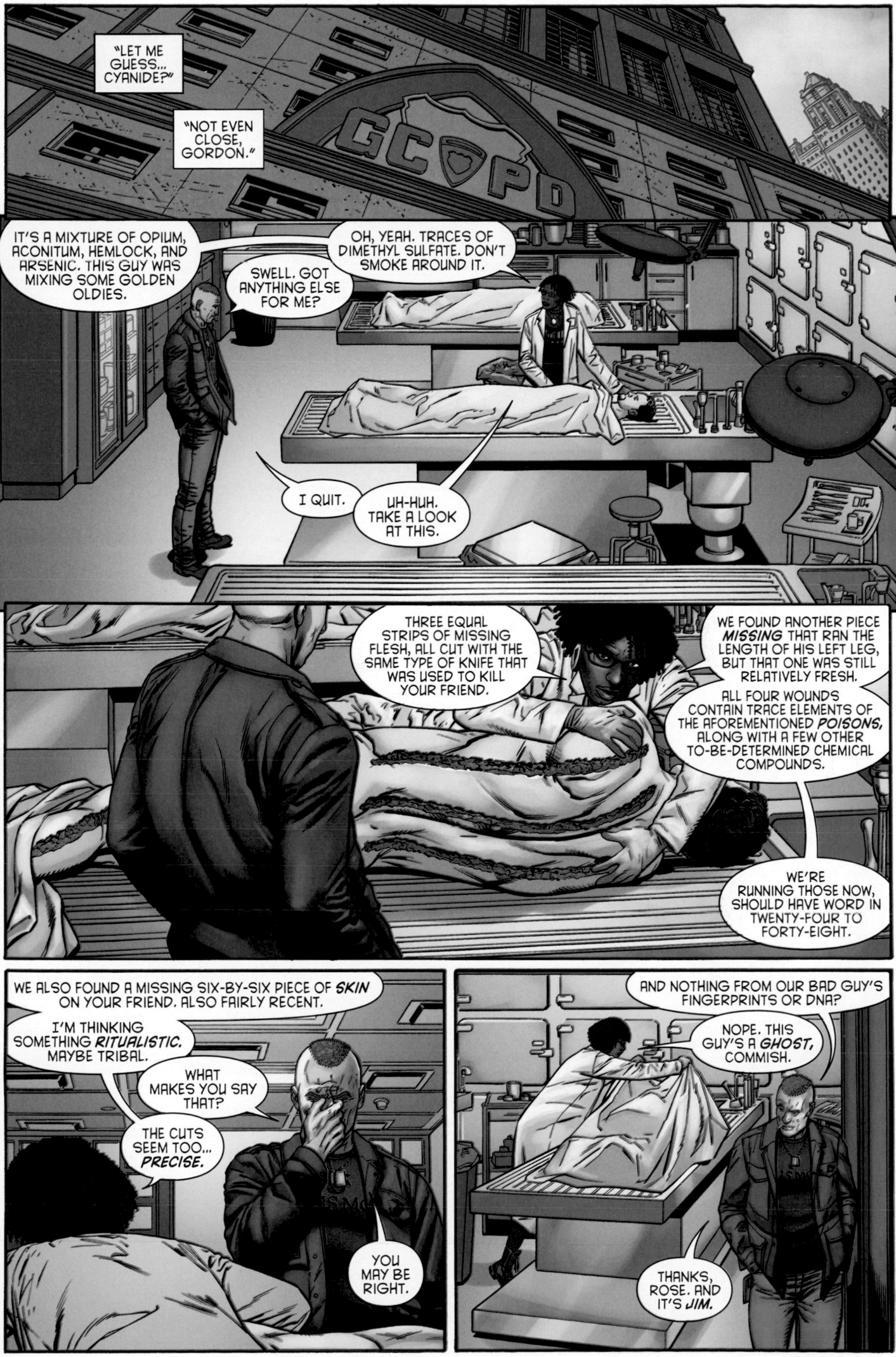
"LET ME GUESS... CYANIDE?"
"NOT EVEN CLOSE, GORDON."
IT'S A MIXTURE OF OPIUM, ACONITUM, HEMLOCK, AND ARSENIC. THIS GUY WAS MIXING SOME GOLDEN OLDIES.
SWELL. GOT ANYTHING ELSE FOR ME?
OH, YEAH. TRACES OF DIMETHYL SULFATE. DON'T SMOKE AROUND IT.
I QUIT.
UH-HUH. TAKE A LOOK AT THIS.
THREE EQUAL STRIPS OF MISSING FLESH, ALL CUT WITH THE SAME TYPE OF KNIFE THAT WAS USED TO KILL YOUR FRIEND.
WE FOUND ANOTHER PIECE MISSING THAT RAN THE LENGTH OF HIS LEFT LEG, BUT THAT ONE WAS STILL RELATIVELY FRESH.
ALL FOUR WOUNDS CONTAIN TRACE ELEMENTS OF THE AFOREMENTIONED POISONS, ALONG WITH A FEW OTHER TO-BE-DETERMINED CHEMICAL COMPOUNDS.
WE'RE RUNNING THOSE NOW, SHOULD HAVE WORD IN TWENTY-FOUR TO FORTY-EIGHT.
WE ALSO FOUND A MISSING SIX-BY-SIX PIECE OF SKIN ON YOUR FRIEND. ALSO FAIRLY RECENT.
I'M THINKING SOMETHING RITUALISTIC. MAYBE TRIBAL.
WHAT MAKES YOU SAY THAT?
THE CUTS SEEM TOO... PRECISE.
YOU MAY BE RIGHT.
AND NOTHING FROM OUR BAD GUY'S FINGERPRINTS OR DNA?
NOPE. THIS GUY'S A GHOST, COMMISH.
THANKS, ROSE. AND IT'S JIM.

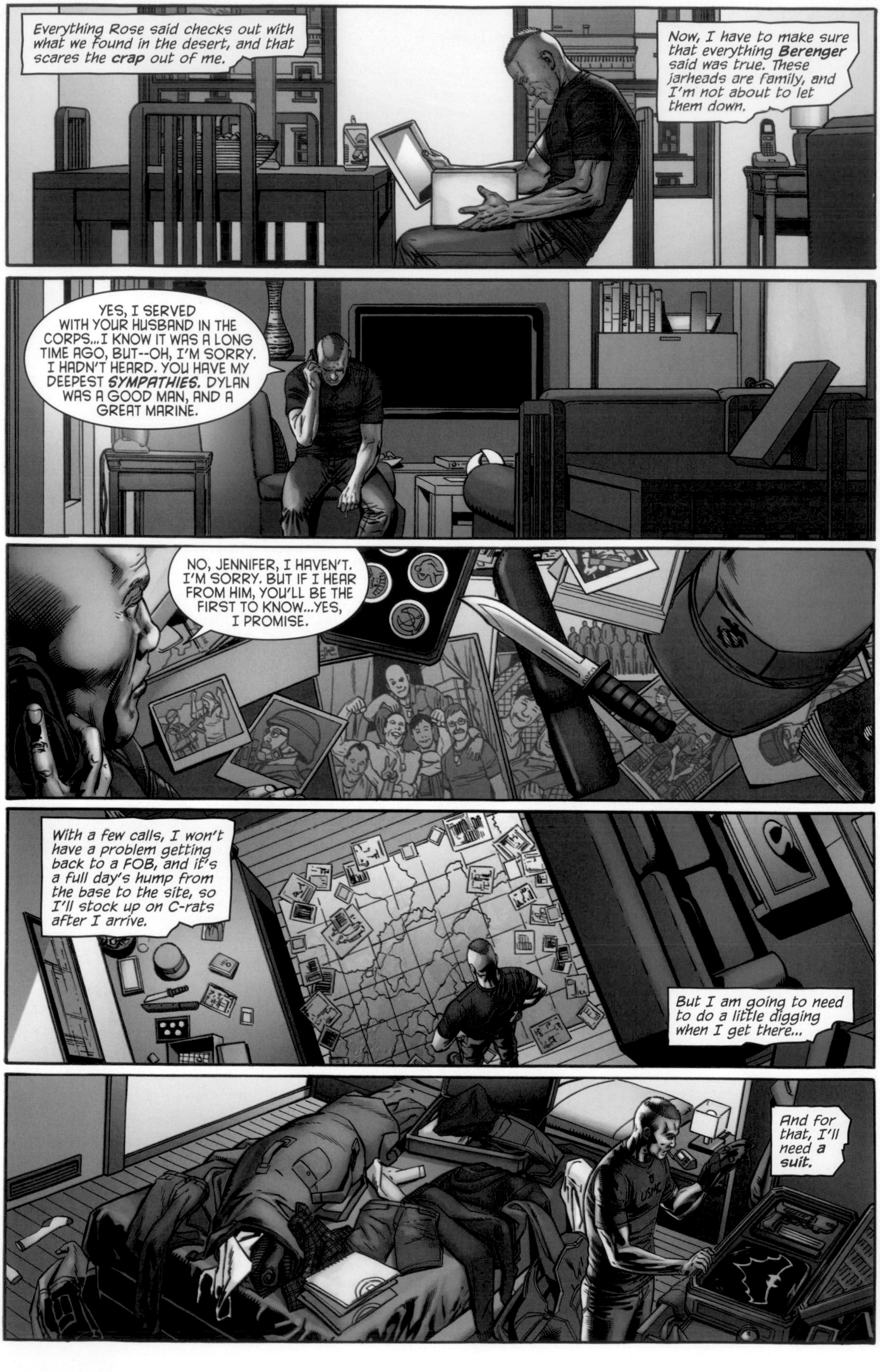
Everything Rose said checks out with what we found in the desert, and that scares the **crap** out of me.
Now, I have to make sure that everything **Berenger** said was true. These jarheads are family, and I'm not about to let them down.
YES, I SERVED WITH YOUR HUSBAND IN THE CORPS...I KNOW IT WAS A LONG TIME AGO, BUT--OH, I'M SORRY. I HADN'T HEARD. YOU HAVE MY DEEPEST ***SYMPATHIES.*** DYLAN WAS A GOOD MAN, AND A GREAT MARINE.
NO, JENNIFER, I HAVEN'T. I'M SORRY. BUT IF I HEAR FROM HIM, YOU'LL BE THE FIRST TO KNOW...YES, I PROMISE.
With a few calls, I won't have a problem getting back to a FOB, and it's a full day's hump from the base to the site, so I'll stock up on C-rats after I arrive.
But I am going to need to do a little digging when I get there...
And for that, I'll need a **suit.**
USMC

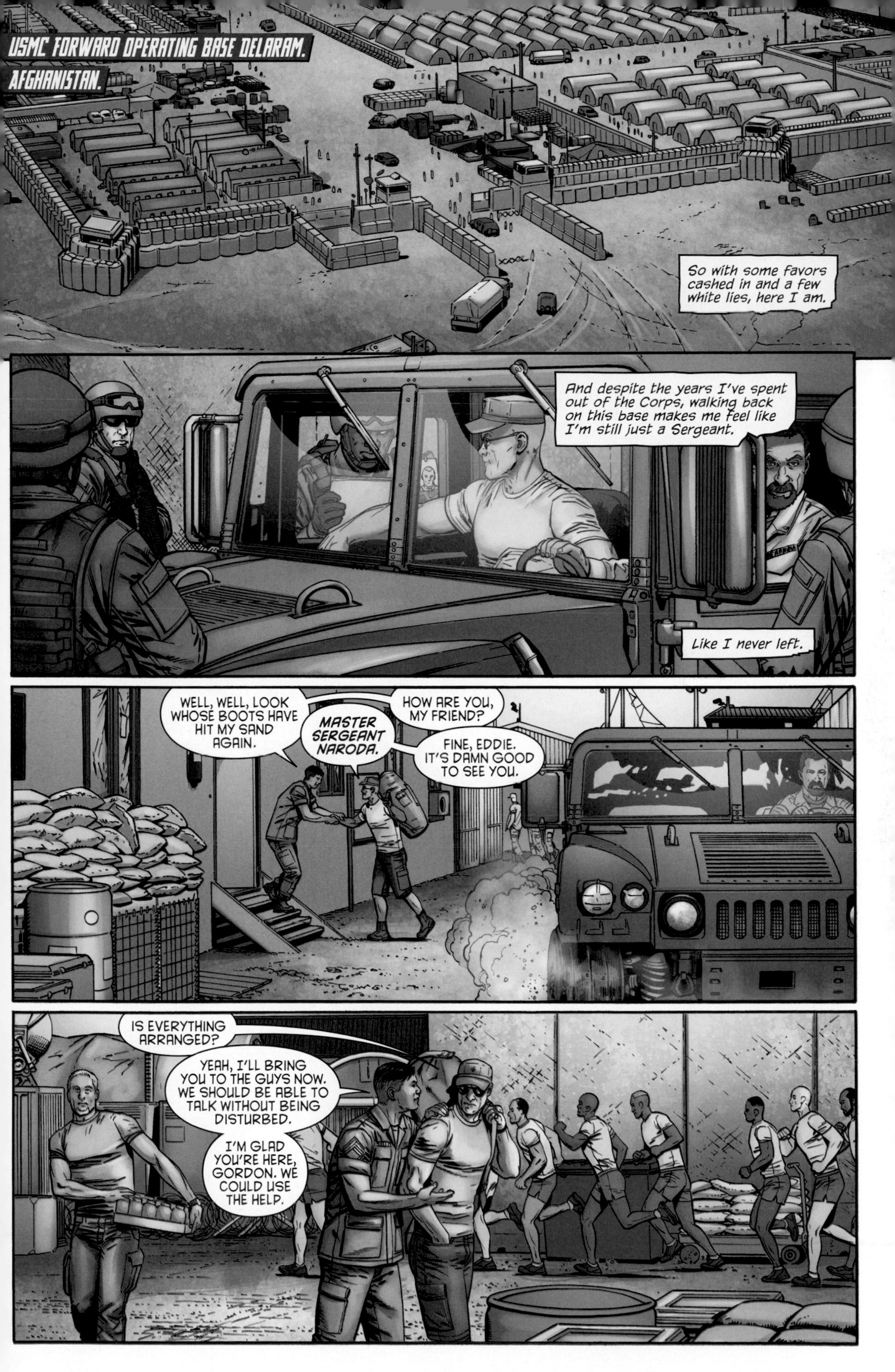
USMC FORWARD OPERATING BASE DELARAM.
AFGHANISTAN.
So with some favors cashed in and a few white lies, here I am.
And despite the years I've spent out of the Corps, walking back on this base makes me feel like I'm still just a Sergeant.
Like I never left.
WELL, WELL, LOOK WHOSE BOOTS HAVE HIT MY SAND AGAIN.
MASTER SERGEANT NARODA.
HOW ARE YOU, MY FRIEND?
FINE, EDDIE. IT'S DAMN GOOD TO SEE YOU.
IS EVERYTHING ARRANGED?
YEAH, I'LL BRING YOU TO THE GUYS NOW. WE SHOULD BE ABLE TO TALK WITHOUT BEING DISTURBED.
I'M GLAD YOU'RE HERE, GORDON. WE COULD USE THE HELP.

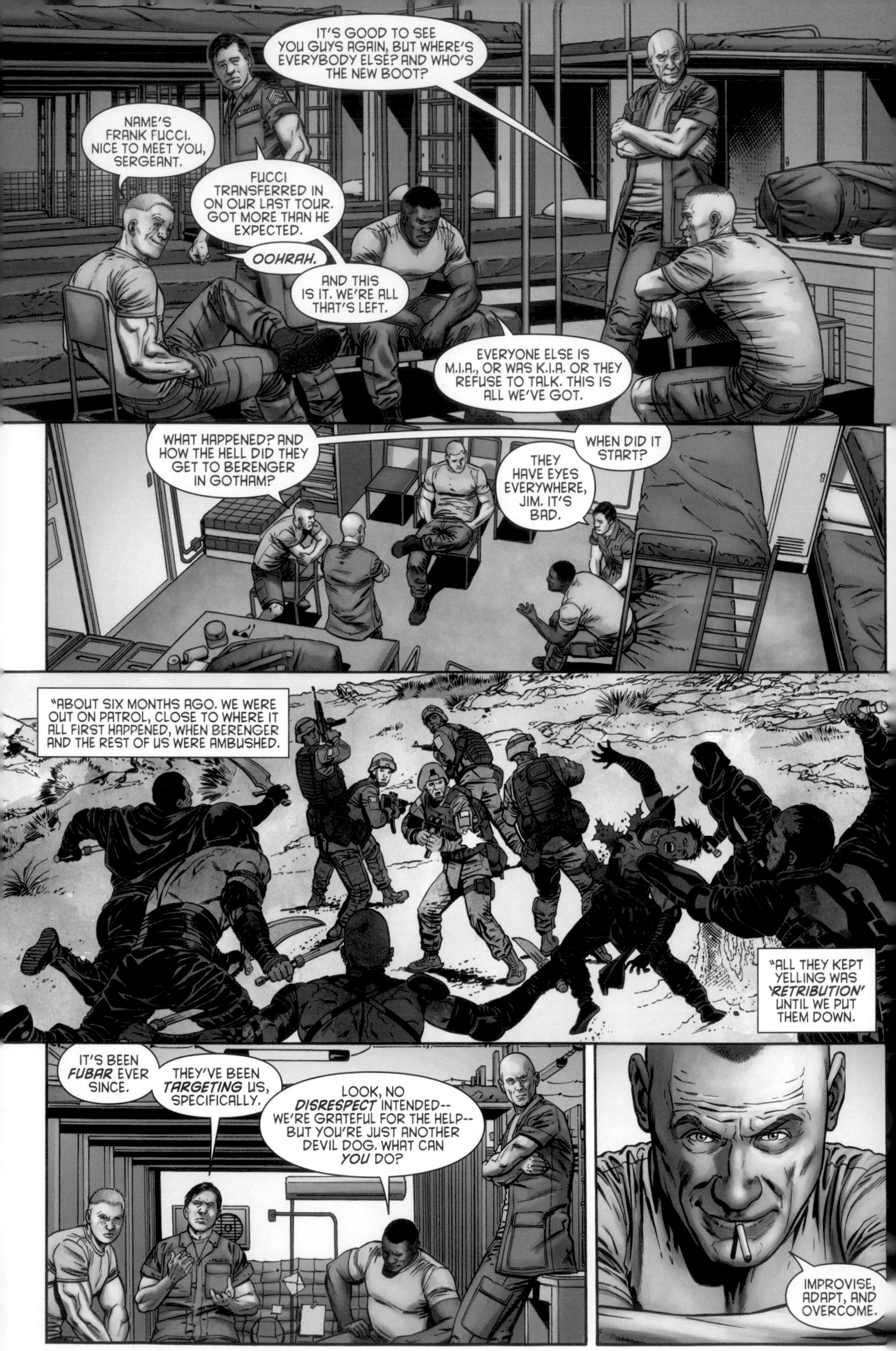
IT'S GOOD TO SEE YOU GUYS AGAIN, BUT WHERE'S EVERYBODY ELSE? AND WHO'S THE NEW BOOT?
NAME'S FRANK FUCCI. NICE TO MEET YOU, SERGEANT.
FUCCI TRANSFERRED IN ON OUR LAST TOUR. GOT MORE THAN HE EXPECTED.
OOHRAH.
AND THIS IS IT. WE'RE ALL THAT'S LEFT.
EVERYONE ELSE IS M.I.A., OR WAS K.I.A. OR THEY REFUSE TO TALK. THIS IS ALL WE'VE GOT.
WHAT HAPPENED? AND HOW THE HELL DID THEY GET TO BERENGER IN GOTHAM?
WHEN DID IT START?
THEY HAVE EYES EVERYWHERE, JIM. IT'S BAD.
"ABOUT SIX MONTHS AGO. WE WERE OUT ON PATROL, CLOSE TO WHERE IT ALL FIRST HAPPENED, WHEN BERENGER AND THE REST OF US WERE AMBUSHED.
"ALL THEY KEPT YELLING WAS 'RETRIBUTION' UNTIL WE PUT THEM DOWN.
IT'S BEEN FUBAR EVER SINCE.
THEY'VE BEEN TARGETING US, SPECIFICALLY.
LOOK, NO DISRESPECT INTENDED-- WE'RE GRATEFUL FOR THE HELP-- BUT YOU'RE JUST ANOTHER DEVIL DOG. WHAT CAN YOU DO?
IMPROVISE, ADAPT, AND OVERCOME.

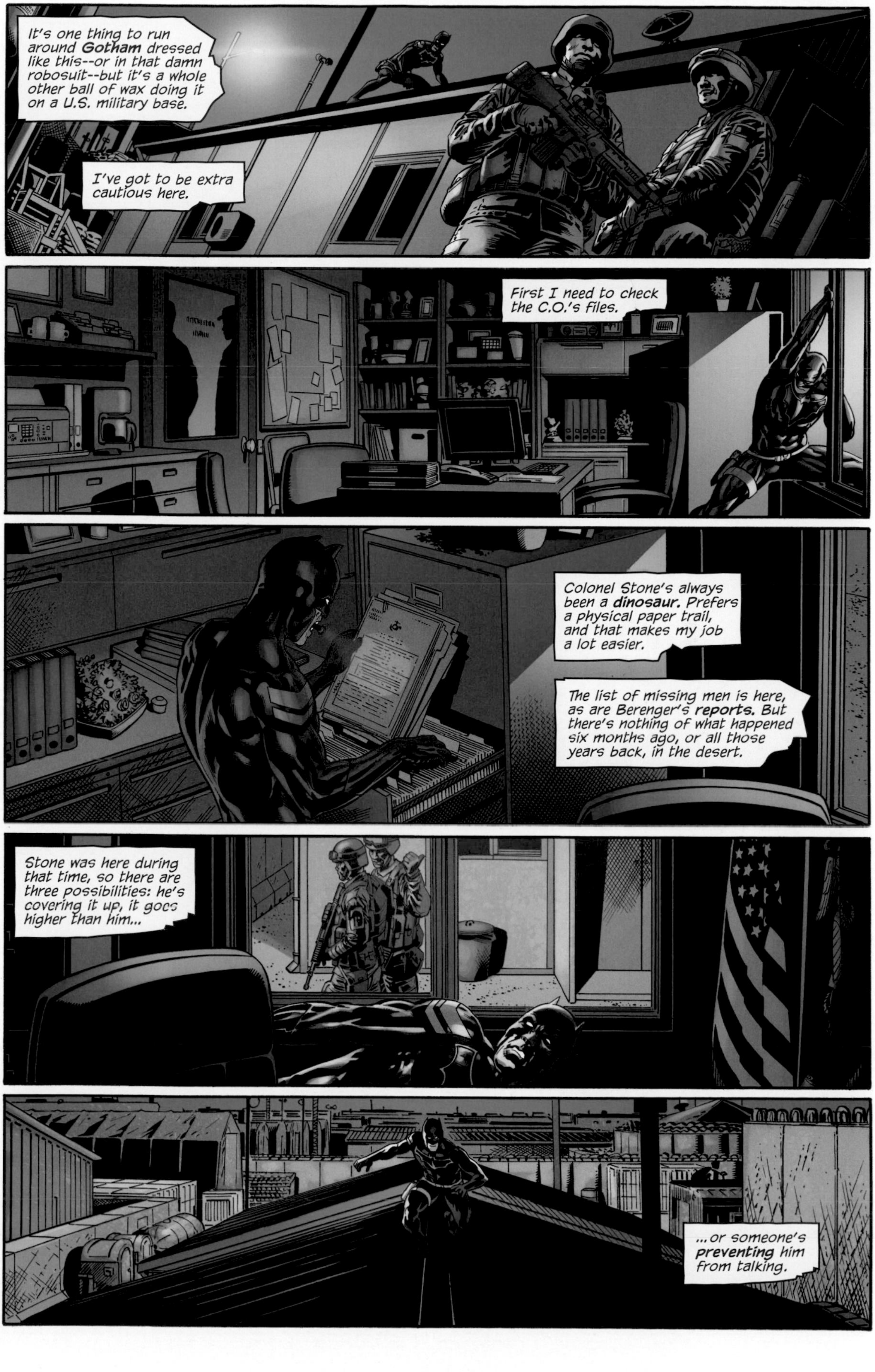
It's one thing to run around Gotham dressed like this--or in that damn robosuit--but it's a whole other ball of wax doing it on a U.S. military base.
I've got to be extra cautious here.
First I need to check the C.O.'s files.
Colonel Stone's always been a dinosaur. Prefers a physical paper trail, and that makes my job a lot easier.
The list of missing men is here, as are Berenger's reports. But there's nothing of what happened six months ago, or all those years back, in the desert.
Stone was here during that time, so there are three possibilities: he's covering it up, it goes higher than him...
...or someone's preventing him from talking.

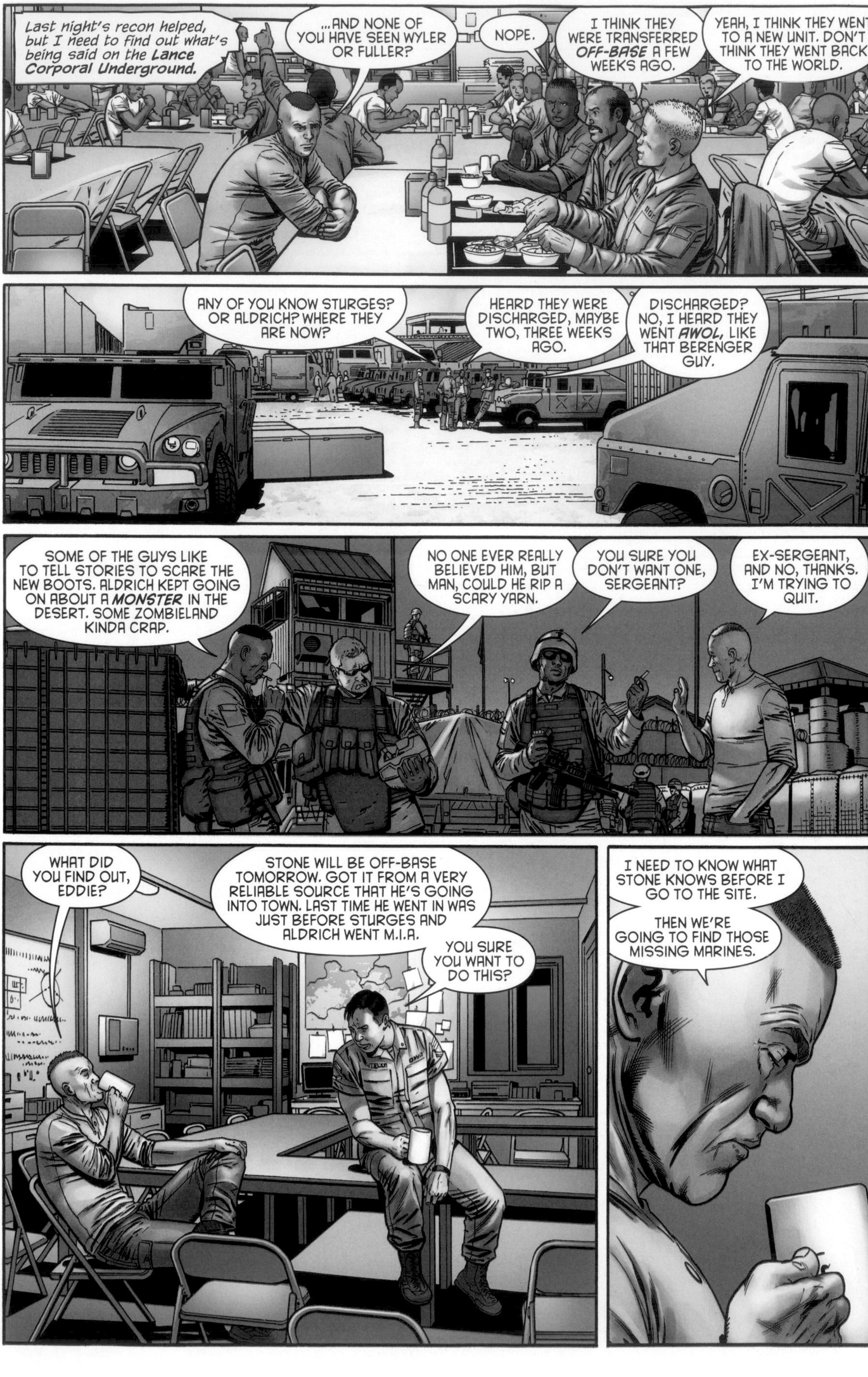
Last night's recon helped, but I need to find out what's being said on the Lance Corporal Underground.
...AND NONE OF YOU HAVE SEEN WYLER OR FULLER?
NOPE.
I THINK THEY WERE TRANSFERRED OFF-BASE A FEW WEEKS AGO.
YEAH, I THINK THEY WENT TO A NEW UNIT. DON'T THINK THEY WENT BACK TO THE WORLD.
ANY OF YOU KNOW STURGES? OR ALDRICH? WHERE THEY ARE NOW?
HEARD THEY WERE DISCHARGED, MAYBE TWO, THREE WEEKS AGO.
DISCHARGED? NO, I HEARD THEY WENT AWOL, LIKE THAT BERENGER GUY.
SOME OF THE GUYS LIKE TO TELL STORIES TO SCARE THE NEW BOOTS. ALDRICH KEPT GOING ON ABOUT A MONSTER IN THE DESERT. SOME ZOMBIELAND KINDA CRAP.
NO ONE EVER REALLY BELIEVED HIM, BUT MAN, COULD HE RIP A SCARY YARN.
YOU SURE YOU DON'T WANT ONE, SERGEANT?
EX-SERGEANT, AND NO, THANKS. I'M TRYING TO QUIT.
WHAT DID YOU FIND OUT, EDDIE?
STONE WILL BE OFF-BASE TOMORROW. GOT IT FROM A VERY RELIABLE SOURCE THAT HE'S GOING INTO TOWN. LAST TIME HE WENT IN WAS JUST BEFORE STURGES AND ALDRICH WENT M.I.A.
YOU SURE YOU WANT TO DO THIS?
I NEED TO KNOW WHAT STONE KNOWS BEFORE I GO TO THE SITE.
THEN WE'RE GOING TO FIND THOSE MISSING MARINES.

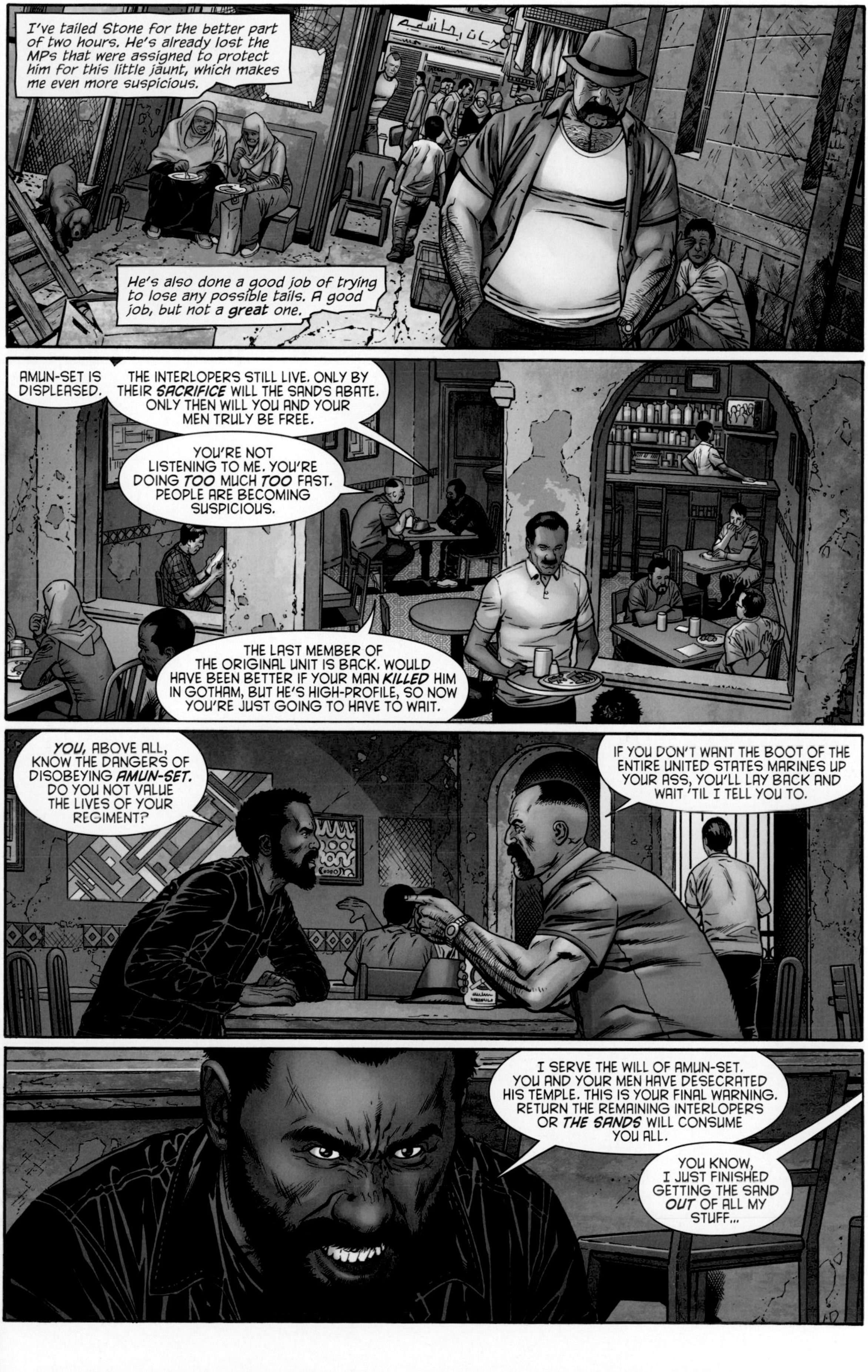
I've tailed Stone for the better part of two hours. He's already lost the MPs that were assigned to protect him for this little jaunt, which makes me even more suspicious.
He's also done a good job of trying to lose any possible tails. A good job, but not a **great** one.
AMUN-SET IS DISPLEASED.
THE INTERLOPERS STILL LIVE. ONLY BY THEIR ***SACRIFICE*** WILL THE SANDS ABATE. ONLY THEN WILL YOU AND YOUR MEN TRULY BE FREE.
YOU'RE NOT LISTENING TO ME. YOU'RE DOING ***TOO*** MUCH ***TOO*** FAST. PEOPLE ARE BECOMING SUSPICIOUS.
THE LAST MEMBER OF THE ORIGINAL UNIT IS BACK. WOULD HAVE BEEN BETTER IF YOUR MAN ***KILLED*** HIM IN GOTHAM, BUT HE'S HIGH-PROFILE, SO NOW YOU'RE JUST GOING TO HAVE TO WAIT.
YOU, ABOVE ALL, KNOW THE DANGERS OF DISOBEYING ***AMUN-SET.*** DO YOU NOT VALUE THE LIVES OF YOUR REGIMENT?
IF YOU DON'T WANT THE BOOT OF THE ENTIRE UNITED STATES MARINES UP YOUR ASS, YOU'LL LAY BACK AND WAIT 'TIL I TELL YOU TO.
I SERVE THE WILL OF AMUN-SET. YOU AND YOUR MEN HAVE DESECRATED HIS TEMPLE. THIS IS YOUR FINAL WARNING. RETURN THE REMAINING INTERLOPERS OR ***THE SANDS*** WILL CONSUME YOU ALL.
YOU KNOW, I JUST FINISHED GETTING THE SAND ***OUT*** OF ALL MY STUFF...

...HEY, COLONEL, MIND IF I JOIN YOU AND YOUR FRIEND?

AN AMBUSH, COLONEL? YOU WILL *SUFFER* FOR THIS!

SLASH

I DIDN'T KNOW HE WAS HERE!

EASY THERE, GORDON. LET'S JUST ALL CALM DOWN BEFORE ANYONE DOES ANYTHING THEY'LL REGRET.

I DON'T THINK SO, COLONEL. HOW ABOUT THE THREE OF US FIND THOSE MPs YOU SHOOK LOOSE AND HEAD BACK TO BASE?

YOU WILL *DIE* IN THE NAME OF AMUN-SET.

YEAH, I'VE HEARD THAT BEFORE.

INTERLOPER!

AND THAT ONE-- *ARRGH!*

KRAKK

YOUR MOVE, COLONEL.

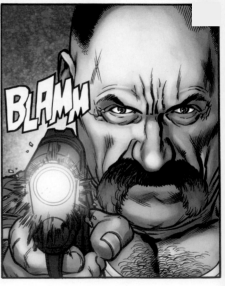

BLAMM

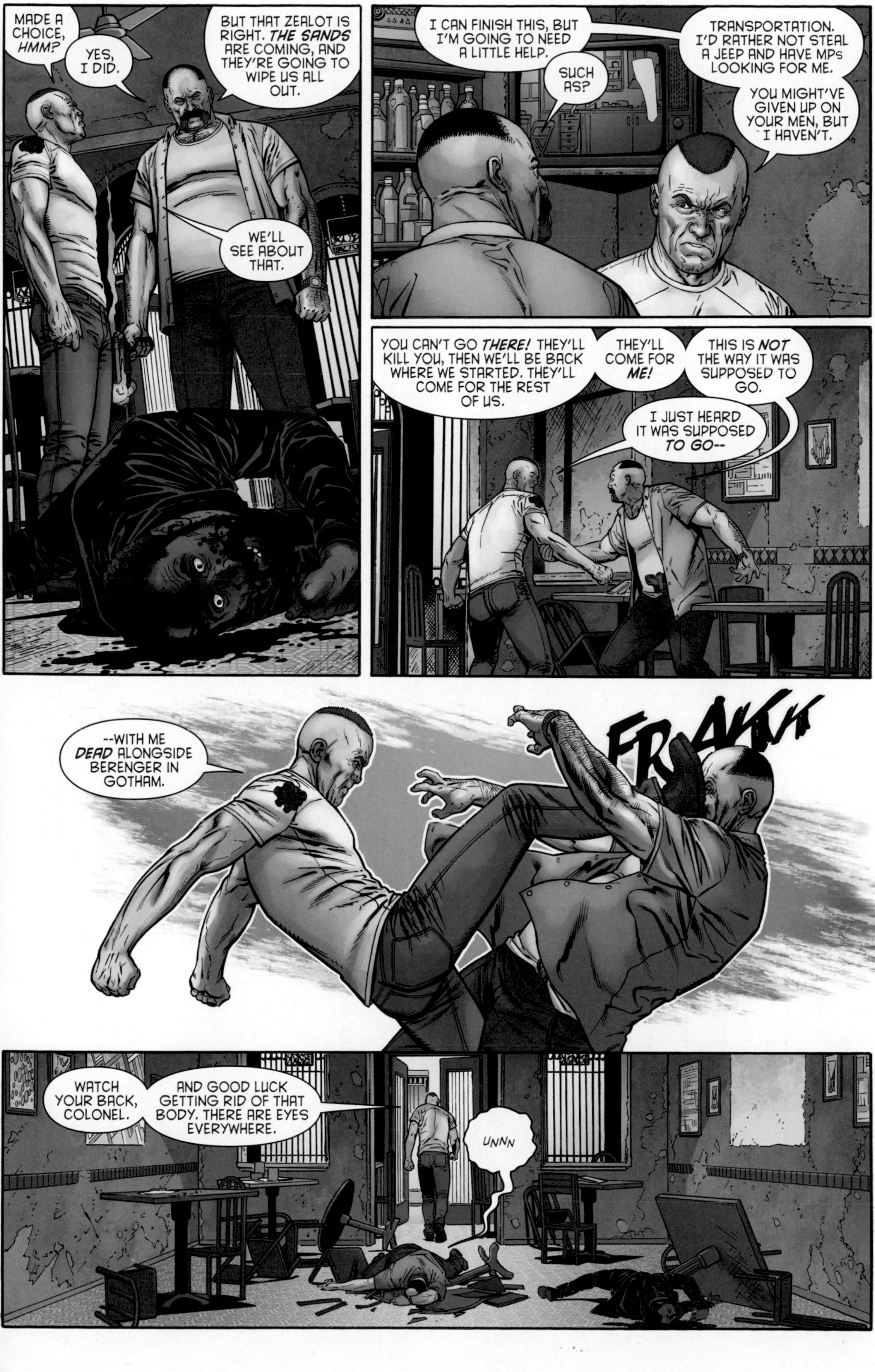
MADE A CHOICE, HMM?
YES, I DID.
BUT THAT ZEALOT IS RIGHT. THE SANDS ARE COMING, AND THEY'RE GOING TO WIPE US ALL OUT.
WE'LL SEE ABOUT THAT.
I CAN FINISH THIS, BUT I'M GOING TO NEED A LITTLE HELP.
SUCH AS?
TRANSPORTATION. I'D RATHER NOT STEAL A JEEP AND HAVE MPs LOOKING FOR ME.
YOU MIGHT'VE GIVEN UP ON YOUR MEN, BUT I HAVEN'T.
YOU CAN'T GO THERE! THEY'LL KILL YOU, THEN WE'LL BE BACK WHERE WE STARTED. THEY'LL COME FOR THE REST OF US.
THEY'LL COME FOR ME!
THIS IS NOT THE WAY IT WAS SUPPOSED TO GO.
I JUST HEARD IT WAS SUPPOSED TO GO--
--WITH ME DEAD ALONGSIDE BERENGER IN GOTHAM.
FRAKK
WATCH YOUR BACK, COLONEL.
AND GOOD LUCK GETTING RID OF THAT BODY. THERE ARE EYES EVERYWHERE.
UNNN

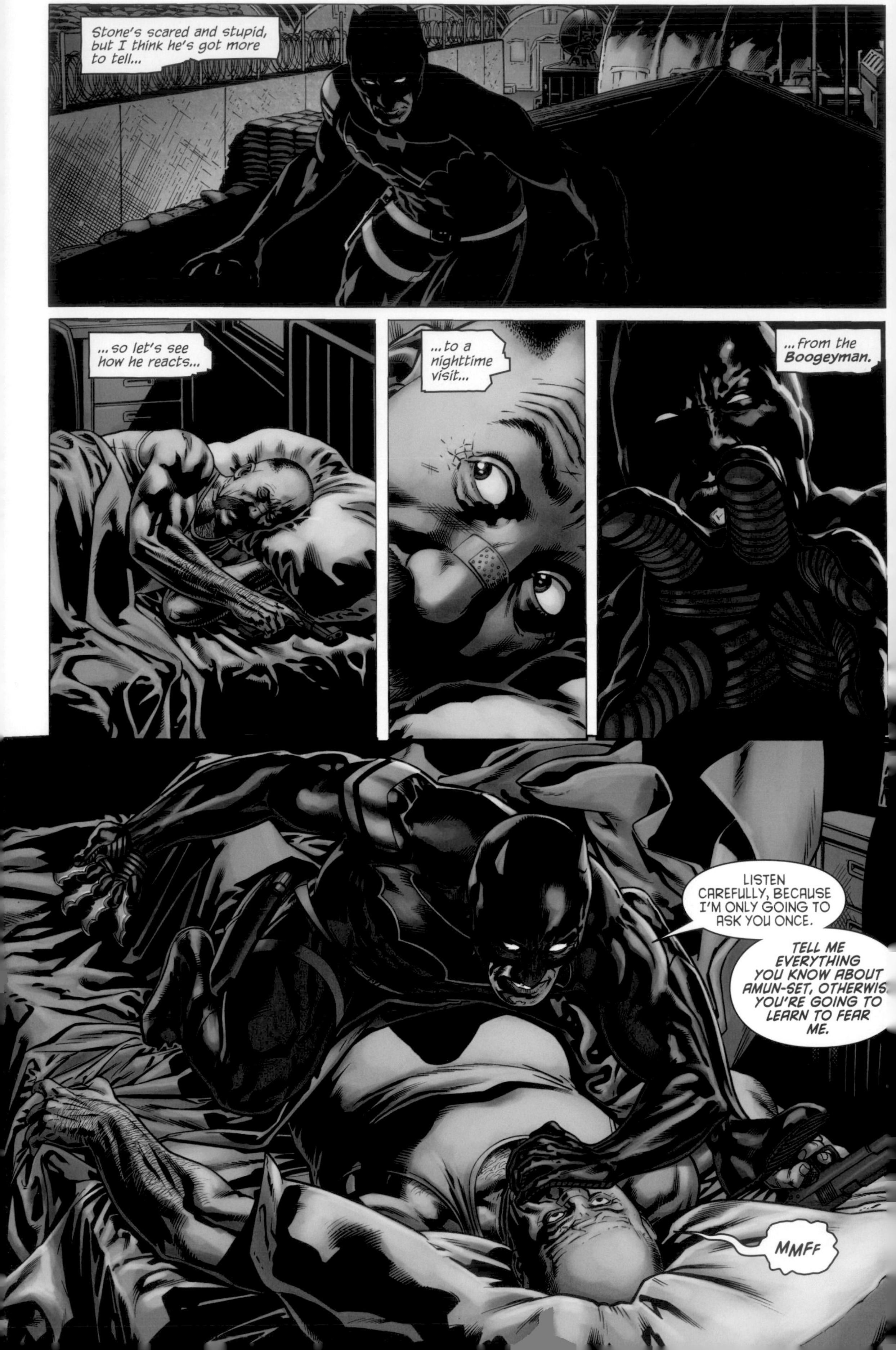
Stone's scared and stupid, but I think he's got more to tell...
...so let's see how he reacts...
...to a nighttime visit...
...from the Boogeyman.
LISTEN CAREFULLY, BECAUSE I'M ONLY GOING TO ASK YOU ONCE.
TELL ME EVERYTHING YOU KNOW ABOUT AMUN-SET, OTHERWISE YOU'RE GOING TO LEARN TO FEAR ME.
MMFF

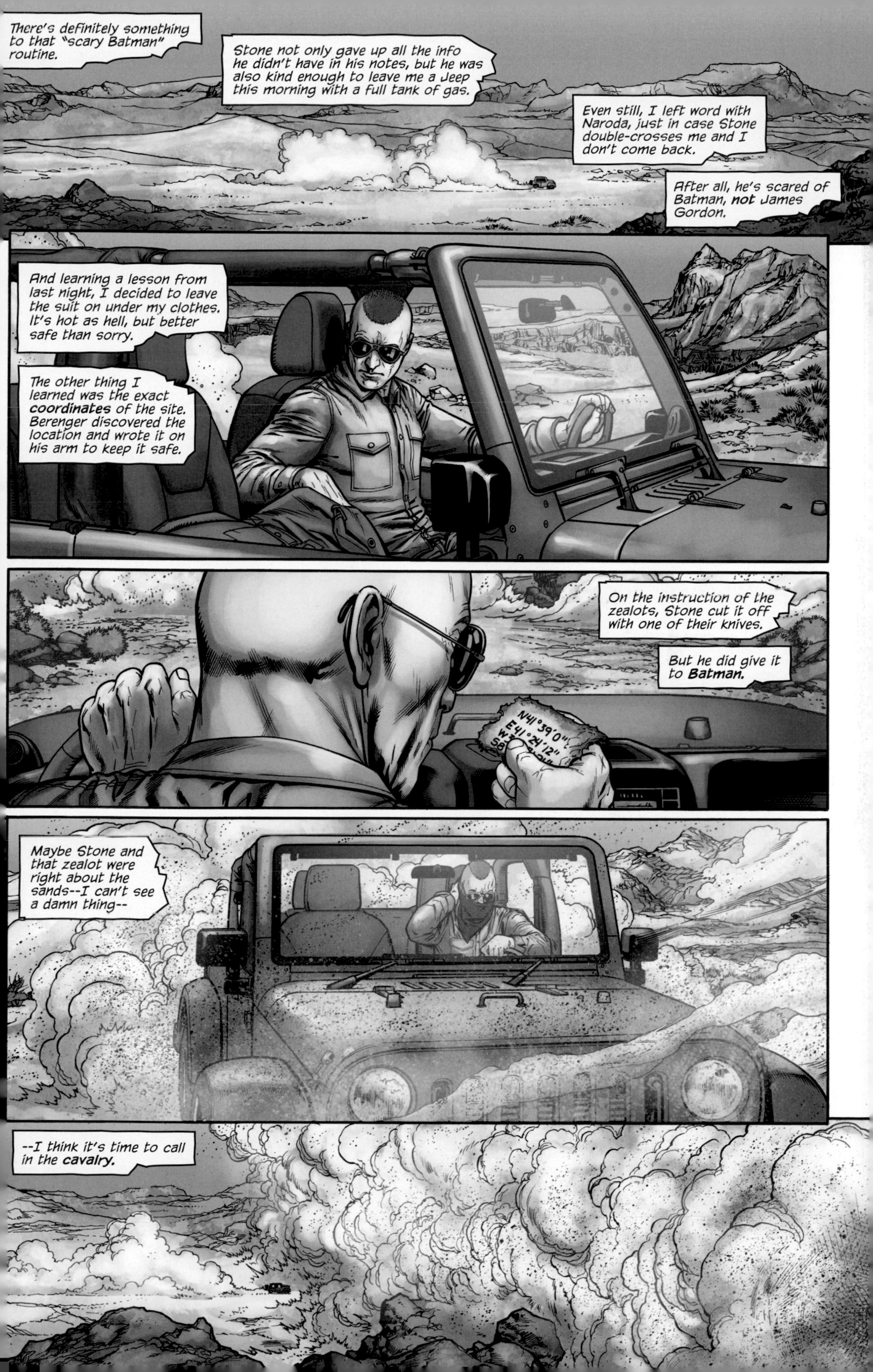
There's definitely something to that "scary Batman" routine.
Stone not only gave up all the info he didn't have in his notes, but he was also kind enough to leave me a Jeep this morning with a full tank of gas.
Even still, I left word with Naroda, just in case Stone double-crosses me and I don't come back.
After all, he's scared of Batman, **not** James Gordon.
And learning a lesson from last night, I decided to leave the suit on under my clothes. It's hot as hell, but better safe than sorry.
The other thing I learned was the exact **coordinates** of the site. Berenger discovered the location and wrote it on his arm to keep it safe.
On the instruction of the zealots, Stone cut it off with one of their knives.
But he did give it to **Batman.**
N41°39'0"
E41°24'12"
Maybe Stone and that zealot were right about the sands--I can't see a damn thing--
--I think it's time to call in the **cavalry.**

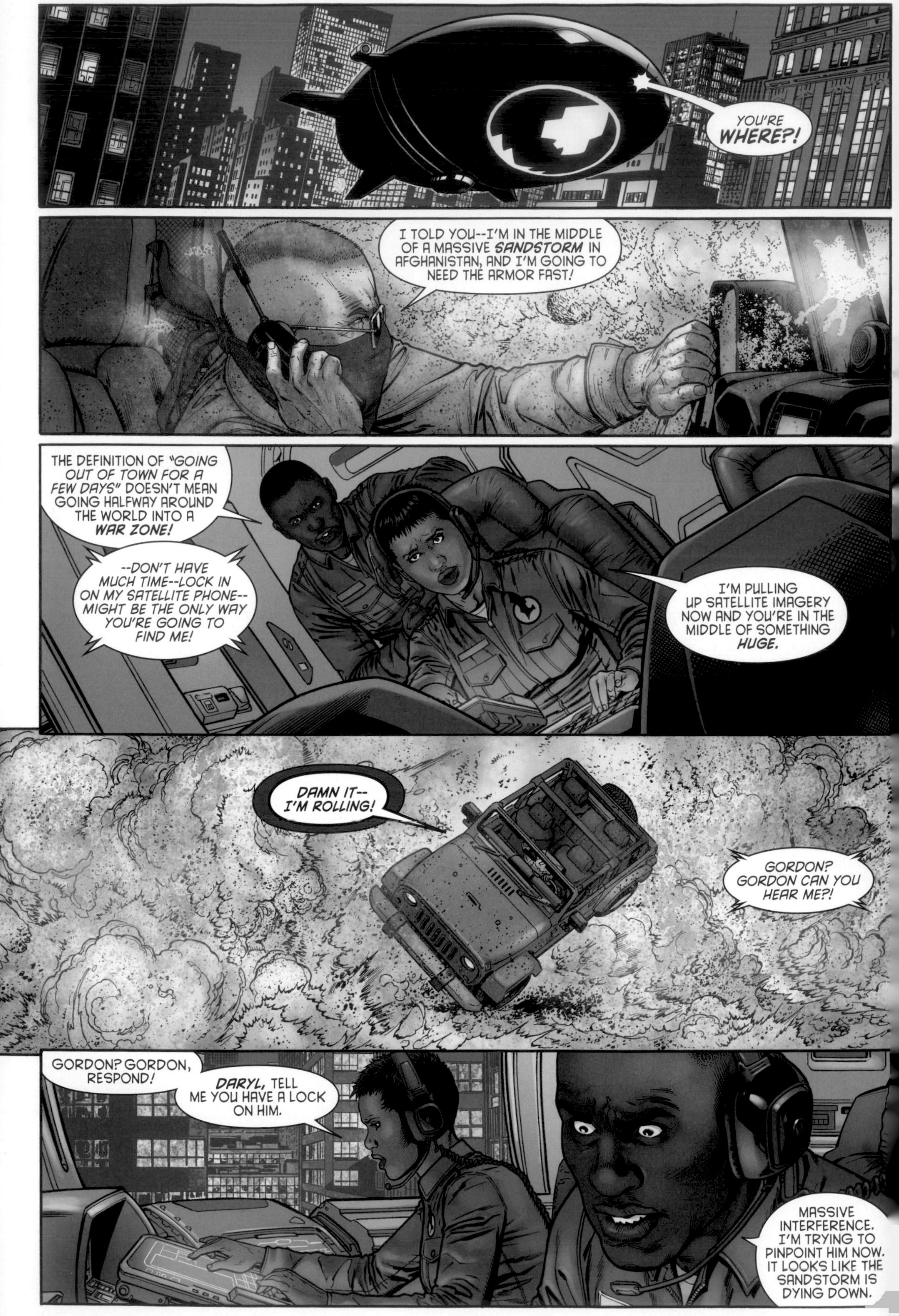
YOU'RE WHERE?!
I TOLD YOU--I'M IN THE MIDDLE OF A MASSIVE SANDSTORM IN AFGHANISTAN, AND I'M GOING TO NEED THE ARMOR FAST!
THE DEFINITION OF "GOING OUT OF TOWN FOR A FEW DAYS" DOESN'T MEAN GOING HALFWAY AROUND THE WORLD INTO A WAR ZONE!
--DON'T HAVE MUCH TIME--LOCK IN ON MY SATELLITE PHONE--MIGHT BE THE ONLY WAY YOU'RE GOING TO FIND ME!
I'M PULLING UP SATELLITE IMAGERY NOW AND YOU'RE IN THE MIDDLE OF SOMETHING HUGE.
DAMN IT-- I'M ROLLING!
GORDON? GORDON CAN YOU HEAR ME?!
GORDON? GORDON, RESPOND!
DARYL, TELL ME YOU HAVE A LOCK ON HIM.
MASSIVE INTERFERENCE. I'M TRYING TO PINPOINT HIM NOW. IT LOOKS LIKE THE SANDSTORM IS DYING DOWN.

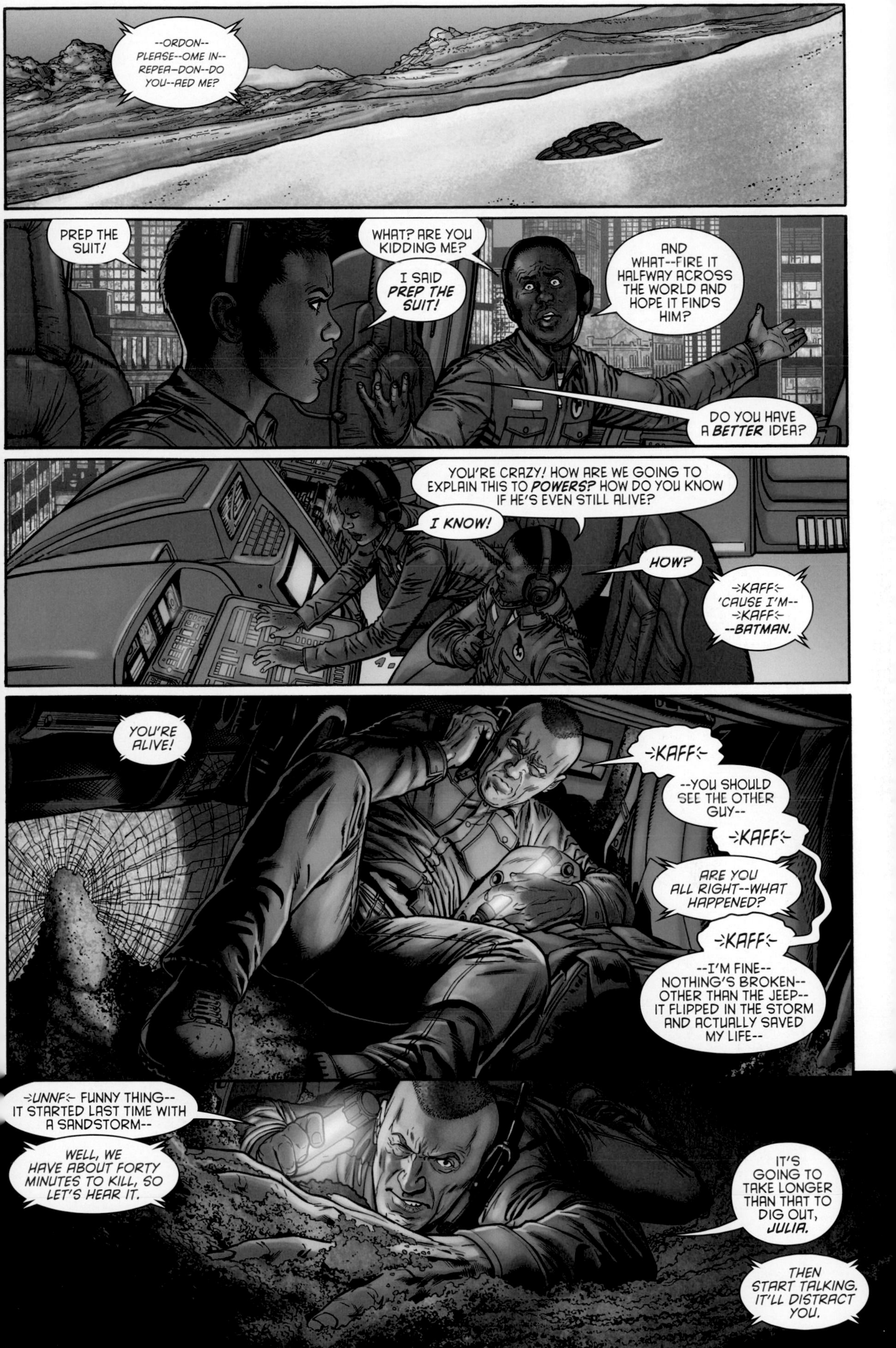

--ORDON-- PLEASE--OME IN-- REPEA--DON--DO YOU--AED ME?
PREP THE SUIT!
WHAT? ARE YOU KIDDING ME?
I SAID PREP THE SUIT!
AND WHAT--FIRE IT HALFWAY ACROSS THE WORLD AND HOPE IT FINDS HIM?
DO YOU HAVE A BETTER IDEA?
YOU'RE CRAZY! HOW ARE WE GOING TO EXPLAIN THIS TO POWERS? HOW DO YOU KNOW IF HE'S EVEN STILL ALIVE?
I KNOW!
HOW?
-KAFF- 'CAUSE I'M-- -KAFF- --BATMAN.
YOU'RE ALIVE!
-KAFF-
--YOU SHOULD SEE THE OTHER GUY--
-KAFF-
ARE YOU ALL RIGHT--WHAT HAPPENED?
-KAFF-
--I'M FINE-- NOTHING'S BROKEN-- OTHER THAN THE JEEP-- IT FLIPPED IN THE STORM AND ACTUALLY SAVED MY LIFE--
-UNNF- FUNNY THING-- IT STARTED LAST TIME WITH A SANDSTORM--
WELL, WE HAVE ABOUT FORTY MINUTES TO KILL, SO LET'S HEAR IT.
IT'S GOING TO TAKE LONGER THAN THAT TO DIG OUT, JULIA.
THEN START TALKING. IT'LL DISTRACT YOU.

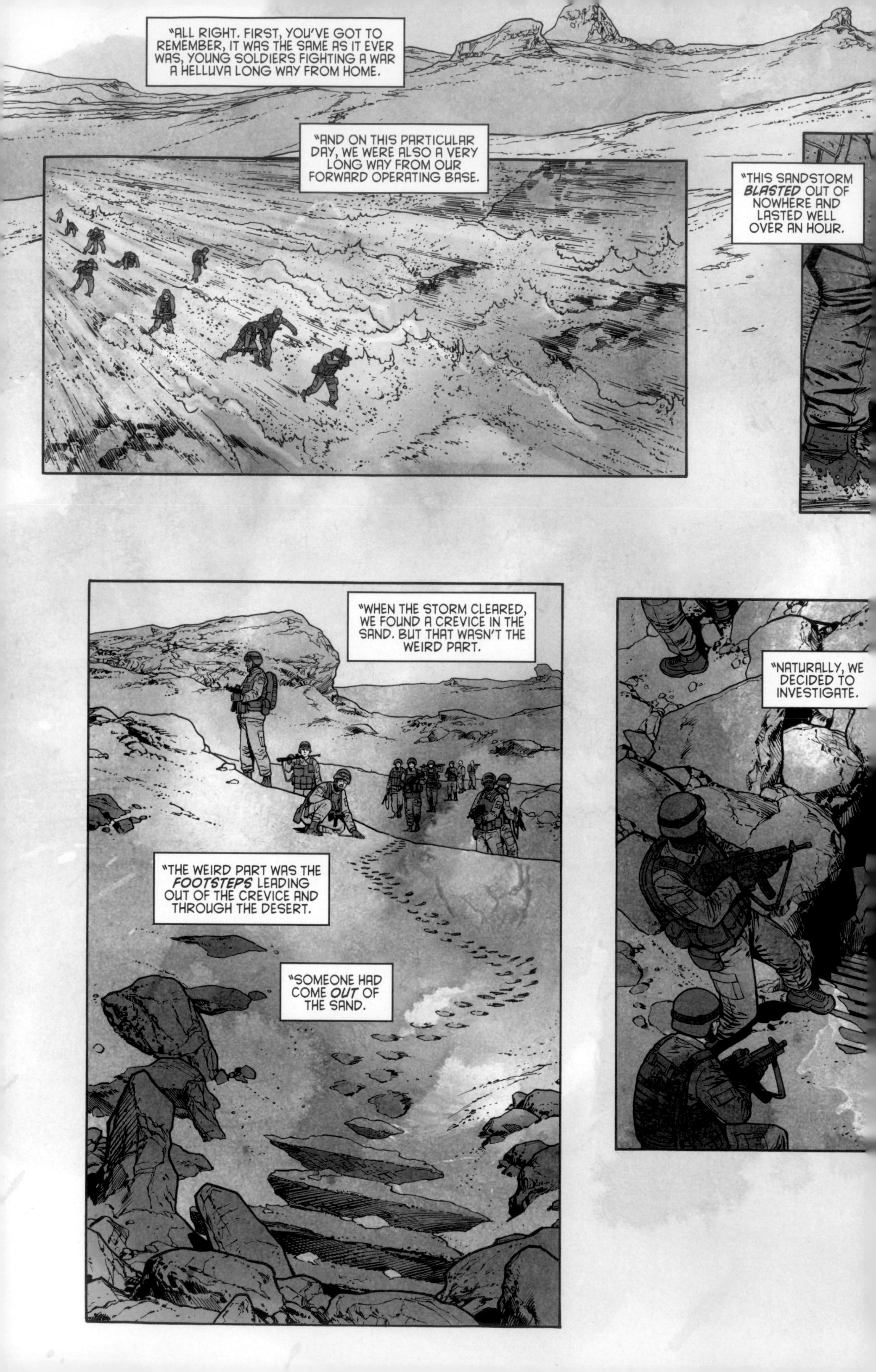
"ALL RIGHT. FIRST, YOU'VE GOT TO REMEMBER, IT WAS THE SAME AS IT EVER WAS, YOUNG SOLDIERS FIGHTING A WAR A HELLUVA LONG WAY FROM HOME.
"AND ON THIS PARTICULAR DAY, WE WERE ALSO A VERY LONG WAY FROM OUR FORWARD OPERATING BASE.
"THIS SANDSTORM BLASTED OUT OF NOWHERE AND LASTED WELL OVER AN HOUR.
"WHEN THE STORM CLEARED, WE FOUND A CREVICE IN THE SAND. BUT THAT WASN'T THE WEIRD PART.
"THE WEIRD PART WAS THE FOOTSTEPS LEADING OUT OF THE CREVICE AND THROUGH THE DESERT.
"SOMEONE HAD COME OUT OF THE SAND.
"NATURALLY, WE DECIDED TO INVESTIGATE.

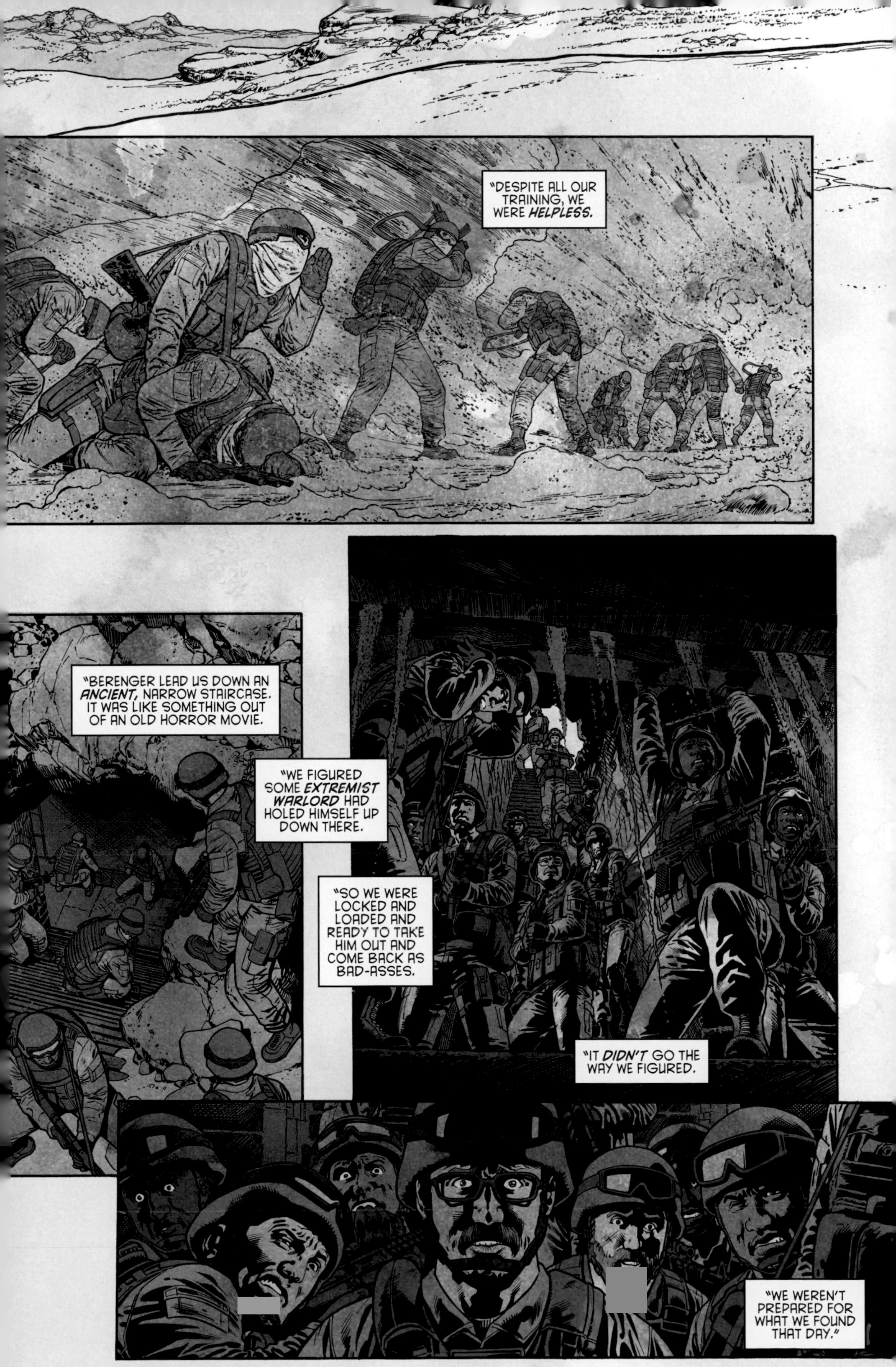
"DESPITE ALL OUR TRAINING, WE WERE HELPLESS.
"BERENGER LEAD US DOWN AN ANCIENT, NARROW STAIRCASE. IT WAS LIKE SOMETHING OUT OF AN OLD HORROR MOVIE.
"WE FIGURED SOME EXTREMIST WARLORD HAD HOLED HIMSELF UP DOWN THERE.
"SO WE WERE LOCKED AND LOADED AND READY TO TAKE HIM OUT AND COME BACK AS BAD-ASSES.
"IT DIDN'T GO THE WAY WE FIGURED.
"WE WEREN'T PREPARED FOR WHAT WE FOUND THAT DAY."

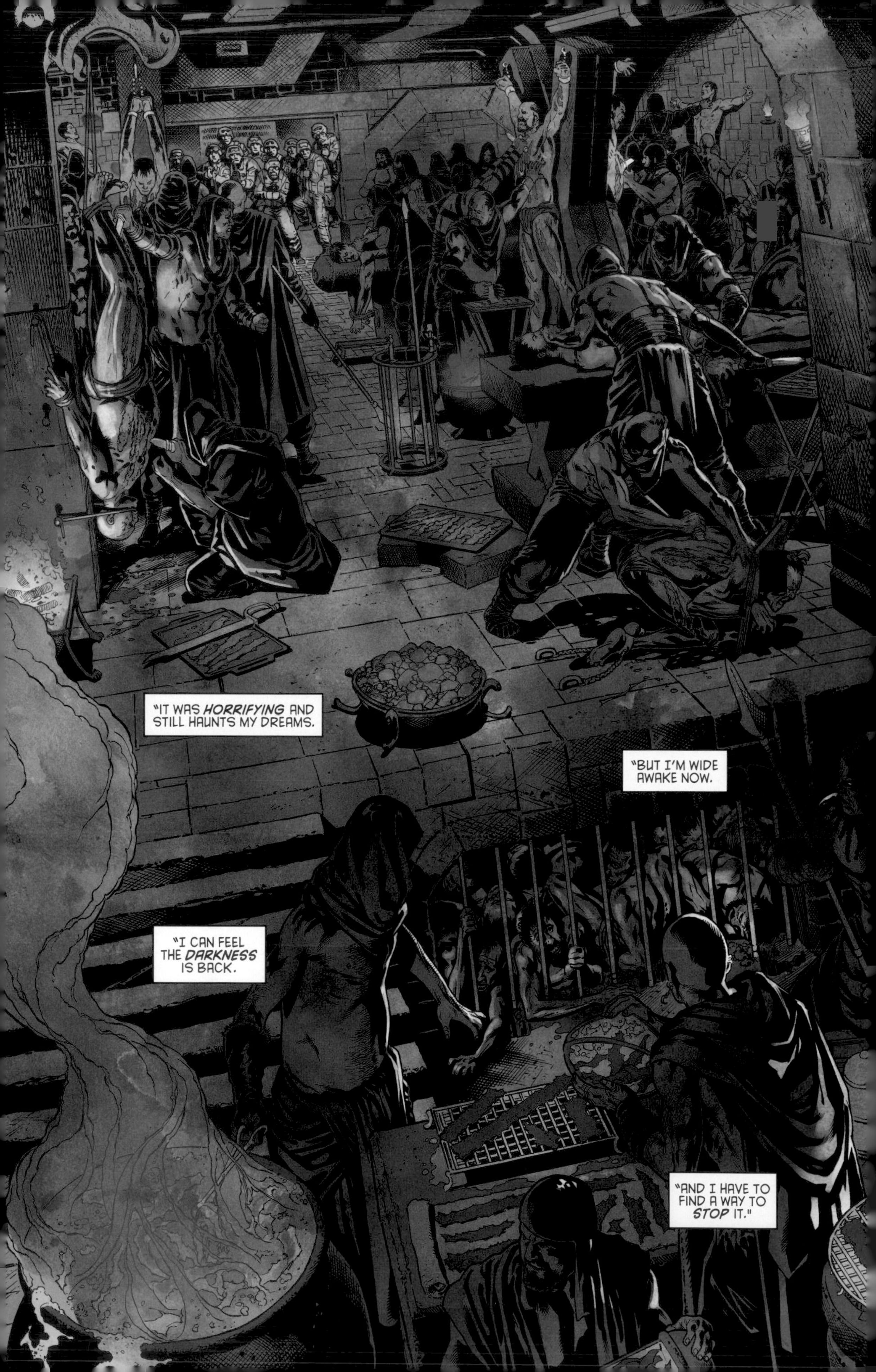
"IT WAS HORRIFYING AND STILL HAUNTS MY DREAMS.
"BUT I'M WIDE AWAKE NOW.
"I CAN FEEL THE DARKNESS IS BACK.
"AND I HAVE TO FIND A WAY TO STOP IT."

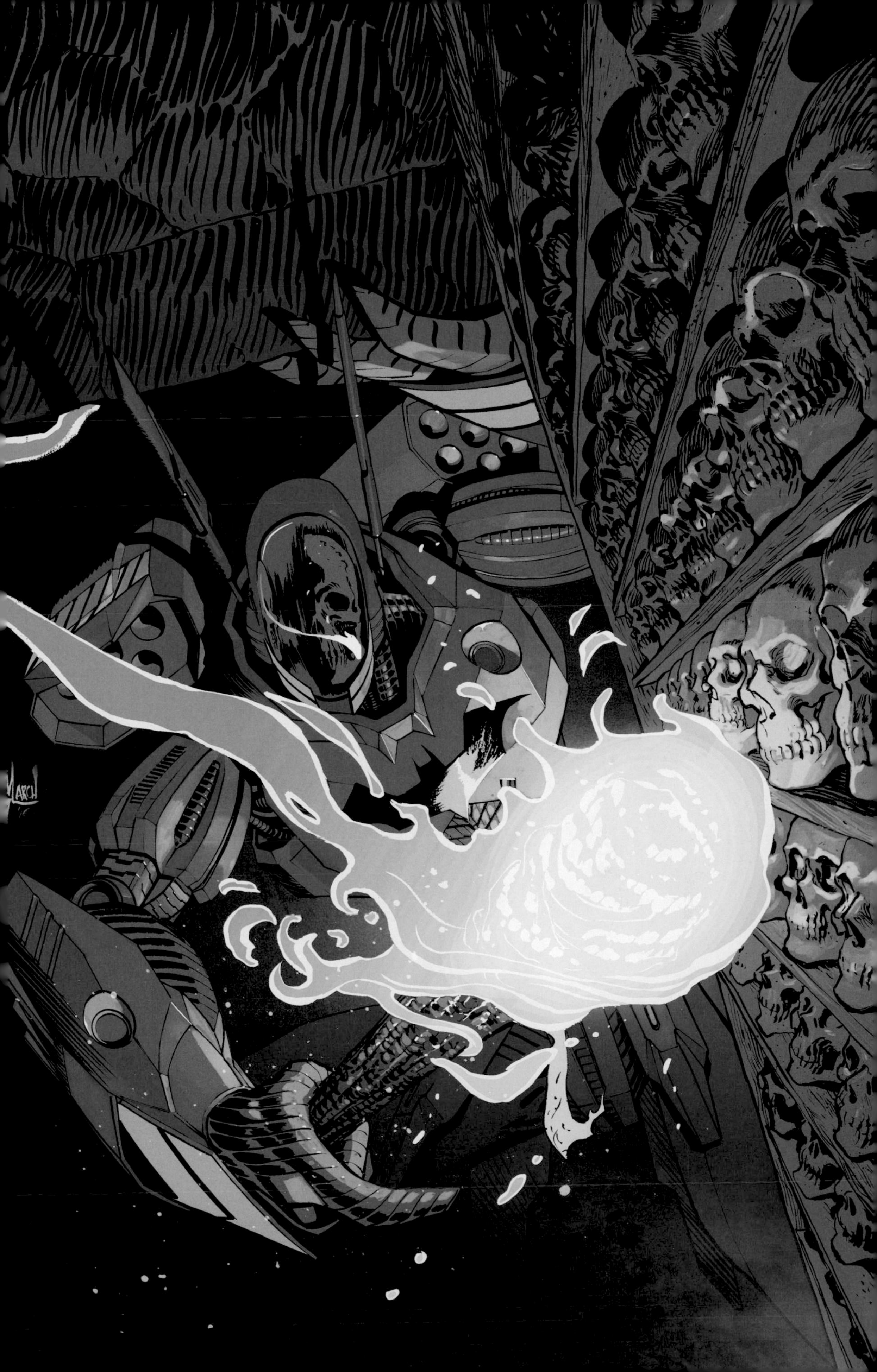

OUR GORDON AT WAR, PART 2

PETER J. TOMASI writer FERNANDO PASARIN penciller MATT RYAN inker CHRIS SOTOMAYOR colorist WES ABBOTT letterer GUILLEM MARCH cover

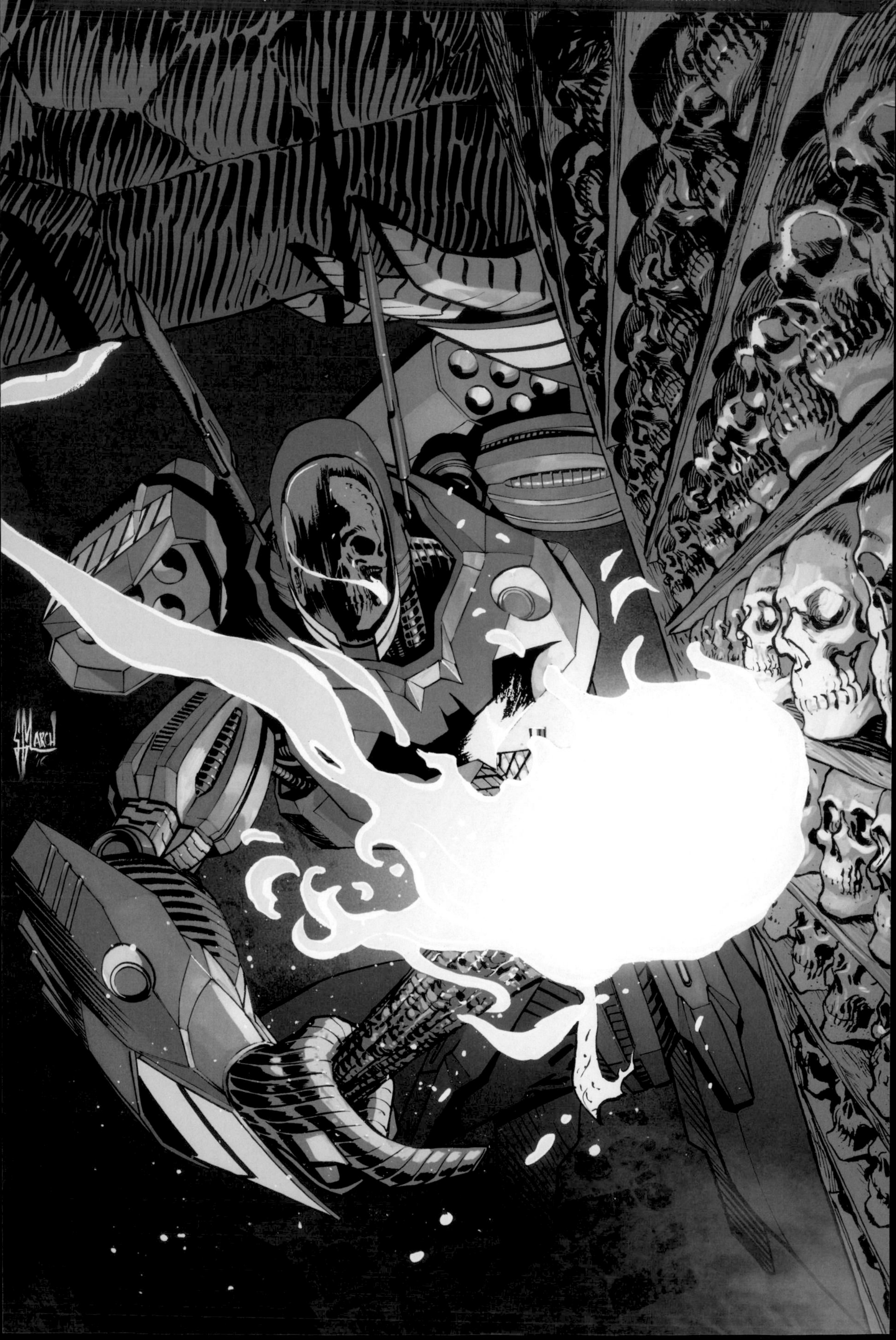

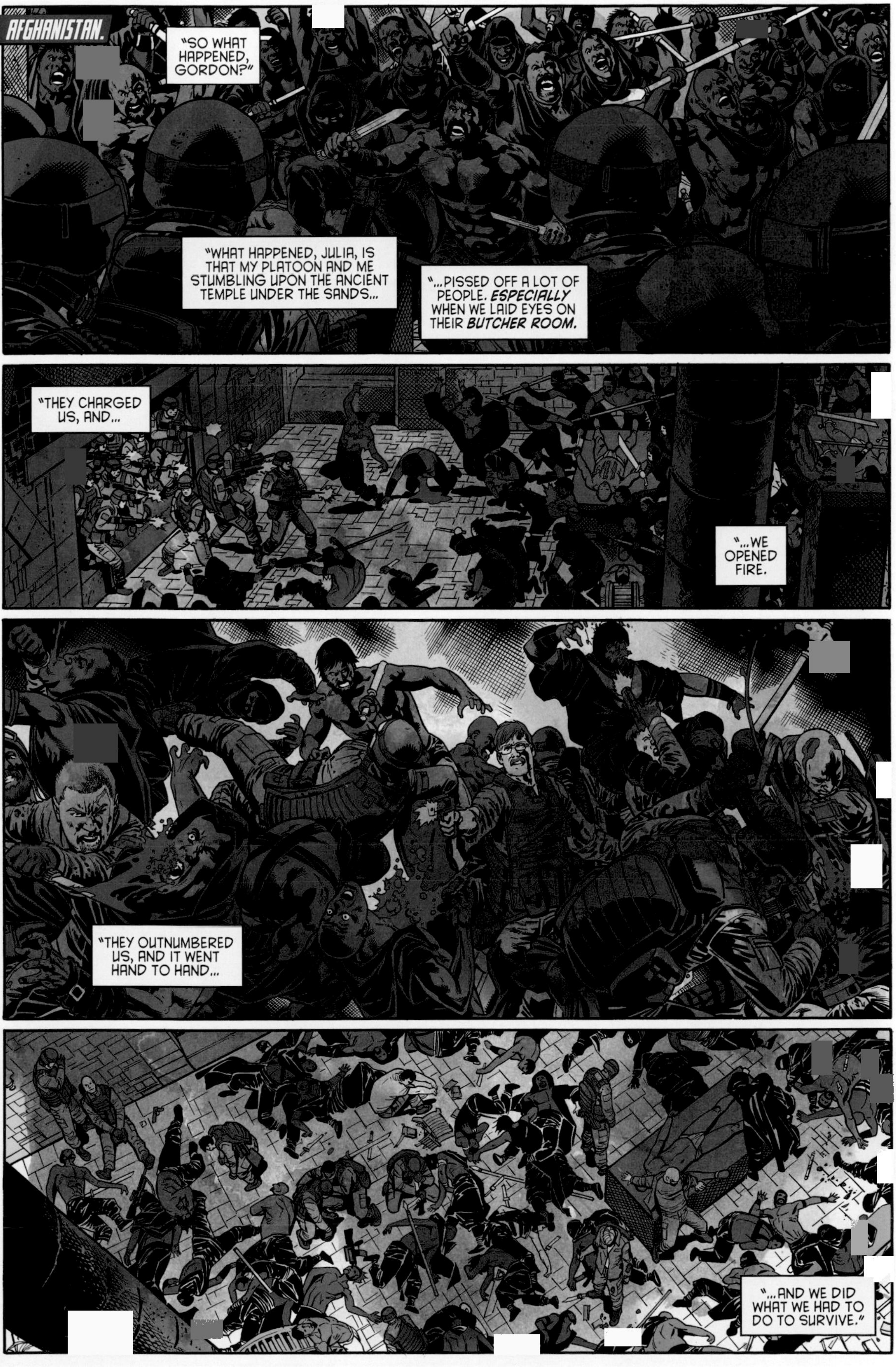
AFGHANISTAN.
"SO WHAT HAPPENED, GORDON?"
"WHAT HAPPENED, JULIA, IS THAT MY PLATOON AND ME STUMBLING UPON THE ANCIENT TEMPLE UNDER THE SANDS...
"...PISSED OFF A LOT OF PEOPLE. *ESPECIALLY* WHEN WE LAID EYES ON THEIR *BUTCHER ROOM.*
"THEY CHARGED US, AND...
"...WE OPENED FIRE.
"THEY OUTNUMBERED US, AND IT WENT HAND TO HAND...
"...AND WE DID WHAT WE HAD TO DO TO SURVIVE."

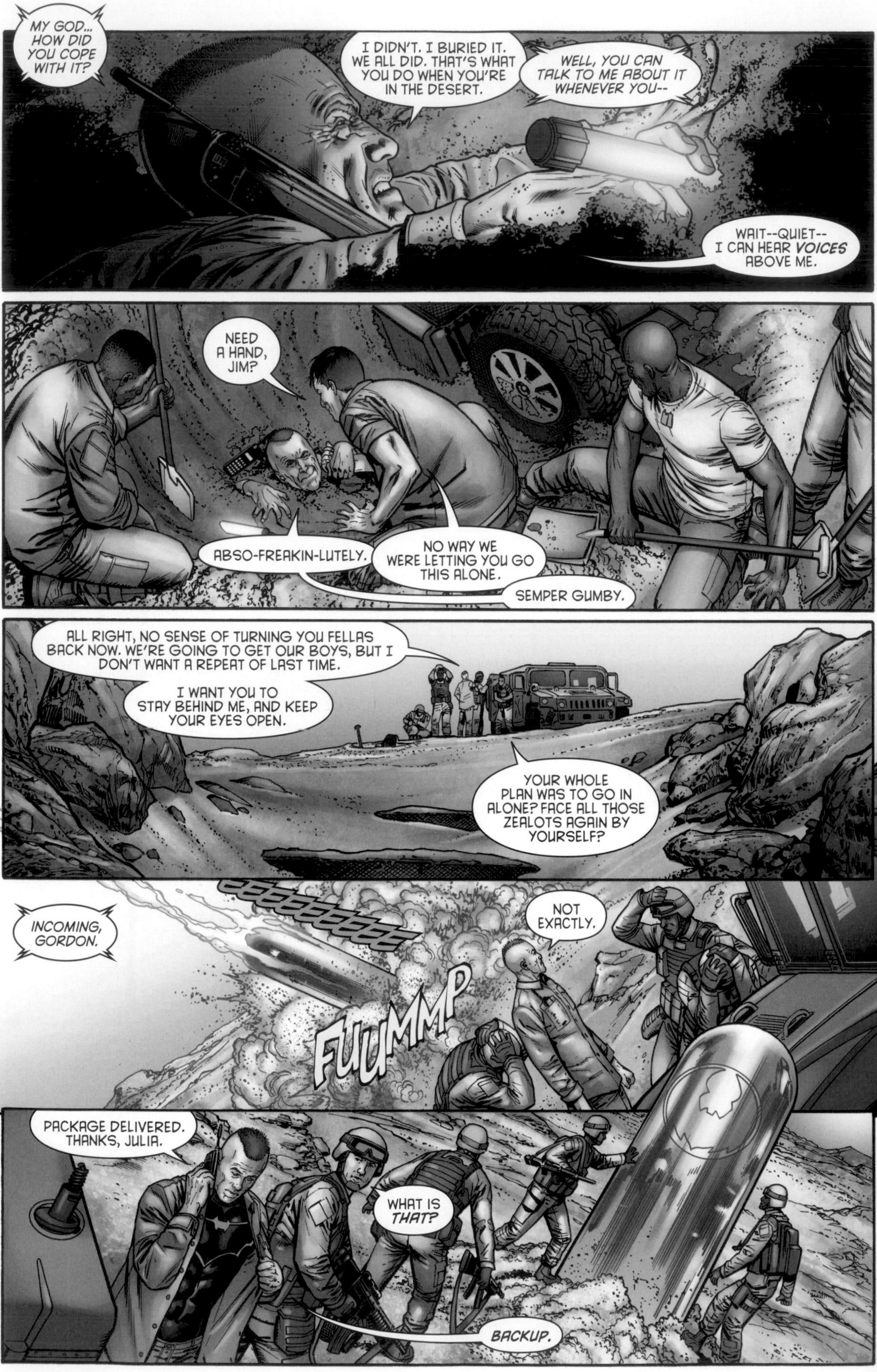
MY GOD... HOW DID YOU COPE WITH IT?
I DIDN'T. I BURIED IT. WE ALL DID. THAT'S WHAT YOU DO WHEN YOU'RE IN THE DESERT.
WELL, YOU CAN TALK TO ME ABOUT IT WHENEVER YOU--
WAIT--QUIET-- I CAN HEAR VOICES ABOVE ME.
NEED A HAND, JIM?
ABSO-FREAKIN-LUTELY.
NO WAY WE WERE LETTING YOU GO THIS ALONE.
SEMPER GUMBY.
ALL RIGHT, NO SENSE OF TURNING YOU FELLAS BACK NOW. WE'RE GOING TO GET OUR BOYS, BUT I DON'T WANT A REPEAT OF LAST TIME.
I WANT YOU TO STAY BEHIND ME, AND KEEP YOUR EYES OPEN.
YOUR WHOLE PLAN WAS TO GO IN ALONE? FACE ALL THOSE ZEALOTS AGAIN BY YOURSELF?
INCOMING, GORDON.
NOT EXACTLY.
FUUMMP
PACKAGE DELIVERED. THANKS, JULIA.
WHAT IS THAT?
BACKUP.

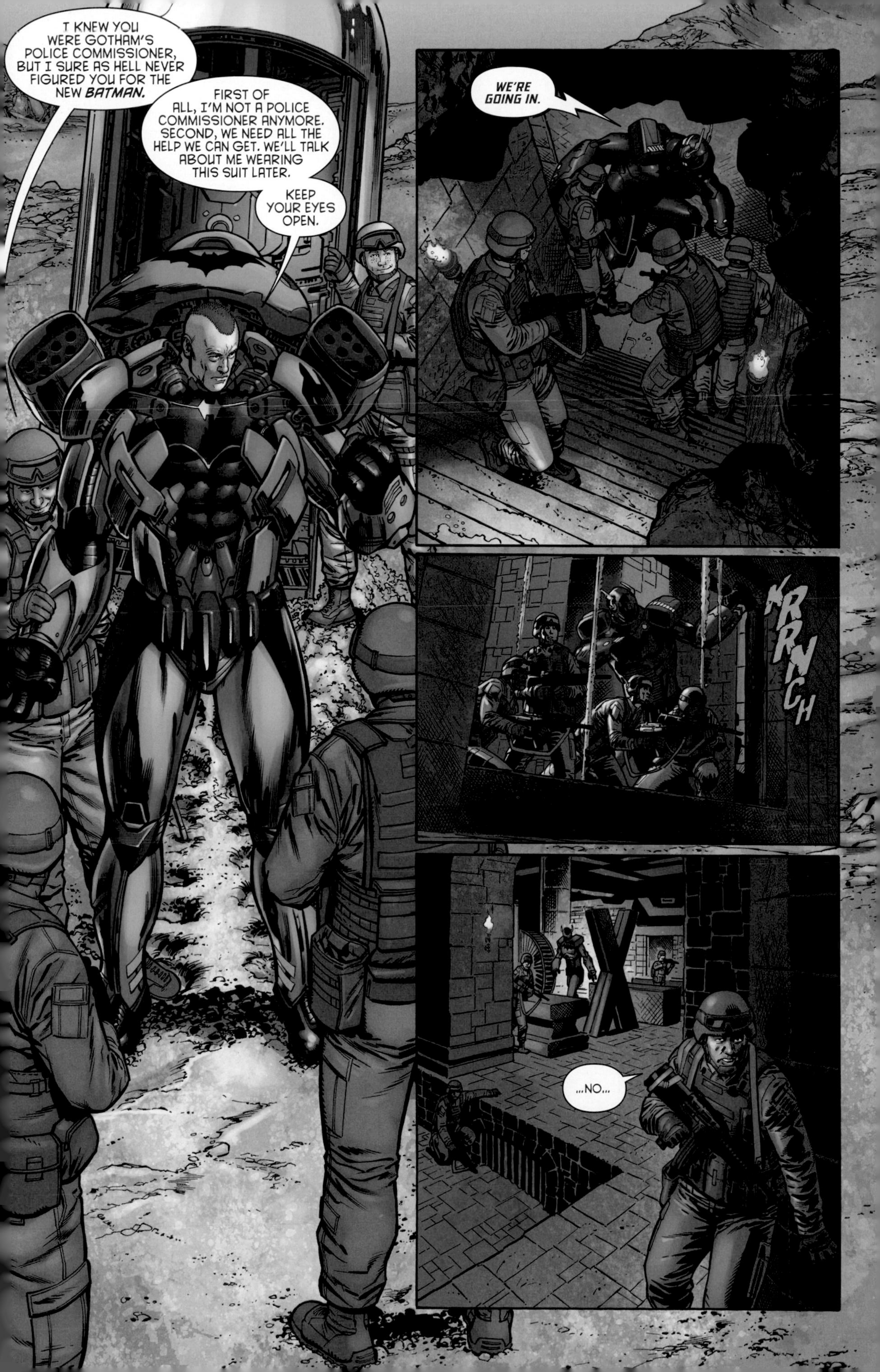
I KNEW YOU WERE GOTHAM'S POLICE COMMISSIONER, BUT I SURE AS HELL NEVER FIGURED YOU FOR THE NEW BATMAN.
FIRST OF ALL, I'M NOT A POLICE COMMISSIONER ANYMORE. SECOND, WE NEED ALL THE HELP WE CAN GET. WE'LL TALK ABOUT ME WEARING THIS SUIT LATER.
KEEP YOUR EYES OPEN.
WE'RE GOING IN.
KRRNCH
...NO...

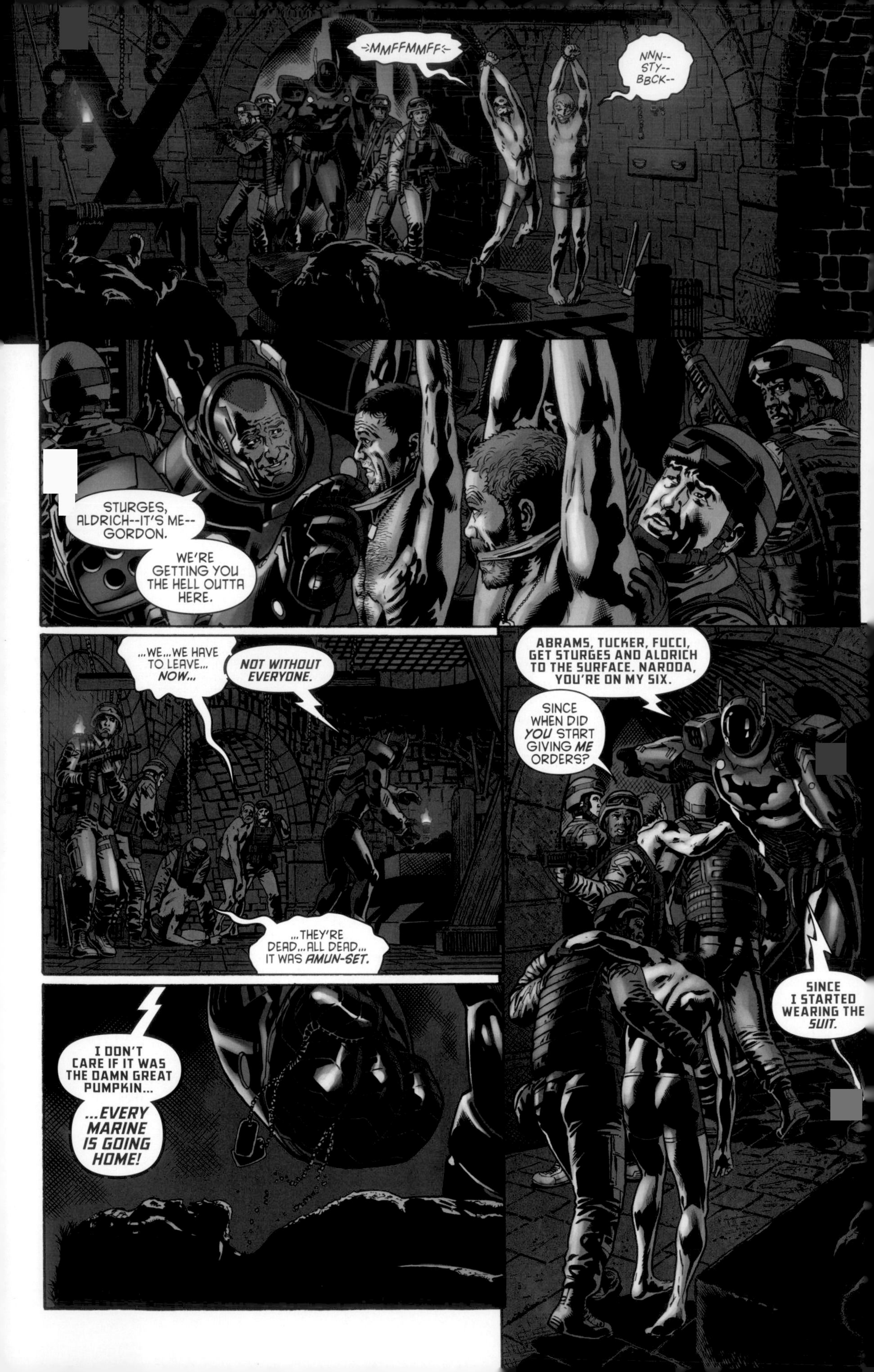
-MMFFMMFF-
NNN-- STY-- BBCK--
STURGES, ALDRICH--IT'S ME--GORDON.
WE'RE GETTING YOU THE HELL OUTTA HERE.
...WE...WE HAVE TO LEAVE... NOW...
NOT WITHOUT EVERYONE.
...THEY'RE DEAD...ALL DEAD... IT WAS AMUN-SET.
I DON'T CARE IF IT WAS THE DAMN GREAT PUMPKIN...
...EVERY MARINE IS GOING HOME!
ABRAMS, TUCKER, FUCCI, GET STURGES AND ALDRICH TO THE SURFACE. NARODA, YOU'RE ON MY SIX.
SINCE WHEN DID YOU START GIVING ME ORDERS?
SINCE I STARTED WEARING THE SUIT.

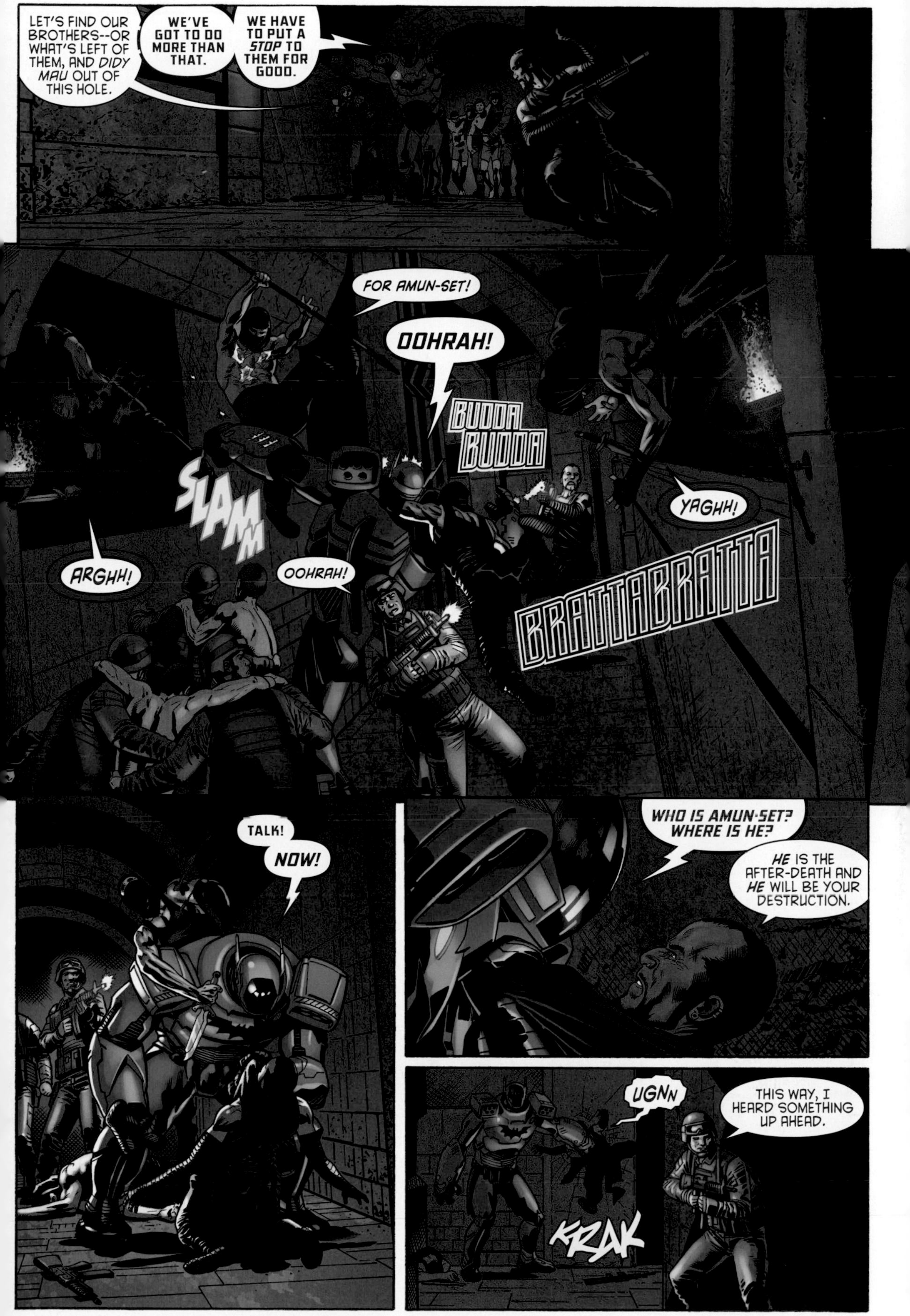
LET'S FIND OUR BROTHERS--OR WHAT'S LEFT OF THEM, AND DIDY MAU OUT OF THIS HOLE.
WE'VE GOT TO DO MORE THAN THAT.
WE HAVE TO PUT A STOP TO THEM FOR GOOD.
FOR AMUN-SET!
OOHRAH!
BUDDA BUDDA
SLAMM
ARGHH!
OOHRAH!
YAGHH!
BRATTABRATTA
TALK!
NOW!
WHO IS AMUN-SET? WHERE IS HE?
HE IS THE AFTER-DEATH AND HE WILL BE YOUR DESTRUCTION.
UGNN
KRAK
THIS WAY, I HEARD SOMETHING UP AHEAD.

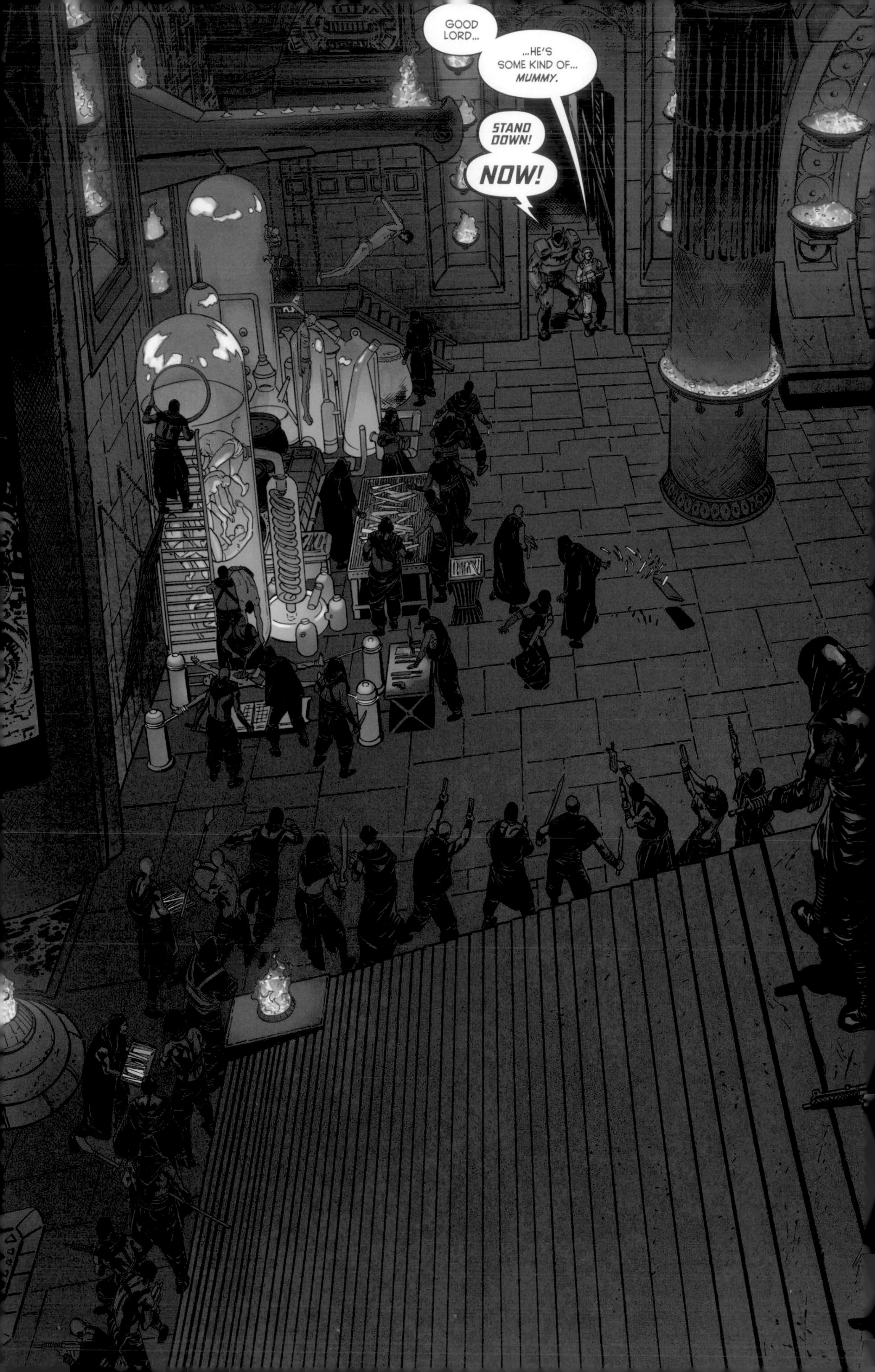
GOOD LORD...
...HE'S SOME KIND OF... MUMMY.
STAND DOWN!
NOW!

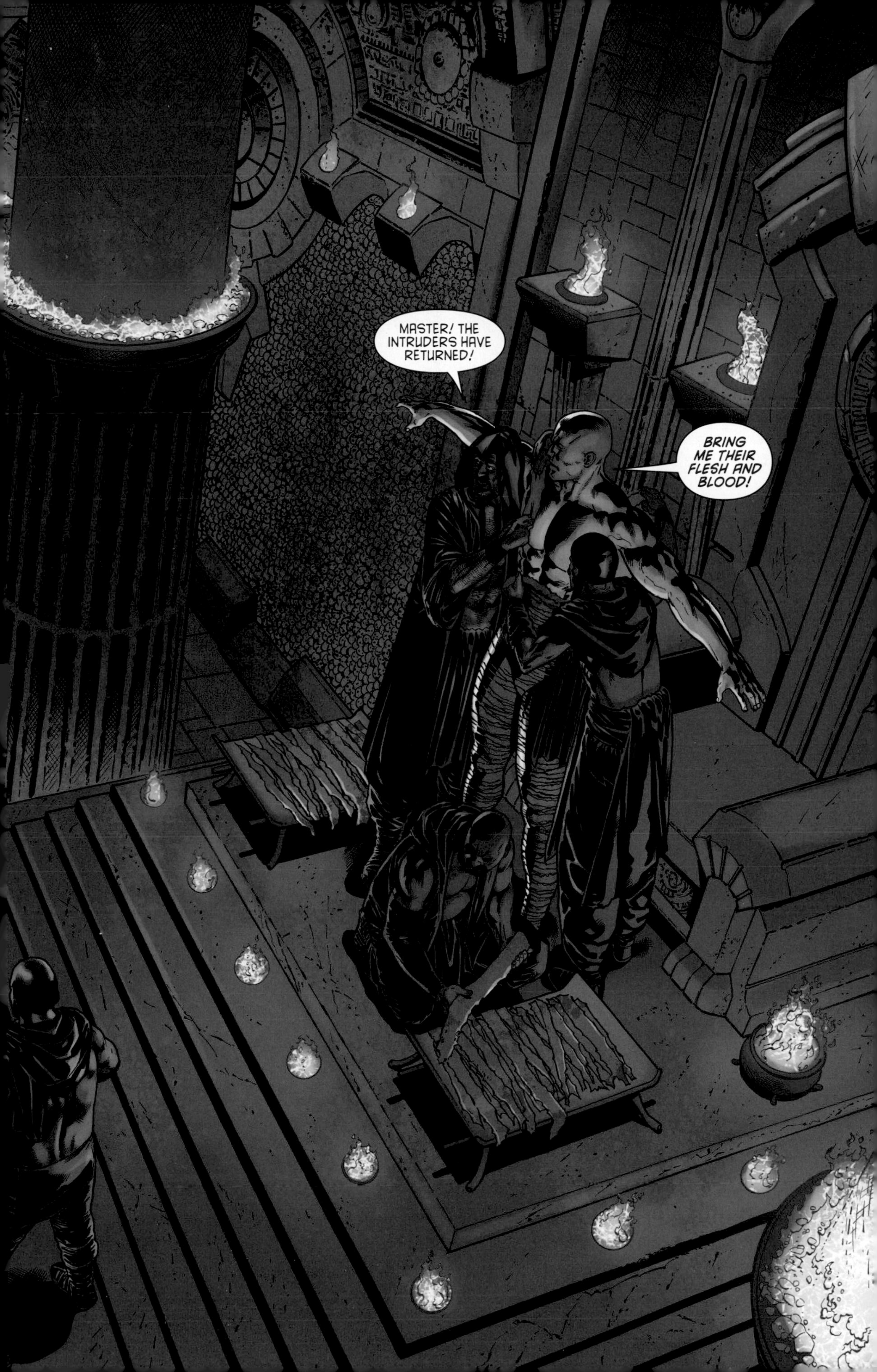
MASTER! THE INTRUDERS HAVE RETURNED!
BRING ME THEIR FLESH AND BLOOD!

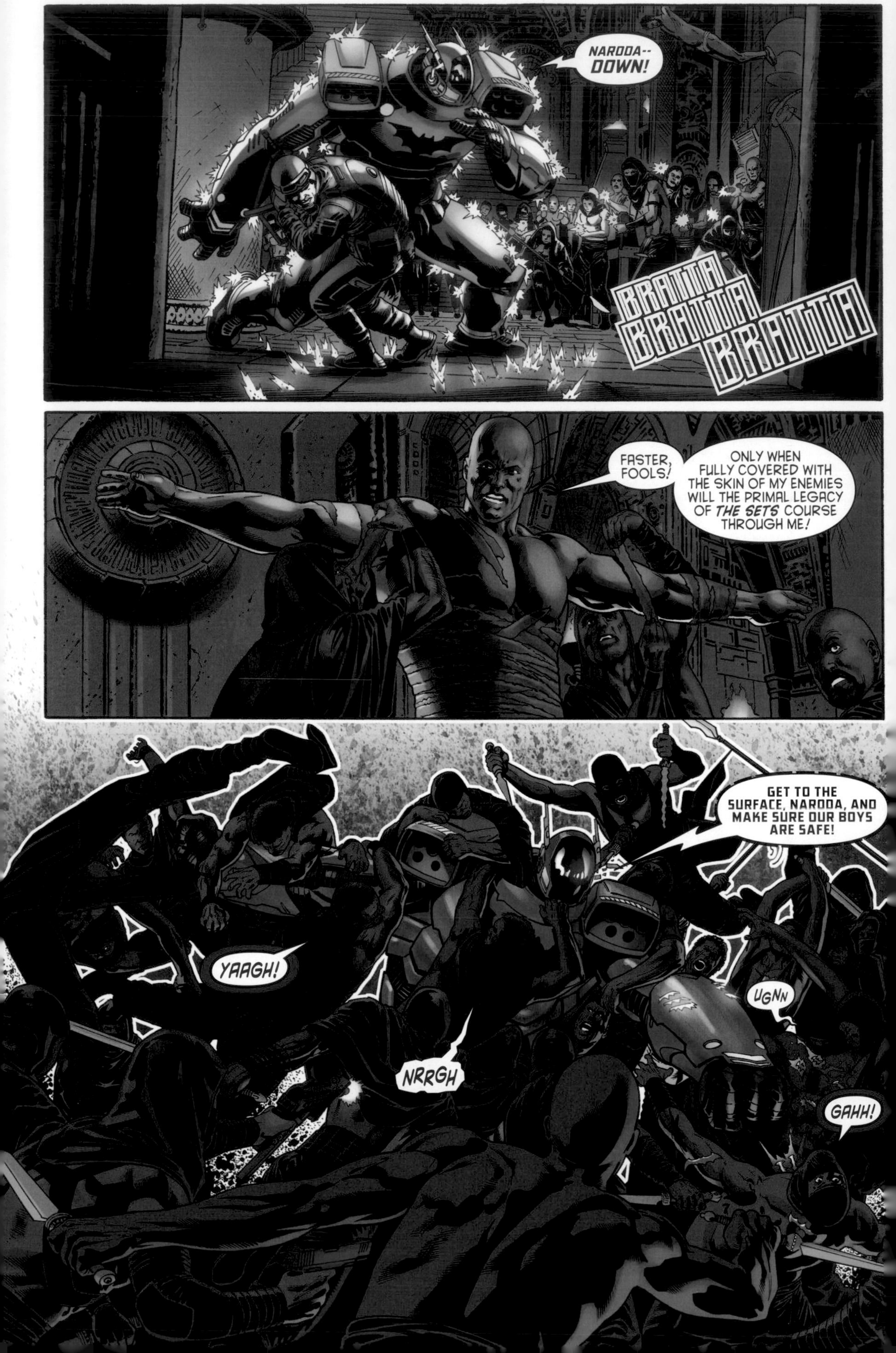
NARODA--
DOWN!
BRATTA BRATTA BRATTA
FASTER, FOOLS!
ONLY WHEN FULLY COVERED WITH THE SKIN OF MY ENEMIES WILL THE PRIMAL LEGACY OF THE SETS COURSE THROUGH ME!
GET TO THE SURFACE, NARODA, AND MAKE SURE OUR BOYS ARE SAFE!
YAAGH!
UGNN
NRRGH
GAHH!

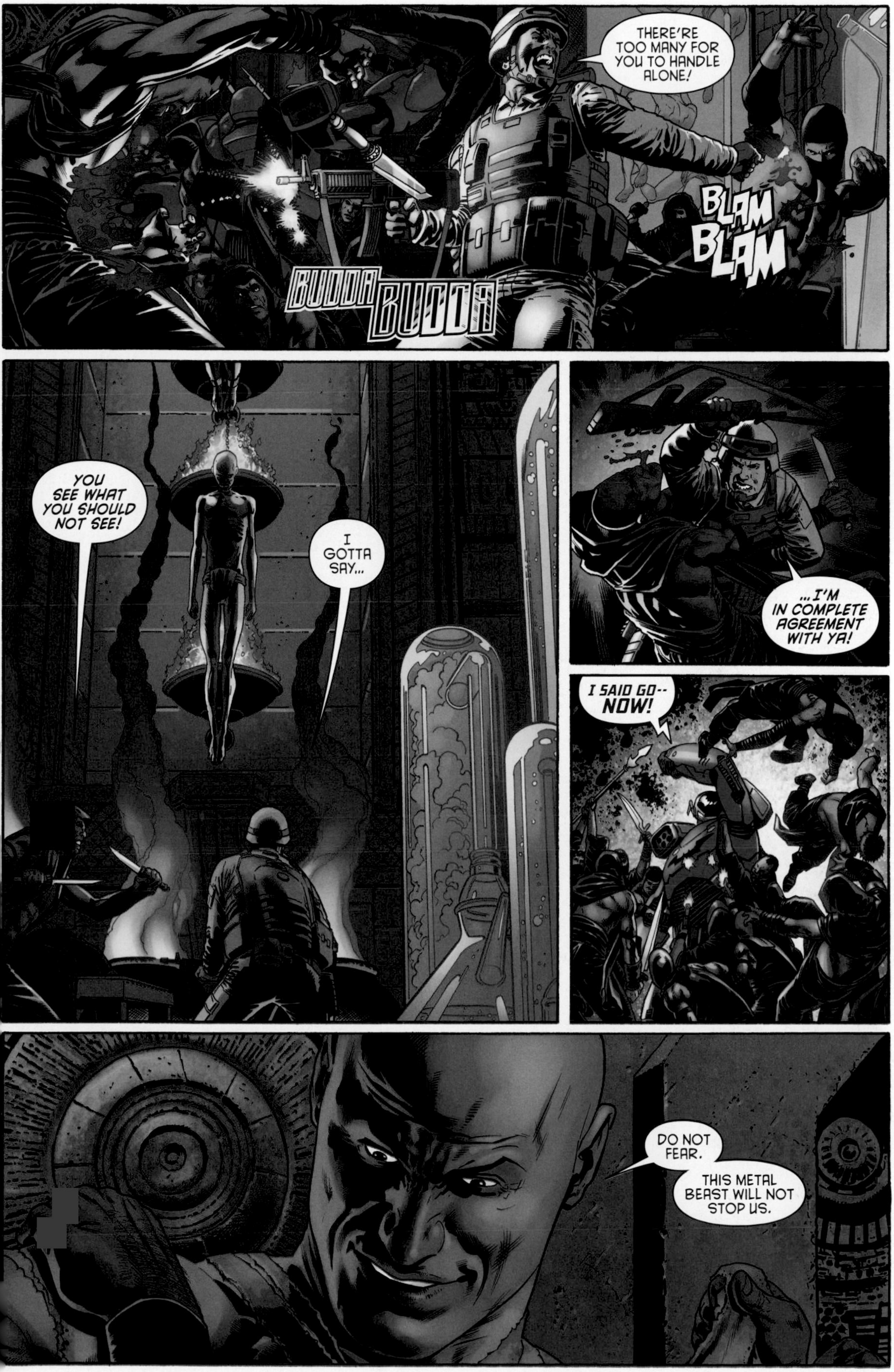
THERE'RE TOO MANY FOR YOU TO HANDLE ALONE!
BLAM BLAM
BUDDA BUDDA
YOU SEE WHAT YOU SHOULD NOT SEE!
I GOTTA SAY...
...I'M IN COMPLETE AGREEMENT WITH YA!
I SAID GO-- NOW!
DO NOT FEAR.
THIS METAL BEAST WILL NOT STOP US.

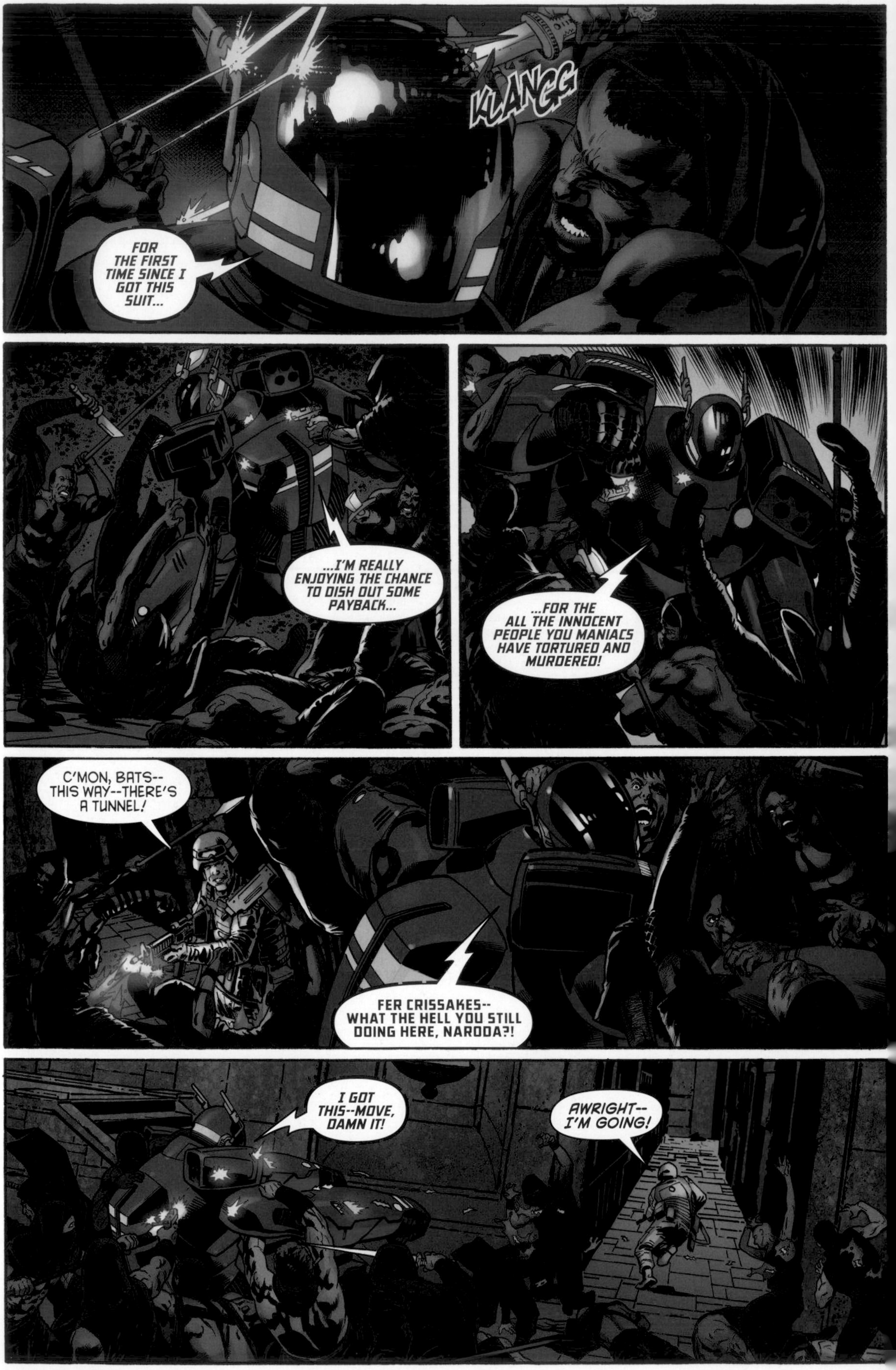
KLANGG
FOR THE FIRST TIME SINCE I GOT THIS SUIT...
...I'M REALLY ENJOYING THE CHANCE TO DISH OUT SOME PAYBACK...
...FOR THE ALL THE INNOCENT PEOPLE YOU MANIACS HAVE TORTURED AND MURDERED!
C'MON, BATS--THIS WAY--THERE'S A TUNNEL!
FER CRISSAKES--WHAT THE HELL YOU STILL DOING HERE, NARODA?!
I GOT THIS--MOVE, DAMN IT!
AWRIGHT--I'M GOING!

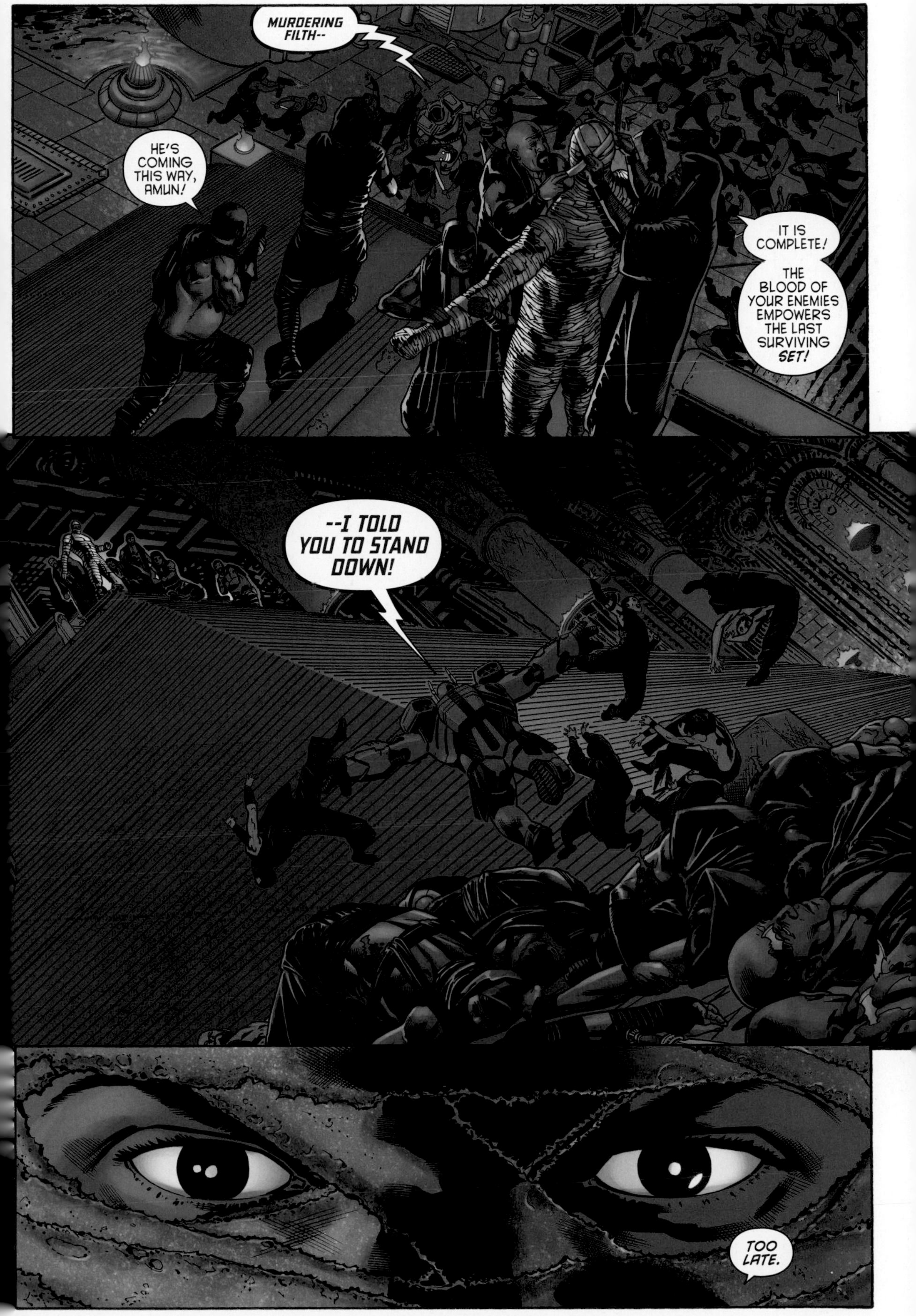
MURDERING FILTH--
HE'S COMING THIS WAY, AMUN!
IT IS COMPLETE!
THE BLOOD OF YOUR ENEMIES EMPOWERS THE LAST SURVIVING SET!
--I TOLD YOU TO STAND DOWN!
TOO LATE.

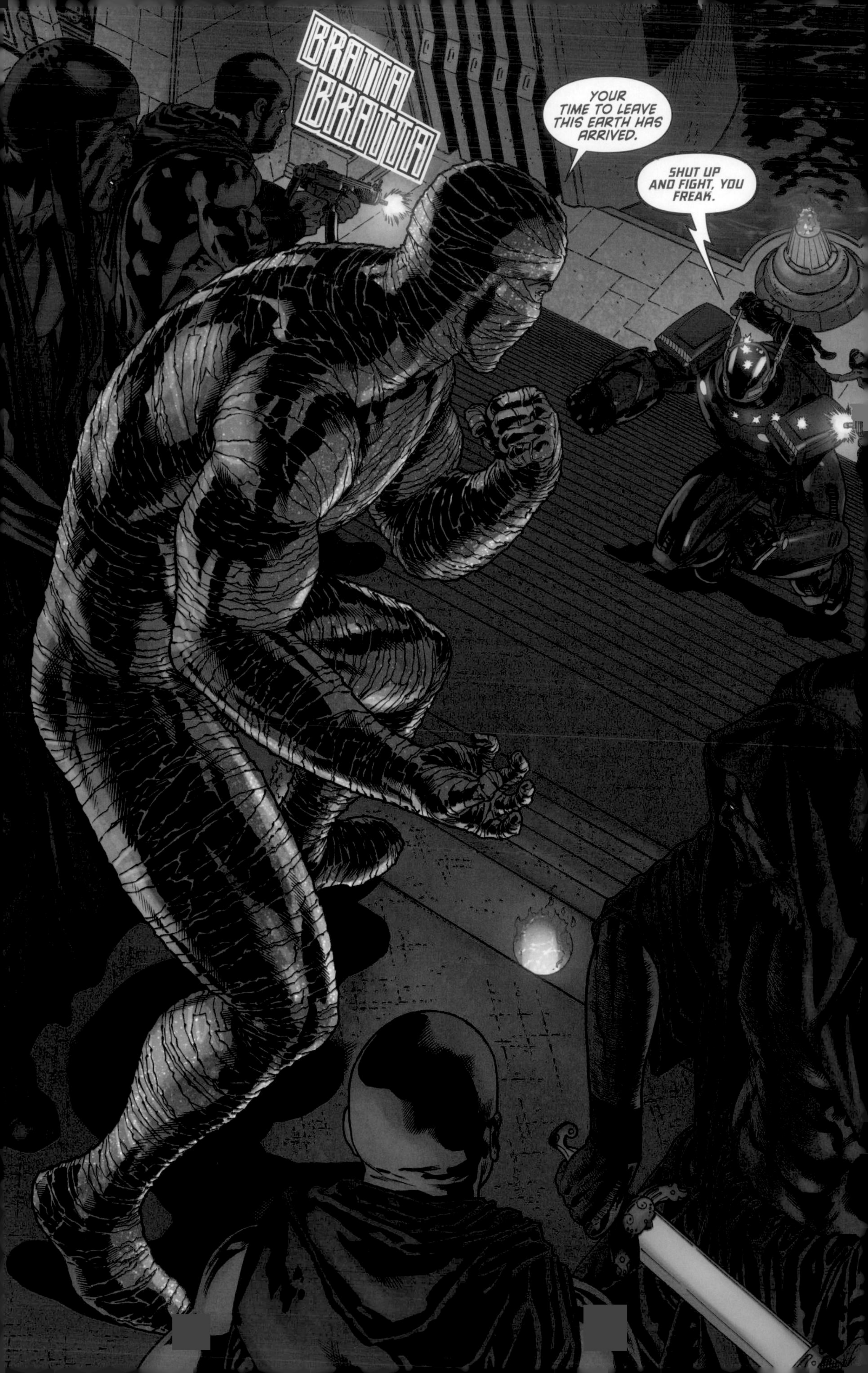
BRATTA BRATTA
YOUR TIME TO LEAVE THIS EARTH HAS ARRIVED.
SHUT UP AND FIGHT, YOU FREAK.

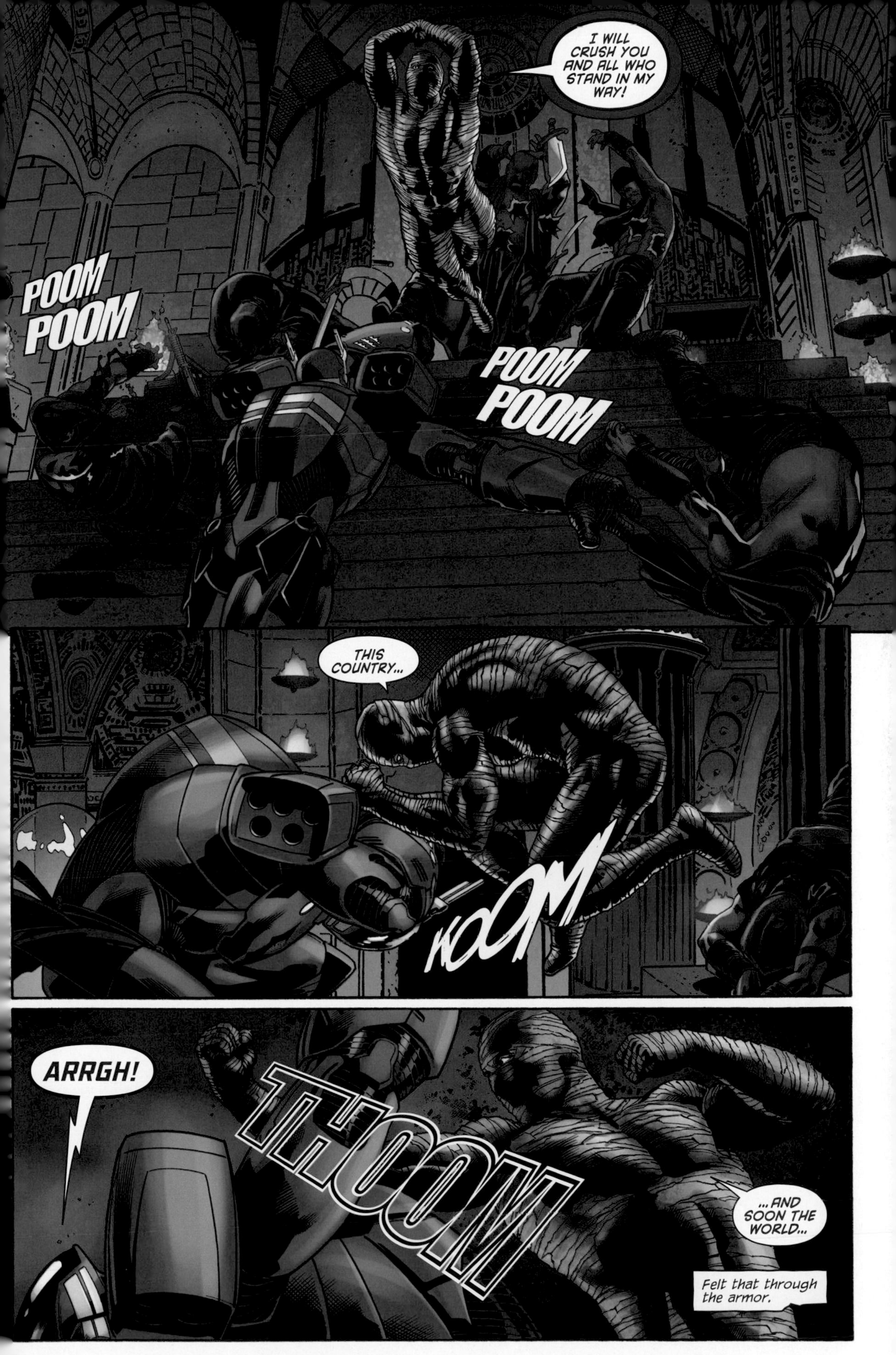
I WILL CRUSH YOU AND ALL WHO STAND IN MY WAY!
POOM POOM
POOM POOM
THIS COUNTRY...
KOOM
ARRGH!
THOOM
...AND SOON THE WORLD...
Felt that through the armor.

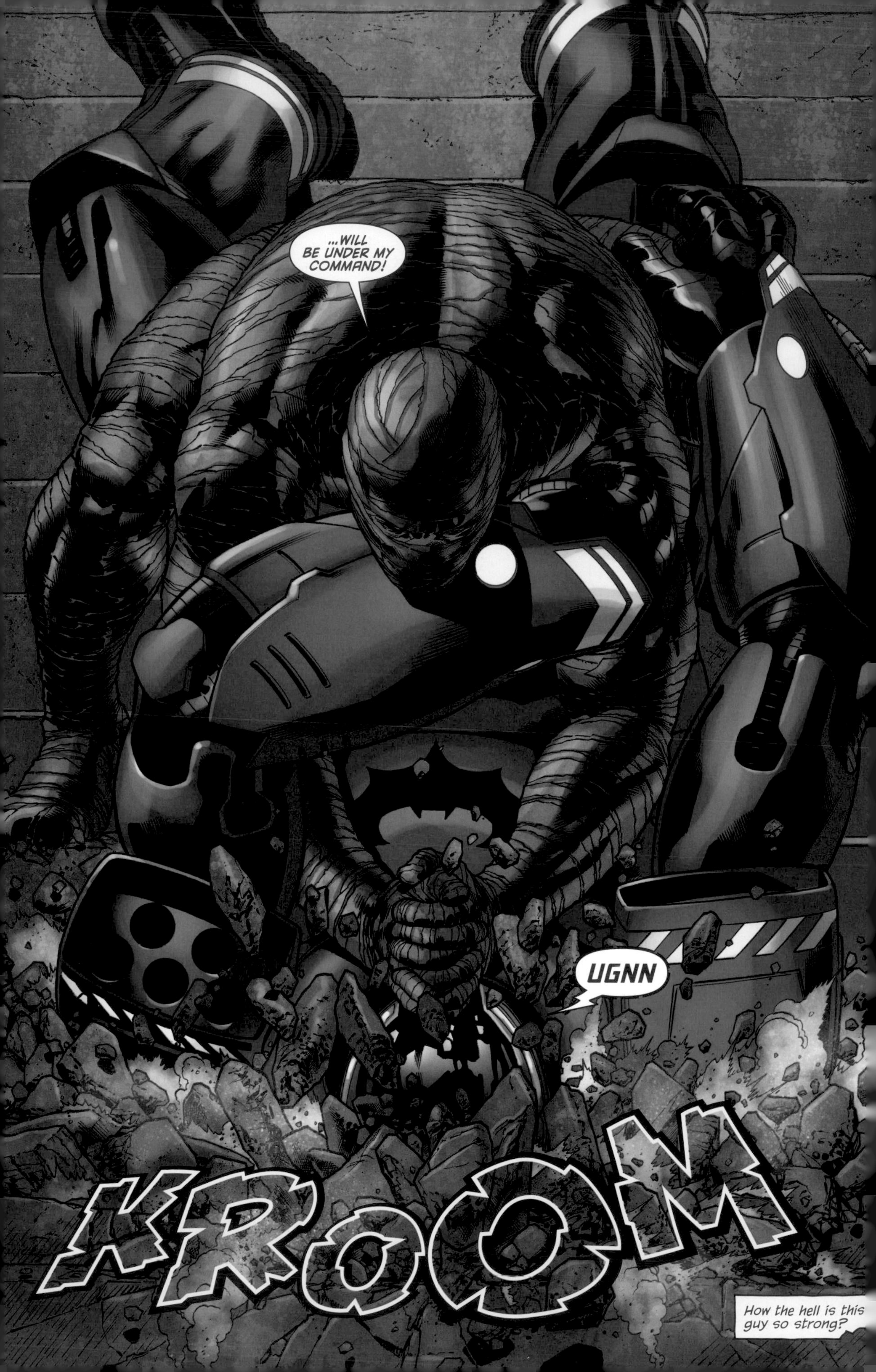
...WILL BE UNDER MY COMMAND!
UGNN
KROOM
How the hell is this guy so strong?

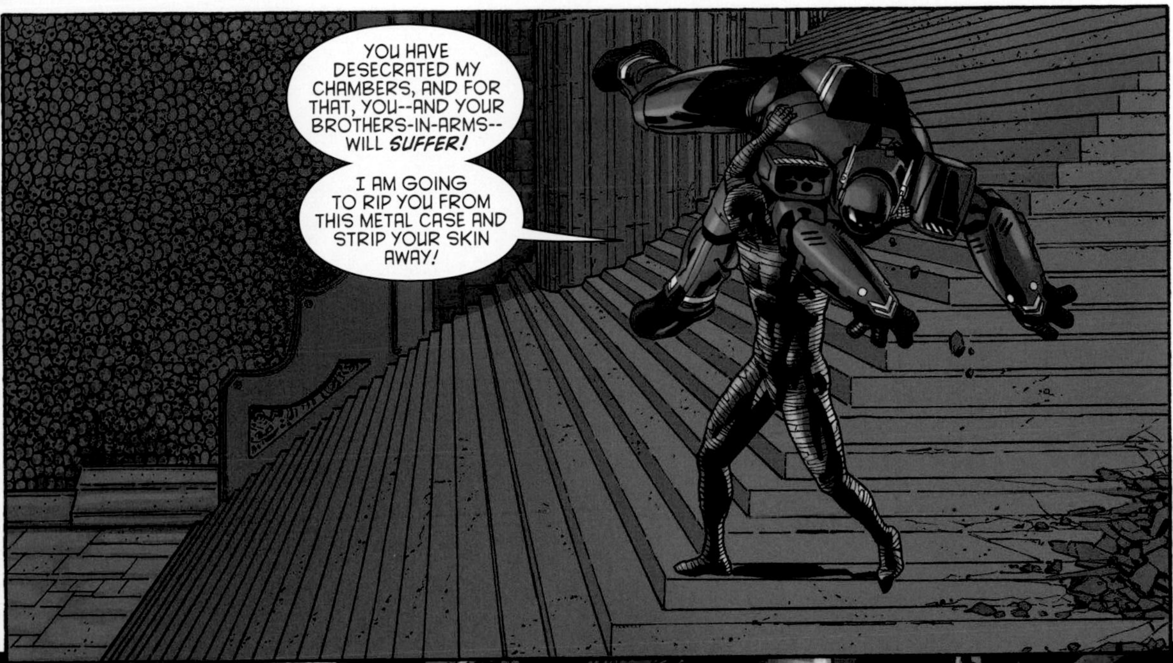
YOU HAVE DESECRATED MY CHAMBERS, AND FOR THAT, YOU--AND YOUR BROTHERS-IN-ARMS--WILL *SUFFER!*
I AM GOING TO RIP YOU FROM THIS METAL CASE AND STRIP YOUR SKIN AWAY!

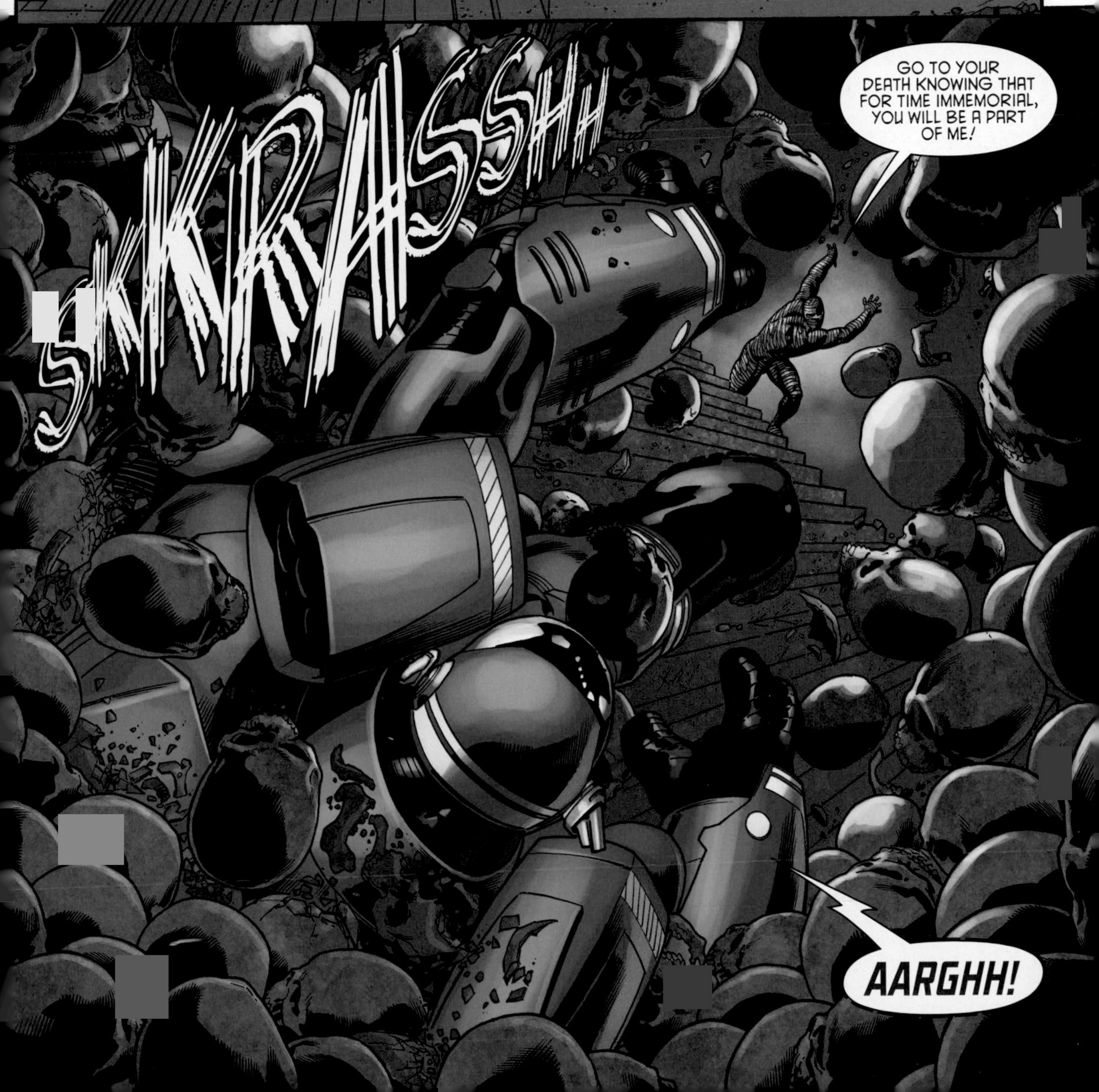
SKRASSHH
GO TO YOUR DEATH KNOWING THAT FOR TIME IMMEMORIAL, YOU WILL BE A PART OF ME!
AARGHH!

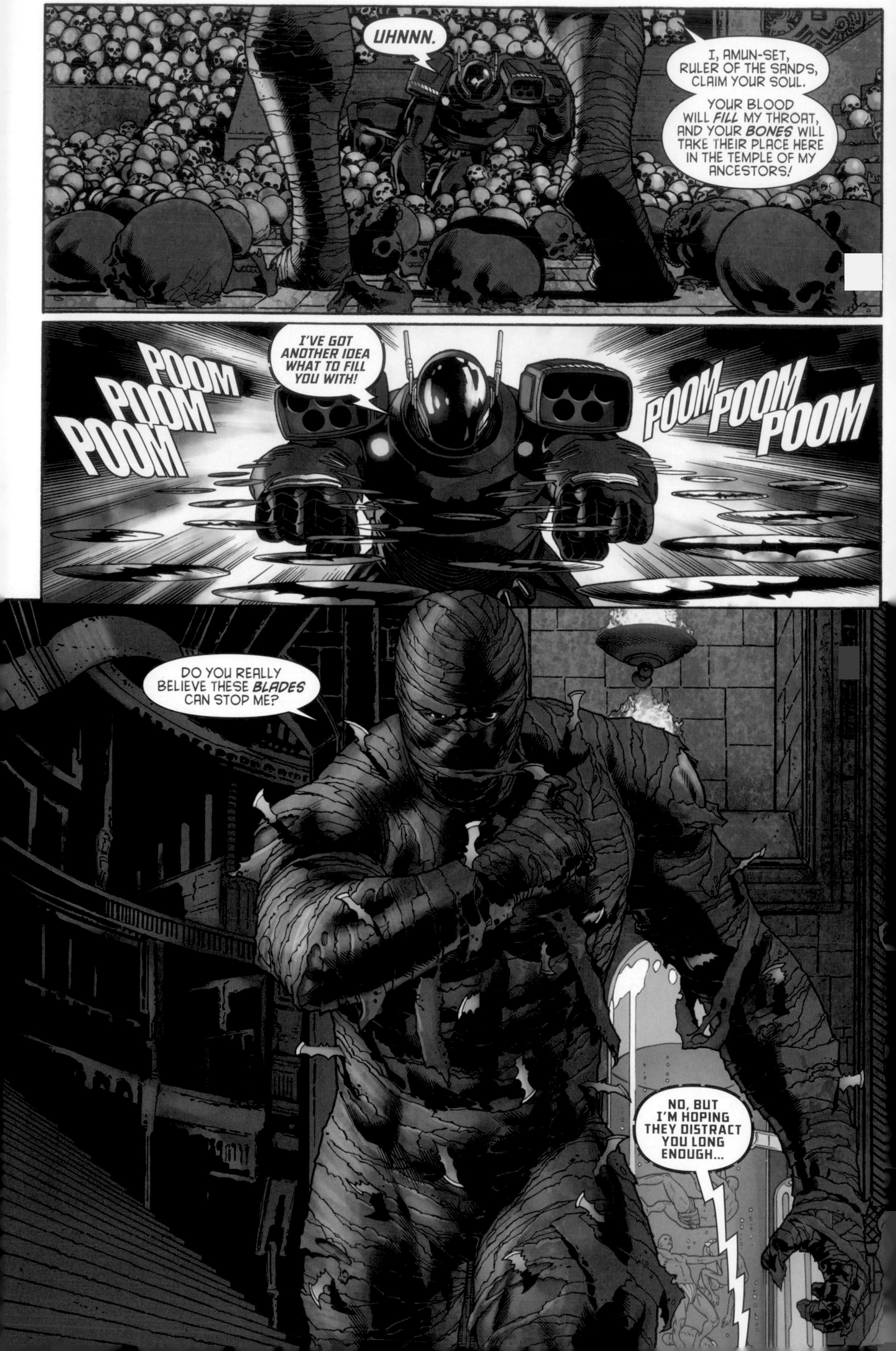
UHNNN.
I, AMUN-SET, RULER OF THE SANDS, CLAIM YOUR SOUL.
YOUR BLOOD WILL FILL MY THROAT, AND YOUR BONES WILL TAKE THEIR PLACE HERE IN THE TEMPLE OF MY ANCESTORS!
POOM POOM POOM
I'VE GOT ANOTHER IDEA WHAT TO FILL YOU WITH!
POOM POOM POOM
DO YOU REALLY BELIEVE THESE BLADES CAN STOP ME?
NO, BUT I'M HOPING THEY DISTRACT YOU LONG ENOUGH...

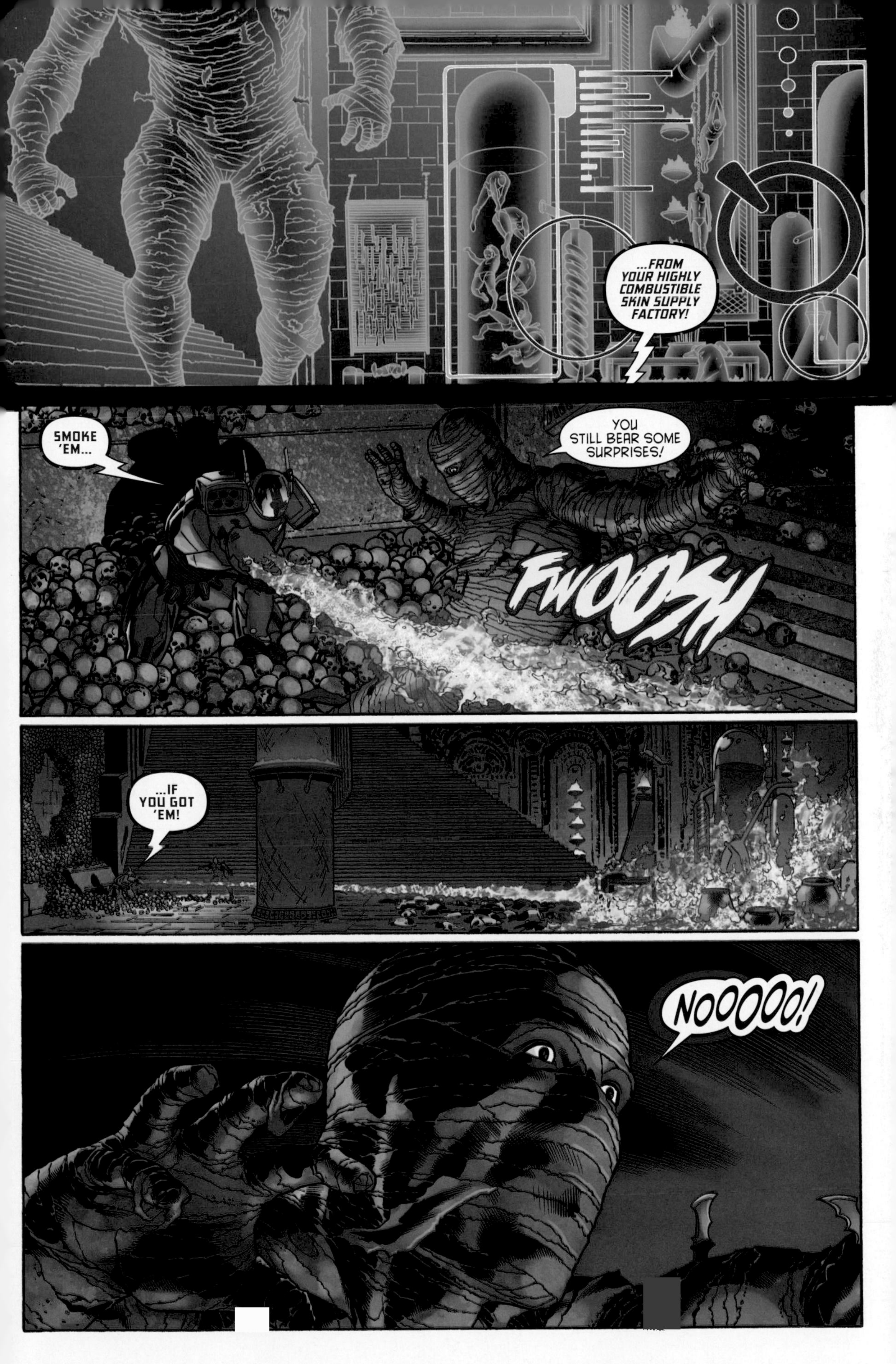
...FROM YOUR HIGHLY COMBUSTIBLE SKIN SUPPLY FACTORY!
SMOKE 'EM...
YOU STILL BEAR SOME SURPRISES!
FWOOSH
...IF YOU GOT 'EM!
NOOOOO!

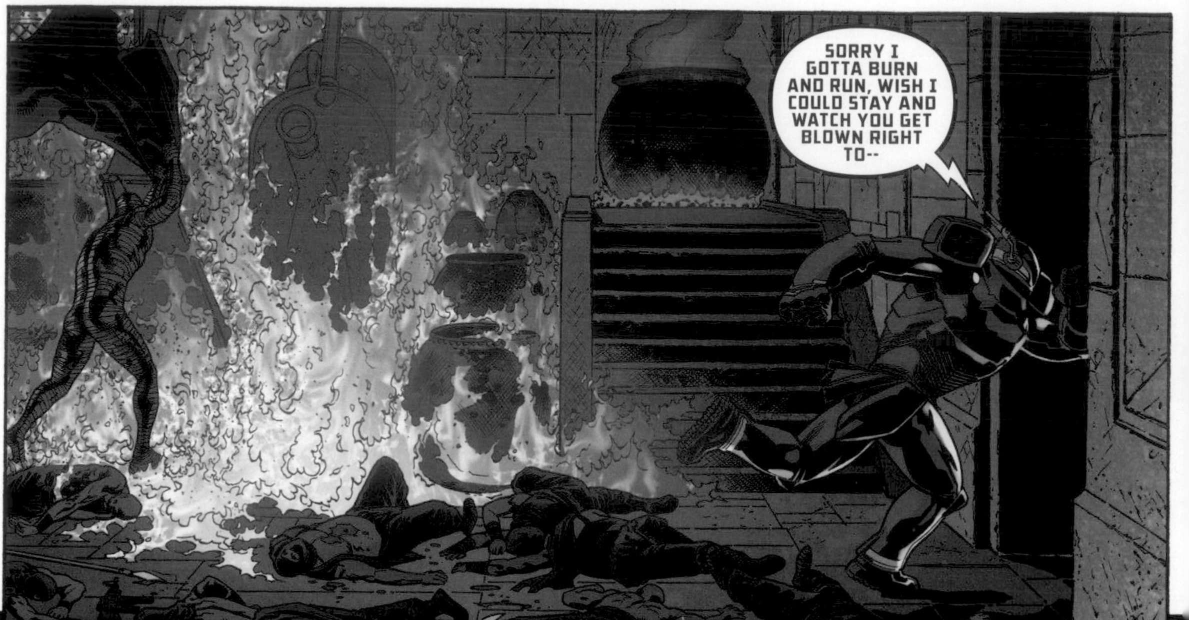
SORRY I GOTTA BURN AND RUN, WISH I COULD STAY AND WATCH YOU GET BLOWN RIGHT TO--

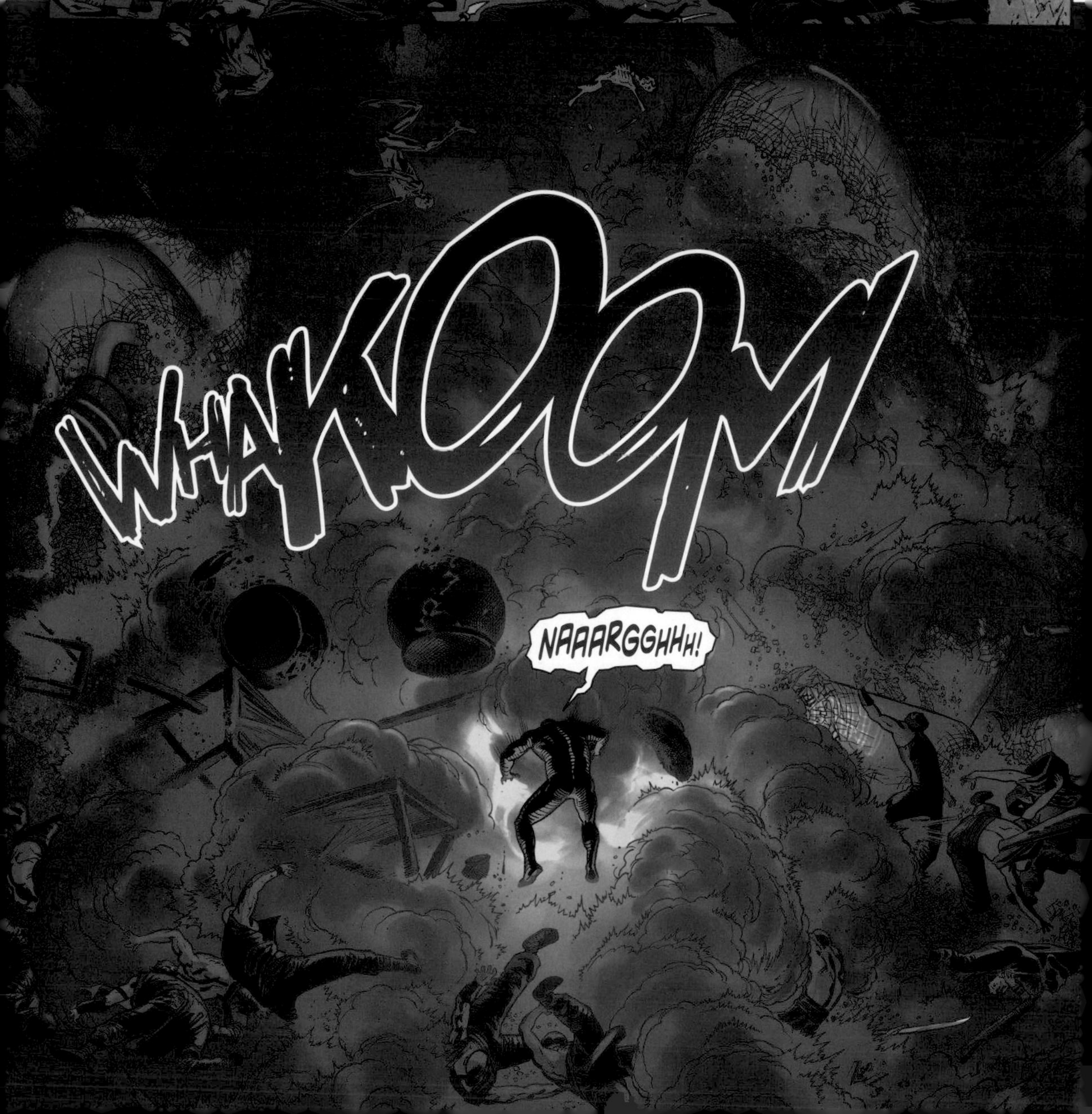
WHAKOOM
NAAARGGHH!

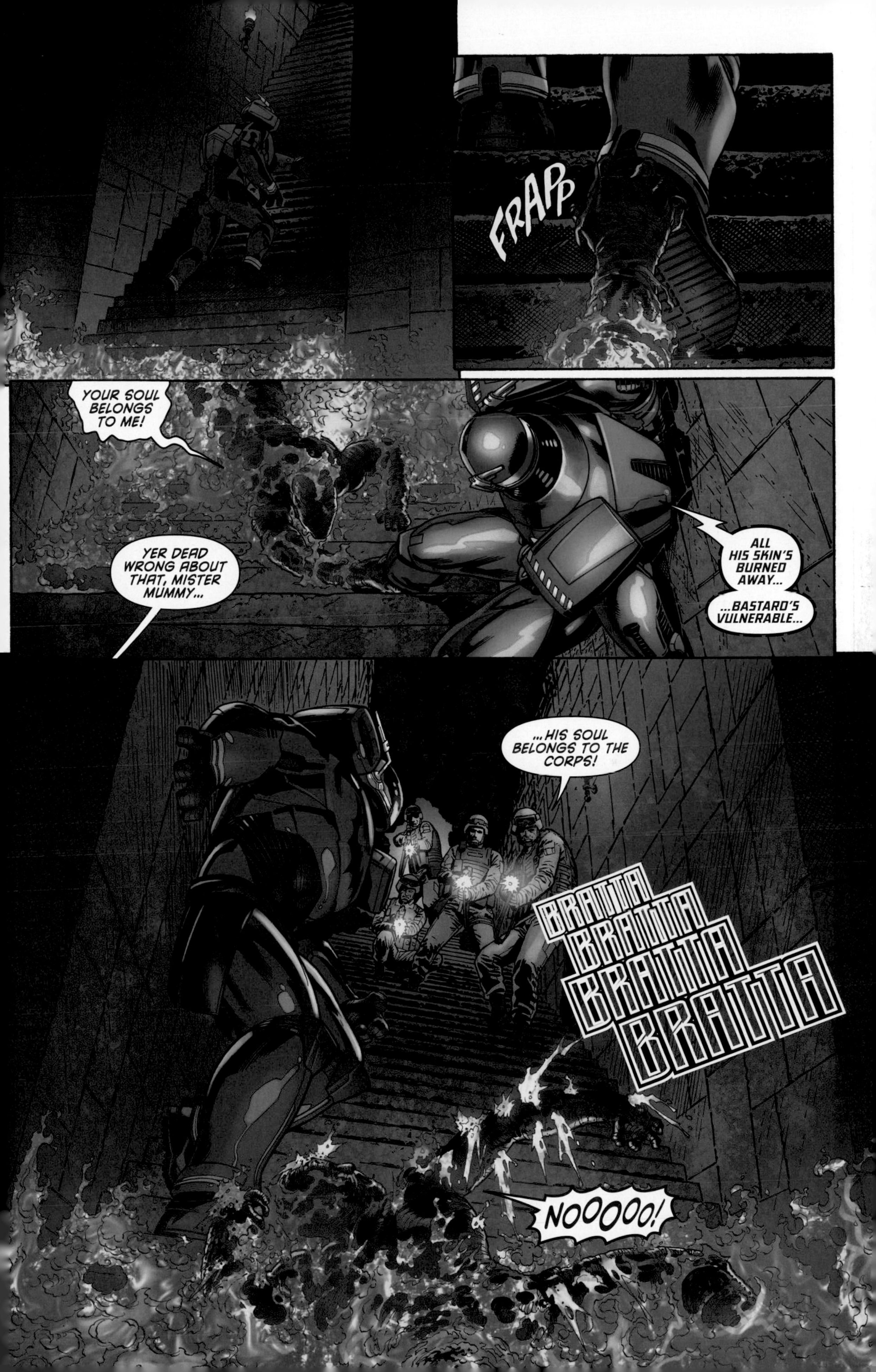
FRAPP
YOUR SOUL BELONGS TO ME!
ALL HIS SKIN'S BURNED AWAY...
...BASTARD'S VULNERABLE...
YER DEAD WRONG ABOUT THAT, MISTER MUMMY...
...HIS SOUL BELONGS TO THE CORPS!
BRATTA BRATTA BRATTA BRATTA
NOOOOO!

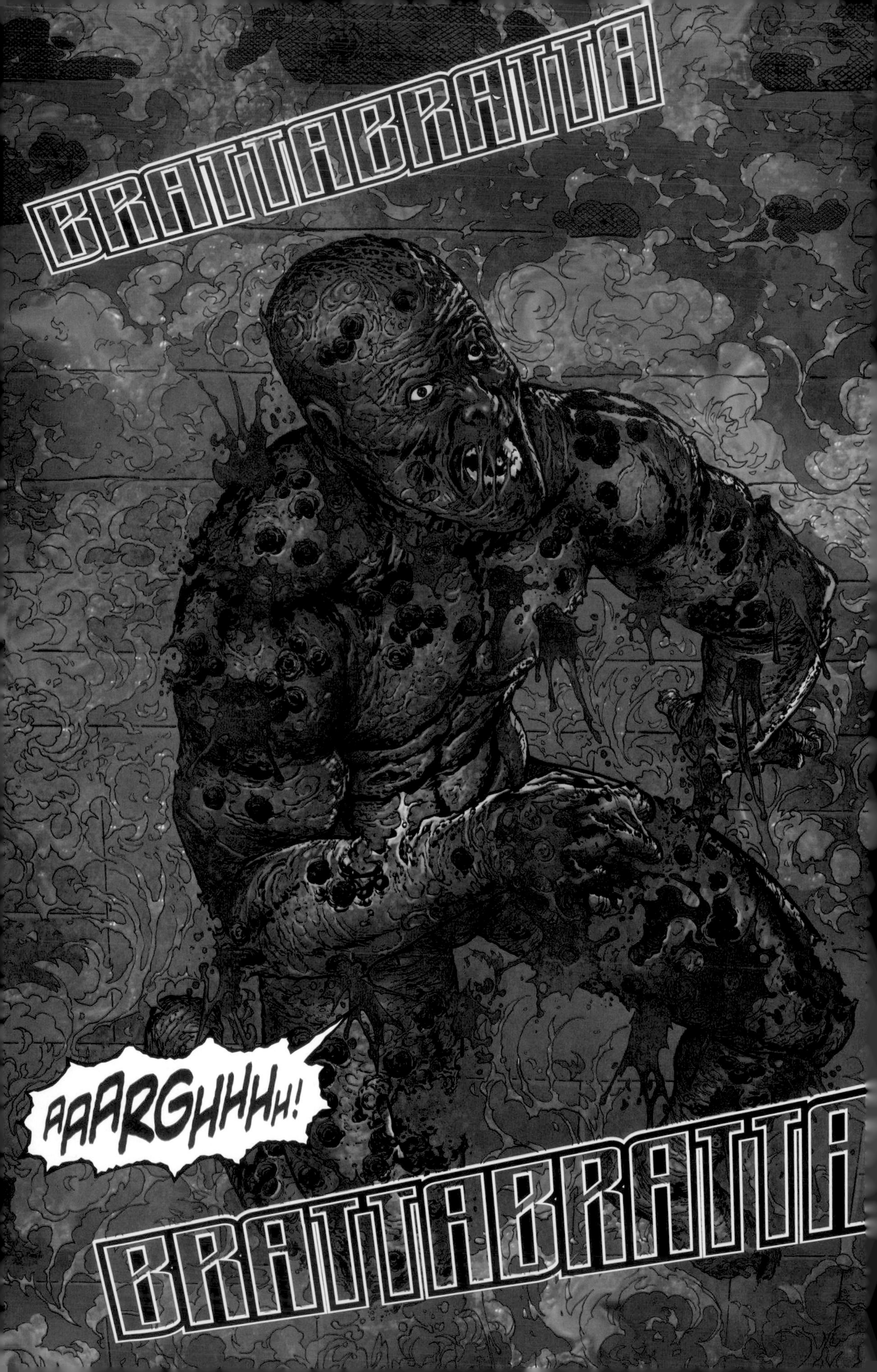
BRATTABRATTA
AAARGHHHH!
BRATTABRATTA

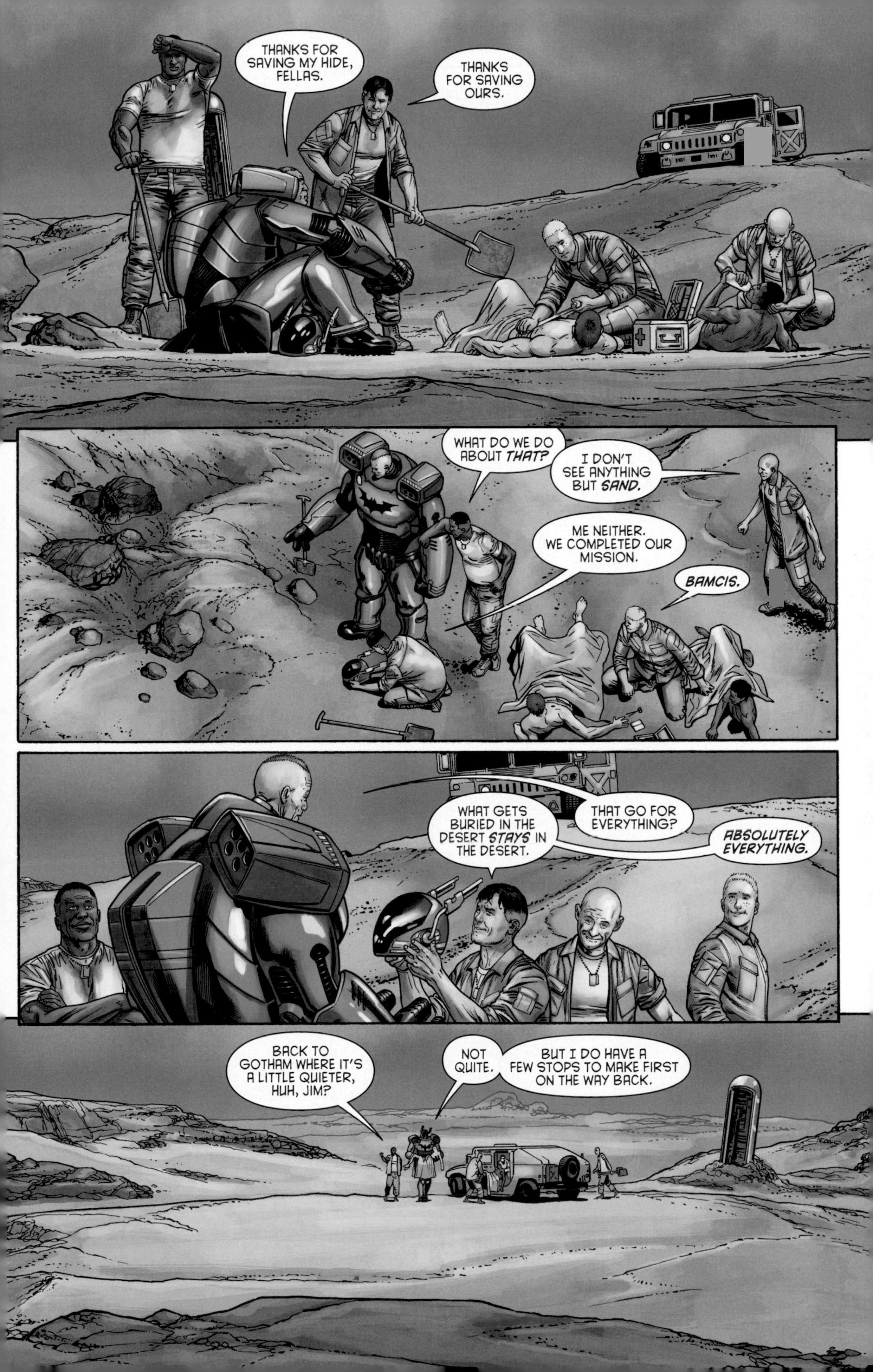
THANKS FOR SAVING MY HIDE, FELLAS.
THANKS FOR SAVING OURS.
WHAT DO WE DO ABOUT THAT?
I DON'T SEE ANYTHING BUT SAND.
ME NEITHER. WE COMPLETED OUR MISSION.
BAMCIS.
THAT GO FOR EVERYTHING?
WHAT GETS BURIED IN THE DESERT STAYS IN THE DESERT.
ABSOLUTELY EVERYTHING.
BACK TO GOTHAM WHERE IT'S A LITTLE QUIETER, HUH, JIM?
NOT QUITE.
BUT I DO HAVE A FEW STOPS TO MAKE FIRST ON THE WAY BACK.

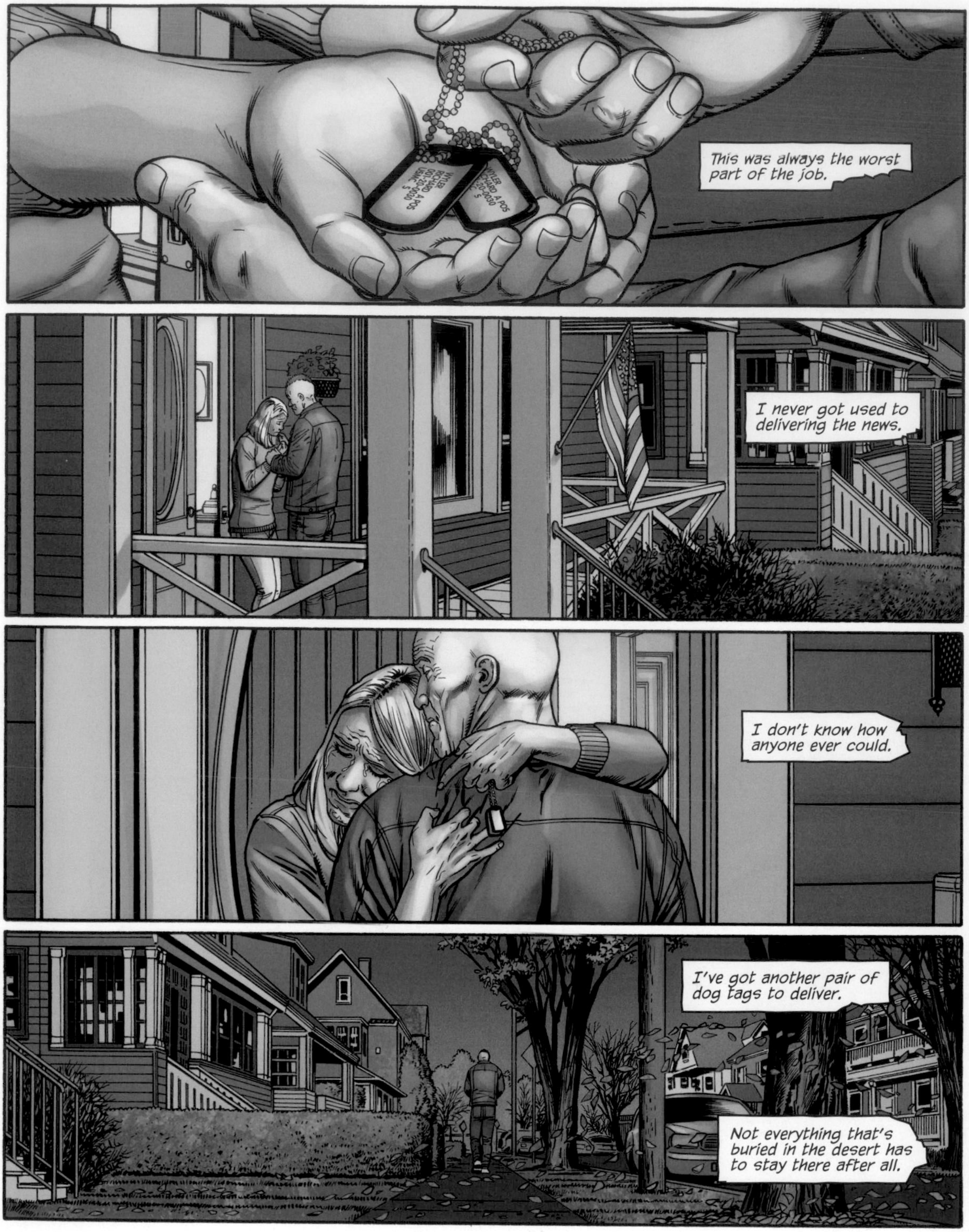
This was always the worst part of the job.
I never got used to delivering the news.
I don't know how anyone ever could.
I've got another pair of dog tags to deliver.
Not everything that's buried in the desert has to stay there after all.

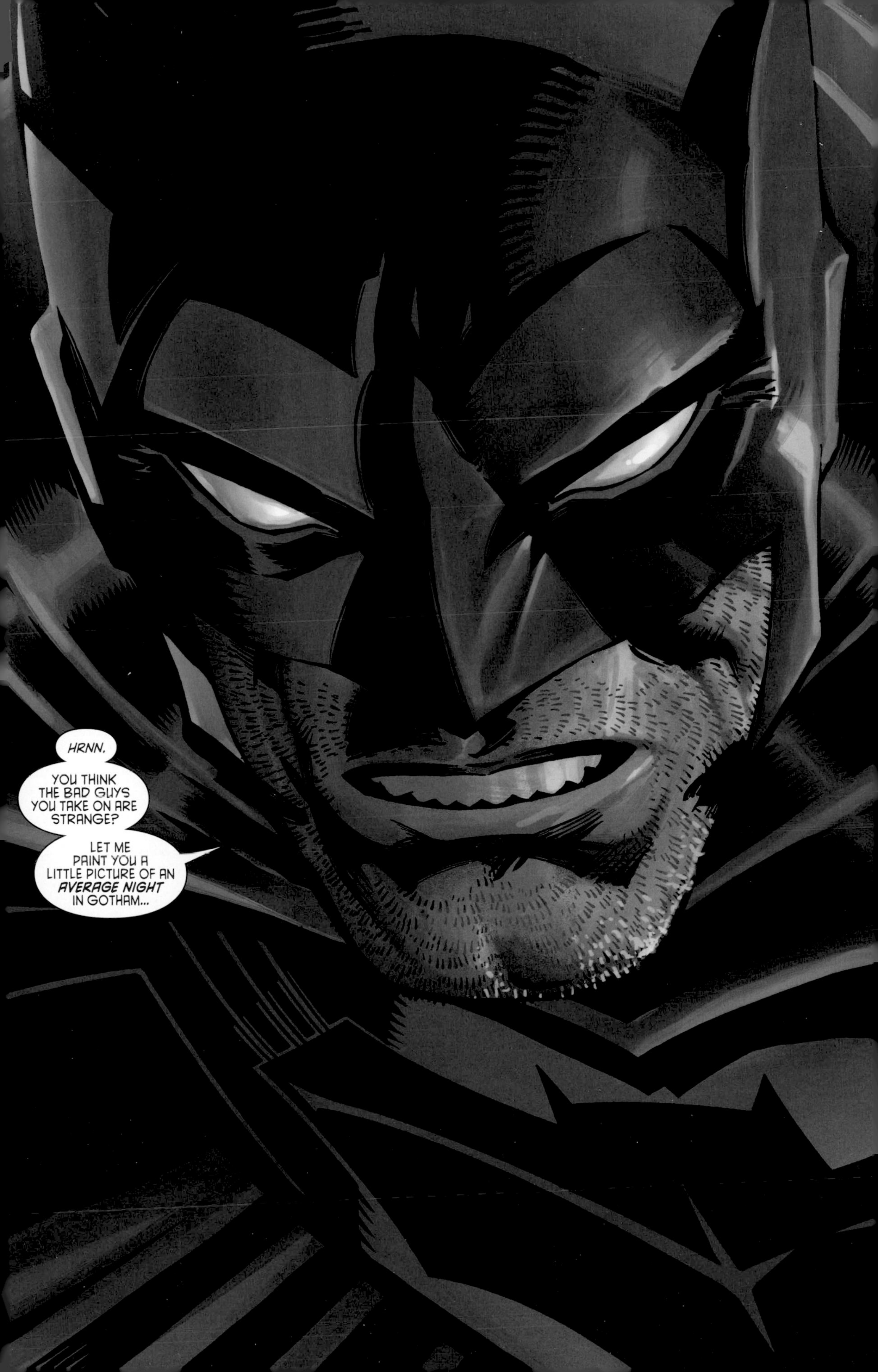
HRNN.
YOU THINK THE BAD GUYS YOU TAKE ON ARE STRANGE?
LET ME PAINT YOU A LITTLE PICTURE OF AN *AVERAGE NIGHT* IN GOTHAM...

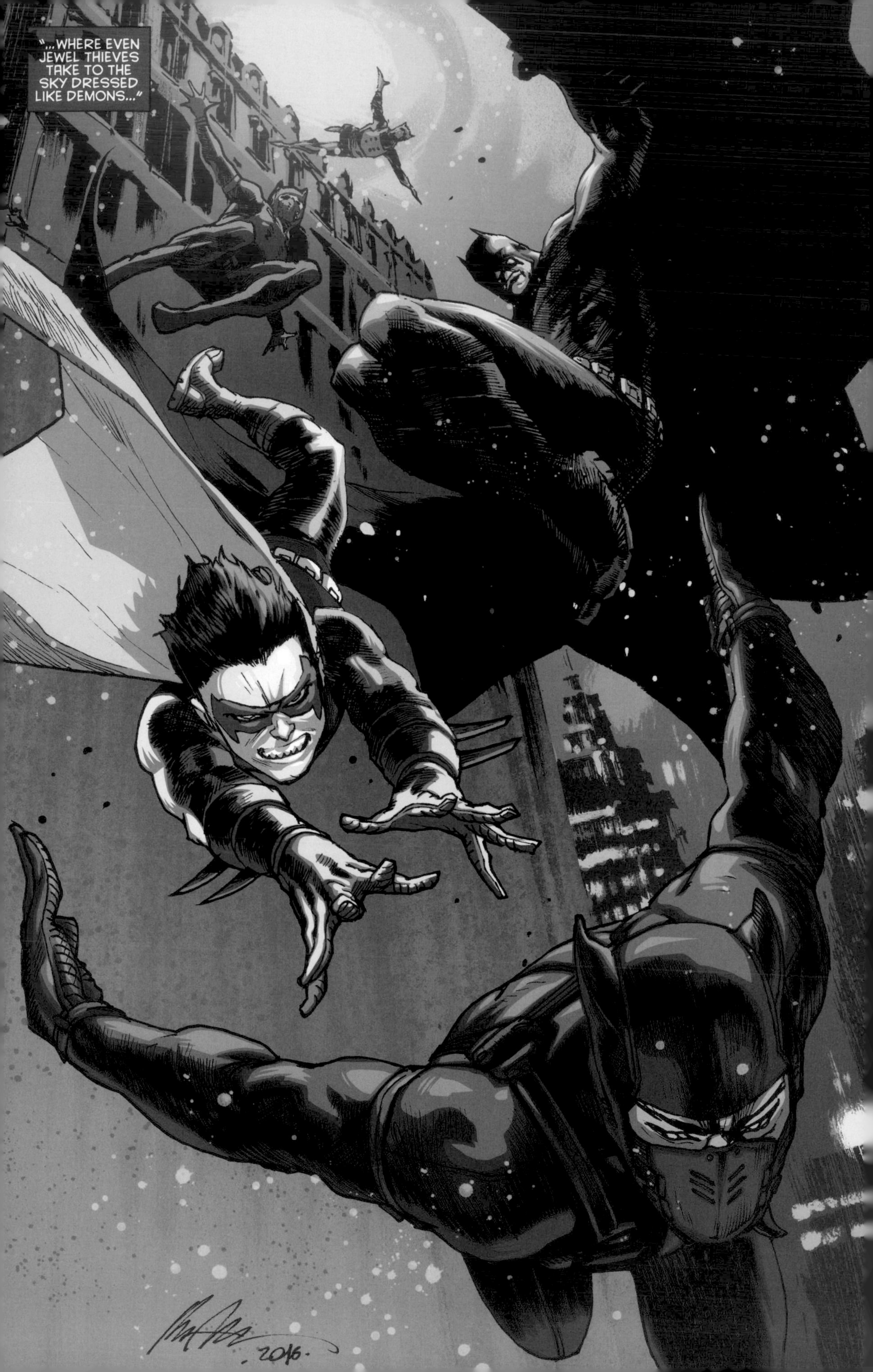
"...WHERE EVEN JEWEL THIEVES TAKE TO THE SKY DRESSED LIKE DEMONS..."
2016

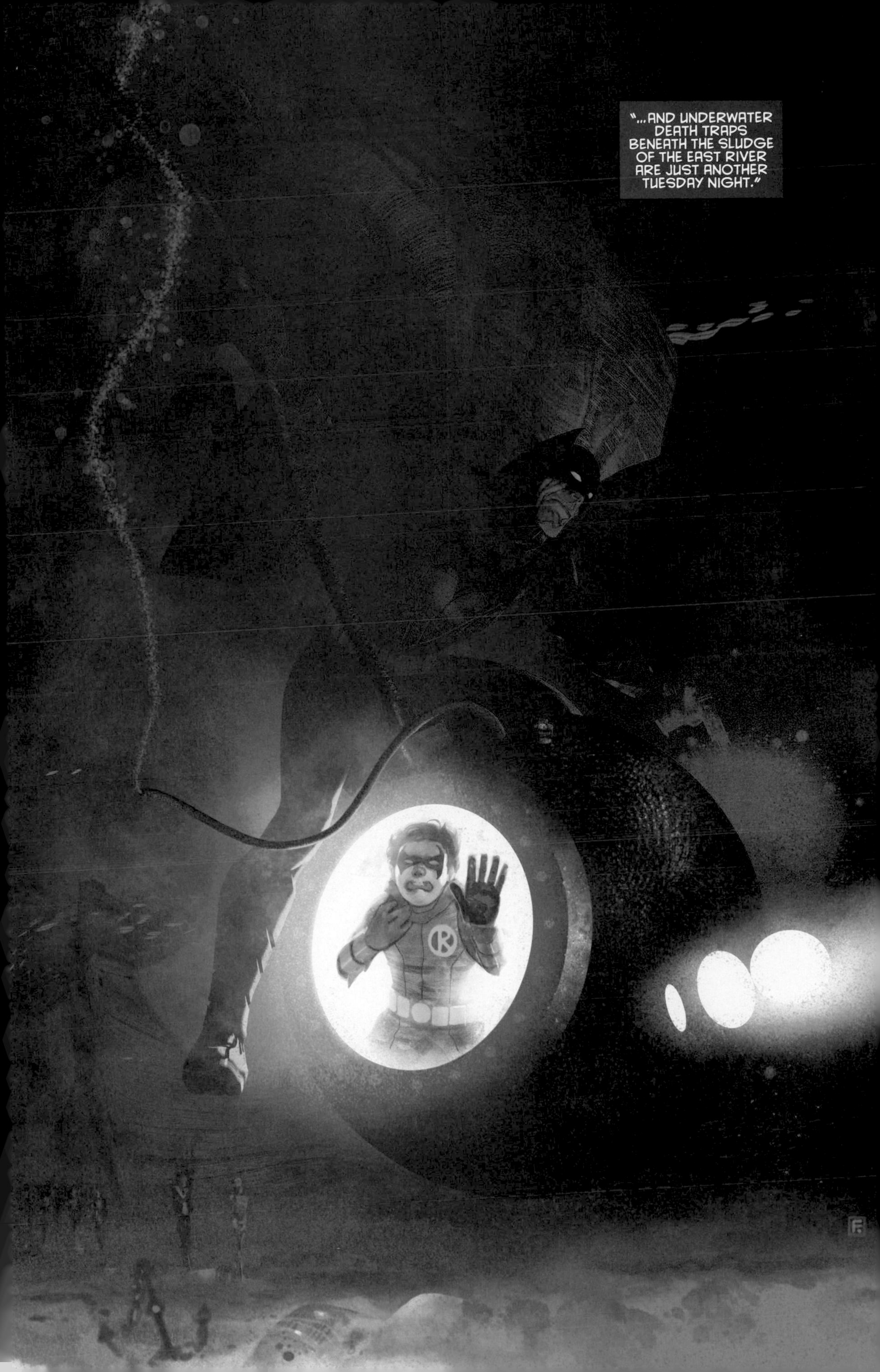
"...AND UNDERWATER DEATH TRAPS BENEATH THE SLUDGE OF THE EAST RIVER ARE JUST ANOTHER TUESDAY NIGHT."

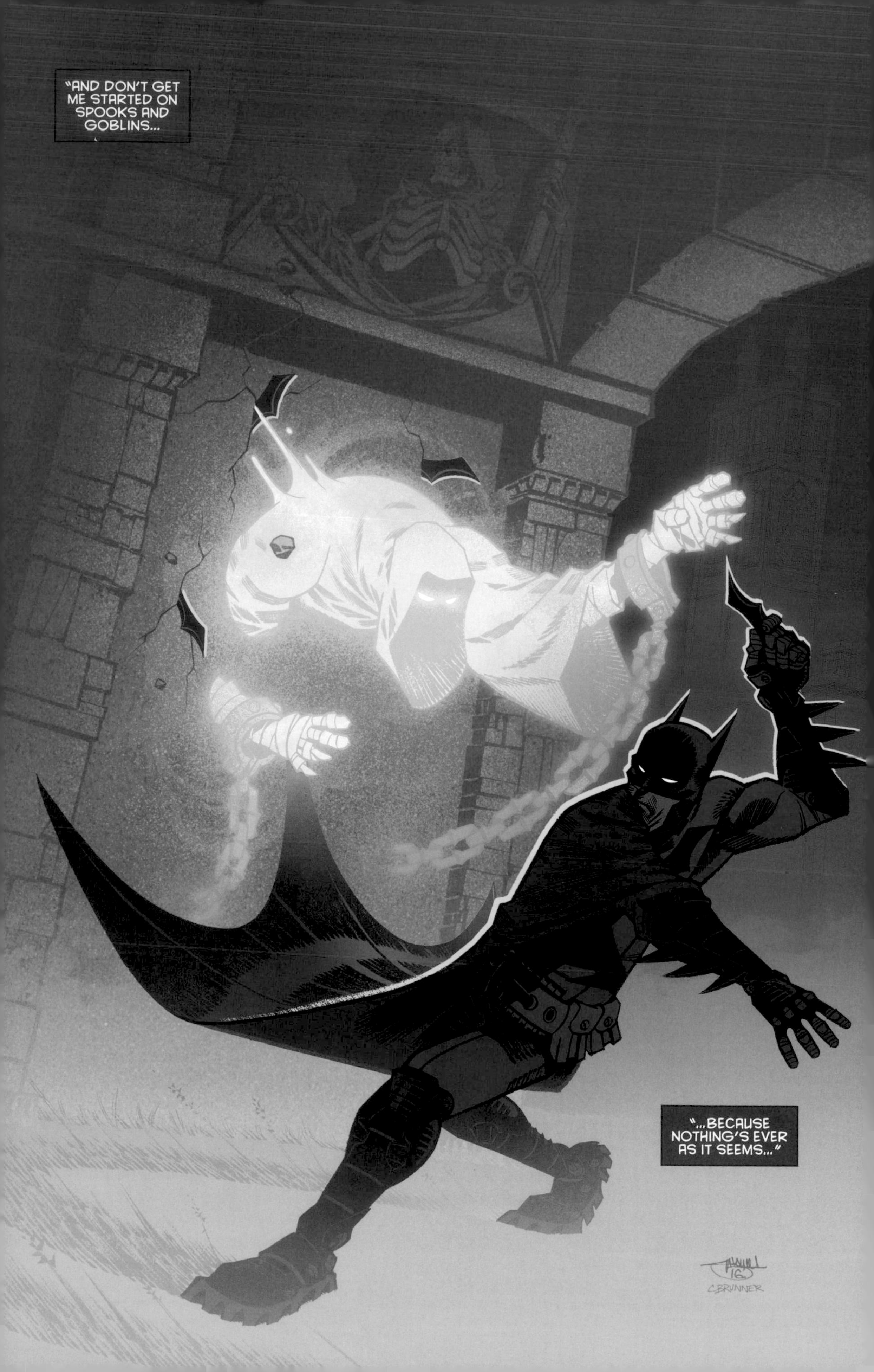
"AND DON'T GET ME STARTED ON SPOOKS AND GOBLINS...
"...BECAUSE NOTHING'S EVER AS IT SEEMS..."
C.BRUNNER

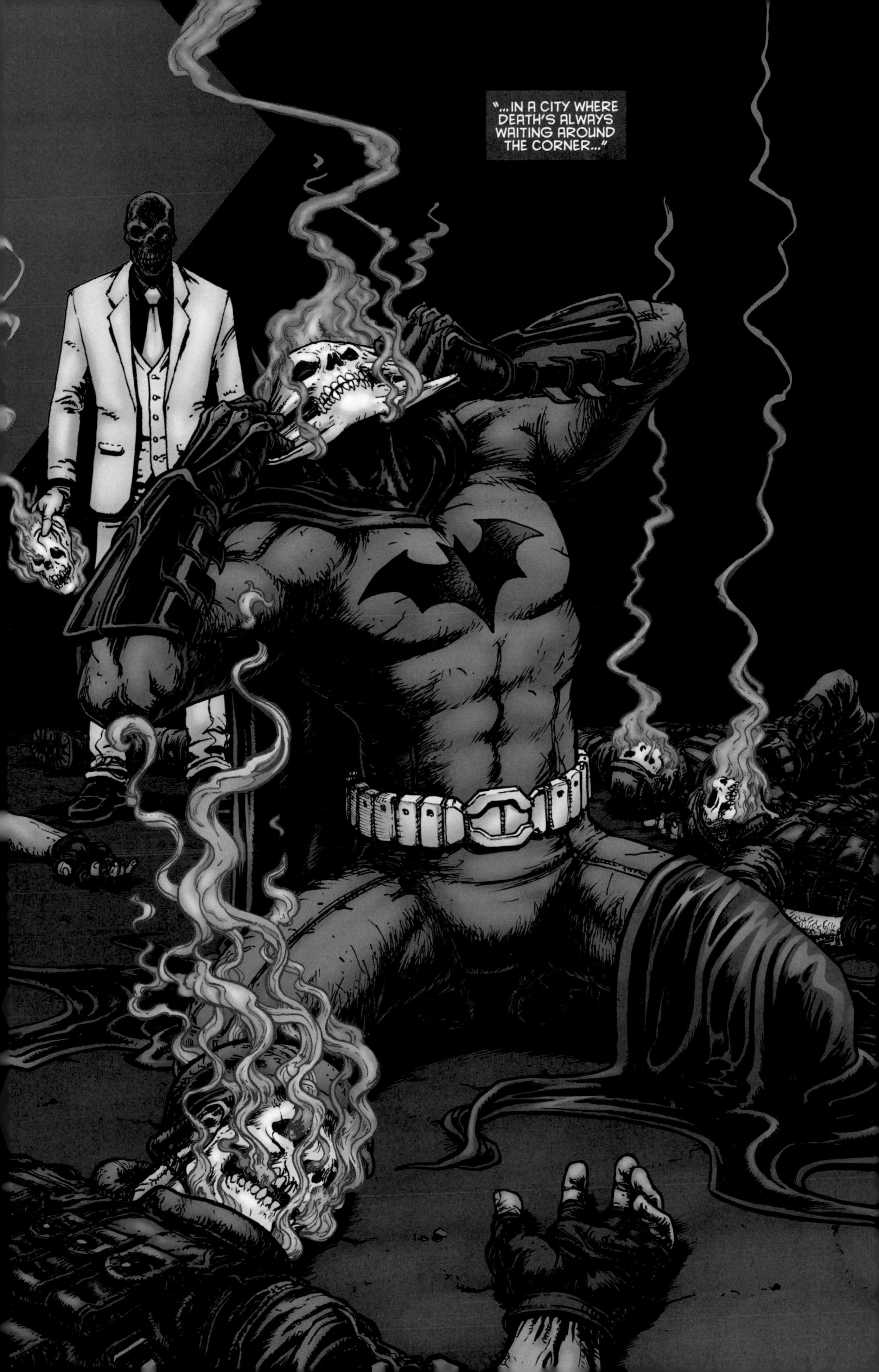
"...IN A CITY WHERE DEATH'S ALWAYS WAITING AROUND THE CORNER..."

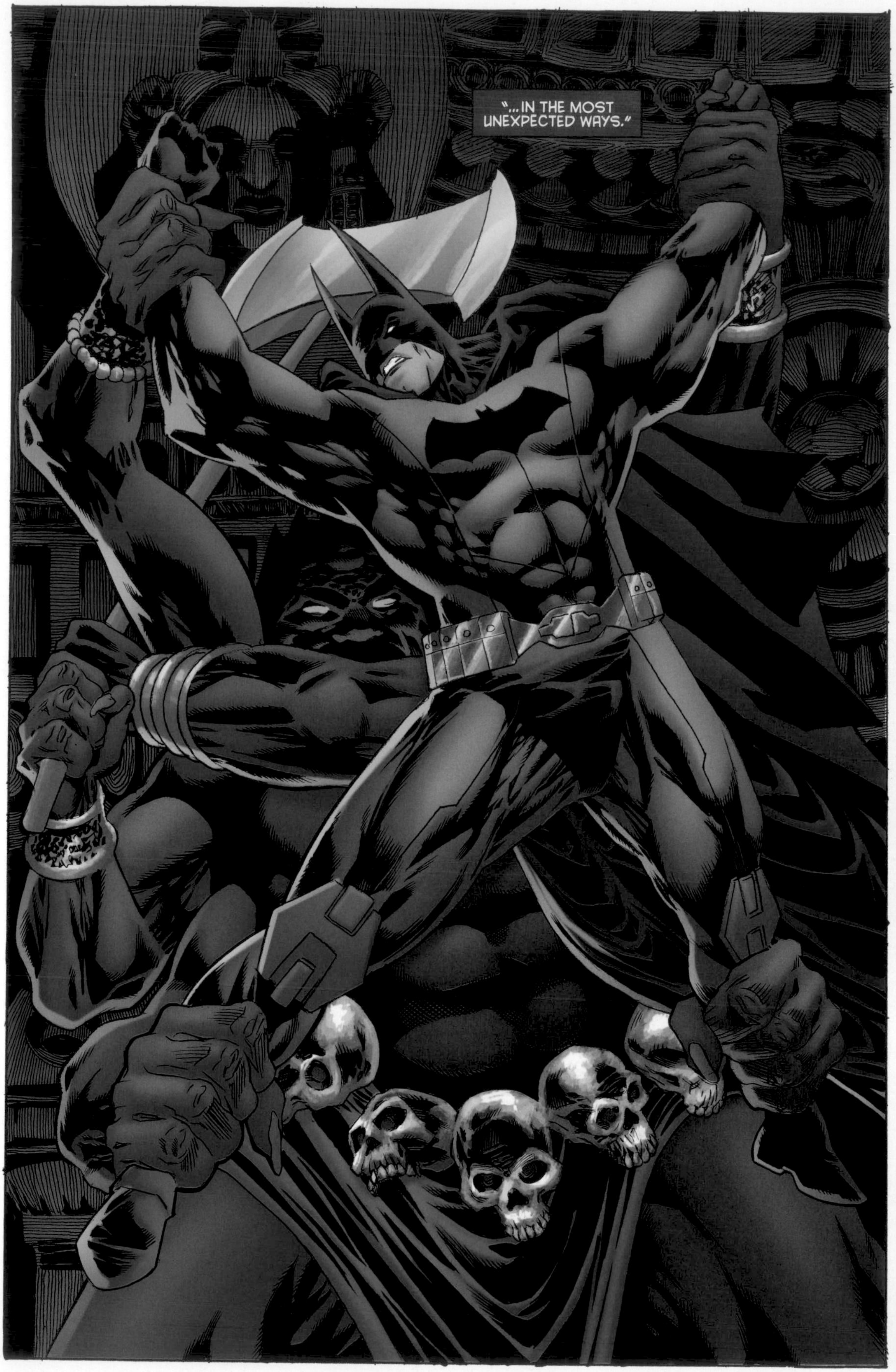
"...IN THE MOST UNEXPECTED WAYS."

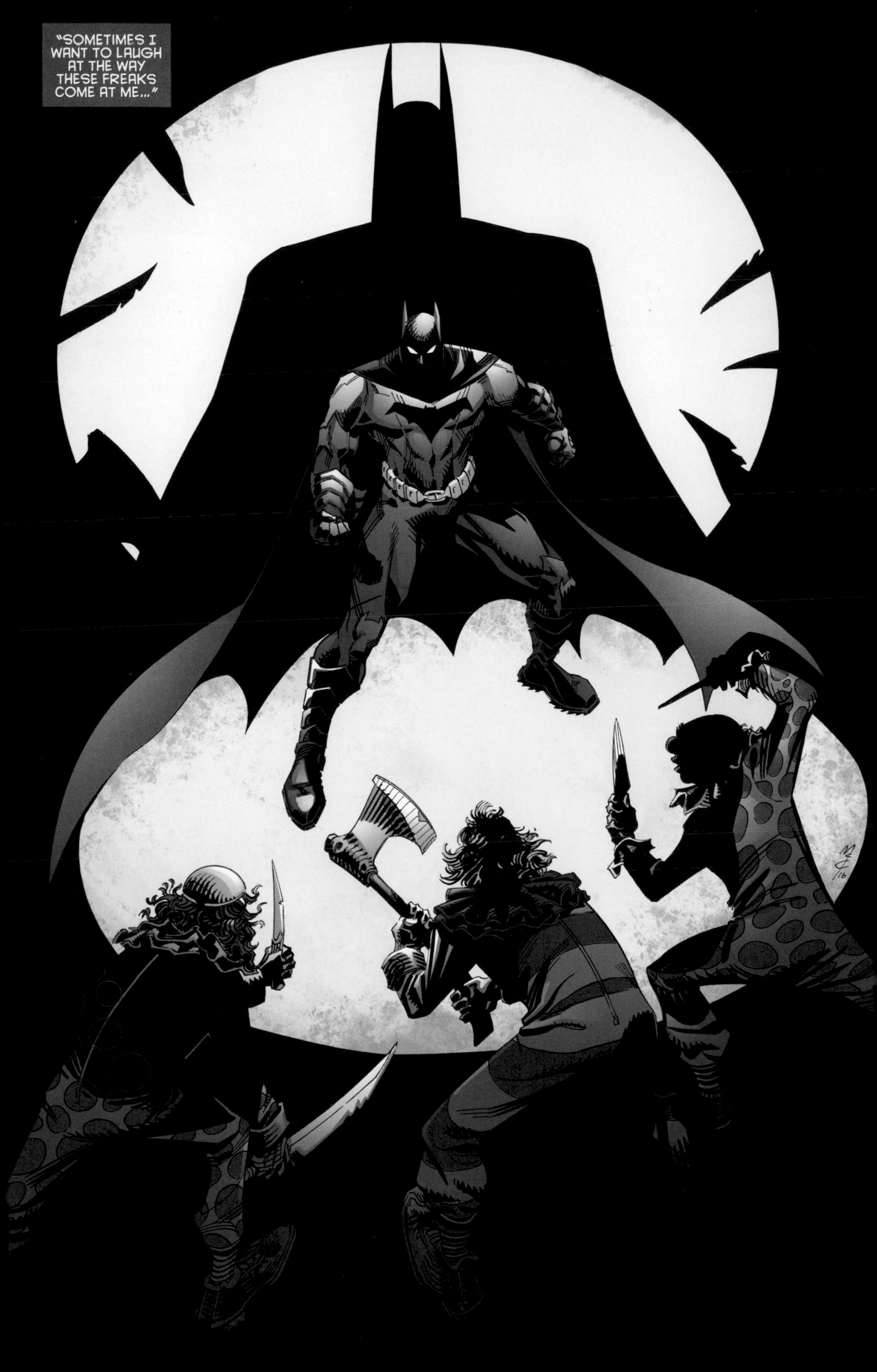
"SOMETIMES I WANT TO LAUGH AT THE WAY THESE FREAKS COME AT ME..."

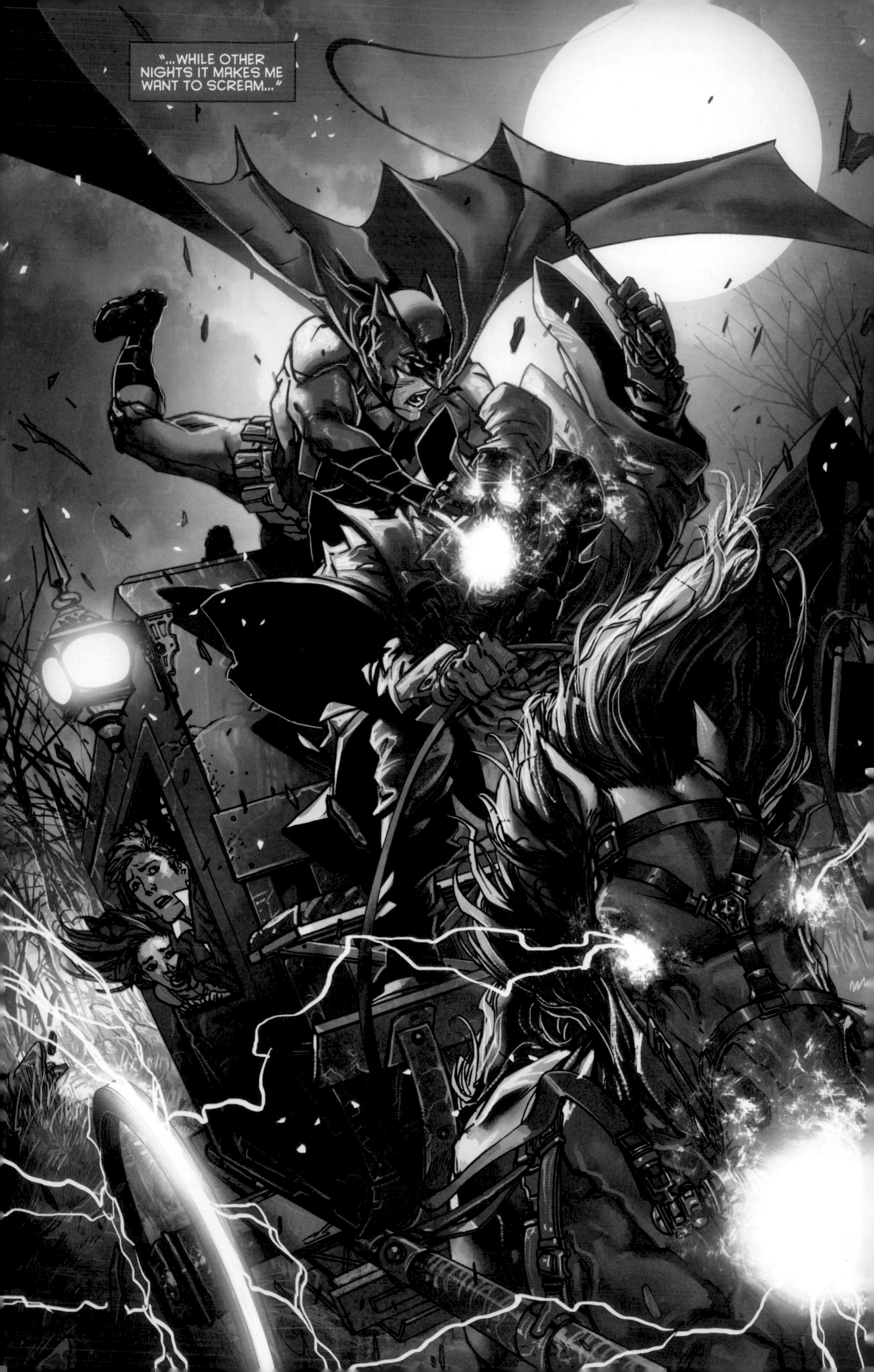
"...WHILE OTHER NIGHTS IT MAKES ME WANT TO SCREAM..."

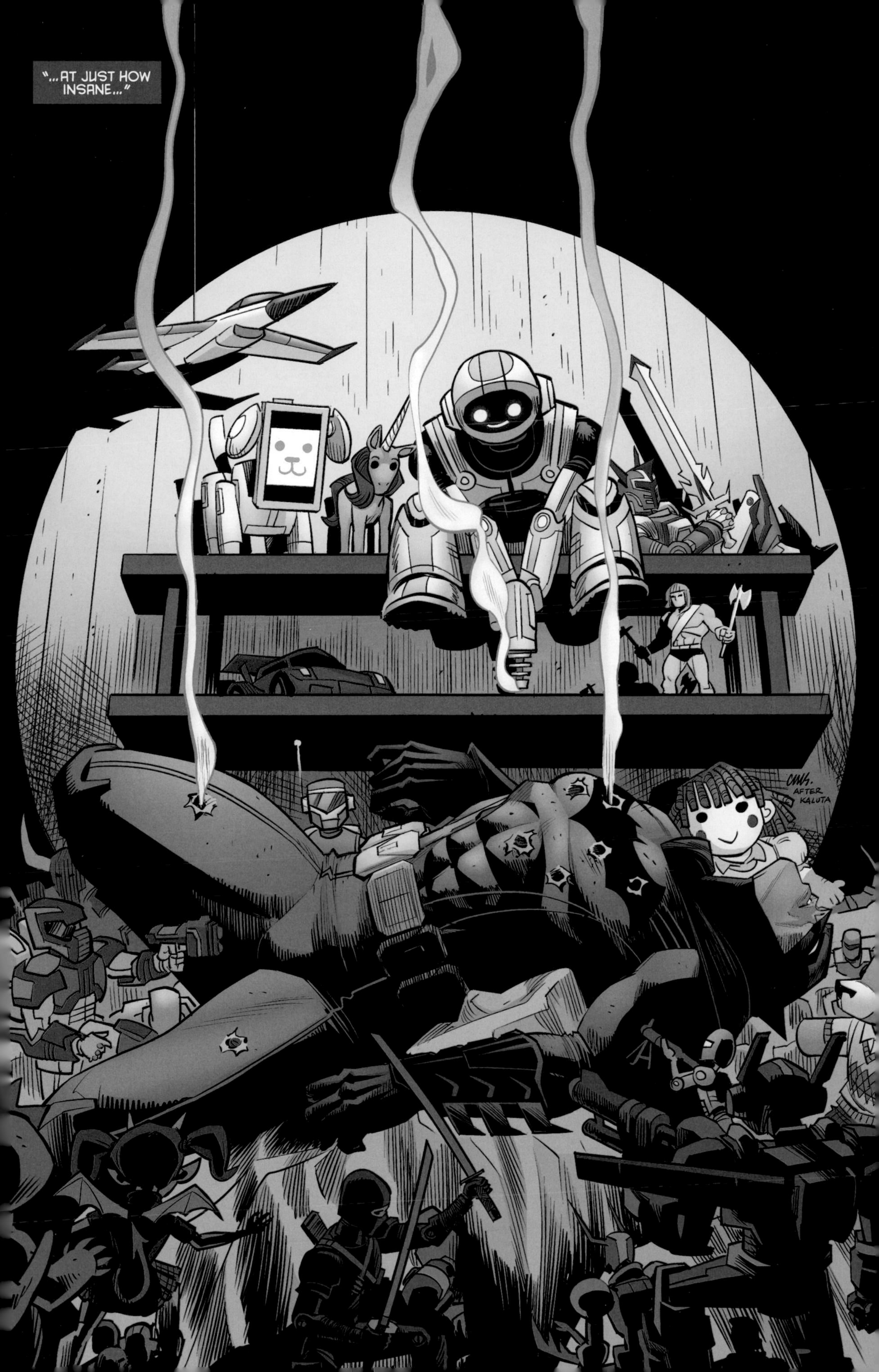
"...AT JUST HOW INSANE..."
AFTER KALUTA

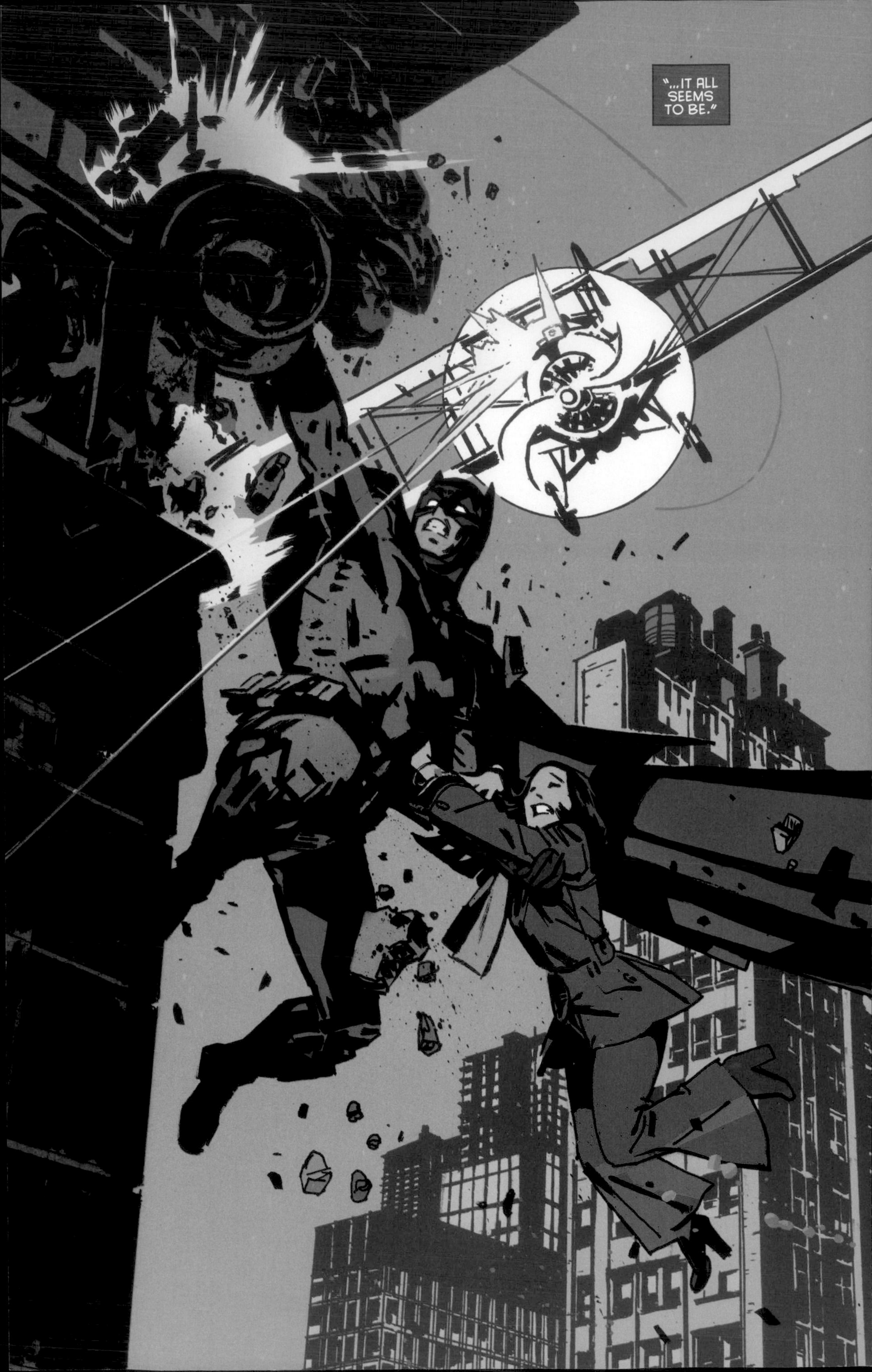
"...IT ALL SEEMS TO BE."

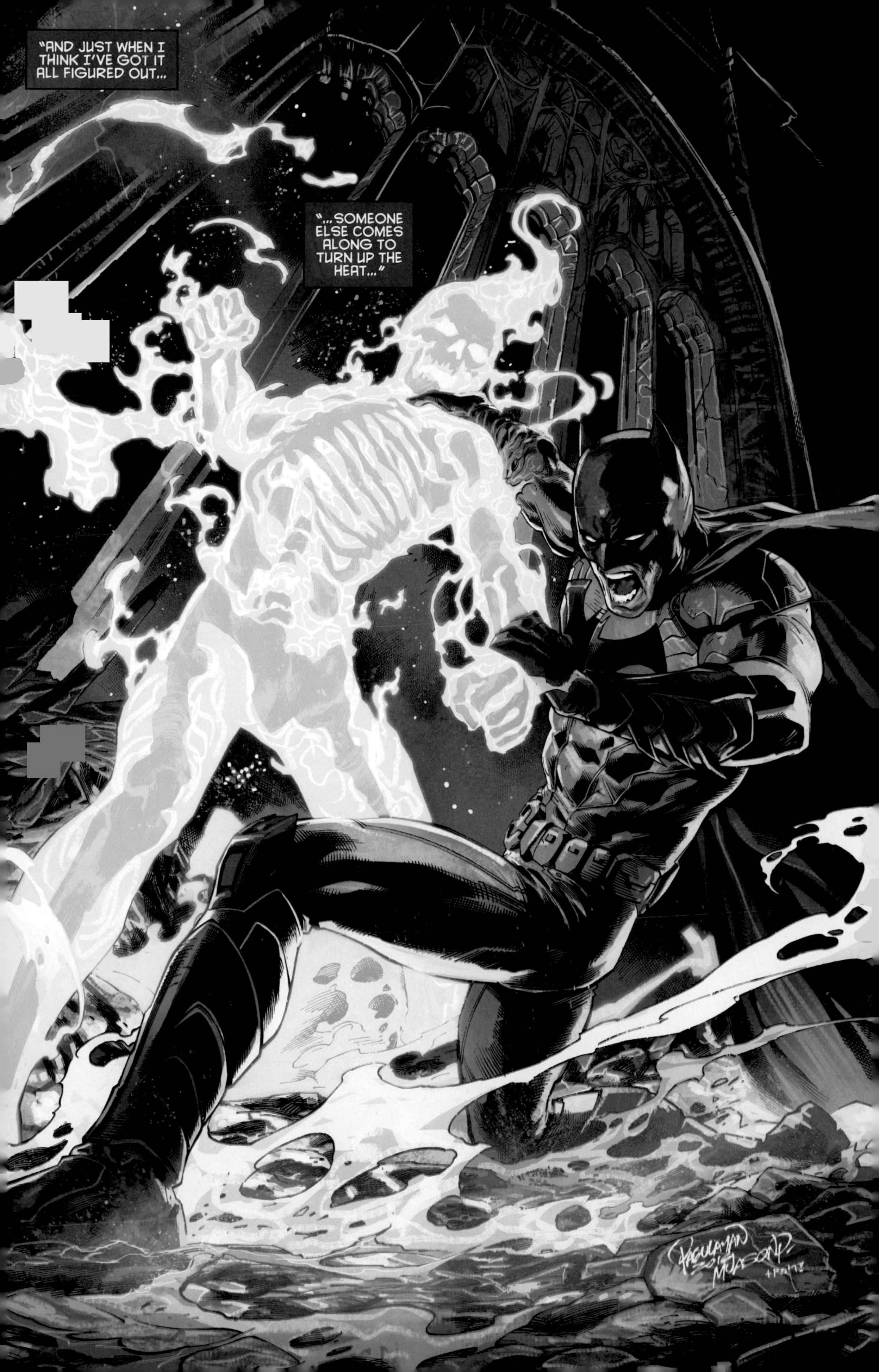
"AND JUST WHEN I THINK I'VE GOT IT ALL FIGURED OUT...
"...SOMEONE ELSE COMES ALONG TO TURN UP THE HEAT..."

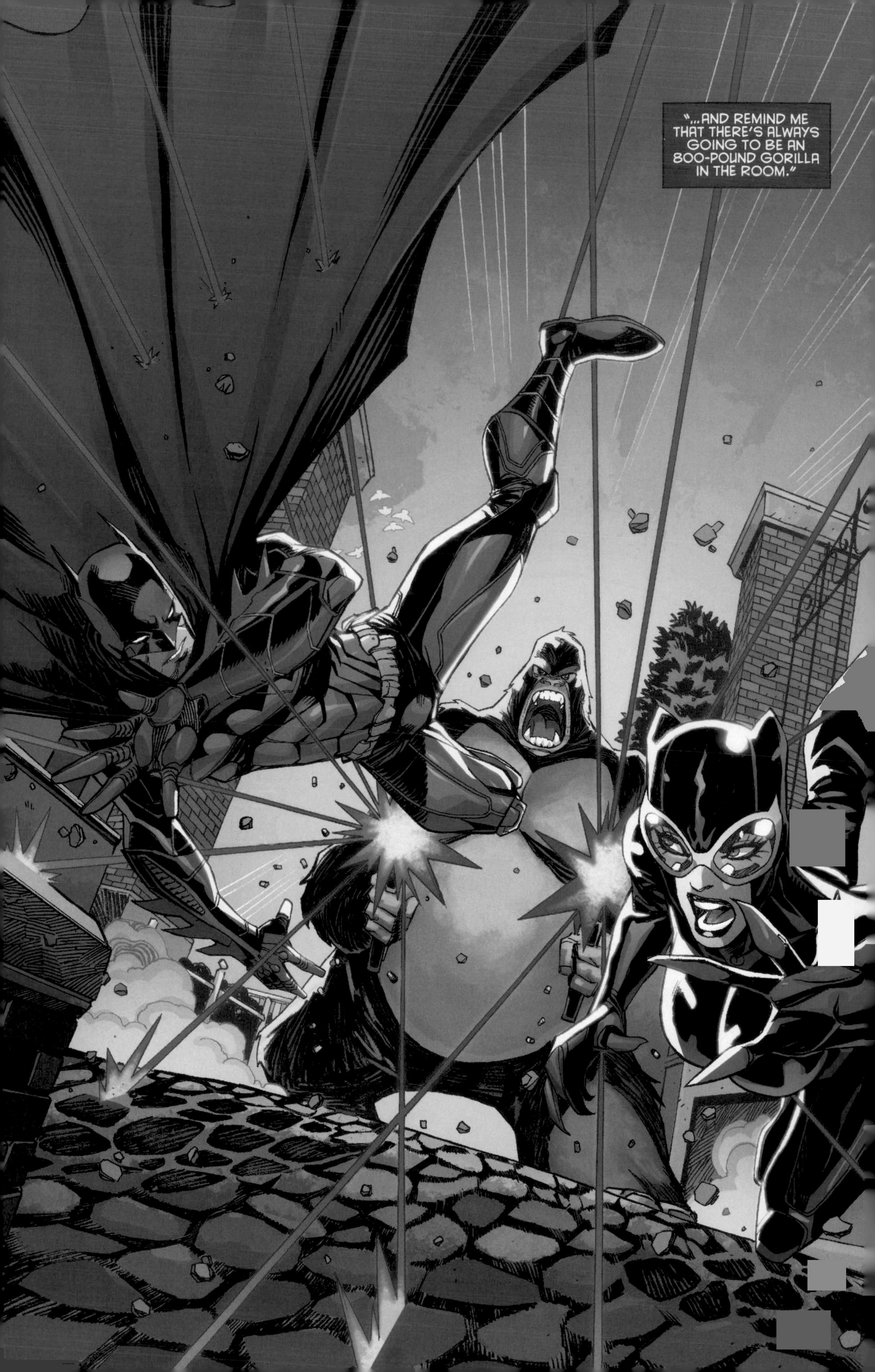
"...AND REMIND ME THAT THERE'S ALWAYS GOING TO BE AN 800-POUND GORILLA IN THE ROOM."

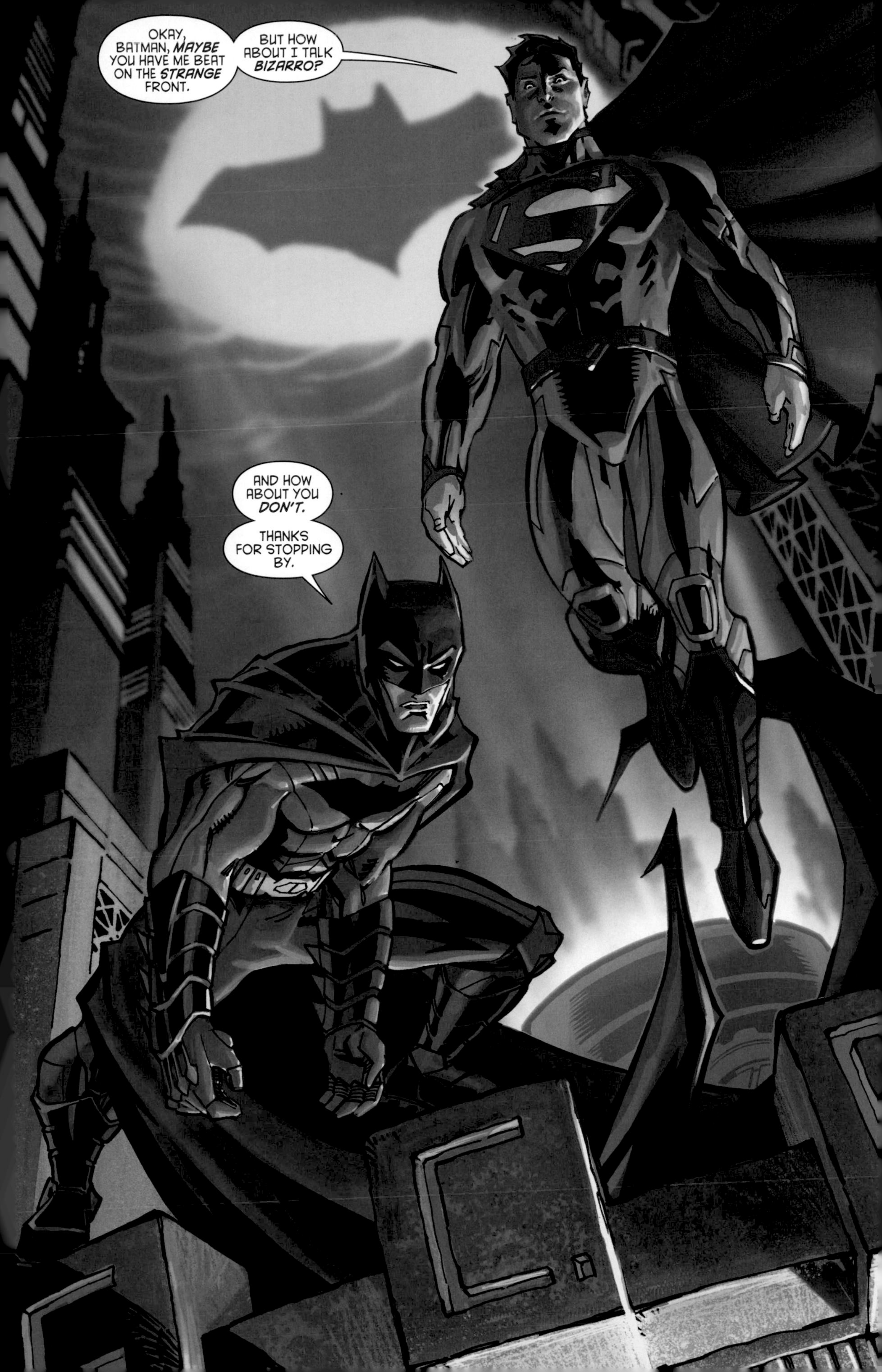
OKAY, BATMAN, MAYBE YOU HAVE ME BEAT ON THE STRANGE FRONT.
BUT HOW ABOUT I TALK BIZARRO?
AND HOW ABOUT YOU DON'T.
THANKS FOR STOPPING BY.

THE 11 CURIOUS CASES OF BATMAN

PETER J. TOMASI: WRITER SCOTT MCDANIEL & DEAN WHITE: ARTISTS (PAGES 129 & 141)

WES ABBOTT: LETTERER DAVE WIELGOSZ: ASSISTANT EDITOR REBECCA TAYLOR: ASSOCIATE EDITOR

MARK DOYLE: EDITOR BATMAN CREATED BY BOB KANE WITH BILL FINGER

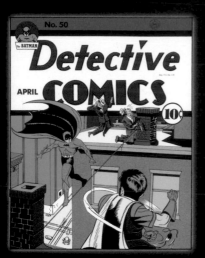

No. 50
The BATMAN
Detective COMICS
APRIL
10¢

PAGE 130 BY RAFAEL ALBUQUERQUE + DAVE MCCAIG AFTER BOB KANE + JERRY ROBINSON

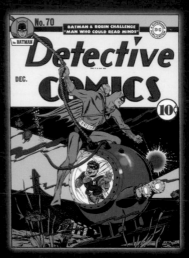

No. 70
BATMAN & ROBIN CHALLENGE "MAN WHO COULD READ MINDS"
The BATMAN
Detective COMICS
DEC.
10¢

PAGE 131 BY FRAZER IRVING AFTER JERRY ROBINSON

DC
THRILLING MYSTERY TALES
20¢
Detective COMICS
NO. 434 APR.
NO CHAINS CAN BIND ME— NO WALLS CONTAIN ME!
I COME AND GO AS I PLEASE—FOR I AM—
THE SPOOK!
The CAPED CRUSADER TACKLES THE PHANTOM PERIL of "the SPOOK THAT STALKED BATMAN!"
HAWKMAN
The WINGED DETECTIVE SOLVES "the RIDDLE of the RED-HANDED ROBBER!"

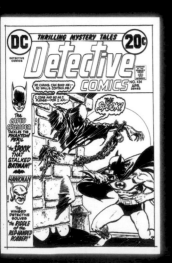

PAGE 132 BY SHAWN CRYSTAL + CHRIS BRUNNER AFTER

DC
Detective Comics
STARRING
BATMAN
BY DOUG MOENCH & KLAUS JANSON
THE MASK OF THE BLACK DEATH!
JANSON

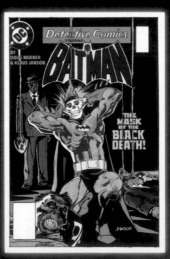

PAGE 133 BY CHRIS BURNHAM + NATHAN FAIRBAIRN AFTER KLAUS JANSON

DC
Detective COMICS
ALAN GRANT
NORM BREYFOGLE
STEVE MITCHELL

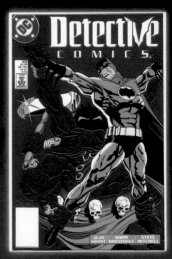

PAGE 134 BY KELLEY JONES + MICHELLE MADSEN AFTER NORM BREYFOGLE

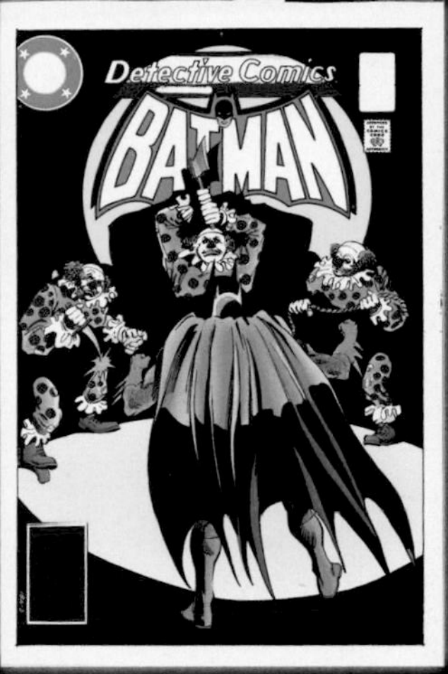
Detective Comics
BATMAN

PAGE 135 BY JOHN McCREA + JOHN KALISZ AFTER GENE COLAN + DICK GIORDANO

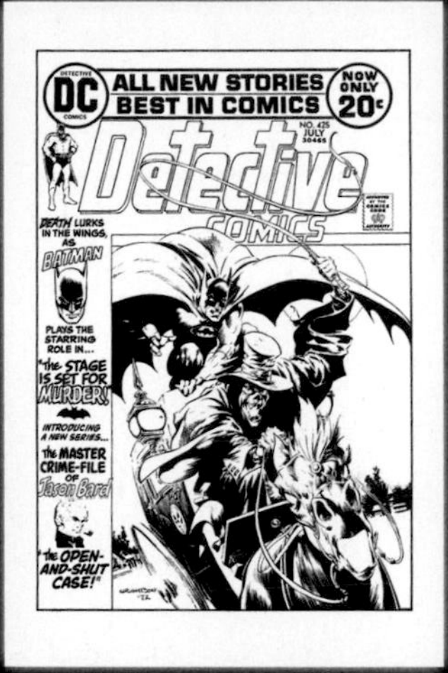
DC
ALL NEW STORIES
BEST IN COMICS
NOW ONLY 20¢
NO. 425
JULY
Detective
COMICS
DEATH LURKS IN THE WINGS, AS BATMAN PLAYS THE STARRING ROLE IN...
"The STAGE IS SET FOR MURDER!"
INTRODUCING A NEW SERIES...
The MASTER CRIME-FILE OF Jason Bard
"The OPEN-AND-SHUT CASE!"

PAGE 136 BY CARMINE DI GIANDOMENICO + ROMULO FAJARDO, JR. AFTER BERNIE WRIGHTSON

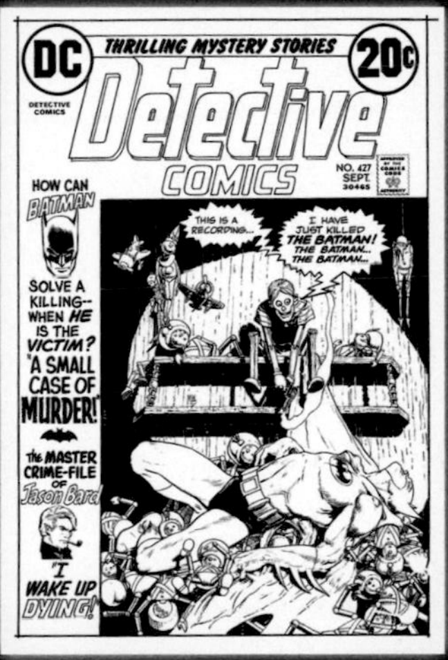
DC
THRILLING MYSTERY STORIES
20¢
Detective
COMICS
NO. 427
SEPT.
HOW CAN BATMAN SOLVE A KILLING--WHEN HE IS THE VICTIM?
"A SMALL CASE OF MURDER!"
THIS IS A RECORDING...
I HAVE JUST KILLED THE BATMAN! THE BATMAN... THE BATMAN...
The MASTER CRIME-FILE OF Jason Bard
"I WAKE UP DYING!"

PAGE 137 BY CAMERON STEWART + NATHAN FAIRBAIRN AFTER MICHAEL KALUTA

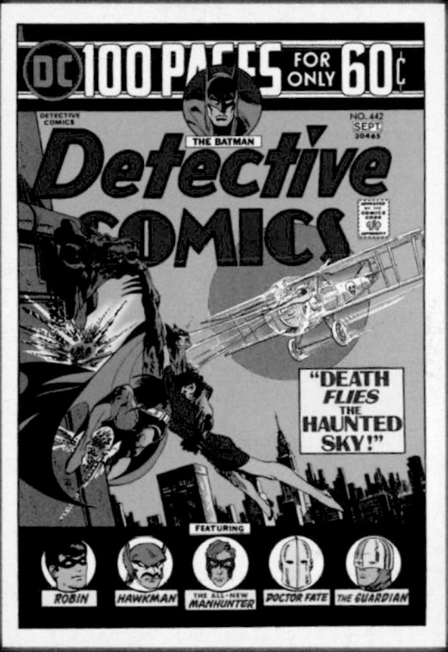
DC
100 PAGES FOR ONLY 60¢
THE BATMAN
NO. 442
SEPT
Detective
COMICS
"DEATH FLIES THE HAUNTED SKY!"
FEATURING
ROBIN
HAWKMAN
THE ALL-NEW MANHUNTER
DOCTOR FATE
THE GUARDIAN

PAGE 138 BY JOHN PAUL LEON AFTER JIM APARO

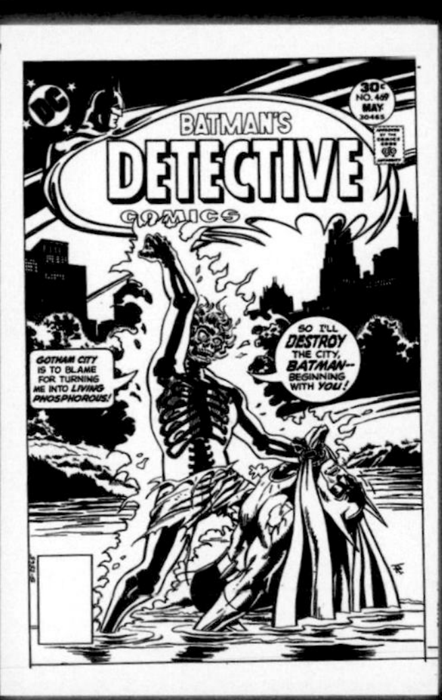
30¢
NO. 469
MAY
BATMAN'S
DETECTIVE
COMICS
GOTHAM CITY IS TO BLAME FOR TURNING ME INTO LIVING PHOSPHOROUS!
SO I'LL DESTROY THE CITY, BATMAN-- BEGINNING WITH YOU!

PAGE 139 BY CARLO PAGULAYAN, JASON PAZ + ROMULO FAJARDO, JR. AFTER JIM APARO

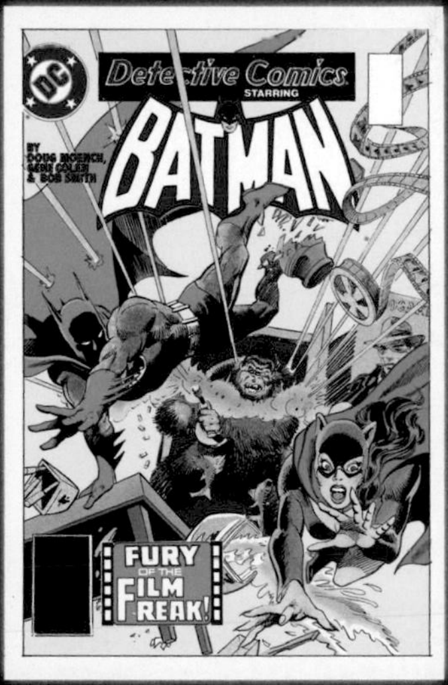
DC
Detective Comics
STARRING
BATMAN
FURY OF THE FILM FREAK!

PAGE 140 BY JOHN TIMMS + HI-FI AFTER GENE COLAN, DICK GIORDANO + ED HANNIGAN

VARIANT COVER GALLERY

DETECTIVE COMICS #48
COLORING BOOK VARIANT BY
TIMOTHY GREEN

DETECTIVE COMICS #49
VARIANT BY
NEAL ADAMS WITH
BRENT ANDERSON
& LAURA MARTIN

DETECTIVE COMICS #50
BATMAN V SUPERMAN
VARIANT BY RAFAEL GRAMPÁ

DETECTIVE COMICS #51
VARIANT BY
JOHN ROMITA JR. WITH
SCOTT HANNA
& DEAN WHITE

DETECTIVE COMICS #52
THE NEW 52 VARIANT BY
FRANCIS MANAPUL

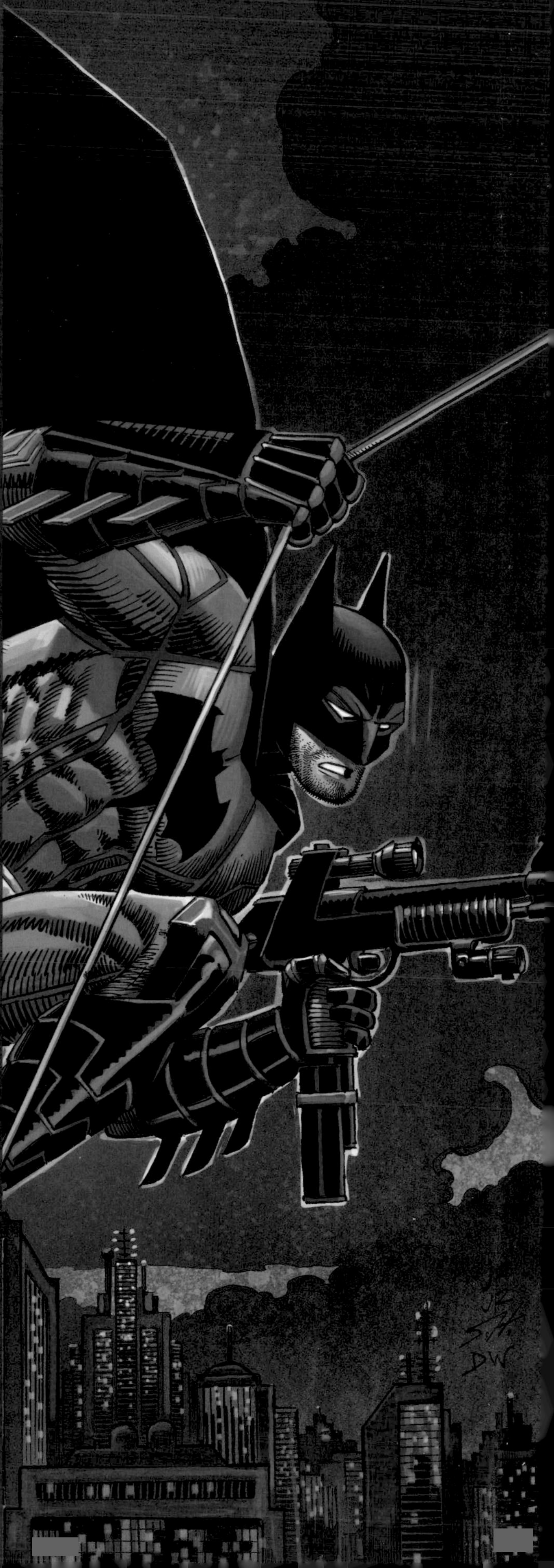

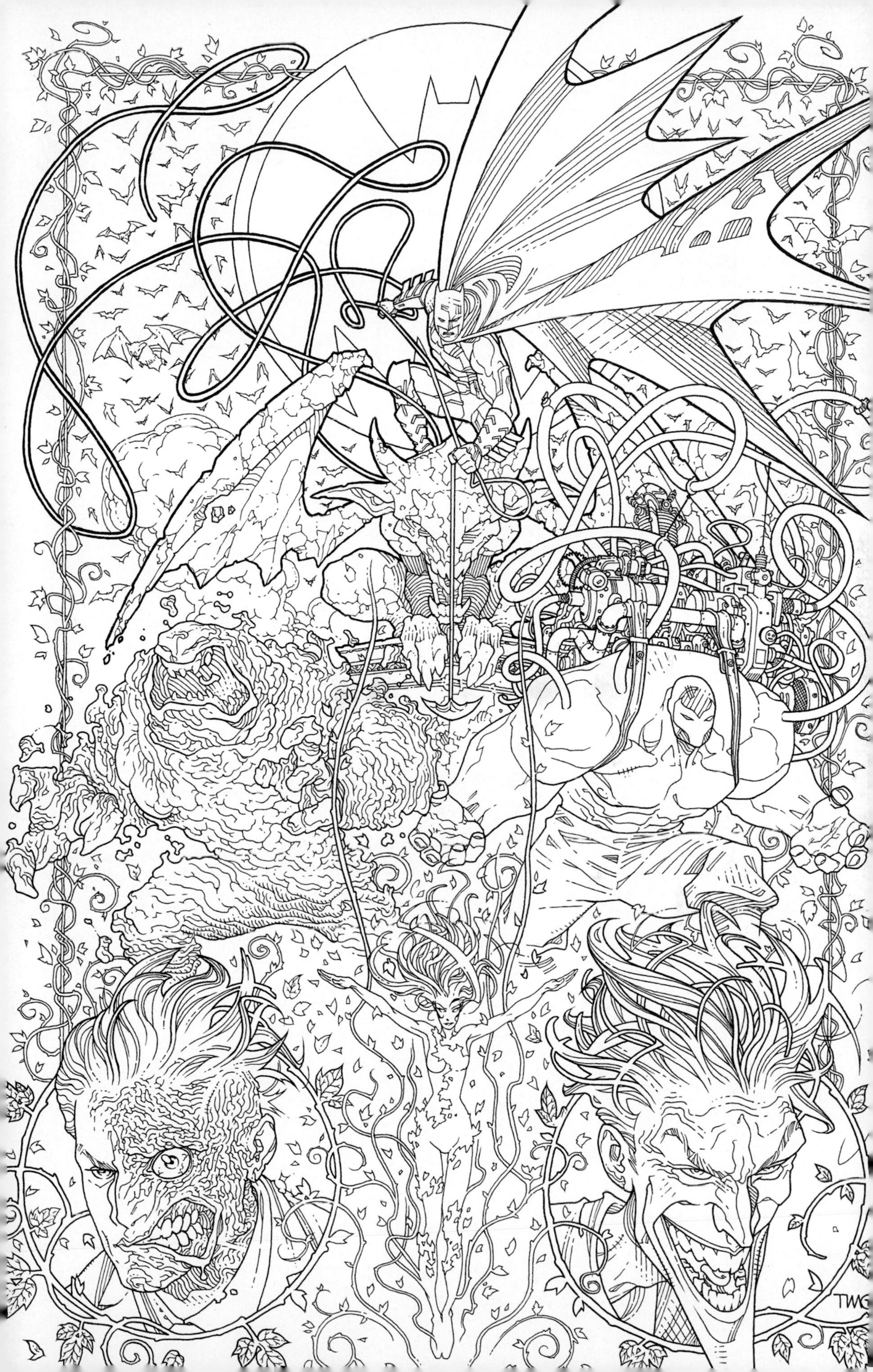
TWG

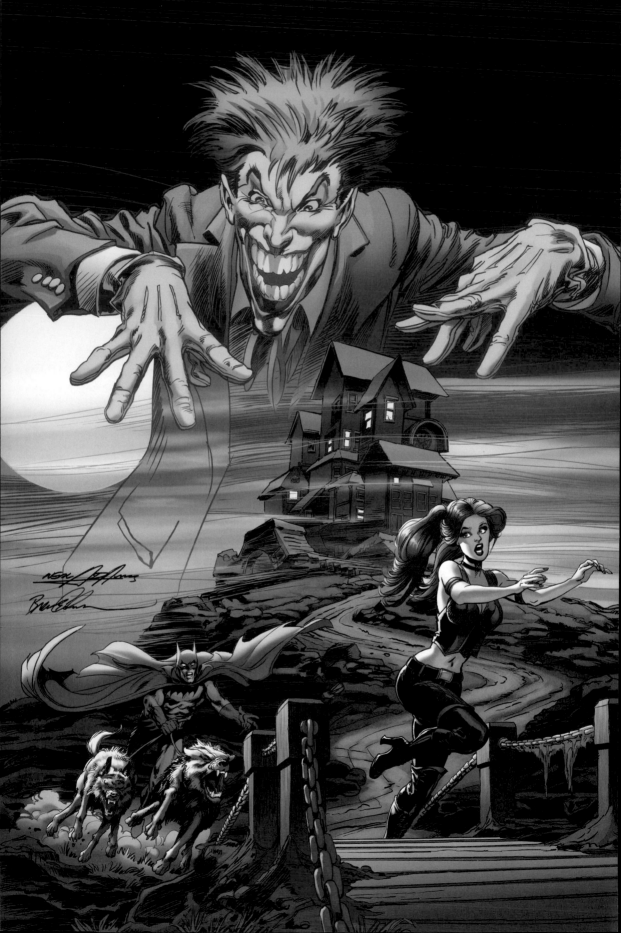

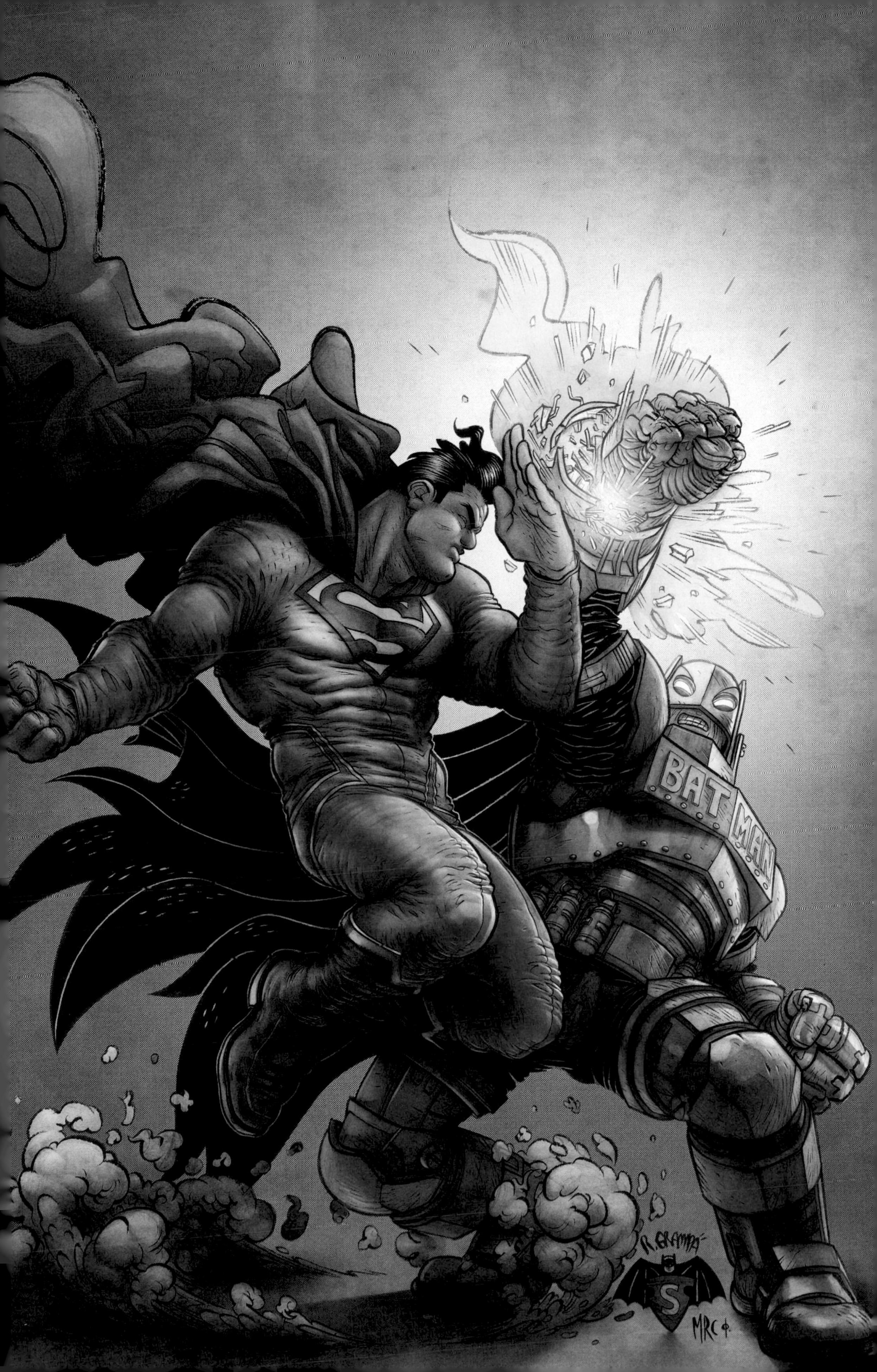
BAT
MAN

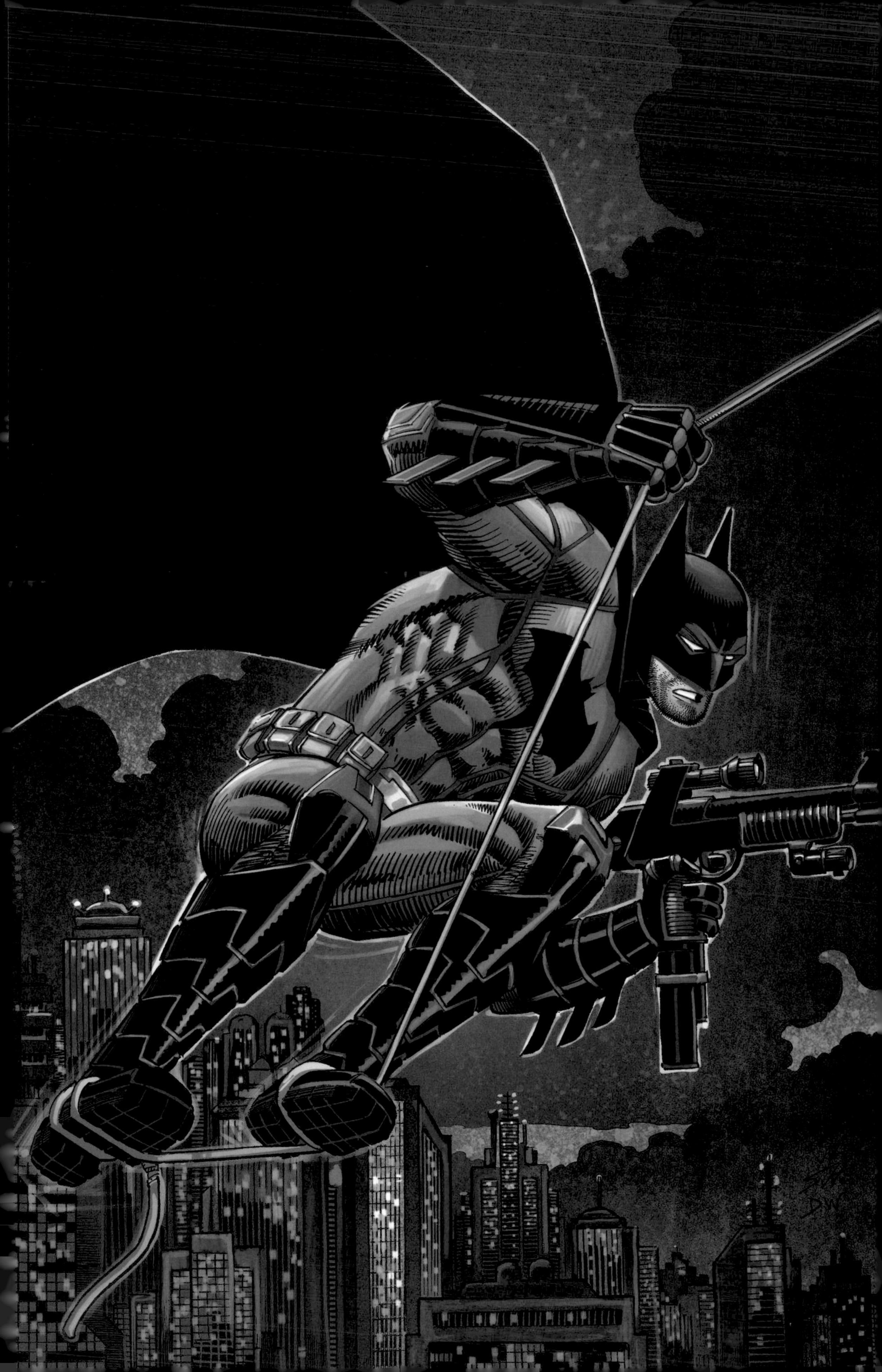

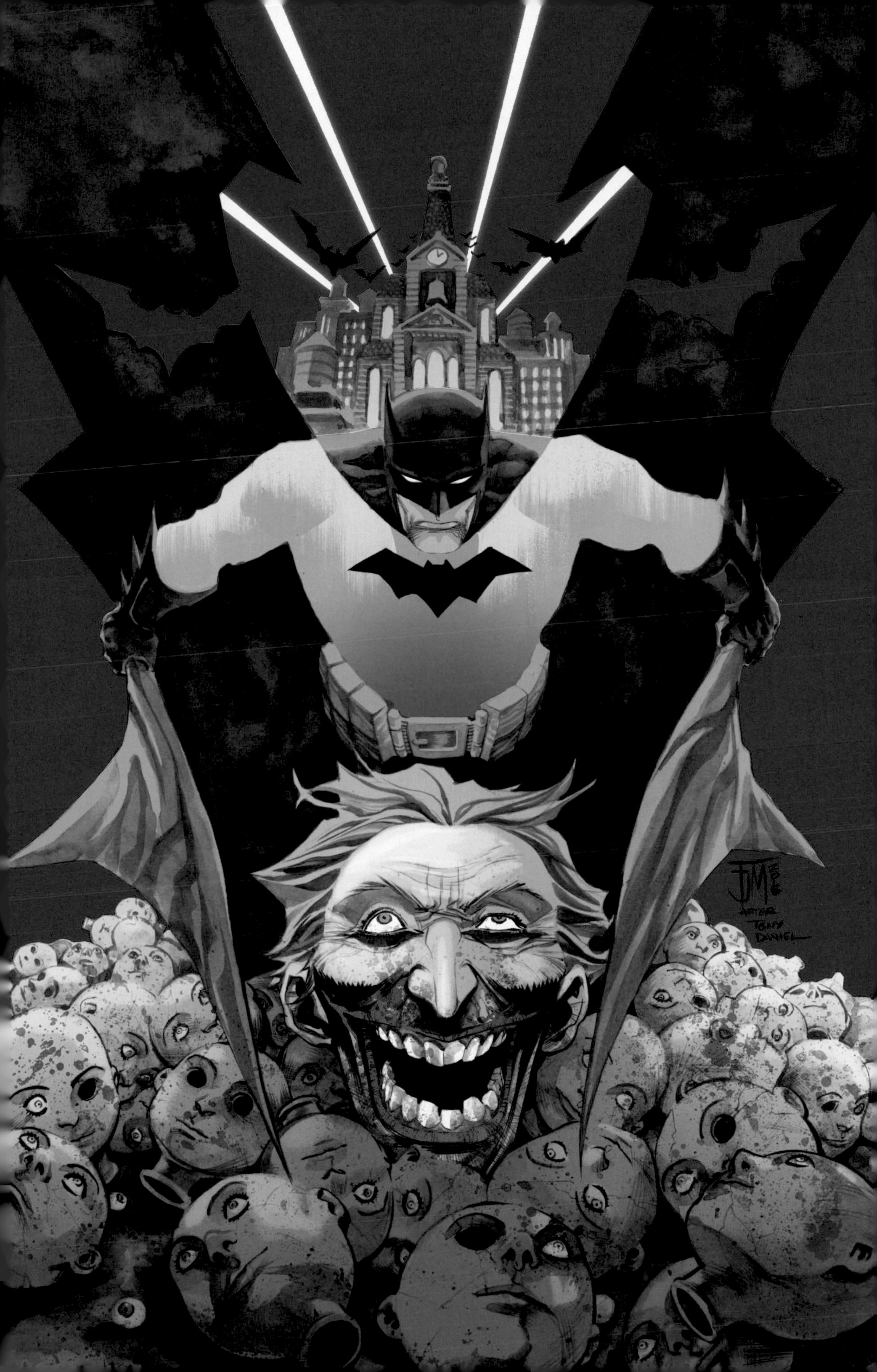
FJM 2016
AFTER TONY DANIEL

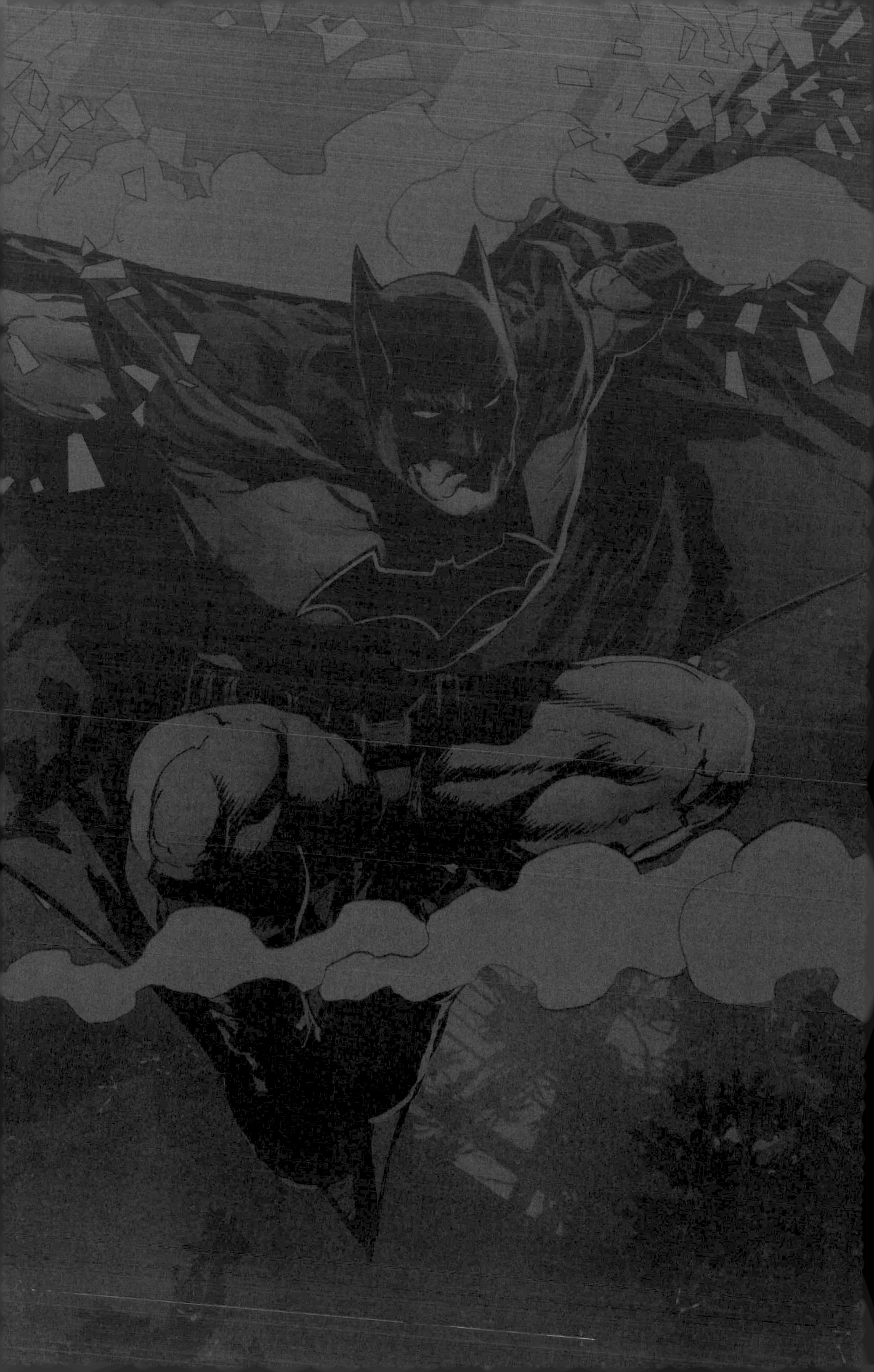

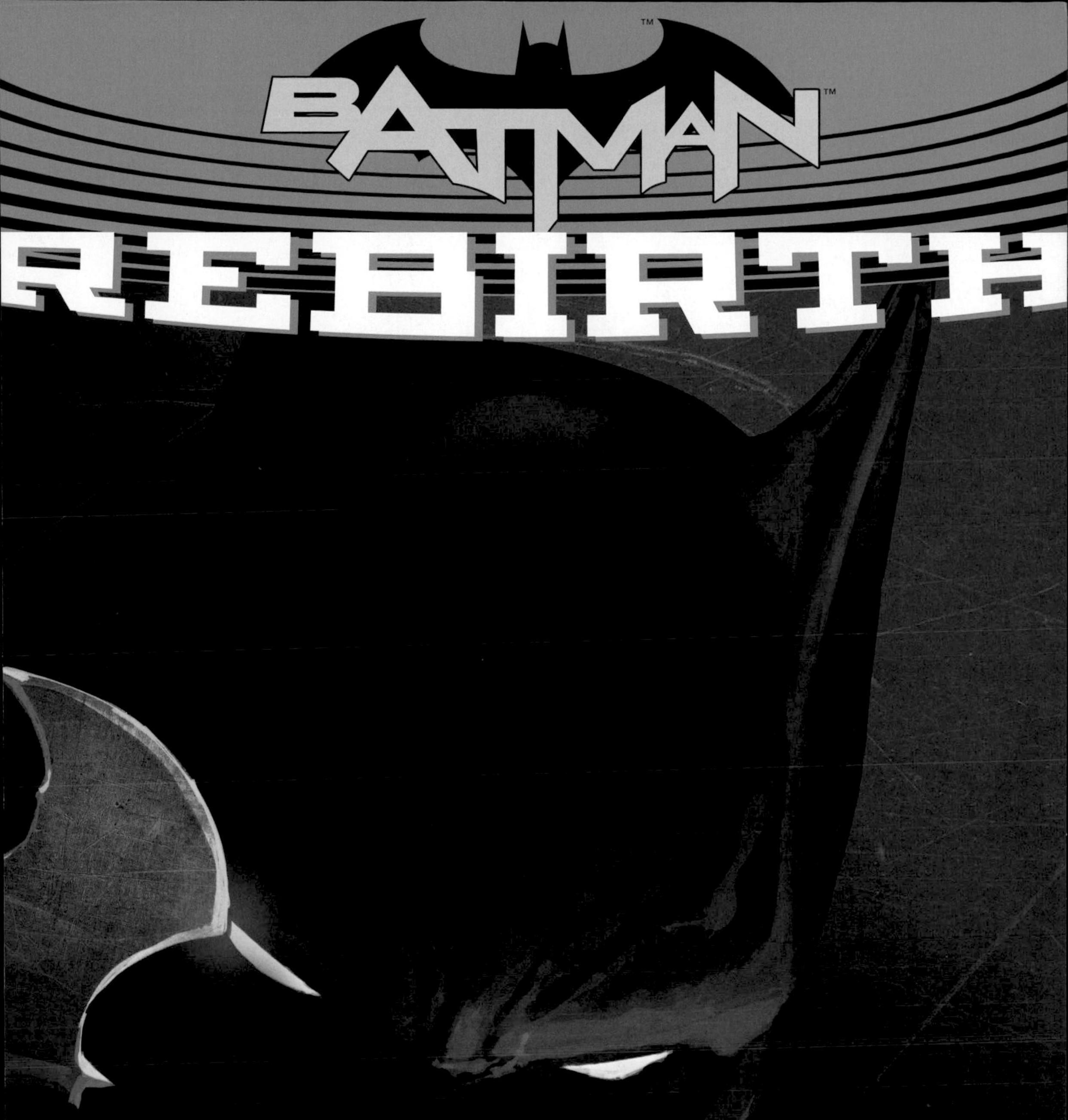
BATMAN™
REBIRTH

The future (and past) of the DC Universe starts with DC UNIVERSE: REBIRTH!

Explore the changing world of Batman in this special bonus preview of **BATMAN: REBIRTH #1**.

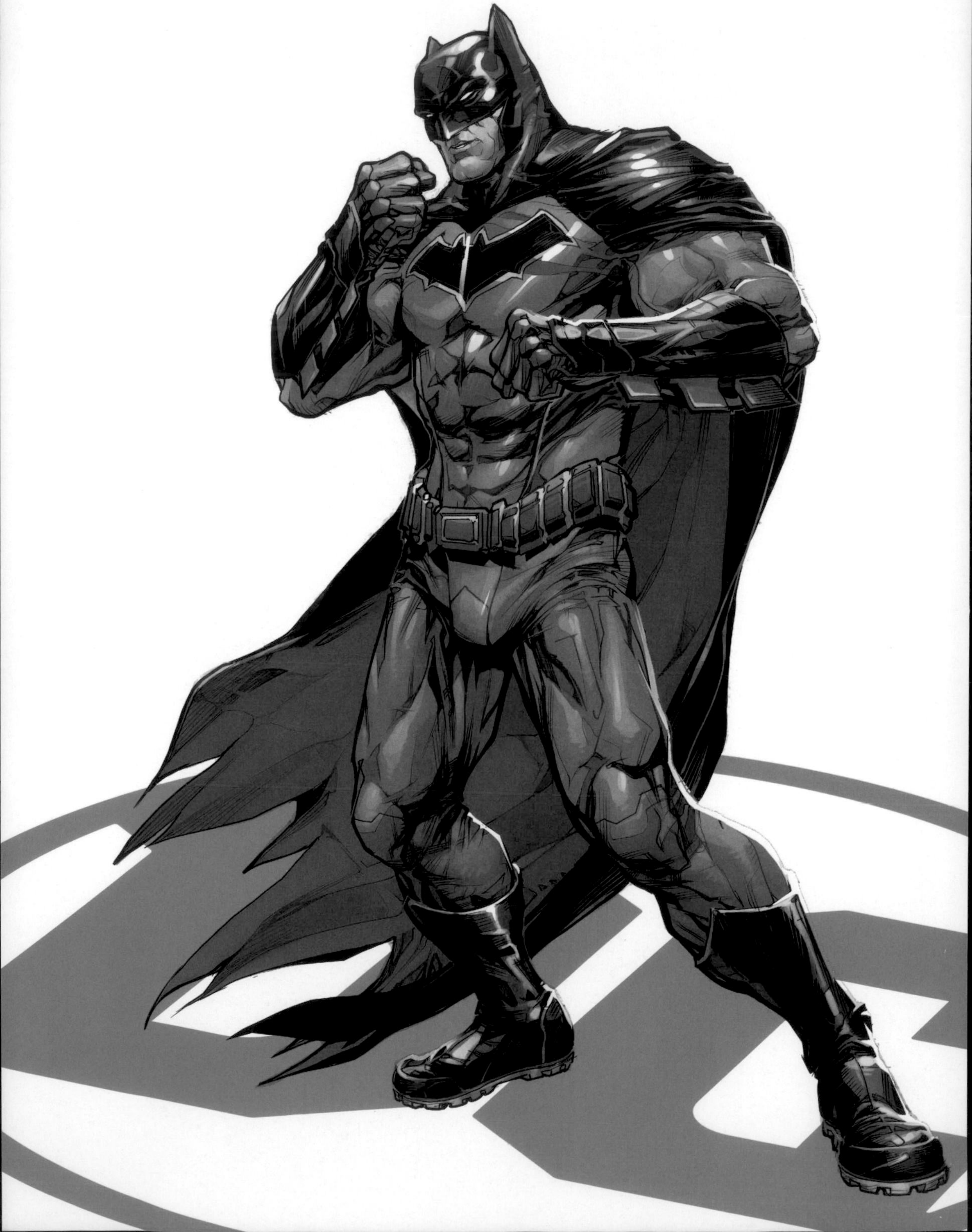

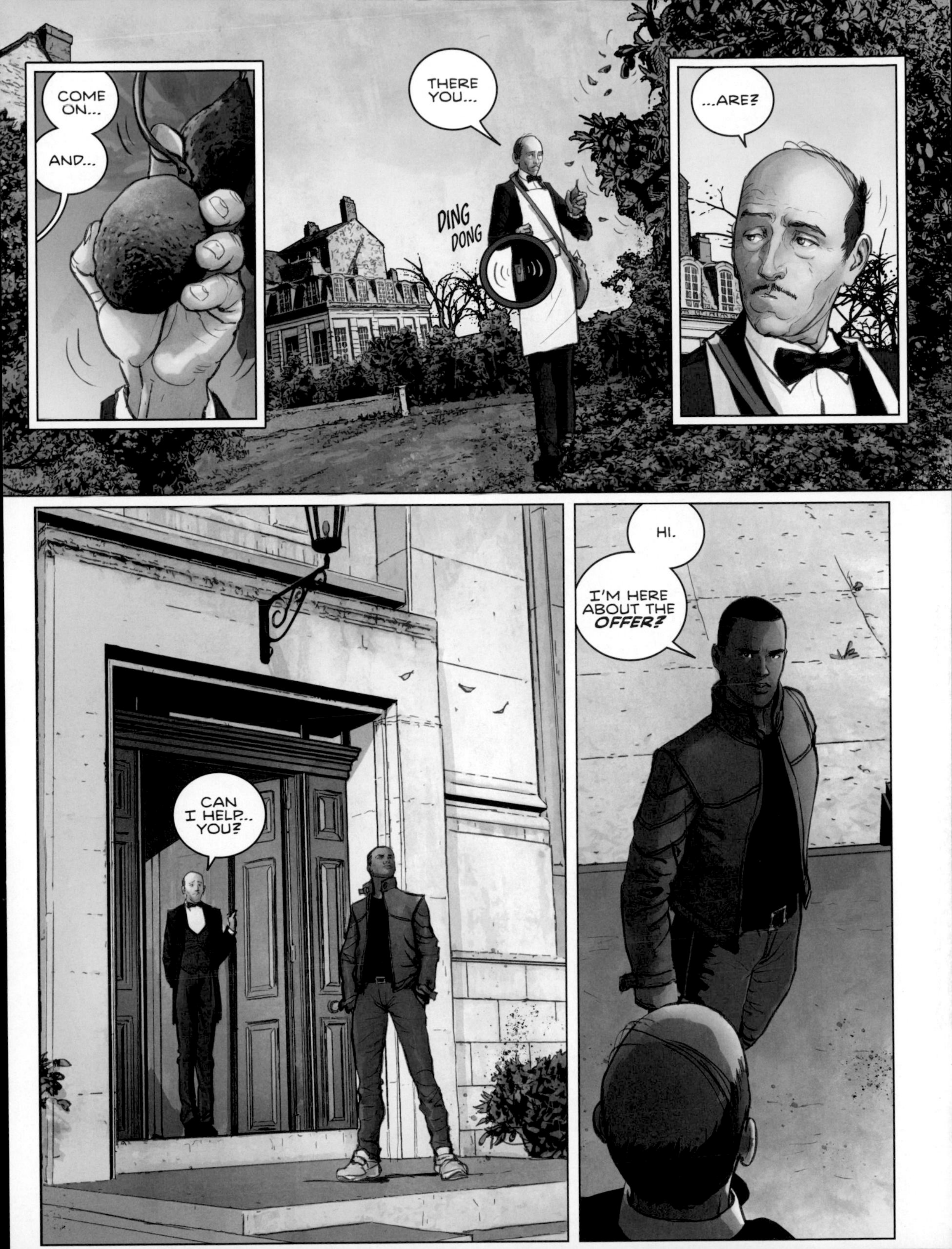
COME ON...
AND...
THERE YOU...
DING DONG
...ARE?
CAN I HELP... YOU?
HI.
I'M HERE ABOUT THE OFFER?

MONDAY: SPRING.

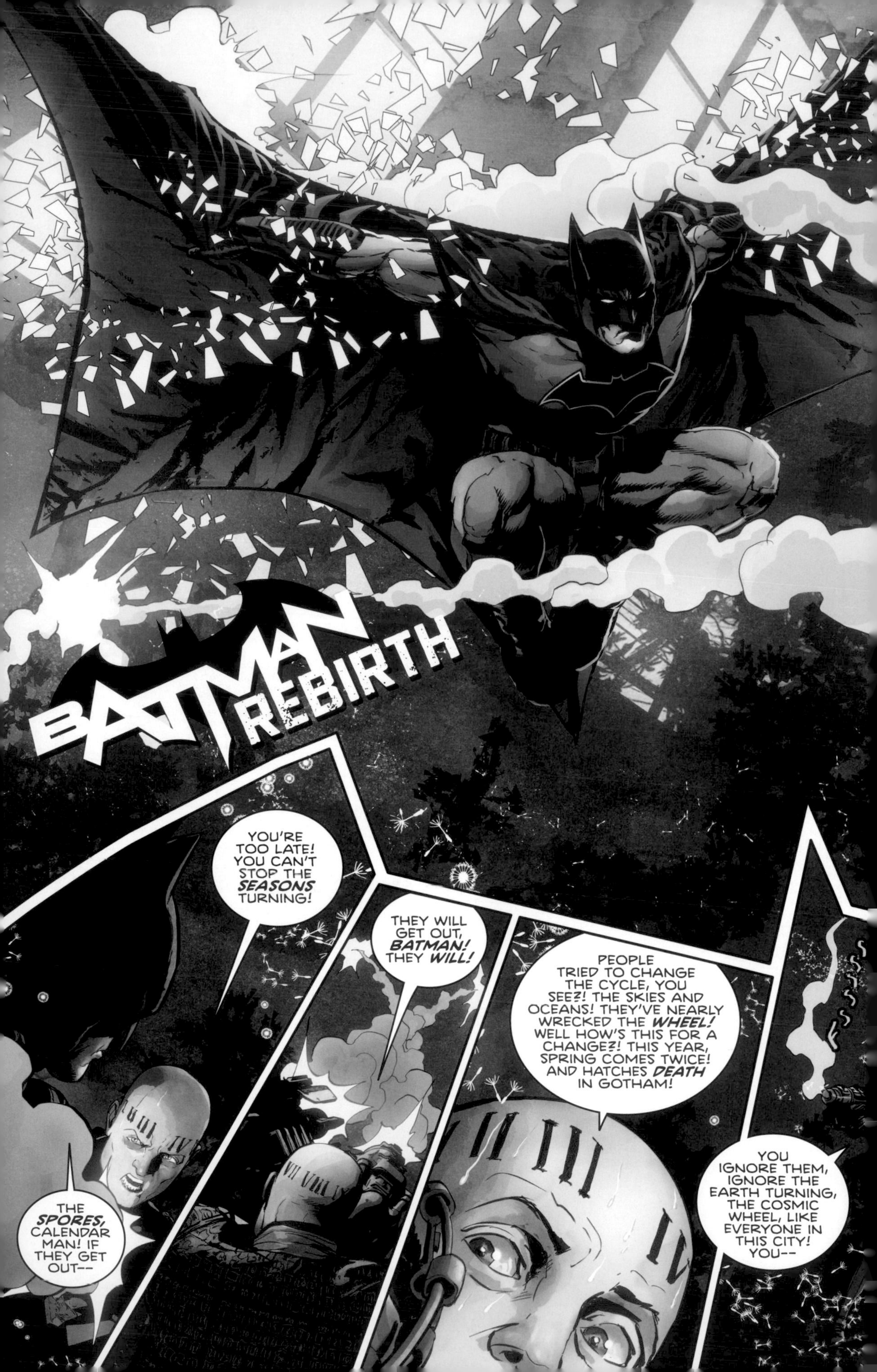
BATMAN REBIRTH
YOU'RE TOO LATE! YOU CAN'T STOP THE SEASONS TURNING!
THE SPORES, CALENDAR MAN! IF THEY GET OUT--
THEY WILL GET OUT, BATMAN! THEY WILL!
PEOPLE TRIED TO CHANGE THE CYCLE, YOU SEE?! THE SKIES AND OCEANS! THEY'VE NEARLY WRECKED THE WHEEL! WELL HOW'S THIS FOR A CHANGE?! THIS YEAR, SPRING COMES TWICE! AND HATCHES DEATH IN GOTHAM!
YOU IGNORE THEM, IGNORE THE EARTH TURNING, THE COSMIC WHEEL, LIKE EVERYONE IN THIS CITY! YOU--

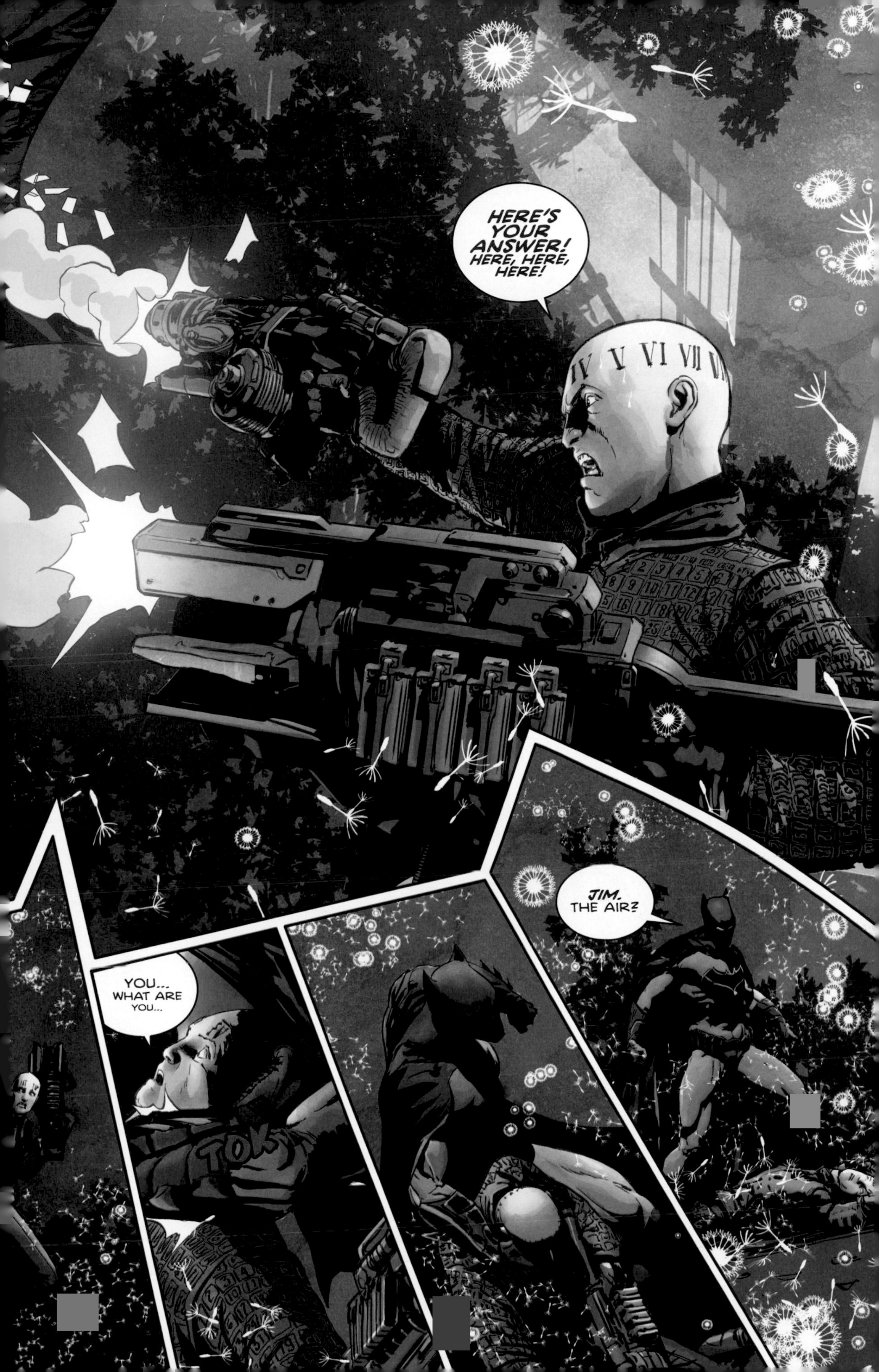
HERE'S YOUR ANSWER! HERE, HERE, HERE!
JIM. THE AIR?
YOU... WHAT ARE YOU...
TOK

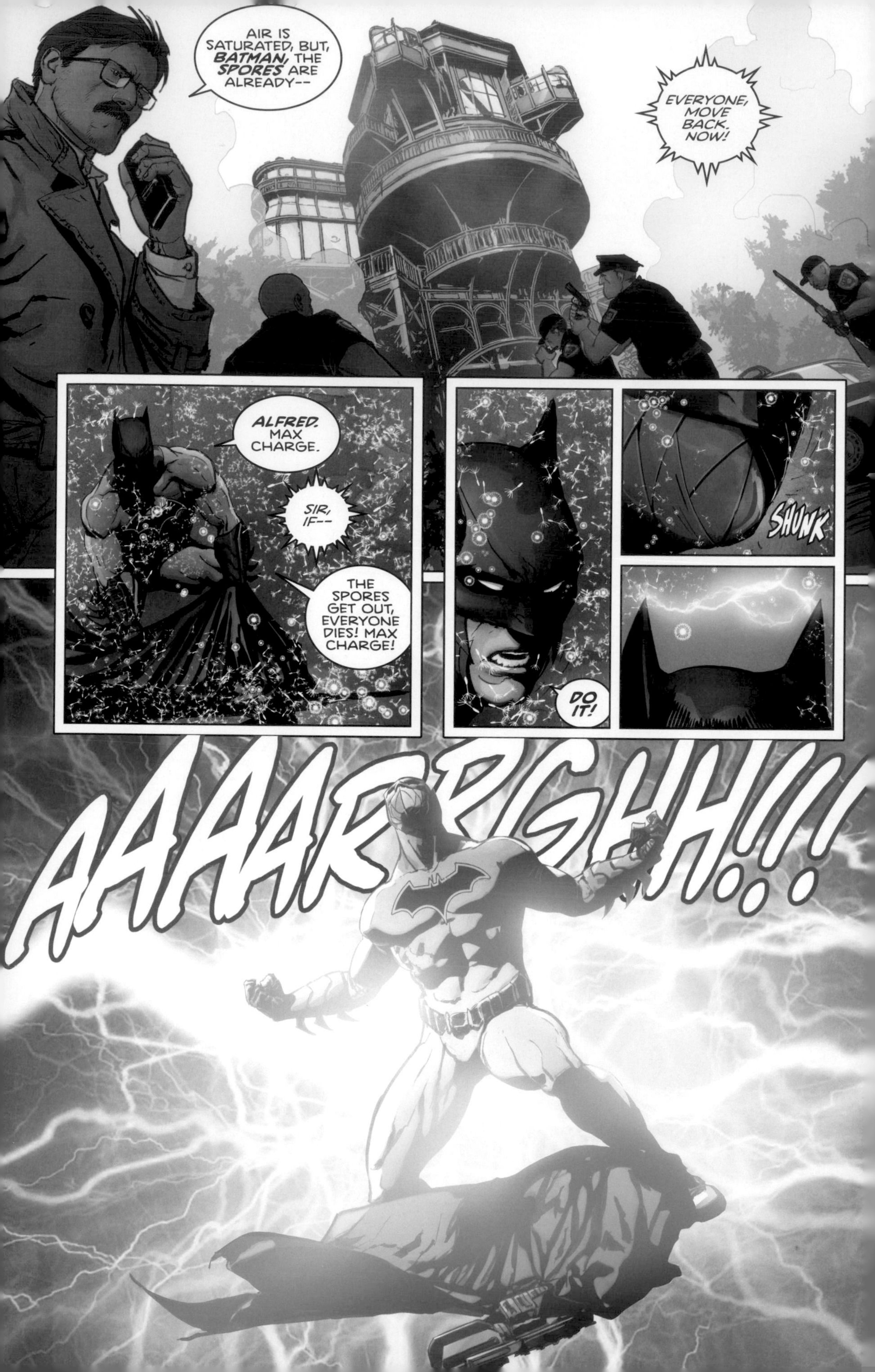
AIR IS SATURATED, BUT, BATMAN, THE SPORES ARE ALREADY--
EVERYONE, MOVE BACK. NOW!
ALFRED. MAX CHARGE.
SIR, IF--
THE SPORES GET OUT, EVERYONE DIES! MAX CHARGE!
DO IT!
SHUNK
AAAARRGHH!!!

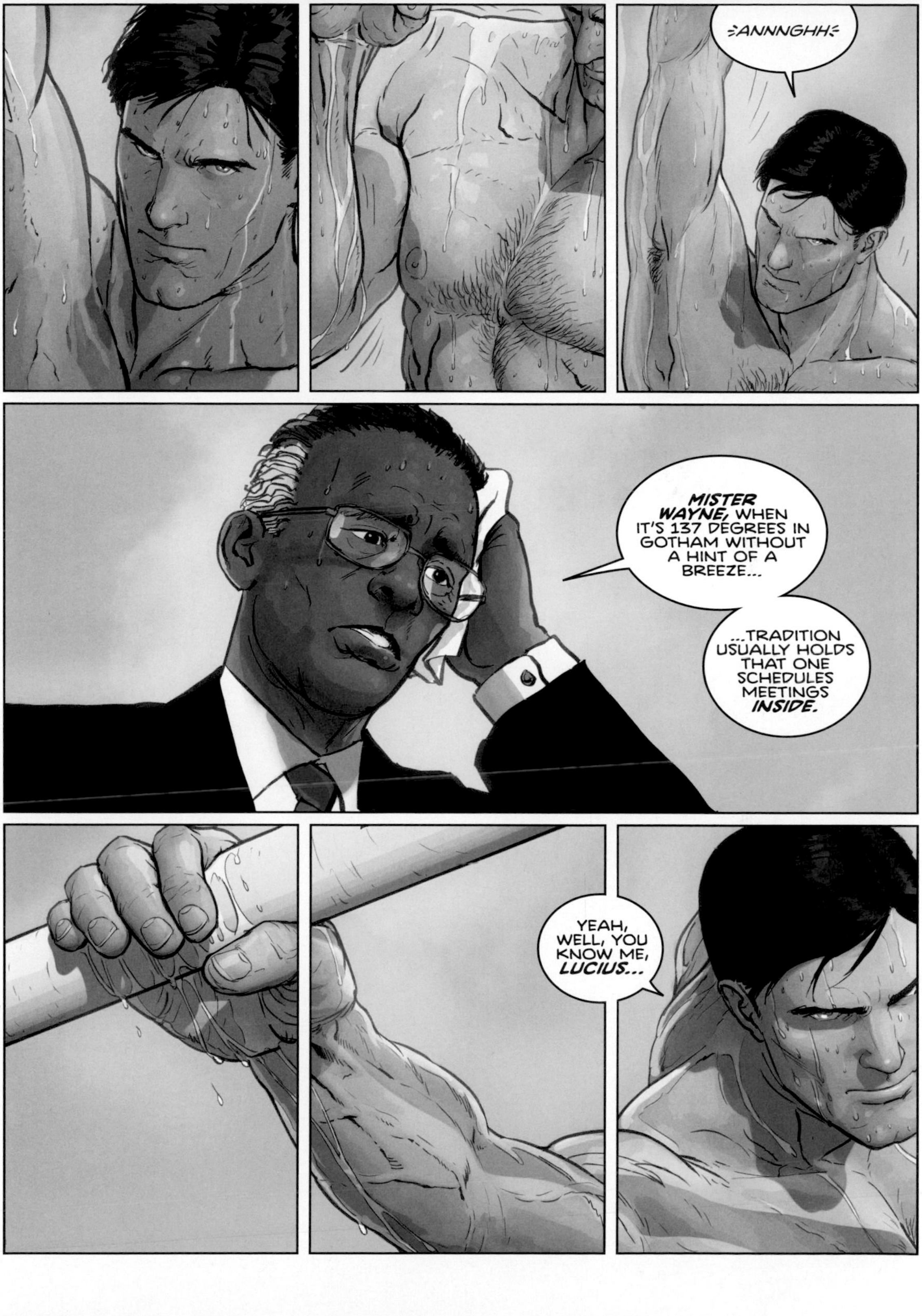

ANNNGHH
MISTER WAYNE, WHEN IT'S 137 DEGREES IN GOTHAM WITHOUT A HINT OF A BREEZE...
...TRADITION USUALLY HOLDS THAT ONE SCHEDULES MEETINGS INSIDE.
YEAH, WELL, YOU KNOW ME, LUCIUS...

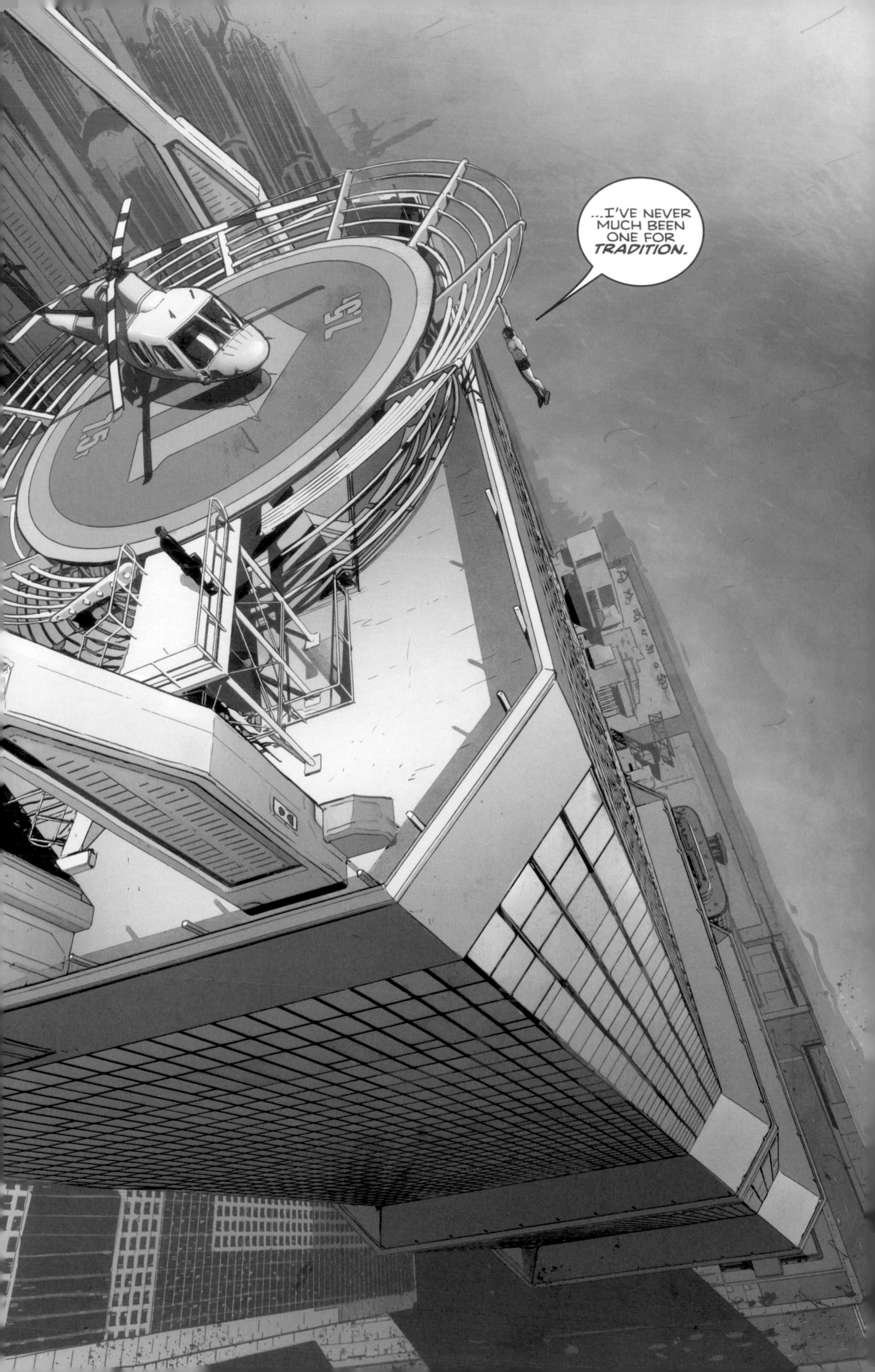
...I'VE NEVER MUCH BEEN ONE FOR TRADITION.

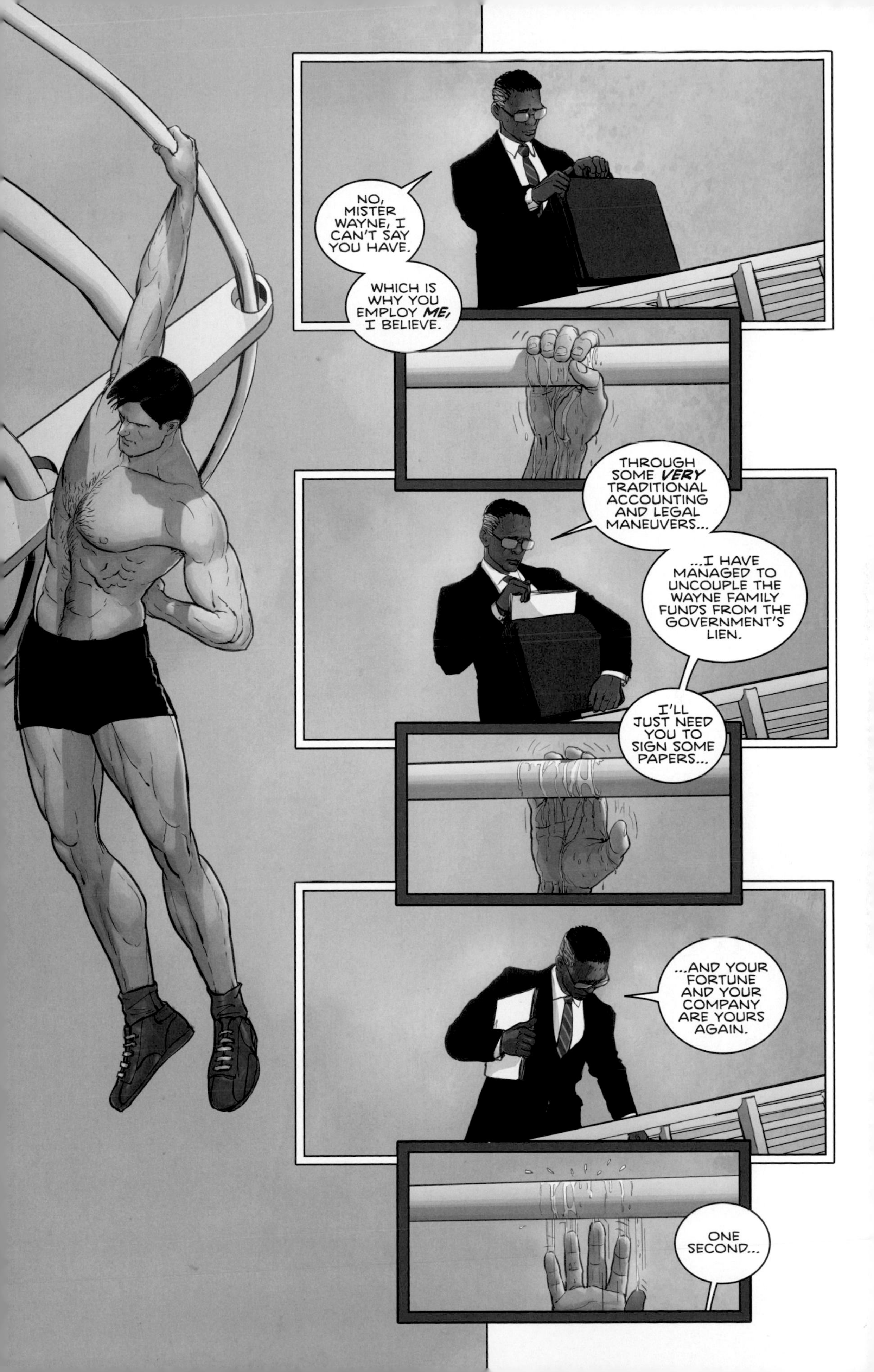
NO, MISTER WAYNE, I CAN'T SAY YOU HAVE.
WHICH IS WHY YOU EMPLOY ME, I BELIEVE.
THROUGH SOME VERY TRADITIONAL ACCOUNTING AND LEGAL MANEUVERS...
...I HAVE MANAGED TO UNCOUPLE THE WAYNE FAMILY FUNDS FROM THE GOVERNMENT'S LIEN.
I'LL JUST NEED YOU TO SIGN SOME PAPERS...
...AND YOUR FORTUNE AND YOUR COMPANY ARE YOURS AGAIN.
ONE SECOND...

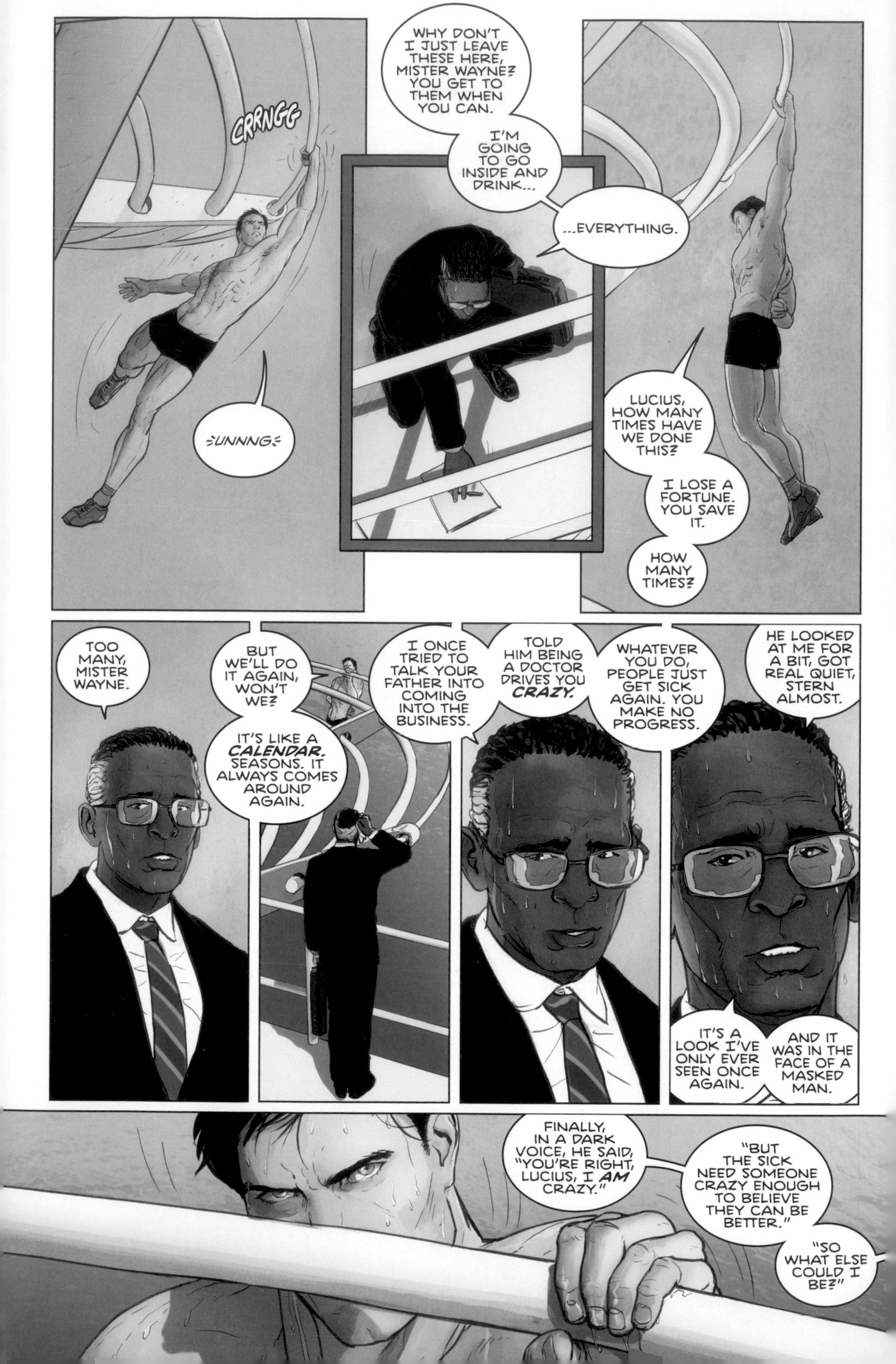
CRRNGG
WHY DON'T I JUST LEAVE THESE HERE, MISTER WAYNE? YOU GET TO THEM WHEN YOU CAN.
I'M GOING TO GO INSIDE AND DRINK...
...EVERYTHING.
UNNNG
LUCIUS, HOW MANY TIMES HAVE WE DONE THIS?
I LOSE A FORTUNE. YOU SAVE IT.
HOW MANY TIMES?
TOO MANY, MISTER WAYNE.
BUT WE'LL DO IT AGAIN, WON'T WE?
IT'S LIKE A CALENDAR. SEASONS. IT ALWAYS COMES AROUND AGAIN.
I ONCE TRIED TO TALK YOUR FATHER INTO COMING INTO THE BUSINESS.
TOLD HIM BEING A DOCTOR DRIVES YOU CRAZY.
WHATEVER YOU DO, PEOPLE JUST GET SICK AGAIN. YOU MAKE NO PROGRESS.
HE LOOKED AT ME FOR A BIT, GOT REAL QUIET, STERN ALMOST.
IT'S A LOOK I'VE ONLY EVER SEEN ONCE AGAIN.
AND IT WAS IN THE FACE OF A MASKED MAN.
FINALLY, IN A DARK VOICE, HE SAID, "YOU'RE RIGHT, LUCIUS, I AM CRAZY."
"BUT THE SICK NEED SOMEONE CRAZY ENOUGH TO BELIEVE THEY CAN BE BETTER."
"SO WHAT ELSE COULD I BE?"

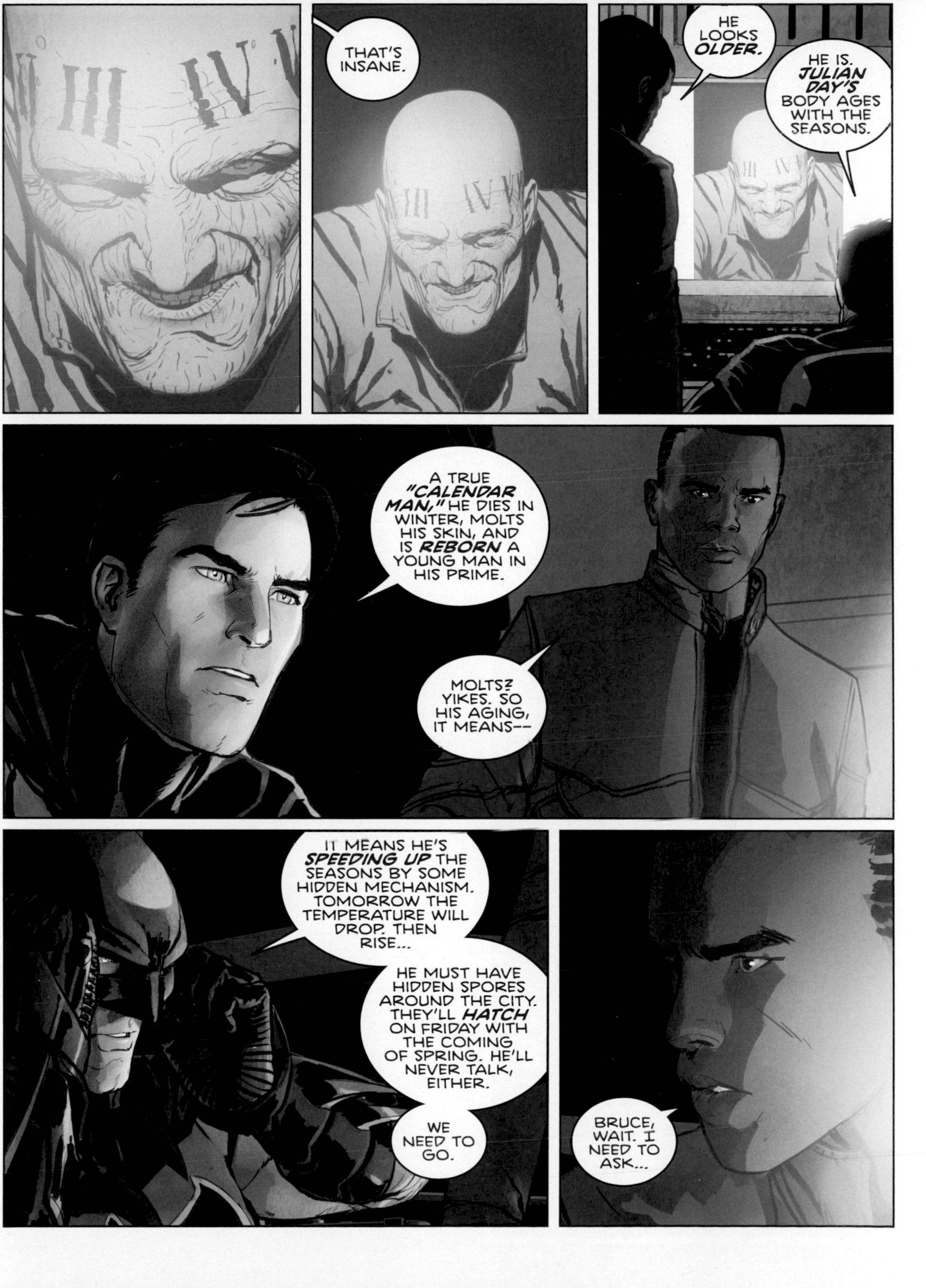
THAT'S INSANE.
HE LOOKS OLDER.
HE IS. JULIAN DAY'S BODY AGES WITH THE SEASONS.
A TRUE "CALENDAR MAN," HE DIES IN WINTER, MOLTS HIS SKIN, AND IS REBORN A YOUNG MAN IN HIS PRIME.
MOLTS? YIKES. SO HIS AGING, IT MEANS--
IT MEANS HE'S SPEEDING UP THE SEASONS BY SOME HIDDEN MECHANISM. TOMORROW THE TEMPERATURE WILL DROP. THEN RISE...
HE MUST HAVE HIDDEN SPORES AROUND THE CITY. THEY'LL HATCH ON FRIDAY WITH THE COMING OF SPRING. HE'LL NEVER TALK, EITHER.
WE NEED TO GO.
BRUCE, WAIT. I NEED TO ASK...

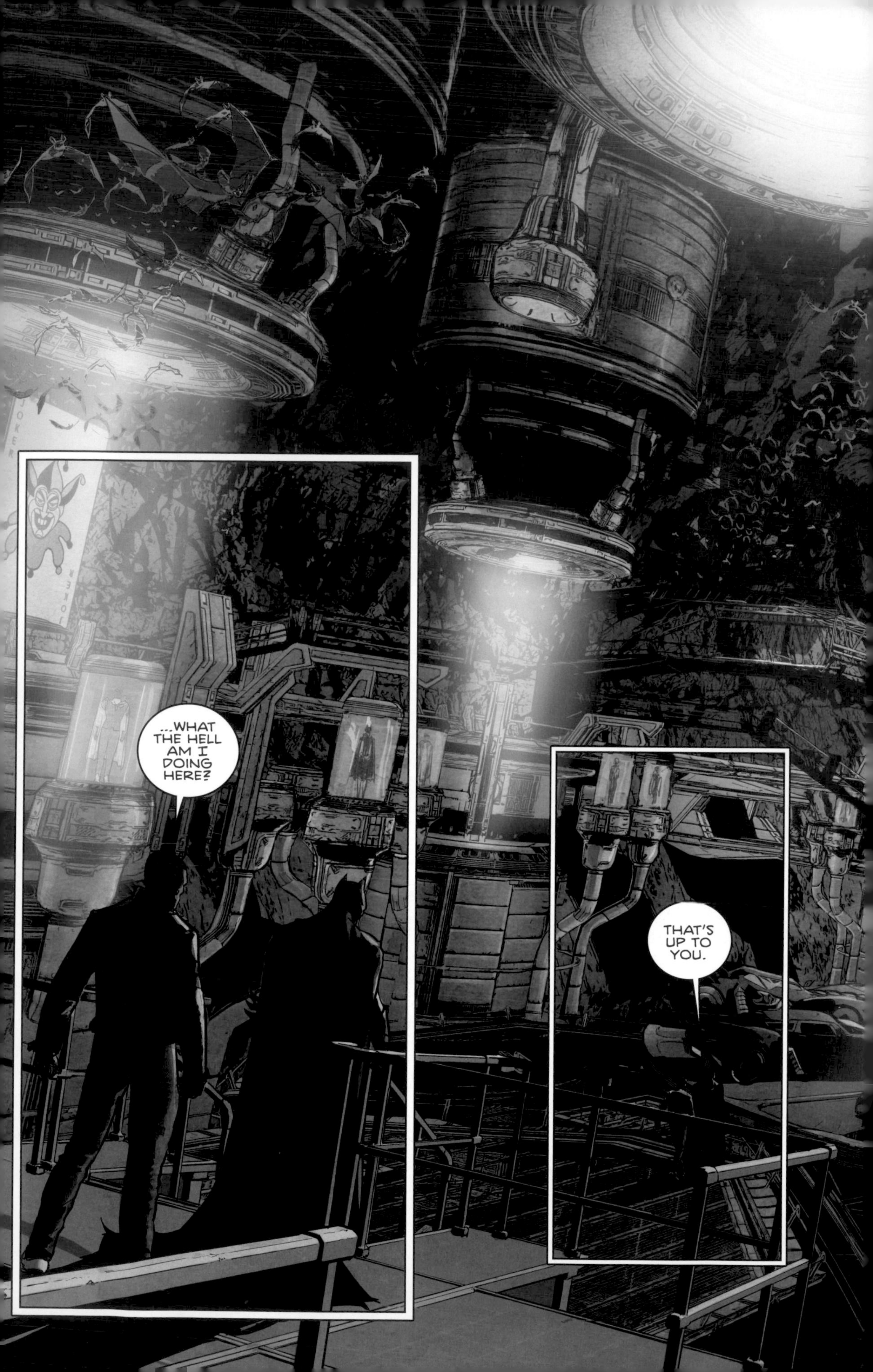
JOKER
...WHAT THE HELL AM I DOING HERE?
THAT'S UP TO YOU.

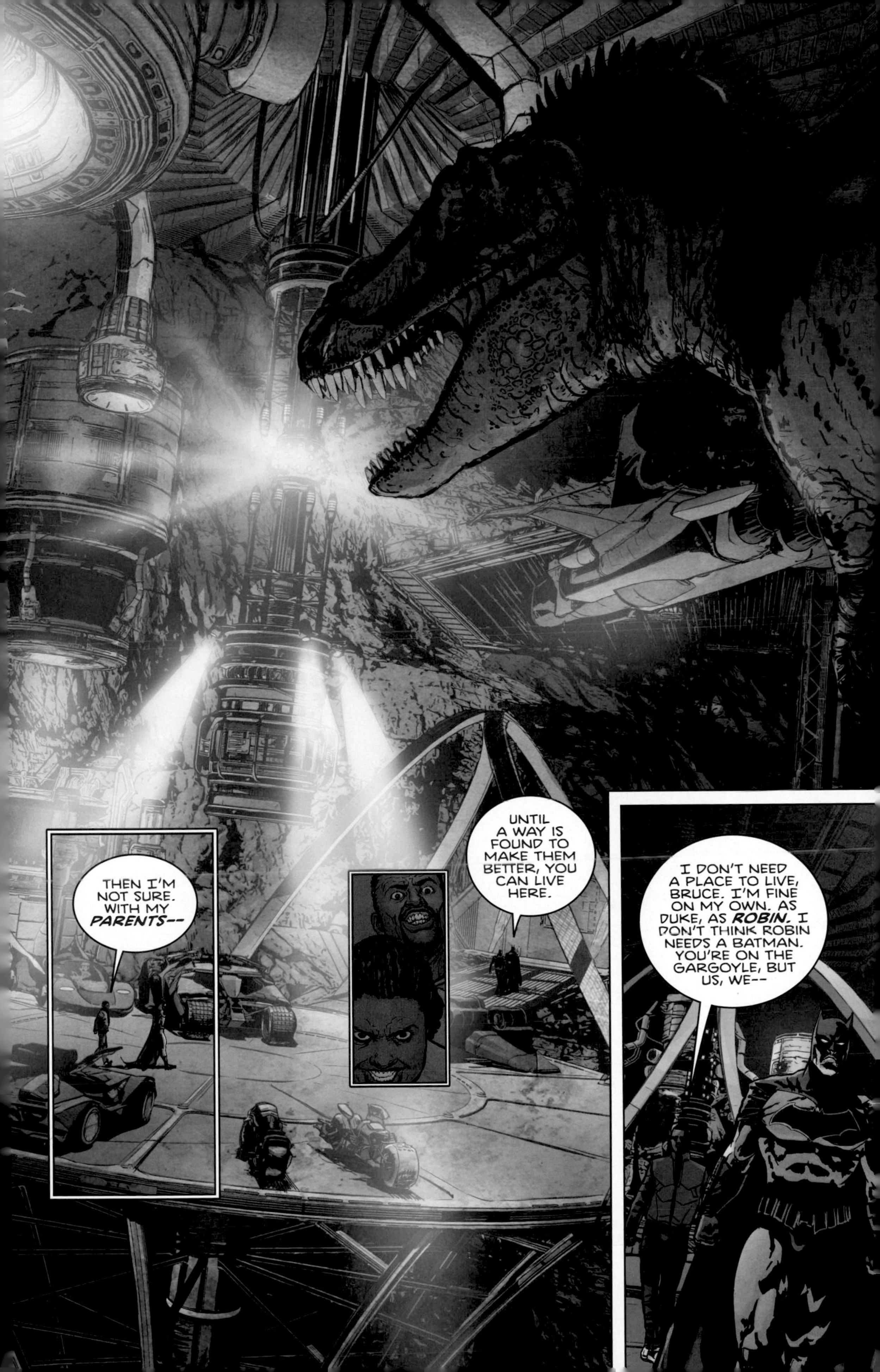
THEN I'M NOT SURE. WITH MY PARENTS--
UNTIL A WAY IS FOUND TO MAKE THEM BETTER, YOU CAN LIVE HERE.
I DON'T NEED A PLACE TO LIVE, BRUCE. I'M FINE ON MY OWN. AS DUKE, AS ROBIN. I DON'T THINK ROBIN NEEDS A BATMAN. YOU'RE ON THE GARGOYLE, BUT US, WE--

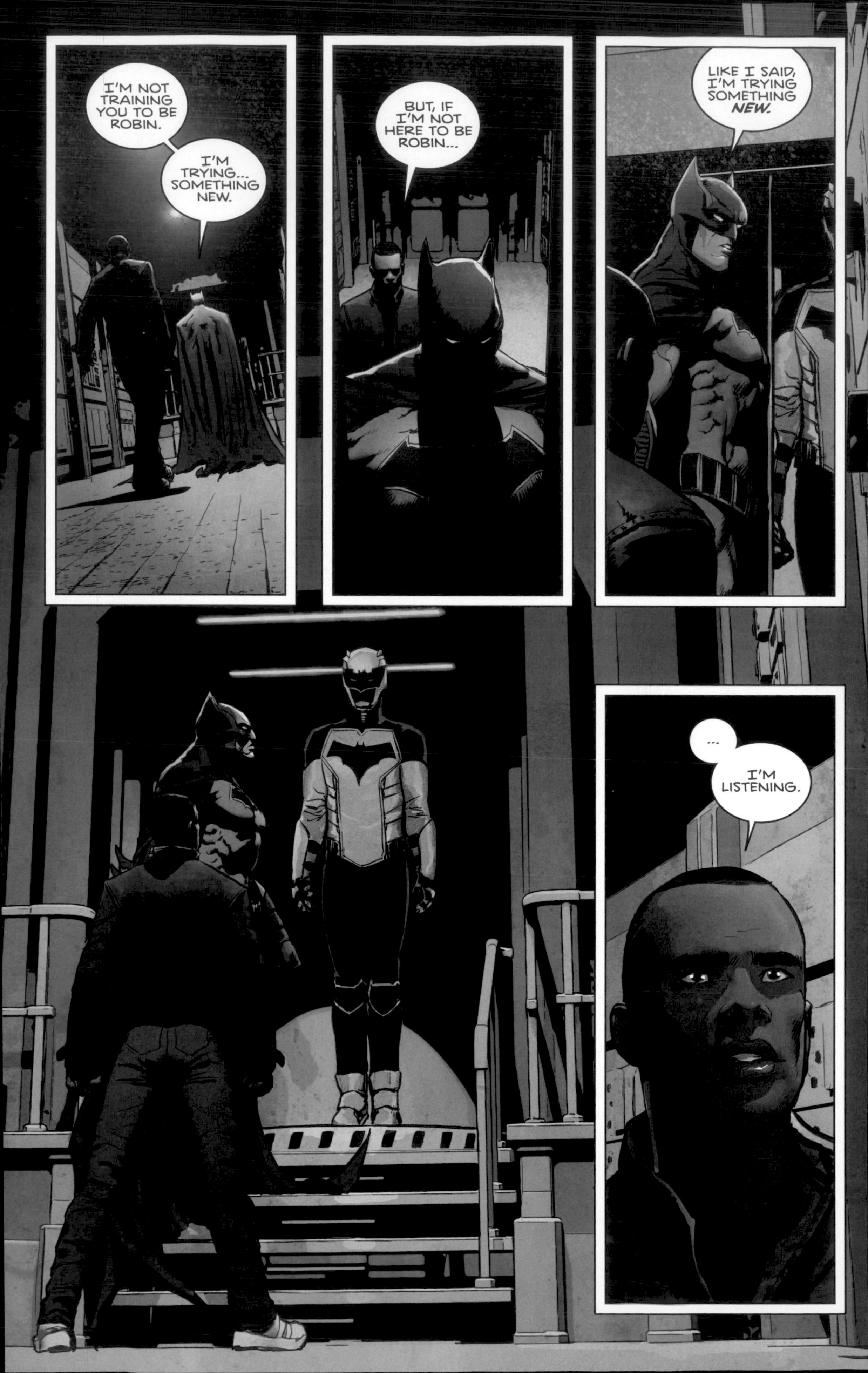
I'M NOT TRAINING YOU TO BE ROBIN.
I'M TRYING... SOMETHING NEW.
BUT, IF I'M NOT HERE TO BE ROBIN...
LIKE I SAID, I'M TRYING SOMETHING NEW.
...
I'M LISTENING.

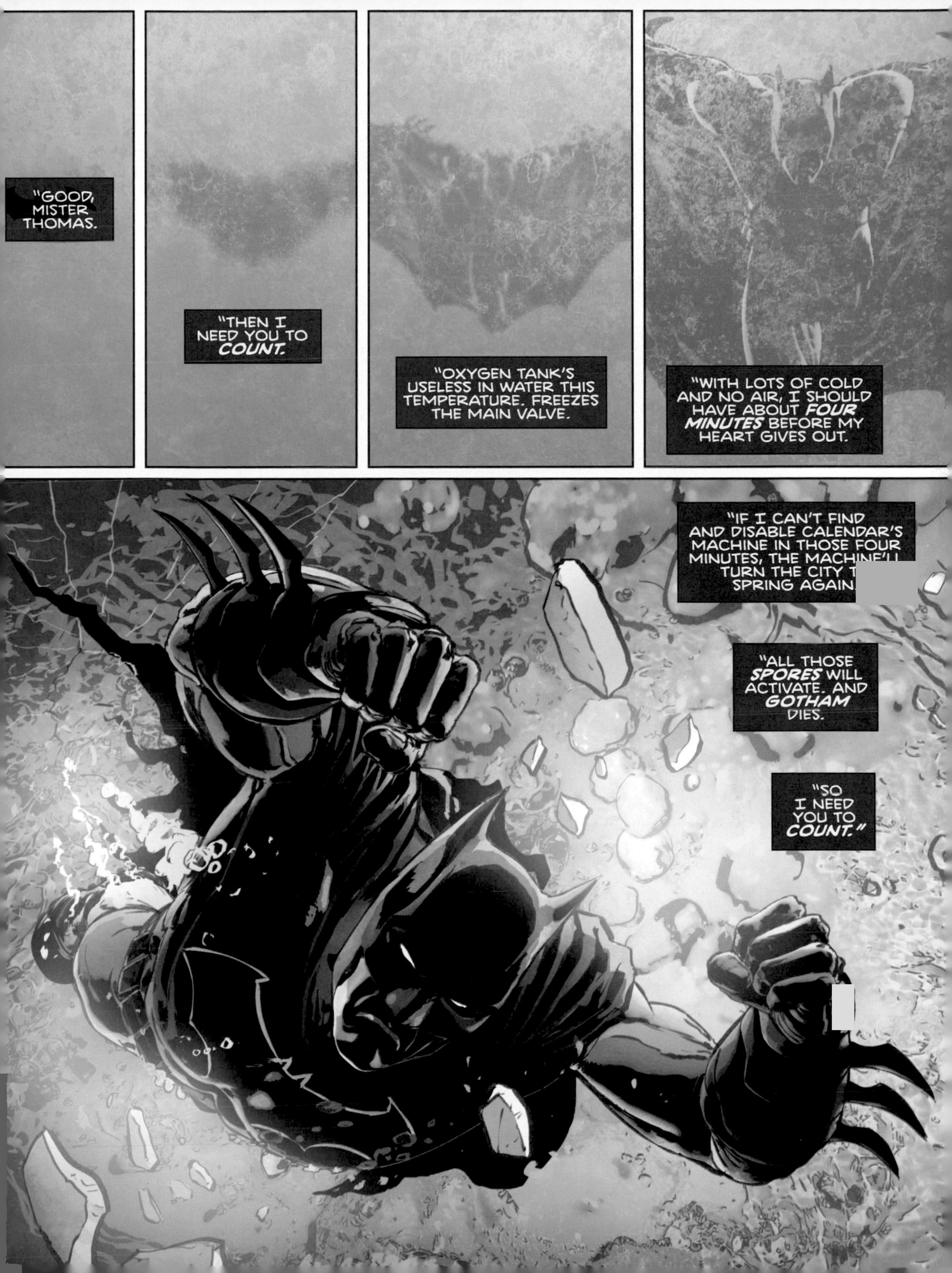
"GOOD, MISTER THOMAS.
"THEN I NEED YOU TO COUNT.
"OXYGEN TANK'S USELESS IN WATER THIS TEMPERATURE. FREEZES THE MAIN VALVE.
"WITH LOTS OF COLD AND NO AIR, I SHOULD HAVE ABOUT FOUR MINUTES BEFORE MY HEART GIVES OUT.
"IF I CAN'T FIND AND DISABLE CALENDAR'S MACHINE IN THOSE FOUR MINUTES, THE MACHINE'LL TURN THE CITY T SPRING AGAIN
"ALL THOSE SPORES WILL ACTIVATE. AND GOTHAM DIES.
"SO I NEED YOU TO COUNT."

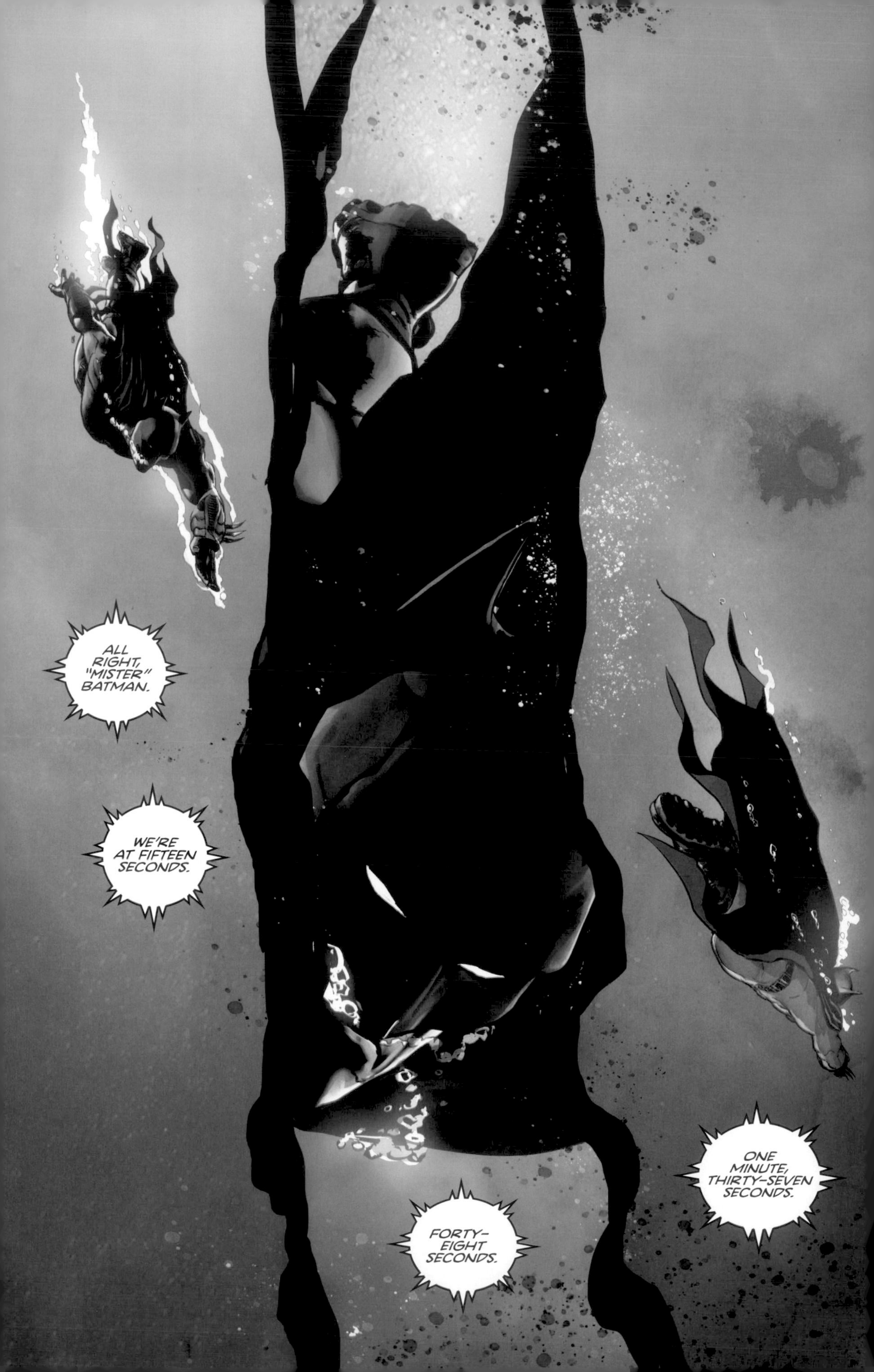
ALL RIGHT, "MISTER" BATMAN.
WE'RE AT FIFTEEN SECONDS.
FORTY-EIGHT SECONDS.
ONE MINUTE, THIRTY-SEVEN SECONDS.

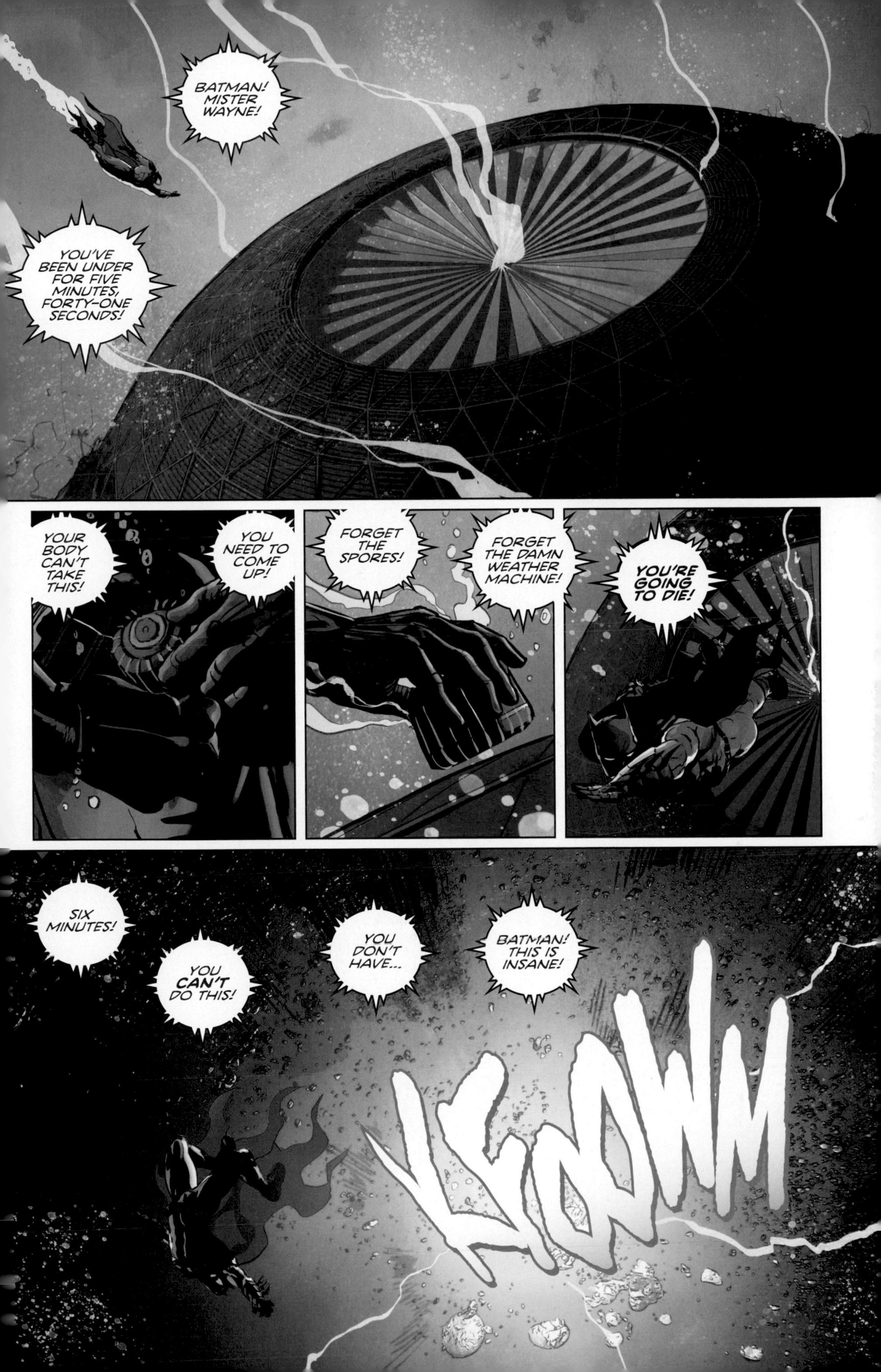
BATMAN! MISTER WAYNE!
YOU'VE BEEN UNDER FOR FIVE MINUTES, FORTY-ONE SECONDS!
YOUR BODY CAN'T TAKE THIS!
YOU NEED TO COME UP!
FORGET THE SPORES!
FORGET THE DAMN WEATHER MACHINE!
YOU'RE GOING TO DIE!
SIX MINUTES!
YOU CAN'T DO THIS!
YOU DON'T HAVE...
BATMAN! THIS IS INSANE!
KRAWM

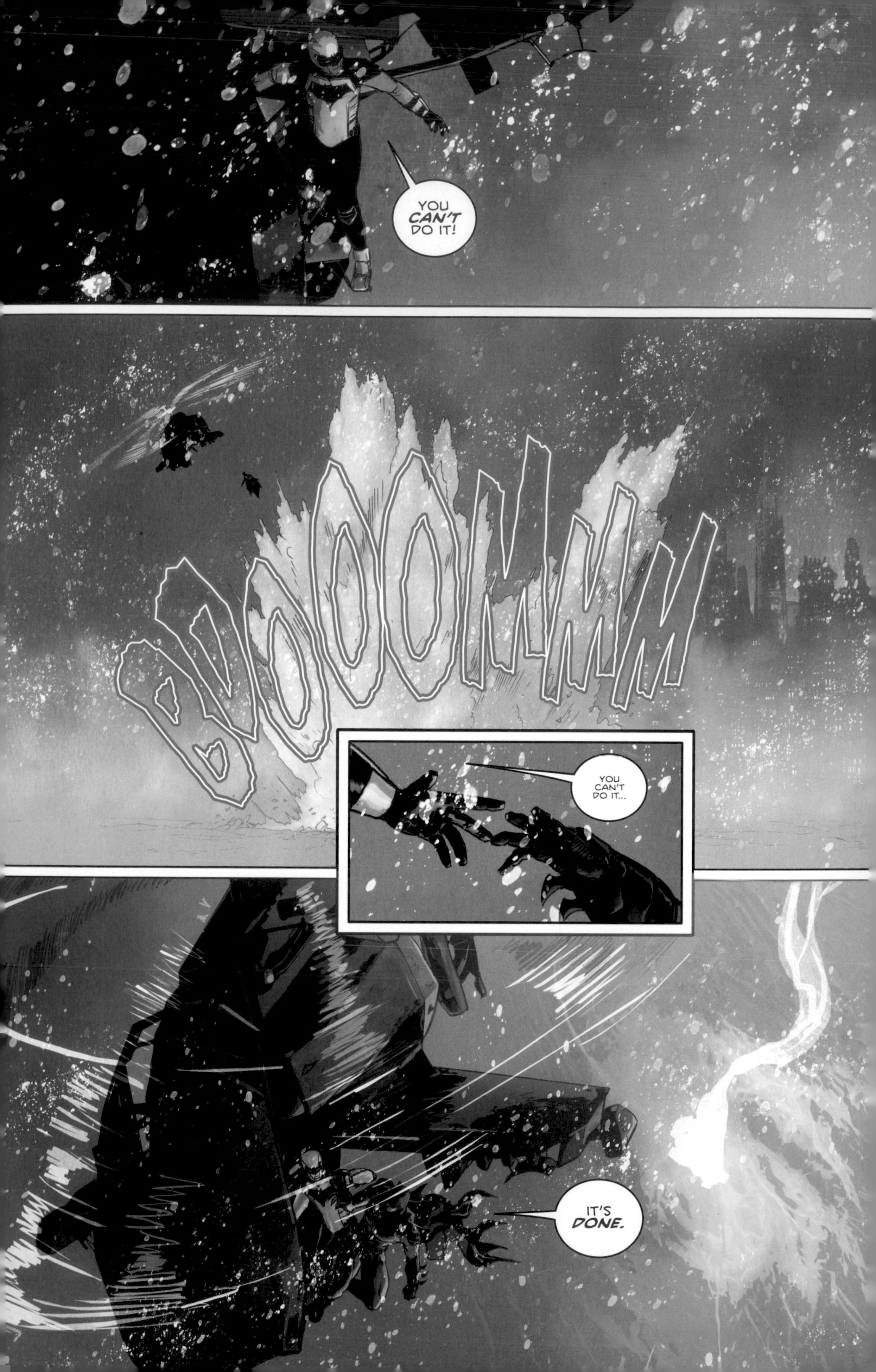
YOU CAN'T DO IT!
BOOOOMMMM
YOU CAN'T DO IT...
IT'S DONE.

FRIDAY. SPRING.

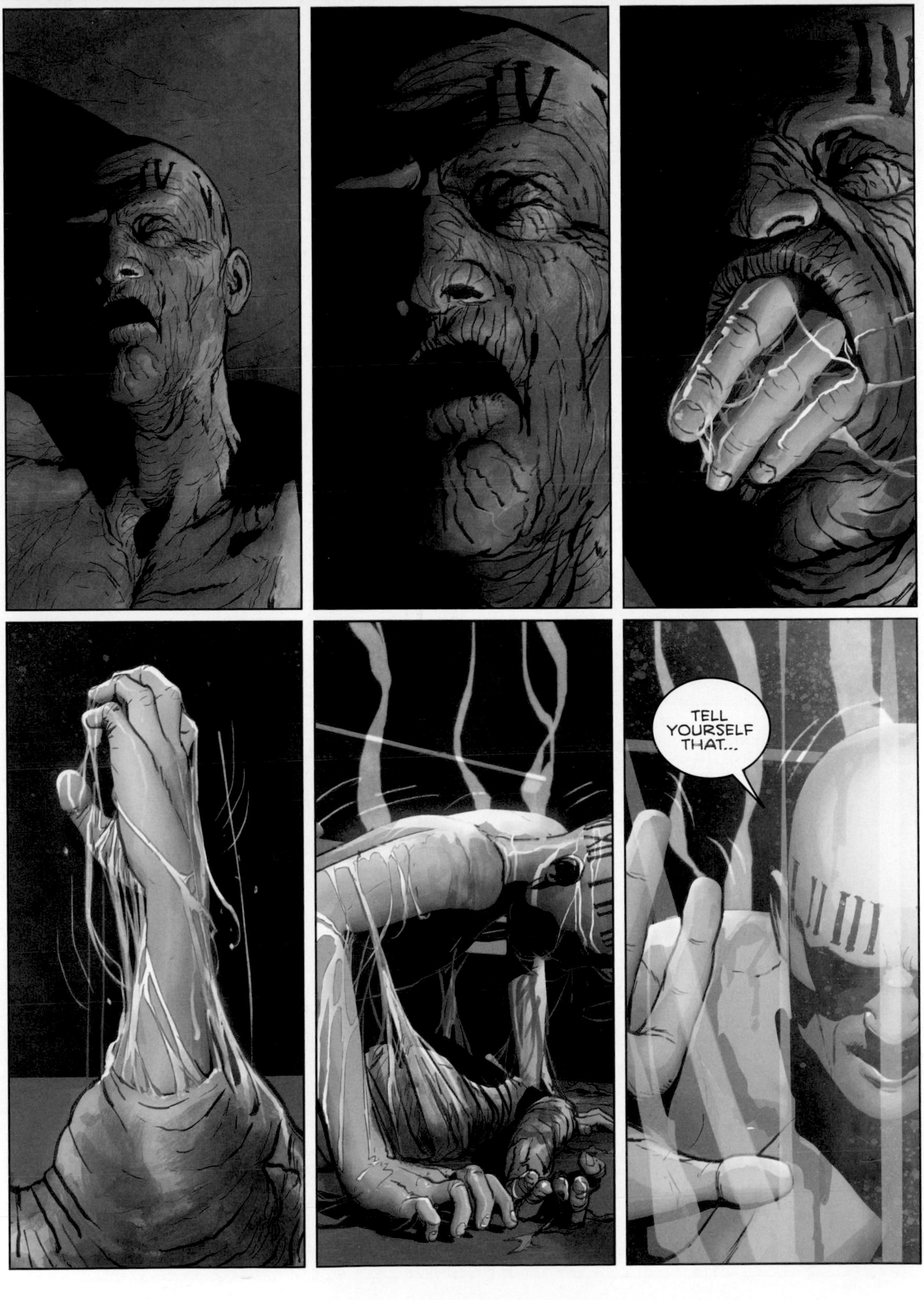
TELL YOURSELF THAT...

"...TELL YOURSELF IT'S DONE.

"BUT IT'S NEVER *DONE*."

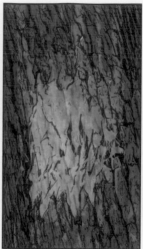

AGAIN.

HE'S BACK. RIGHT ABOUT NOW, HE'S... *HATCHING*. I WAS LOOKING AT THE FILE ON HIM.

IT SAYS THAT EVERY TIME HE COMES BACK, HE COMES BACK SLIGHTLY DIFFERENT, HIS DNA ALTERED. HE'S A DIFFERENT PERSON, BUT HE RETAINS ALL THE MEMORIES HE HAD LAST TIME.

HE'LL COME UP WITH NEW IDEAS.

THE TREE IS WINNING. YOUR POINT?

JUST THAT, HE COMES BACK *BETTER* EVERY TIME. HOW ARE WE SUPPOSED TO COMBAT THAT?

EASY. *WE* COME BACK BETTER EACH TIME, TOO.

...

YOU'RE CRAZY, YOU KNOW THAT, RIGHT?

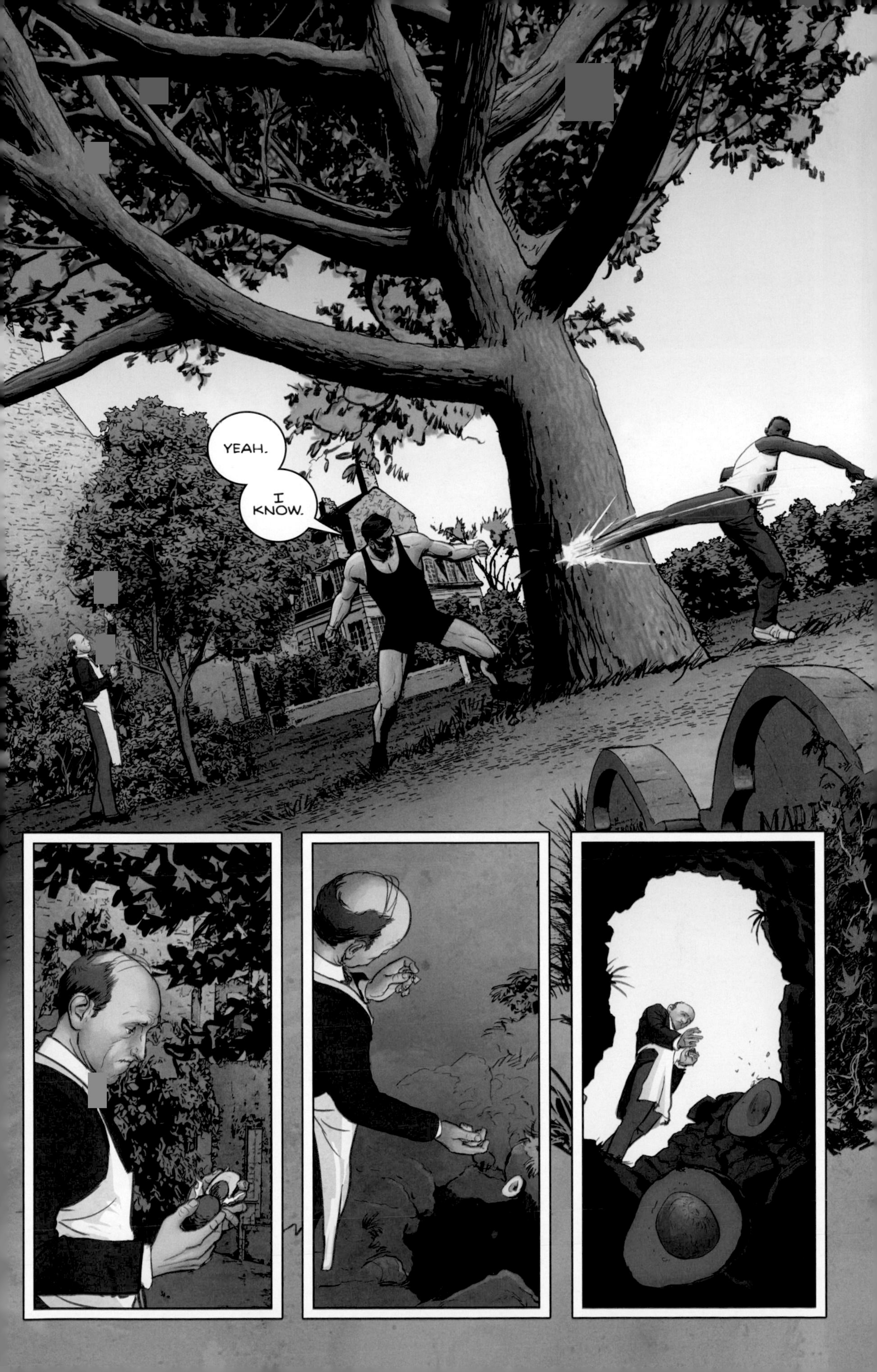
YEAH.
I KNOW.

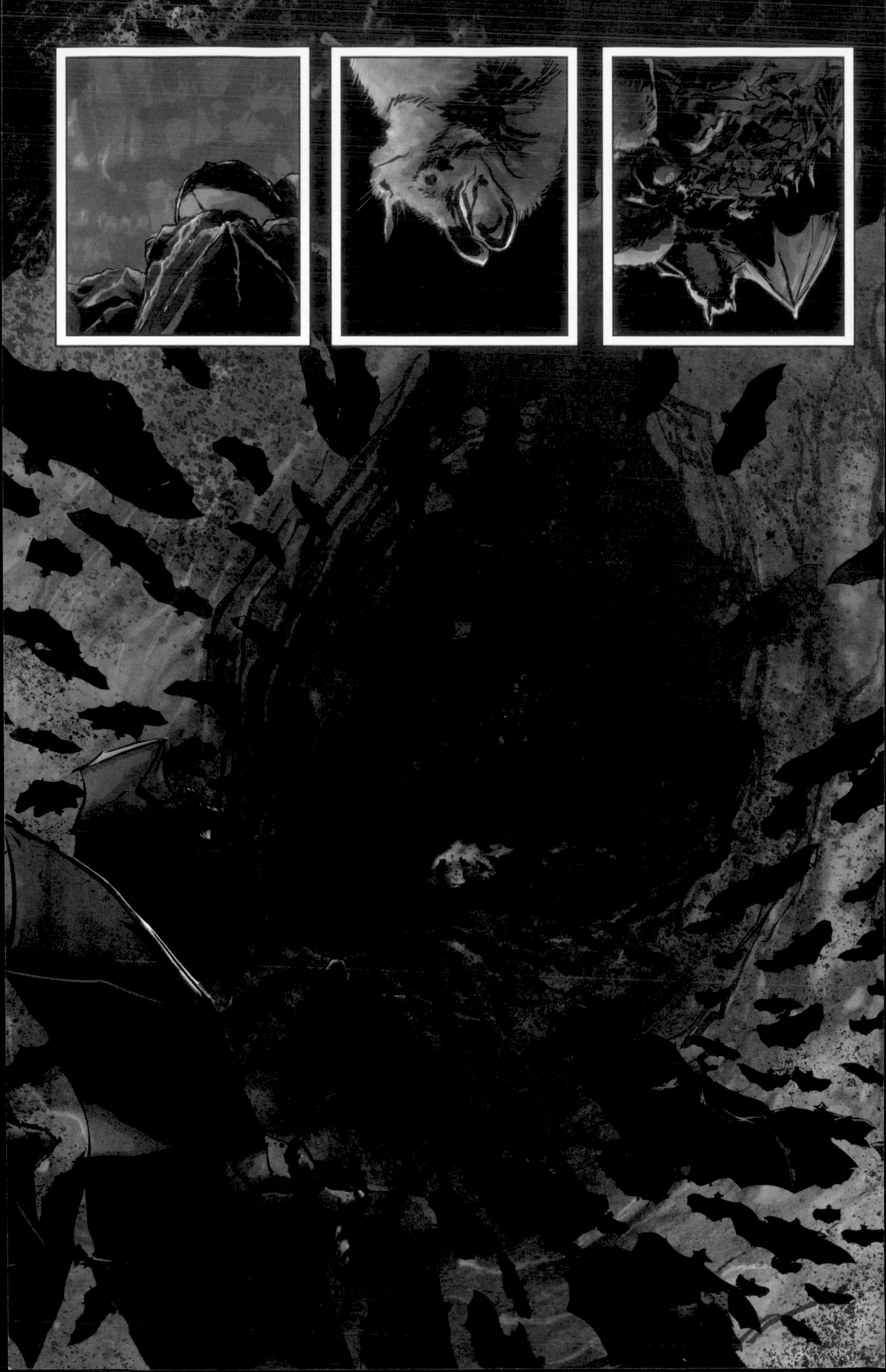

"This is your go-to book."—ENTERTAINMENT WEEKLY

"DETECTIVE COMICS is head-spinningly spectacular from top to bottom."—MTV GEEK

START AT THE BEGINNING!

BATMAN:
DETECTIVE COMICS
VOLUME 1: FACES OF DEATH

**BATMAN:
DETECTIVE COMICS
VOL. 2: SCARE TACTICS**

**BATMAN:
DETECTIVE COMICS
VOL. 3: EMPEROR
PENGUIN**

**THE JOKER:
DEATH OF THE FAMILY**

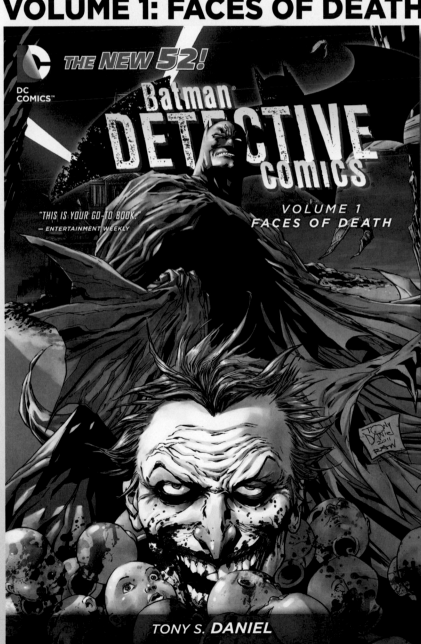

DC COMICS™

START AT THE BEGINNING!

BATMAN VOLUME 1: THE COURT OF OWLS

BATMAN & ROBIN
VOLUME 1:
BORN TO KILL

PETER J. TOMASI PATRICK GLEASON MICK GRAY

BATMAN: DETECTIVE
COMICS VOLUME 1:
FACES OF DEATH

TONY S. DANIEL

BATMAN: THE DARK
KNIGHT VOLUME 1:
KNIGHT TERRORS

DAVID FINCH PAUL JENKINS RICHARD FRIEND

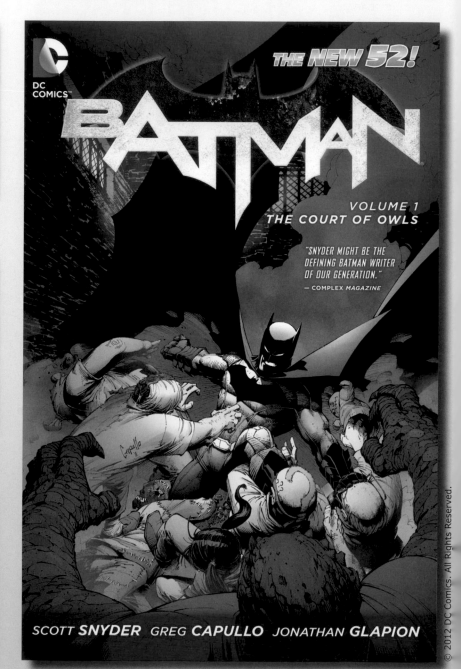

SCOTT **SNYDER**   GREG **CAPULLO**   JONATHAN **GLAPION**

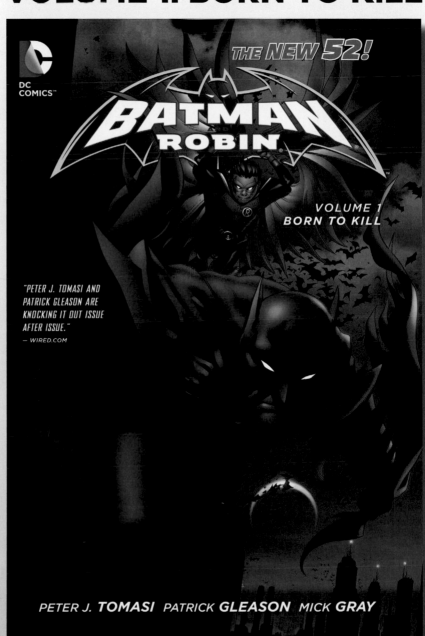

"Rock solid."—IGN

"This is the kind of Batman story I like to read: an actual mystery with an emotional hook."
—THE ONION/AV CLUB

START AT THE BEGINNING!

BATMAN & ROBIN
VOLUME 1: BORN TO KILL

**BATMAN & ROBIN
VOL. 2: PEARL**

**BATMAN & ROBIN
VOL. 3: DEATH OF THE
FAMILY**

**BATMAN
INCORPORATED
VOL. 1: DEMON STAR**

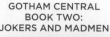

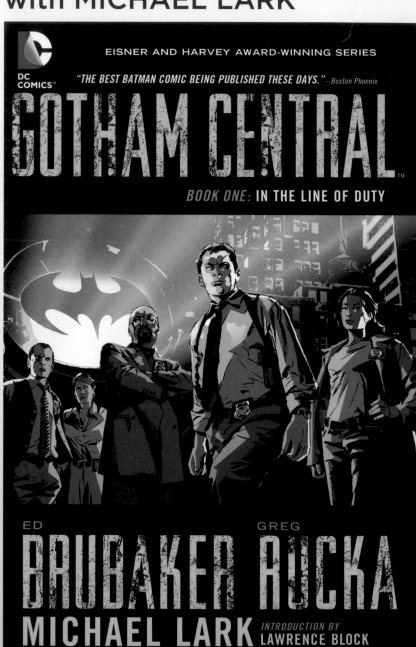